Lecture Notes in Computer Science   11637

Commenced Publication in 1973
Founding and Former Series Editors:
Gerhard Goos, Juris Hartmanis, and Jan van Leeuwen

Editorial Board Members

More information about this series at http://www.springer.com/series/7409

Guojun Wang · Jun Feng ·
Md Zakirul Alam Bhuiyan ·
Rongxing Lu (Eds.)

Security, Privacy, and Anonymity in Computation, Communication, and Storage

SpaCCS 2019 International Workshops
Atlanta, GA, USA, July 14–17, 2019
Proceedings

 Springer

Editors
Guojun Wang (iD)
Guangzhou University
Guangzhou, China

Md Zakirul Alam Bhuiyan (iD)
Fordham University
New York City, NY, USA

Jun Feng (iD)
Huazhong University of Science
and Technology
Wuhan, China

Rongxing Lu (iD)
University of New Brunswick
Fredericton, NB, Canada

ISSN 0302-9743   ISSN 1611-3349   (electronic)
Lecture Notes in Computer Science
ISBN 978-3-030-24899-4   ISBN 978-3-030-24900-7   (eBook)
https://doi.org/10.1007/978-3-030-24900-7

LNCS Sublibrary: SL3 – Information Systems and Applications, incl. Internet/Web, and HCI

This Springer imprint is published by the registered company Springer Nature Switzerland AG
The registered company address is: Gewerbestrasse 11, 6330 Cham, Switzerland

Preface

A very warm welcome to the 12th International Conference on Security, Privacy, and Anonymity in Computation, Communication, and Storage (SpaCCS 2019), held in Atlanta, USA, during July 14–17, 2019. SpaCCS 2019 was jointly organized by Guangzhou University, Georgia State University, and St. Francis Xavier University.

SpaCCS 2019 and its associated symposiums and workshops provide a forum for international and national scholars to gather and share their research findings, ideas, and emerging trends in cyberspace security research. Previous SpaCCS conferences were successfully held in Melbourne, Australia (2018), Guangzhou, China (2017), Zhangjiajie, China (2016), Helsinki, Finland (2015), Beijing, China (2014), Melbourne, Australia (2013), Liverpool, UK (2012), and Changsha, China (2011).

The workshop program this year consisted of six symposiums and workshops covering a broad range of research topics on security, privacy and anonymity in computation, communication, and storage:

(1) The 8th International Symposium on Security and Privacy on Internet of Things (SPIoT 2019)
(2) The 9th International Symposium on Trust, Security and Privacy for Emerging Applications (TSP 2019)
(3) The 5th International Symposium on Sensor-Cloud Systems (SCS 2019)
(4) The 11th International Symposium on UbiSafe Computing (UbiSafe 2019)
(5) The 11th International Workshop on Security in e-Science and e-Research (ISSR 2019)
(6) The 2019 International Workshop on Cybersecurity Metrics and Risk Modeling (CMRM 2019)

SpaCCS 2019 symposiums and workshops attracted 75 submissions from different countries and institutions around the globe. All submissions received at least 3 reviews by highly qualified experts, resulting in 26 papers being selected for oral presentation at the conference (i.e., an acceptance rate of 34.7%).

In addition to the technical presentations, the workshop program includes a number of keynote speeches by world-renowned researchers. We would like to thank the keynote speakers for their time and willingness to share their expertise with the conference attendees.

This event would not have been possible without the contributions of many experts who volunteered and devoted their time and expertise to make this happen. We would like to thank the symposium and workshop organizers for their hard work in soliciting high-quality submissions, assembling the Program Committee, managing the peer-review process, and planning the symposium and workshop agenda. We would also like to acknowledge the strong support of the Organizing Committee of SpaCCS 2019, and in particular the Steering Chairs, Prof. Guojun Wang and Prof. Gregorio Martinez. We would like to offer our gratitude to the General Chairs, Prof. Kim-Kwang

Raymond Choo, Prof. Mark Last, and Prof. Yanqing Zhang, for their tremendous support and advice in ensuring the success of the conference. Thanks also go to: Program Chairs, Md Zakirul Alam Bhuiyan, Jun Feng, and Rongxing Lu; Workshop Chair, Wm. Bradley Glisson; Publicity Chairs, Peter Mueller, Reza M. Parizi, and Yogachandran Rahulamathavan; Local Chair, Yubao Wu; and Web Chairs, Zihao Jiang and Xin Nie.

It is worth noting that SpaCCS 2019 was held jointly with the 12th IEEE International Conference on Internet of Things (iThings 2019), the 12th IEEE International Conference on Cyber, Physical, and Social Computing (CPSCom 2019), the 15th IEEE International Conference on Green Computing and Communications (GreenCom 2019), the 5th IEEE International Conference on Smart Data (SmartData 2019), and the 2nd IEEE International Conference on Blockchain (Blockchain 2019).

Finally, we thank you for your contribution to and/or participation in SpaCCS 2019 and hope that you found the conference to be a stimulating and exciting forum. Hopefully, you will also have enjoyed the beautiful city of Atlanta, USA.

July 2019

Guojun Wang
Jun Feng
Md Zakirul Alam Bhuiyan
Rongxing Lu

Organization

SpaCCS 2019 Organizing and Program Committees

General Chairs

Kim-Kwang Raymond Choo	University of Texas at San Antonio, USA
Mark Last	Ben-Gurion University of the Negev, Israel
Yanqing Zhang	Georgia State University, USA

Program Chairs

Md Zakirul Alam Bhuiyan	Fordham University, USA
Jun Feng	Huazhong University of Science and Technology, China
Rongxing Lu	University of New Brunswick, Canada

Workshop Chair

Wm. Bradley Glisson	Sam Houston State University, USA

Publicity Chairs

Peter Mueller	IBM Zurich Research Laboratory, Switzerland
Reza M. Parizi	Kennesaw State University, USA
Yogachandran Rahulamathavan	Loughborough University London, UK

Local Chair

Yubao Wu	Georgia State University, USA

Web Chairs

Zihao Jiang	St. Francis Xavier University, Canada
Xin Nie	Huazhong University of Science and Technology, China

Program Committee

Habtamu Abie	Norwegian Computing Center, Norway
Avishek Adhikari	University of Calcutta, India
Hamid Alasadi	Basra University, Iraq
Abdul Halim Ali	Universiti Kuala Lumpur, Malaysia
Flora Amato	University of Napoli Federico II, Italy
Kamran Arshad	Ajman University, UAE and University of Greenwich, UK

Zubair Baig	Data61 CSIRO, Australia
Cataldo Basile	Politecnico di Torino, Italy
Alessandra De Benedictis	University of Napoli Federico II, Italy
Jorge Bernal Bernabe	University of Murcia, Spain
Sulabh Bhattarai	Dakota State University, USA
Carlo Blundo	Università di Salerno, Italy
Larbi Boubchir	University of Paris VIII, France
Salah Bourennane	Ecole Centrale Marseille, France
Eddy Caron	ENS de Lyon, France
Arcangelo Castiglione	University of Salerno, Italy
Sudip Chakraborty	Valdosta State University, USA
Anupam Chattopadhyay	National Technological University, Singapore
Ankit Chaudhary	Northwest Missouri State University, USA
Pin-Yu Chen	IBM T. J. Watson Research Center, USA
Thomas Chen	City, University of London, UK
Felix J. Garcia Clemente	University of Murcia, Spain
Stefano Cresci	Istituto di Informatica e Telematica, CNR, Italy
Hai Dao	Hanoi University of Industry, Vietnam
Ashok Kumar Das	International Institute of Information Technology, India
Isabel de la Torre Díez	University of Valladolid, Spain
Subrata Dutta	Haldia Institute of Technology, India
Oscar Esparza	Universitat Politècnica de Catalunya, Spain
Jun Feng	Huazhong University of Science and Technology, China
Josep Domingo-Ferrer	Universitat Rovira i Virgili, Spain
Massimo Ficco	University of Campania Luigi Vanvitelli, Italy
Ugo Fiore	University of Napoli Federico II, Italy
Juan Pedro Munoz-Gea	Universidad Politécnica de Cartagena, Spain
Dimitris Geneiatakis	European Commission, Joint Research Centre, Italy
Angelo Genovese	Universita degli Studi di Milano, Italy
Kalman Graffi	Heinrich-Heine-Universität Düsseldorf, Germany
Yao Guo	Peking University, China
Hovhannes Harutyunyan	Concordia University, Canada
Selena He	Kennesaw State University, USA
Abdessamad Imine	Lorraine University, France
Pedro R. M. Inácio	Univsersidade da Beira Interior, Portugal
Celestine Iwendi	Bangor College, WSN Consults Ltd, Sweden, China
Biju Issac	Teesside University, UK
Linzhi Jiang	University of Surrey, UK
Vana Kalogeraki	Athens University of Economics and Business, Greece
Rajgopal Kannan	University of Southern California, USA
George Karakostas	McMaster University, Canada
Dimitrios Karras	Sterea Hellas Institute of Technology, Greece
Zaheer Khan	University of the West of England, UK
Asad Masood Khattak	Zayed University, UAE
Nikos Komninos	City, University of London, UK

Ruidong Li	National Institute of Information and Communications Technology, Japan
Xin Li	Nanjing University of Aeronautics and Astronautics, China
Feng Lin	University of Colorado Denver, USA
Giovanni Livraga	Universitá degli Studi di Milano, Italy
Pascal Lorenz	University of Haute Alsace, France
Pavel Loskot	Swansea University, UK
Leandros Maglaras	De Montfort University, UK
Wissam Mallouli	Montimage, France
Mirco Marchetti	University of Modena and Reggio Emilia, Italy
Guazzone Marco	University of Piemonte Orientale, Italy
Antonio Ruiz-Martínez	University of Murcia, Spain
Ilaria Matteucci	Istituto di Informatica e Telematica, CNR, Italy
Christoph Meinel	Hasso-Plattner-Institute, Germany
Aleksandra Mileva	University Goce Delcev, Macedonia
Moeiz Miraoui	University of Gafsa, Tunisia
Jose Andre Morales	Carnegie Mellon University, USA
Vincenzo Moscato	University of Napoli Federico II, Italy
Roberto Nardone	University of Napoli Federico II, Italy
Mohammadreza Nasiriavanaki	Wayne State University, USA
Keyurkumar Patel	Australian Defence Force, Australia
Changgen Peng	Guizhou University, China
Thinagaran Perumal	Universiti Putra Malaysia, Malaysia
Antonio Pescape'	University of Napoli Federico II, Italy
Roberto Di Pietro	University of Padova, Italy
Vaibhav Rastogi	University of Wisconsin-Madison, India
Mubashir Husain Rehmani	COMSATS, Institute of Information Technology, Pakistan
Vincent Roca	Inria, France
Altair Santin	Pontifical Catholic University of Parana, Brazil
Andrea Saracino	Istituto di Informatica e Telematica, CNR, Italy
Saratha Sathasivam	Universiti Sains Malaysia, Malaysia
Frank Schulz	SAP SE, Germany
Patrick Siarry	Universite Paris-Est Creteil, France
Jorge SA Silva	University of Coimbra, Portugal
Nicolas Sklavos	University of Patras, Greece
Martin Strohmeier	University of Oxford, UK
Junggab Son	Kennesaw State University, USA
Traian Marius Truta	Northern Kentucky University, USA
Omair Uthmani	Glasgow Caledonian University, UK
Quoc-Tuan Vien	Middlesex University, UK
Zhiwei Wang	Nanjing University of Posts and Telecommunication, China
Yubao Wu	Georgia State University, USA

Ping Yang	State University of New York at Binghamton, USA
Yong Yu	Shaanxi Normal University, China
Go Yun	HWUM, Malaysia
Nicola Zannone	Eindhoven University of Technology, The Netherlands
Sherali Zeadally	University of Kentucky, USA
Mingwu Zhang	Hubei University of Technology, China
Shunli Zhang	Huazhong University of Science and Technology, China
Xinliang Zheng	Frostburg State University, USA
Natasa Zivic	University of Siegen, Germany

Steering Committee

Guojun Wang (Chair)	Guangzhou University, China
Gregorio Martinez (Chair)	University of Murcia, Spain
Jemal H. Abawajy	Deakin University, Australia
Jose M. Alcaraz Calero	University of the West of Scotland, UK
Jiannong Cao	Hong Kong Polytechnic University, SAR China
Hsiao-Hwa Chen	National Cheng Kung University, Taiwan
Jinjun Chen	Swinburne University of Technology, Australia
Kim-Kwang Raymond Choo	University of Texas at San Antonio, USA
Robert Deng	Singapore Management University, Singapore
Mario Freire	The University of Beira Interior, Portugal
Minyi Guo	Shanghai Jiao Tong University, China
Weijia Jia	University of Macau, SAR China
Wei Jie	University of West London, UK
Georgios Kambourakis	University of the Aegean, Greece
Ryan Ko	Queensland University, Australia
Constantinos Kolias	University of Idaho, USA
Jianbin Li	North China Electric Power University, China
Jie Li	Shanghai Jiao Tong University, China
Jianhua Ma	Hosei University, Japan
Felix Gomez Marmol	University of Murcia, Spain
Geyong Min	University of Exeter, UK
Peter Mueller	IBM Zurich Research Laboratory, Switzerland
Indrakshi Ray	Colorado State University, USA
Kouichi Sakurai	Kyushu University, Japan
Juan E. Tapiador	The University Carlos III of Madrid, Spain
Sabu M. Thampi	Indian Institute of Information Technology and Management, India
Jie Wu	Temple University, USA
Yang Xiao	The University of Alabama, USA
Yang Xiang	Swinburne University of Technology, Australia

Zheng Yan   Aalto University, Finland and Xidian University, China
Laurence T. Yang   St. Francis Xavier University, Canada
Wanlei Zhou   University of Technology Sydney, Australia

Sponsors

Contents

The 5th International Symposium on Sensor-Cloud Systems (SCS 2019)

The 8th International Symposium on Security and Privacy on Internet of Things (SPIoT 2019)

SPIoT 2019 Organizing and Program Committees

Program Chairs

Marios Anagnostopoulos	Norwegian University of Science and Technology (NTNU), Norway
Georgios Kambourakis	University of the Aegean, Greece
Constantinos Kolias	University of Idaho, USA

Program Committee

Afrand Agah	West Chester University of Pennsylvania, USA
Mohamad Badra	Zayed University, UAE
Cataldo Basile	Politecnico di Torino, Italy
Fernando Pereniguez Garcia	University Centre of Defence, Spanish Air Force Academy, Spain
Dan Garcia-Carrillo	University of Murcia, Spain
Dimitris Geneiatakis	European Commission, Joint Research Centre, Italy
Vasileios Gkioulos	Norwegian University of Science and Technology (NTNU), Norway
Hsiang-Cheh Huang	National University of Kaohsiung, Taiwan
Youssef Iraqi	Khalifa, University of Science, Technology, and Research, UAE
Georgios Karopoulos	University of Athens, Greece
Vinh Hoa La	Telecom SudParis, France
Riccardo Lazzeretti	Sapienza University of Rome, Italy
Wissam Mallouli	Montimage, France
Daisuke Mashima	Advanced Digital Sciences Center, Singapore
Sofia Anna Menesidou	Democritus University of Thrace, Greece
Weizhi Meng	Technical University of Denmark, Denmark
Edmundo Monteiro	University of Coimbra, Portugal
Juan Pedro Munoz-Gea	Universidad Politecnica de Cartagena, Spain
Renita Murimi	Oklahoma Baptist University, USA
Christoforos Ntantogian	University of Piraeus, Greece
Dimitrios Papamartzivanos	University of the Aegean, Greece
Zeeshan Pervez	University of the West of Scotland, UK
Roger Piqueras Jover	Bloomberg Lp-Security Research Lab, USA
Rodrigo Roman	University of Malaga, Spain
Asaf Shabtai	Ben-Gurion University, Israel

Georgios Spathoulas	University of Thessaly, Greece
Lanier A. Watkins	The Johns Hopkins University, USA
Peng Zhou	Shanghai University, China

Steering Committee

Guojun Wang (Chair)	Guangzhou University, China
Gregorio Martinez (Chair)	University of Murcia, Spain
Mauro Conti	University of Padua, Italy
Hua Wang	Victoria University, Australia
Vasilis Katos	Bournemouth University, UK
Jaime Lloret Mauri	Polytechnic University of Valencia, Spain
Yongdong Wu	Institute for Infocomm Research, Singapore
Zhoujun Li	Beihang University, China

Robust Hybrid Lightweight Cryptosystem for Protecting IoT Smart Devices

Ahmed Ragab$^{(\boxtimes)}$, Gamal Selim, Abdelmoniem Wahdan,
and Ahmed Madani

Arab Academy for Science, Technology and Maritime Transport,
Cairo, Egypt
a.abdelhamid92@gmail.com, wahdan73@gmail.com,
{dgamalselim, madani82}@aast.edu

Abstract. There are limited numbers of reliable hybrid cryptosystems that can be used to protect IoT smart devices, specifically in smart cities, smart hospitals, smart homes, and industrial fields. Therefore, much related work has to be performed. The aim is to study the trade-off between performance and security in these constrained environments and to achieve more secure hybrid cryptosystem with high demanded performance. Several types of recommended lightweight encryption algorithms will be investigated. These hybrid cryptosystems combine symmetric encryption algorithms such as TEA, XTEA, XXTEA, and asymmetric encryption algorithms such as RSA and ECC. They have the capability to protect IoT smart devices from internet attacks. They can efficiently achieve confidentiality, authenticity, integrity, and non-repudiation. Comparative analysis and evaluation are achieved; hence a robust hybrid cryptosystem was proposed. It uses chaotic theory to generate random keys. The analysis included the most important factors that have to be tackled in case of using lightweight ciphers to suit limited resources of IoT smart devices. Among these factors are security level, memory size, power consumption, encryption time, decryption time, and throughput. Results show that the proposed hybrid cryptosystem that combined ECC and XXTEA gives better security and higher performance than RSA and XXTEA with 40%.

Keywords: Hybrid cryptosystems · Protecting IoT smart devices ·
Lightweight ciphers analysis · RSA · ECC · XXTEA

1 Introduction

There is extensive diversity of IoT devices, including sensor-enabled smart devices, and all types of wearables smart devices connect to the Internet. The cost of technology has decreased, in every area, we demand access to the internet which delivers a quantity of information in real time. IoTs are applied in several applications including smart homes, smart hospitals, smart industry, and smart cities. Moreover, some environments exist only on the internet, such as social networks, where all information is in the cloud. Several advanced technologies, such as smart sensors, networks, wireless communications, data analysis techniques, and cloud computing, have been developed to realize the potential of IoT with different smart systems [1]. As technology rapidly rises at

© Springer Nature Switzerland AG 2019
G. Wang et al. (Eds.): SpaCCS 2019 Workshops, LNCS 11637, pp. 5–19, 2019.
https://doi.org/10.1007/978-3-030-24900-7_1

radio-frequency identification (RFID), Internet approaches have gained momentum in connecting everyday things to the internet and facilitating communication from machine to human and from machine to machine with the physical world [2]. The main advantages of IoT smart devices include enhanced data collection, provides real-world information and technology optimization. However, vulnerabilities that face IoT smart devices may include security, privacy, and complexity. IoT smart devices are vulnerable to security attacks [3]. So that protection techniques using encryption techniques are required to protect these devices. It is important to secure data from different kinds of attacks that have made the role of information security more important than before. Encryption techniques are normally used to secure information.

Symmetric encryption technologies provide cost-effective means and efficiency to secure data without compromising security [4]; however, sharing a secret key is a problem. On the other hand, asymmetric technologies resolve the encryption key distribution problem; however, they are slow compared to symmetric encryption and consume more computer resources [5]. Hence, one of the best possible solutions for encryption is the complementary use of both symmetric and asymmetric encryption techniques [6]. In this paper, a hybrid model combines two different cryptography; symmetric and asymmetric algorithms; to ensure the confidentiality, authenticity, integrity, and non-repudiation will be tackled. The problem statement that has to be tackled in this paper is to propose a lightweight hybrid cryptosystem to protect IoT smart devices efficiently. To solve this problem a suitable block cipher and suitable stream cipher has to be selected to fit with the limited recourse of IoT smart devices. Limited resources mean low memory, limiter power, and energy consumptions.

The rest of the paper is as follows: Sect. 2 discusses related work. Section 3 discusses lightweight ciphers characteristics and security services. Section 4 explains the hybrid cryptosystem proposed. Section 5 discusses the results and performance evaluation of the proposed hybrid cryptosystem. Section 6 is the conclusion.

2   Related Work

There are several hybrid encryption algorithms discussed in many kinds of literature based on different techniques. For example, a hybrid encryption method based on symmetric DES and asymmetric cryptography ECC to ensure the security of the database system in a mobile payment technology was applied in smart travel [7]. The drawback of this system is that it only achieves confidentiality and authenticity. To enhance security, a hybrid encryption technique described in [8] uses the advance encryption standard (AES) and the asymmetric key to enabling strong security and low computational complexity through a combined encryption algorithm. It provides confidentiality, integrity, and non-repudiation on the data transmission for IoT to the database server. The drawback of this system is that AES occupy large size in ROM and RAM at processing [9]; also, the used MD5 is susceptible to differential attack [10]. To increase efficiency and decrease memory consumption, there was a study to implement and observe parameters like time and memory for implementation of multi-level encryption using the data encryption standard (DES) was described [25]. Besides, a modified version of the RSA algorithm was used via the multi-prime RSA [11]. It consumes a larger size in memory to generate a longer key [10]. Another technique (HAN [15]) is used to enhance encryption's speed with less computational complexity. It is based on AES for data encryption and decryption and uses NTRU [16] for key encryption and decryption through the media. It applies new lattice basis reduction techniques to cryptanalyze NTRU to discover the original key to get original text [16].

In [19], a hybrid technique was used to combine the symmetric cryptographic algorithm (AES) and the asymmetric algorithm (RSA) and hashing function (MD5). These algorithms were combined to ensure confidentiality, authentication and data integrity. However, AES occupies large size in ROM and RAM at processing, also MD5 is susceptible to differential attack along with a large size of memory used to process RSA key. In A healthcare security model for securing medical data transmission in IoT environments was investigated [20]. The model secures patients' data using hybrid encryption scheme created from AES and RSA algorithms. In [21] a hybrid model was constructed to ensure security and integrity assurance of the data during the transmission. The model is an implementation of two cryptographic algorithms including the SHA1, hash generation algorithm and AES for encryption and decryption of messages. The work also discussed various other cryptographic algorithms and the reason why AES and SHA1 are preferred in an RFID system. The drawback of this system is that SHA1 is susceptible to collision attacks [22]. In [23] another context introduced a hybrid technique for cryptography using the symmetric algorithms AES and Blowfish. This combination gives high security, it also uses hashing Key based MD5 [24] that make hashing the key in the encryption process and make the same process in decryption. This design causes a CPU overload and memory consumption in the process of double encrypt of plaintext.

To increase the security of hybrid cryptosystem, another methodology was proposed using the lightweight algorithm XTEA for data encryption and ECC for key encryption and PBKDF2 for key generation in IoT and deployed on an Arduino kit for secure transmission between IoT wireless sensor network (WSN) [17]. The drawback of this system is that XTEA got broken and weaknesses within PBKDF2 function due to its susceptibility to Brutal force attack [18].

A cyber security scheme for IoT [12] was proposed to facilitate an additional level of security based on the strength of symmetric and asymmetric algorithms such as AES and RSA for a closed system through tunneling technology to be applied in internet sensitive application and file storage. The drawbacks of this system are that AES consumes more memory and RSA needs more computational power to generate RSA key [26]. It was also shown that the lightweight block cipher XXTEA outperforms the performance of AES. However, XXTEA is susceptible to related key attack [13], this weakness is overcome by enhancing XXTEA encryption algorithm using S-Box, and chaos system key generation as described in our work [27]. To overcome this attack, XXTEA is joined with a chaotic system to produce a more secure algorithm [14]. When the system sends data, it uses a chaotic algorithm to generate key during each transmission. This design only achieves confidentiality of data. Besides the above, Table 1 illustrates the types of cryptographic algorithms used in IoT industrial systems to achieve IoT devices security.

Table 1. Types of security features used in IoT industrial systems.

Security features	Libelium IoT industry hybrid cryptosystem [29]	Amazon IoT industry hybrid cryptosystem [30]	ARM IoT industry hybrid cryptosystem [31]
Authentication	RSA	RSA/ECDHE	RSA
Confidentiality	AES256	AES128	AES128
Integrity	MD5/SHA1	SHA256	SHA
Non-repudiation	RSA key signing message	ECDSA	Not defined

To overcome most drawbacks of the above described cryptographic models we investigate several types of recommended hybrid cryptosystems based on tiny family block ciphers and ECC versus RSA. Then, a robust secure lightweight hybrid cryptosystem is proposed to protect IoT smart devices efficiently, as described in the next sections.

3 Lightweight Ciphers Investigated

Lightweight block ciphers play an indispensable role for security in the context of pervasive computing. However, the performance of resource-constrained devices can be affected dynamically by the selection of suitable crypt-algorithms, especially for the devices in the resource-constrained IoT smart devices and wireless networks. Thus, we study the trade-off between security and performance of several top performing lightweight block ciphers for the demand of resource-constrained IoT smart devices. Then, the software performance evaluation about these ciphers has been carried out in terms of memory occupation, cycles per byte, encryption and decryption time, throughput, and efficiency.

Moreover, the results which show the possibility to resist possible types of different attacks, are presented subsequently. Our results show that XXTEA is the software-oriented lightweight cipher which achieves the best performance in various aspects, and it enjoys a healthy security margin at the same time. Furthermore, RSA, which is usually used as a benchmark for newer hardware-oriented lightweight ciphers, shows that the software performance combined with XXTEA is inadequate when it is implemented. In the real application, there is a need to better understand the resources of dedicated platforms and security requirement, as well as the emphasis and focus. Therefore, this case study can serve as a good reference for the better selection of trade-off between performance and security in constrained environments.

Good Lightweight Ciphers: Designing a good, memory efficient, resource efficient and robust lightweight cipher requires a number of features to be considered. The important features of a good lightweight cipher are as follows [45–47]: (a) Less complexity, (b) Robust architecture, (c) Rich encryption standard, (d) High throughput, (e) Less execution time, (f) Requires less memory software implementation (code size, RAM size), (g) Need smaller hardware implementation, (h) Consumes less power (energy consumption), (i) Good immunity against linear and differential attacks, (j) Prevent possible advance attacks like Biclique attack, Zero correlation attack, Meet-In-The-Middle attack (MITM), and Algebraic attacks.

3.1 Security Features and Services

The main security services that can be achieved using symmetric and asymmetric cryptography is given in Table 2. Sometimes a primitive cannot provide a security service on its own, but when it is used in a mode of operation or in combination with another primitive. The following are the security features that the proposed hybrid cryptosystem has to achieve [46].

Table 2. Security services provided by different symmetric and asymmetric cryptographic primitives implemented in the proposed hybrid cryptosystem.

Primitive	Security service			
	Confidentiality	Integrity	Authentication	Non-repudiation
Block cipher	●	◉	◉	○
Stream cipher	●	◉	◉	○
Hash function	○	◉	◉	○
SHA256	○	●	◉	○
Digital signature	○	●	●	●
Authenticated cipher	●	●	●	○
Public-key encryption	●	◉	●	○

● - using only the primitive
◉ - Using the primitive in a mode of operation or combined with primitives.
○ - not possible

- *Confidentiality.* This security service ensures that only those authorized have access to the content of the information. Hence, it prevents an unauthorized user to access the content of the protected information. It is sometimes referred to as secrecy.
- *Data integrity.* It provides a mean to detect whether data has been manipulated by an unauthorized party since the last time an authorized user created, stored or transmitted it. Data manipulation refers to operations such as insertion, deletion, or substitution.
- *Authentication.* Authentication is related to identification and it is often divided into two classes: data origin authentication and entity authentication.
  - Data origin authentication. It gives assurance that an entity is the original source of a message. Data origin authentication implicitly provides data integrity. Sometimes, it is referred to as message authentication.
  - Entity authentication. Entity authentication assures one entity about the identity of a second entity with which it is interacting. Usually, entity authentication implies data origin authentication.
- *Non-repudiation.* It is a security service that prevents an entity from denying a previous action or commitment. It is very useful in situations that can lead to

disputes. When a dispute arises, a trusted third party is able to provide the evidence required to settle it.

3.2 The Tiny Family Block Ciphers

There are several types of lightweight block ciphers algorithms among these block ciphers, the tiny family ciphers that are investigated in the hybrid cryptosystems in this paper, they include TEA block cipher, XTEA block cipher and XXTEA block cipher [42]. In addition, there are also several lightweight stream ciphers algorithms described in [43]. Among these stream ciphers that will be used in the hybrid cryptosystems investigated in this paper are ECC and RSA.

The XXTEA block cipher [32, 33] is used to achieve confidentiality. The XXTEA is a block cipher comprising at least two 32-bit words, using a 128-bit key. It is designed to correct weaknesses in the original block TEA and XTEA. An XXTEA full cycle is n rounds, where n is the number of words in the block. The number of full cycles to enact over the block is given as 6 + 52/n. The XXTEA memory consumptions and computational cycles (cost) are analyzed and compared with other block ciphers [16, 27, 40]. Table 3 shows a summary of the results. It is clear from these results that XXTEA outperforms AES128 and AES256 because it uses less memory and less computational cycles. For these reasons, the XXTEA is used in the proposed hybrid cryptosystem for data encryption and decryption to achieve confidentiality.

Table 3. Memory consumption and computational cost (cycles)

Memory consumption (bytes) and computational cost (cycles)						
IoT Device Contr.	Mica2			Arduino Pro		
Ciphers	RAM	ROM	Cycles	RAM	ROM	Cycles
XXTEA	542	6312	24064	226	4112	30464
Skipjack	3096	8658	9820	398	4952	12672
RC5	682	6110	53014	350	3184	61504
AES-128	1074	6296	37525	814	3692	43200
AES-256	1822	7932	80344	1014	4190	88896
CGEA	664	6268	67786	548	3228	76212

3.3 ECC and RSA via Comparison

The elliptic curve cryptography (ECC) [34] is asymmetric cryptography engages the use of two keys. A private key used to decrypt messages and sign (create) signatures. And a public key used to encrypt messages and verify signatures. ECC is used to achieve authenticity, integrity, and non-repudiation with the help of some additional algorithms. ECDHE Digital signatures are *used* to verify the *authenticity* of messages and confirm that they have not been altered in transmission. To assure the integrity of the received data, a hashing algorithm is used. The Elliptic Curve Digital Signature Algorithm (ECDSA) algorithm uses ECC to provide a variant of the Digital Signature

Algorithm (DSA). A pair of keys (public and private) are generated from an elliptic curve, and these can be used both for signing or verifying a message's signature. The ECDSA algorithm is used to achieve non-repudiation [30]. It ensures the sender and receiver from denying the sending or receiving of a message and the authenticity of their signature. Equation (1) is used to generate the public key (Q) as follows:

$$Q = d * P; \qquad (1)$$

where: d is the random number chosen within the range (1 to n−1); the private key, P is a point on the curve, and Q is the public key. ECC- Encryption: Let "m" be the message that should be sent. this message has to be represented on the curve. Consider "m" has the point "M" on the curve "E". Randomly select "k" from [1 − (n−1)]. We need to generate two cipher texts (C1 and C2), as shown in Eqs. (2) and (3) and send them.

$$C_1 = k * P \text{ and } C_2 = M + k * Q \qquad (2)$$

ECC- Decryption: We can get the original message using the Eq. (3) as follows:

$$M = C_2 - d * C_1 \qquad (3)$$

Several analyses are made for RSA and ECC to provide most efficient in IoT smart devices [27, 35–40]. Table 4 shows the recommended security bit level provided by NIST [27]. This means that, for the same level of security, significantly smaller key sizes can be used in ECC than RSA. For instance, to achieve 80 bits of security level, the RSA algorithm requires a key size of 1024 bits, while ECC needs a key size of 160 bits. Hence, RSA consumes longer encryption time and uses memory more than ECC. Performance evaluation of the proposed hybrid cryptosystem is discussed next.

Table 4. Comparing ECC and RSA security bit level [27].

Security bit level	RSA key size	ECC key size
80	1024	160
112	2048	224
128	3072	256
192	7680	384
256	15360	512

4 The Hybrid Cryptosystem Proposed

The hybrid cryptosystem proposed consists of three main components including the XXTEA (symmetric block cipher) used to achieve confidentiality, the ECC (asymmetric cipher) used to achieve authenticity, integrity and non-repudiated based digital signature, and the chaotic keys generator used to generate random keys. The aim is to achieve the best performance with a high level of security. The Chaotic systems (Chaos) [34] are used to generate random keys. It has the following advantages.

1. The Chaotic sequences are nonlinear systems that are inevitable.
2. They are very sensitive to change in initial value or seed value.
3. Two isomorphic chaotic systems with exact distinctions in seed values will produce two totally different chaotic sequences within a short period of time.
4. The strings given by chaotic systems are not only random but regenerative.

Because of these features, chaotic equations can be used to implement the key generator in cryptography. Some examples of chaotic equations are sine map, tent map, and Logistic map. One of the most common utilizing is the logistic map that can be given by Eq. (4) as follows:

$$X_{n+1} = 1 - 2X_n^2;$$
$$X_n \ ranges \ from \quad -1 \ to \ 1 \ and \ n = 0, 1_{,...} \tag{4}$$

Figure 1a and b show the component used to implement the hybrid cryptosystem proposed. The following algorithm illustrates the steps of operations of the hybrid cryptosystem.

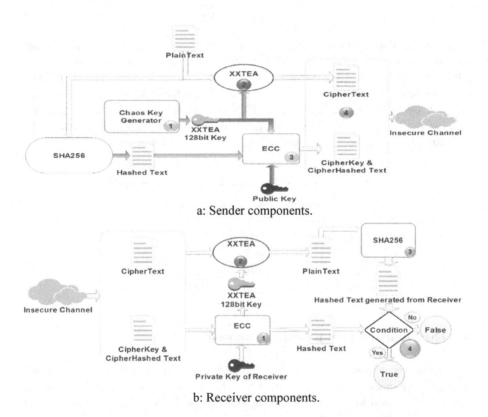

a: Sender components.

b: Receiver components.

Fig. 1. a, b. The design of the hybrid cryptosystem proposed.

1. *First, Sender A and Receiver B exchange their public key using ECC Diffie-Hellman key exchange algorithm.*
2. *Sender A wants to send an encrypted message to Receiver B.*
3. *Sender A constructs 128-bit key for XXTEA through using of the chaos key generator.*
4. *The XXTEA encrypts the desired message using the 128-bit key and ECC encrypt the 128-bit key and hashed message so that cipher text, cipher key, and cipher hashed message are sent to Receiver B.*
5. *Receiver B decrypts the received message that was sent using ECC to obtain the 128-bit key and the hashed message.*
6. *Receiver B receives the encrypted message and decrypts it using the 128-bit key.*
7. *At the receiver side, the 128-bit key derived from Receiver B with same parameters used at Sender A will compare it with the received 128-bit hashed key as well as check received message sent from Sender A, verifying integrity.*

5   Results and Discussions

The proposed hybrid cryptosystem was implemented using IoT simulation running on Laptop intel i-7 core processor with 4 GB RAM. The following sections discuss the results and performance evaluation of the proposed hybrid cryptosystem via comparison with other related tiny family hybrid cryptosystems.

5.1   The Hybrid Cryptosystem Based Tiny Family and RSA: Enc and Dec

Figure 2a and b show results of the performance comparison between the hybrid cryptosystems (TEA & RSA), (XTEA & RSA), and (XXTEA & RSA) as functions of message size (KB) and encryption time (sec) in case of encryption and decryption, respectively. Results show that the hybrid cryptosystem based on (TEA & RSA) consumes less encryption and decryption time while the hybrid cryptosystem based on (XXTEA & RSA) consumes highest encryption and decryption time. This is because of the TEA block cipher algorithm is much simpler than both XTEA and XXTEA block ciphers.

5.2   The Hybrid Cryptosystem Based Tiny Family and ECC: Enc and Dec

Figure 3a and b show results of performance comparison between the hybrid cryptosystems based on (TEA & ECC), (XTEA & ECC), and (XXTEA & ECC) as a function of message size (KB) and encryption time (sec) in case of encryption and decryption, respectively. These data are used to test the hybrid cryptosystems by the simulator for the case of information transfer between IoT devices and between cloud and IoT, ranged from Kbytes to Mbytes, as illustrated in the Figures. Results show that the hybrid cryptosystem based on (TEA & ECC) consumes less encryption and decryption time while the hybrid cryptosystem based on (XXTEA & ECC) consumes highest encryption and decryption time. The XTEA encryption time is longer than TEA

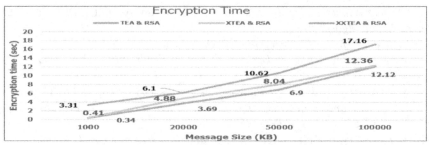

a. Encryption time vs message sizes for hybrid cryptosystems based Tiny Family and RSA.

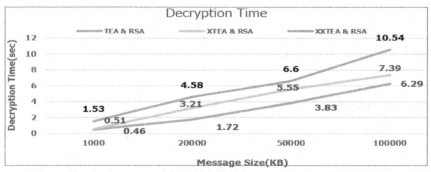

b. Decryption time vs message sizes for hybrid cryptosystems based Tiny Family and RSA.

Fig. 2. a. Encryption time vs message sizes for hybrid cryptosystems based tiny family and RSA. **b.** Decryption time vs message sizes for hybrid cryptosystems based Tiny Family and RSA.

because: there is an additional 11 shift round in XTEA algorithm to make it irregular. Besides, XTEA uses the whole 128 bit-key in the first 2 cycles while TEA uses 2 (32-bit key array) in the first 2 cycles. The XXTEA uses the whole 128 bit-key input next and the previous character in encryption and decryption. This causes little delay to increase security when data encrypted. Although, the hybrid cryptosystem based XXTEA and ECC consumes more time, however, it is recommended to be used for data transmission protection for the IoT smart devices because it is more secure than both TEA and XTEA. It can also be used for encrypting longer messages and for general purposes as well.

5.3   The Throughput Performance Evaluation

Figure 4a and b show results of performance comparison between the hybrid cryptosystems based on (XXTEA & ECC), and (XXTEA & RSA) as a function of message size (KB) and encryption and decryption throughput, respectively. Results show that the hybrid cryptosystem based on (XXTEA & ECC) encryption and decryption

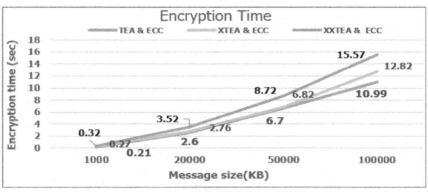

a. Encryption time vs message sizes for hybrid cryptosystems based Tiny Family and ECC.

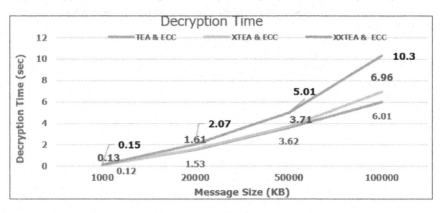

b. Decryption time vs message sizes for hybrid cryptosystems based Tiny Family and ECC.

Fig. 3. a. Encryption time vs message sizes for hybrid cryptosystems based Tiny Family and ECC. **b.** Decryption time vs message sizes for hybrid cryptosystems based Tiny Family and ECC.

throughput is higher than the encryption and decryption throughput of the hybrid cryptosystem based on (XXTEA & RSA). Table 5 shows the average encryption and decryption throughput of theses hybrid cryptosystems. Where:

$$The\ throughput\ (Speed)\ S\ =\ \Sigma\ Message\ Size\ /\ \Sigma\ Total\ time\ taken.$$
$$The\ average\ throughput\ of\ encryption\ and\ decryption$$
$$for\ (XXTEA + ECC)\ =\ 5.73 + 9\ =\ 15\ Mb/s.$$
$$The\ average\ throughput\ of\ encryption\ and\ decryption$$
$$for\ (XXTEA + RSA)\ =\ 3.5 + 5.5\ =\ 9\ Mb/s.$$
$$Hence,\ throughput\ efficiency\ =\ [(15 - 9)/15]\ *\ 100\ =\ 40\%.$$

This result shows that the hybrid cryptosystem based on (XXTEA + ECC) out-performs the hybrid cryptosystem based on (XXTEA + RSA) by 40%.

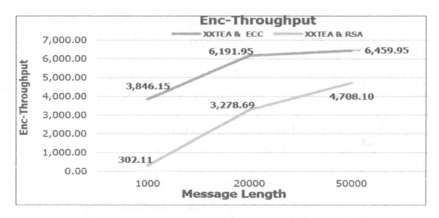

a. Comparing Enc-Throughput vs message sizes for hybrid cryptosystems (XXTEA &ECC) and XXTEA & RSA).

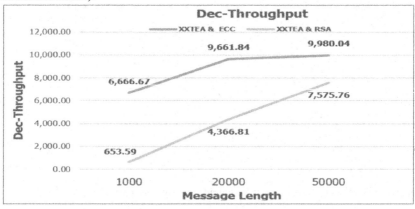

b. Comparing Dec-Throughput vs message sizes for hybrid cryptosystems (XXTEA &ECC) and (XXTEA & RSA).

Fig. 4. a. Comparing Enc-Throughput vs message sizes for hybrid cryptosystems (XXTEA & ECC) and (XXTEA & RSA). **b.** Comparing Dec-Throughput vs message sizes for hybrid cryptosystems (XXTEA & ECC) and (XXTEA & RSA).

Table 5. Shows the encryption and decryption throughput (Speed) of the hybrid cryptosystems.

Enc-speed Mb/s	Message size				
	1000	20000	50000	100000	Avg
XXTE & ECC	3,846.15	6,191.95	6,459.95	6,422.61	5,730.17
XXTE & RSA	302.11	3,278.69	4,708.10	5,827.51	3,529.10
Dec-Speed Mb/s					
	1000	20000	50000	100000	Avg
XXTE & ECC	6,666.67	9,661.84	9,980.04	9,708.74	9,004.32
XXTE & RSA	653.59	4,366.81	7,575.76	9,487.67	5,520.96

6 Conclusion

The work described in this paper showed that the XXTEA lightweight block cipher is more suitable to be used in IoT smart devices for data security since it requires less memory consumption and less computational cycles (cost). Besides, the ECC asymmetric cipher was used because it achieves a high level of bit security at smaller key sizes better than RSA. The ECC cipher was used to achieve authenticity, integrity, and non-repudiation. The XXTEA block cipher was used to achieve confidentiality. In addition, the Chaotic theory was used to generate random keys in each time data is being encrypted and SHA256 was used to achieve data integrity. Performance analysis and evaluation-based on simulation were performed. Results show that the hybrid cryptosystem based on (XXTEA + ECC) outperforms the hybrid cryptosystem based on (XXTEA + RSA) with respect to encryption and decryption time as well as it achieves better throughput by 40%. The proposed hybrid cryptosystem that combines ECC, XXTEA, SHA256, and Chaos random key generator achieve the main demanded characteristics of cryptography, including confidentiality, authenticity, integrity, and non-repudiation. This helps to protect IoT smart devices from vulnerabilities related to security attacks. The hardware realization of the proposed hybrid cryptosystem will be tackled in the near future work.

References

1. Bhardwaj, S., Kole, A.: Review and study of the Internet of Things: it's the future. In: 2016 IEEE International Conference Intelligent Control Power and Instrumentation (ICICPI) (2016)
2. Demblewski, M.: Security Frameworks for Machine-to-Machine Devices and Networks. Ph.D. Thesis, Nova Southeastern University (2015). https://nsuworks.nova.edu/cgi/view content.cgi?article=1068&context=gscis_etd. Accessed 10 Feb 2019
3. Ali, B., Awad, A.: Cyber and physical security vulnerability assessment for IoT-based smart homes. Sensors 18(3), 817 (2018)
4. Chandra, S., Paira, S., Alam, S., Sanya, G.: A comparative survey of symmetric and asymmetric key cryptography. In: International Conference on Electronics, Communication and Computational Engineering (ICECCE) (2014)
5. Kumar, Y., Munjal, R., Sharma, H.: Comparison of symmetric and asymmetric cryptography with existing vulnerabilities and countermeasures. IJCSMS Int. J. Comput. Sci. Manag. Stud. 11(03), (2011)
6. Henriques, M., Vernekar, N.: Using symmetric and asymmetric cryptography to secure communication between devices in IoT. In: 2017 IEEE International Conference IoT and Application (ICIOT) (2017)
7. Ruan, C., Luo, J.: Design and implementation of a mobile payment system for intelligent travel. In: 2014 IEEE 3rd International Conference Cloud Computing and Intelligence Systems (CCIS) (2014)
8. Xin, M.: A mixed encryption algorithm used in the Internet of Things security transmission system. In: 2015 IEEE International Conference Cyber-Enabled Distributed Computing and Knowledge Discovery (CyberC) (2015)

9. Biswas, K., Muthukkumarasamy, V., Wu, X.-W., Singh, K.: Performance evaluation of block ciphers for wireless sensor networks. In: Choudhary, Ramesh K., Mandal, J.K., Auluck, N., Nagarajaram, H.A. (eds.) Advanced Computing and Communication Technologies. AISC, vol. 452, pp. 443–452. Springer, Singapore (2016). https://doi.org/10.1007/978-981-10-1023-1_44

10. Ekera, M.: Differential Cryptanalysis of MD5. Master of Science Thesis Stockholm, Sweden (2009)

11. Kaur, S., et al.: Study of multi-level cryptography algorithm: multi-prime RSA and DES. Int. J. Comput. Netw. Inf. Secur. 9(9), 22 (2017)

12. Darwish, A., El-Gendy, M.M., Hassanien, A.E.: A new hybrid cryptosystem for Internet of Things applications. In: Hassanien, A.E., Fouad, M.M., Manaf, A.A., Zamani, M., Ahmad, R., Kacprzyk, J. (eds.) Multimedia Forensics and Security. ISRL, vol. 115, pp. 365–380. Springer, Cham (2017). https://doi.org/10.1007/978-3-319-44270-9_16

13. Yarrkov, A.: Cryptanalysis of XXTEA, 4 May 2010. https://eprint.iacr.org/2010/254.pdf. Accessed 10 Feb 2019

14. Bhaskar, C., Rupa, C.: An advanced symmetric block cipher based on chaotic systems. In: 2017 IEEE Innovations Power and Advanced Computing Technologies (i-PACT) (2017)

15. Yousefi, A., Jameii, S.: Improving the security of Internet of Things using encryption algorithms. In: 2017 IEEE International Conference IoT and Application (ICIOT) (2017)

16. Singh, S., Padhye, S.: Cryptanalysis of NTRU with n Public Keys. In: ISEA Asia Security and Privacy (ISEASP) (2017)

17. Khomlyak, O.: An investigation of lightweight cryptography and using the key derivation function for a hybrid scheme for security in IoT (2017)

18. Hatzivasilis, A.: Password hashing status in molecular diversity preservation. MDPI Int. J. (2017)

19. Harini, A., et al.: A novel security mechanism using hybrid cryptography algorithms. In: 2017 IEEE International Conference Electrical Instrumentation and Communication Engineering (ICEICE) (2017)

20. Elhoseny, M., et al.: Secure medical data transmission model for IoT-based healthcare systems. IEEE Access 6, 20596–20608 (2018)

21. Njuki, S., et al.: An evaluation on securing cloud systems based on cryptographic key algorithms. In: Proceedings of the 2018 2nd International Conference on Algorithms, ACM Computing and Systems (2018)

22. Shoup, V.: Advances in cryptology-CRYPTO. In: 2005 Proceedings of The 25th Annual International Cryptology Conference, Santa Barbara, California, USA, 14–18 August, vol. 3621. Springer (2005)

23. Abdelminaam, D.: Improving the security of cloud computing by building new hybrid cryptography algorithms. J. Electron. Inf. Eng. 8(1), 40–48 (2018)

24. Sagar, F.: Cryptographic Hashing Functions - MD5, September 2016. http://cs.indstate.edu/~fsagar/doc/paper.pdf. Accessed 20 Apr (2019)

25. Habboush, A.: Multi-level encryption framework. (IJACSA) Int. J. Adv. Comput. Sci. Appl. 9(4), 130–134 (2018)

26. Mahto, D., Khan, D., Yadav, D.: Security analysis of elliptic curve cryptography and RSA. In: Proceedings of the World Congress on Engineering 2016, WCE 2016, 29 June–1 June 2016, London, U.K, vol. I (2016)

27. Ragab, A.: Robust hybrid cryptosystem for protecting smart devices in Internet of Things (IoT), Master thesis, record number 14120399, Dept. of Computer Engineering, Arab Academy for Science, Technology and Maritime Transport, Cairo, Egypt (2019)

28. Bhasher, U., Rupa, C.: An advanced symmetric block cipher based on chaotic systems. In: IEEE International Conference on Innovations in Power and Advanced Computing Technologies (2017)
29. Libelium-Techedge: Smart Industrial Protocols Solution Kit. https://www.the-iot-marketplace.com/libelium-techedge-smart-industrial-protocols-solution-kit. Accessed 10 Feb 2019
30. AWS IoT Device Defender: Security management for IoT devices. https://aws.amazon.com/iot-device-defender/?nc=sn&loc=2&dn=5. Accessed 20 Apr 2019
31. Security on arm. https://developer.arm.com/technologies/security-on-arm. Accessed 20 Apr 2019
32. Wheeler, D., Needham, R.: Correction to XTEA. Computer Laboratory, Cambridge University, England (1998)
33. Andem, V.: A cryptanalysis of the tiny encryption algorithm, Master thesis, Department of Computer Science in the Graduate School of The University of Alabama (2003)
34. Miller, V.S.: Use of elliptic curves in cryptography. In: Williams, H.C. (ed.) CRYPTO 1985. LNCS, vol. 218, pp. 417–426. Springer, Heidelberg (1986). https://doi.org/10.1007/3-540-39799-X_31
35. Kaur, S., Bharadwaj, P., Mankotia, S.: Study of multi-level cryptography algorithm: multi-prime RSA and DES. Modern Education and Computer Science (MECS) Press (2017)
36. Barker, E., Dang, Q.: Recommendation for key management. NIST Special Publication 800-57 Part-3 Revision 1, National Institute of Standards and Technology (NIST), January 2015
37. Percival, C.: Stronger key derivation via sequential memory-hard functions, pp 1–16 (2009)
38. Dunkelman, O., Sekar, G., Preneel, B.: Improved meet-in-the-middle attacks on reduced-round DES. In: Srinathan, K., Rangan, C.P., Yung, M. (eds.) INDOCRYPT 2007. LNCS, vol. 4859, pp. 86–100. Springer, Heidelberg (2007). https://doi.org/10.1007/978-3-540-77026-8_8
39. Stamp, M., Low, R.: Applied Cryptanalysis: Breaking Ciphers in the Real World. Wiley, Hoboken (2017)
40. Albela, M., Lamas, P., Caramés, T.: A practical evaluation on RSA and ECC-based cipher suites for IoT high-security energy-efficient fog and mist computing devices. Sensors 18, 3868 (2018)
41. Ertaul, L., Kaur, M., Gudise, V.: Implementation and performance analysis of PBKDF2, Bcrypt, Scrypt algorithms. In: Proceedings of the International Conference on Wireless Networks (ICWN), Athens, pp. 66–72. Athens (2016)
42. Rajesh, S., Paul, V., Menon, V., Khosravi, M.: A secure and efficient lightweight symmetric encryption scheme for transfer of text files between embedded IoT devices. Symmetry 11, 293 (2019)
43. Shah, A., Engineer, M.: A survey of lightweight cryptographic algorithms for IoT-based applications. In: Tiwari, S., Trivedi, M.C., Mishra, K.K., Misra, A.K., Kumar, K.K. (eds.) Smart Innovations in Communication and Computational Sciences. AISC, vol. 851, pp. 283–293. Springer, Singapore (2019). https://doi.org/10.1007/978-981-13-2414-7_27. Accessed 20 Apr 2019
44. Percival, C.: Stronger key derivation via sequential memory-hard functions. https://www.tarsnap.com/scrypt/scrypt.pdf. Accessed 20 Apr 2019
45. Sehrawat, D., Nasib Gill, N.: Lightweight block ciphers for IoT based applications: a review. Int. J. Appl. Eng. Res. 13(5), 2258–2270 (2018). ISSN 0973-4562
46. Dinu, D.: Efficient and secure implementations of lightweight symmetric cryptographic primitives. Ph.D. Dissertation, Luxembourg University (2017) https://zdoc.pub/2017-in-luxembourg-to-obtain-the-degree-of.html. Accessed 20 Apr 2019
47. Mohd, B., Hayajneh, T.: Lightweight block ciphers for IoT: energy optimization and survivability techniques. IEEE Access 6, 35966–35978 (2018)

A Weighted Risk Score Model for IoT Devices

Shachar Siboni[1(✉)], Chanan Glezer[2], Asaf Shabtai[1],
and Yuval Elovici[1]

[1] Department of Software and Information Systems Engineering,
Ben-Gurion University of the Negev, 84105 Beer-Sheva, Israel
sibonish@post.bgu.ac.il, {shabtaia,elovici}@bgu.ac.il
[2] Department of Industrial Engineering and Management,
Ariel University, 40700 Ariel, Israel
chanang@ariel.ac.il

Abstract. The Internet of Things (IoT) defines a new era where ordinary physical objects are being transformed into smart connected devices. These advanced devices have the ability to sense, compute, and communicate with their surroundings via the Internet. This may result in severe network security breaches, as these devices in-crease the attack surface by exposing new vulnerabilities and infiltration points into restricted networks. One of the major challenges in such deployments is determining the security risks that IoT devices pose to the environment they operated in. This paper proposes an IoT device risk score model, denoted as the Weighted Risk Ranking (WRR) model. The proposed approach focuses on quantifying the static and dynamic properties of a device, in order to define a risk score. Our practical proof of concept demonstrates the use of the WRR scheme for several IoT devices in the context of an enterprise network, showing the feasibility of the suggested solution as a tool for device risk assessment in modern networks where IoT devices are widely deployed.

Keywords: Internet of Things · Security · Device risk assessment ·
Device-centric approach · Security risk score

1 Introduction

The Internet of Things (IoT) defines a new era where physical objects, including home appliances, medical equipment, organizational and industrial infrastructure, wearable devices, and more, are transformed into smart connected digital devices with the ability to sense, compute, and communicate with their surroundings via the Internet [1].

The proliferation of IoT technology and its applications poses major security and privacy risks due to the range of functionalities and capabilities provided by these systems [2]. Specifically, IoT devices are powered by different operating systems and are therefore exposed to various types of security breaches and attacks. Moreover, most of these smart devices are not developed with security in mind and are designed mainly on the basis of features and cost considerations. As low resource devices, in terms of power source, memory size, bandwidth communication, and computational capabilities, standard security solutions are largely not applicable [3].

© Springer Nature Switzerland AG 2019
G. Wang et al. (Eds.): SpaCCS 2019 Workshops, LNCS 11637, pp. 20–34, 2019.
https://doi.org/10.1007/978-3-030-24900-7_2

In addition, as smart connected devices, IoT devices can be continuously connected to the Internet, either directly or indirectly, via dedicated gateways, and therefore they are highly accessible—particularly to attackers [4]. Furthermore, these embedded devices are equipped with advanced sensing and communication capabilities which greatly increases the risk of using such devices on the networks [5]. Moreover, such devices are used in dynamic contexts and states, which significantly complicates the assessment of security and privacy risks they pose to existing environments [6].

Recently, IoT technology has been integrated into corporate and industrial environments, in order to ease the workload of employees, and increase business productivity and efficiency levels [7]. However, as IoT devices become more common in the workplace, different security and privacy risks are raised, both from the employees and the corporate perspectives [3]. The deployment of IoT devices in such environments makes companies much more vulnerable and increases their attack surface; these devices expose new vulnerabilities and infiltration points for attackers. One of the major problems in this situation is to determine the security risk the devices pose to the network [6].

In this paper, a risk score model, denoted as the Weighted Risk Ranking (WRR) model, for IoT devices is proposed. This new technique employs a device-centric approach and uses both static and dynamic features of the device, in order to derive a weighted risk score for IoT devices under test. Static features are device-specific, and include known vulnerabilities and service capabilities elements of an IoT device, which do not change over time (unless an update is performed). Dynamic features are IoT domain-related, and include the contexts in which the IoT device operates. Our practical proof of concept evaluates several IoT devices in the context of an enterprise network and demonstrates the feasibility of the proposed model for device risk assessment.

The rest of the paper is structured as follows. In Sect. 2 we present work related to this study. In Sect. 3, we portray in details the suggested risk score model, followed by a model implementation and operation in Sect. 4. We conclude and suggest possible future work in Sect. 5.

2   Related Work

Security risk assessment for the IoT domain has been investigated extensively in prior research. Different methodologies for assessing risks in the context of the IoT, by considering the dynamics and changes in IoT systems, were presented in [8]. IoT security and privacy risk considerations, helping organizations better characterize IoT devices by their capabilities and used to define the devices' security risks, were defined by [9].

A variety of security risk score definition solutions have been proposed both by academia and industry. In [10] a cyber risk scoring system for medical devices, which relies on a security questionnaire (based on the STRIDE model), is presented. Scientific-based security risk metrics were defined by [11]; these metrics aim to assess the cyber maturity level of governments, organizations, and more, using a modified CVSS base score along with the Analytic Hierarchy Process (AHP) technique.

A weighted risk scoring model for IT environments, which is part of the Nexpose tool, was suggested by [12]. This method considers the number of known vulnerabilities of an asset, the type of and services running by an asset, and the context in which the asset is deployed in the organization, in order to assign risk score.

Risk analysis for different IoT environments has been discussed in various works. In [13], a cyber-related risk assessment within the power grid is suggested. A risk-based adaptive security framework for IoT in the eHealth domain was presented by [14]. Risk analysis for smart homes, which emphasize the security risks and mitigation mechanisms for such IoT deployments was proposed by [15]. Another technique for risk assessment in smart home environments was presented in [16], where a risk-based permission model called Tyche based on domain experts and Mechanical Turk users was suggested to compute a relative ranking of risks associated with device operations, in order to limit the risk that apps pose to smart home users. Enterprise risk factors for IoT deployments were introduced by [6], which used a Delphi expert questionnaire in order to construct and revise the defined risk factors.

3   Weighted Risk Ranking Model Definition

In this section, our proposed risk score model for IoT devices, denoted as the Weighted Risk Ranking (WRR) model, M_{WRR}, is defined. The model consists of three main components, including: (1) the Risk Mapping Database, (2) the Weighted Risk Ranking Method, and (3) the Device Risk Score Calculation, as presented in Fig. 1.

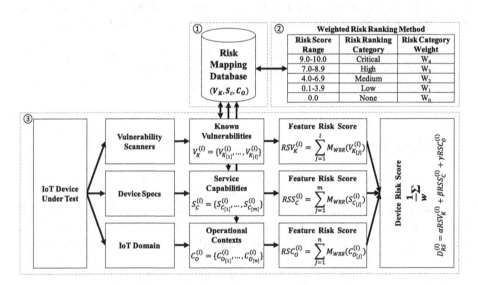

Fig. 1. The Weighted Risk Ranking model for IoT devices.

3.1 Risk Mapping Database

The risk mapping database, denoted as RMD, is a database component of the proposed model that stores all of the information about the model's features and their elements, as well as the base risk scores of these elements, as follows.

Definition of Features The set of features and elements used in our model, as shown in Fig. 1, include: (1) known vulnerabilities, denoted as V_K, this feature refers to the set of known vulnerabilities elements, in terms of software, hardware, and firmware vulnerabilities, such that using this information it is possible to compromise an IoT device and utilize it for further malicious activities and attacks (these elements are obtained from vulnerability scanner tools); (2) service capabilities, denoted as S_C, this feature refers to the set of service capabilities elements, including the means of communication and physical sensors built-in/embedded in IoT devices, such that using this set of capabilities, it is possible to collect private and sensitive information from/via the device, change the state of the environment the device is deployed on, and connect to the device via one of its existing means of communication in order to perform further attacks (these elements are obtained from the specification of an IoT device, based on its type and model); and (3) operational contexts, denoted as C_O, this feature refers to the set of operational contexts elements with respect to the IoT domain use case, such that different operational contexts, specifically locations and time of operation, imply different severity and security risks (these elements are defined for specific IoT domain).

Based on the definitions mentioned above, the RMD component contains three main sub-databases, one for each feature type (V_K, S_C, C_O) in the model. Each sub-database contains the possible risk information associated with its elements, along with the appropriate base risk score for each element. The RMD is a global database of the model, and given that, when assigning a risk score for IoT device i, the definitions of the device's elements and base risk scores with respect to the feature sets of the model are derived from this database, i.e., $V_K^{(i)} \in V_K$, $S_C^{(i)} \in S_C$, and $C_O^{(i)} \in C_O$, as shown in Fig. 1.

3.2 Weighted Risk Ranking Method

In our proposed model, all of the elements of the defined features are assigned a weighted risk score as follows. For each element in the model, a base risk score in the range of 0.1 and 10.0 is defined (see definition of elements' base risk scores in Sect. 4). Then, considering the NVD vulnerability severity ratings table for CVSS v3.0 calculator [17], a weighted version of this method is applied in our model using a risk category weight, as shown in Fig. 1, in order to define a numeric weighted risk score associated with elements of the model. Namely, the base risk score of each element in the model is multiplied by the appropriate weight W_i according to its risk score range shown in Fig. 1 (see assignment for the risk category weights in Sect. 4). Using this approach, we guarantee a higher risk score for devices that have elements with a high risk ranking category. Moreover, this method is applied on all of the elements of the model's features with respect to the proposed weighted version (compared to [17] which only considers known vulnerabilities, without risk category weights).

3.3 Device Risk Score Calculation

The risk score of an IoT device under test is derived from the set of elements of the device, defined as a device-centric approach. The definition of a device risk score based on the model's features and the device's elements is as follows. Given the afore-mentioned device features, the proposed risk score model M_{WRR} assigns a risk score, denoted as D_{RS}, for an IoT device under test such that the final weighted risk score for IoT device i is defined by the following weighted function definition:

$$D_{RS}^{(i)} = \alpha RSV_K^{(i)} + \beta RSS_C^{(i)} + \gamma RSC_O^{(i)} \tag{1}$$

where α, β, and γ are weighted parameters of the model and used for risk score calibration, and $RSV_K^{(i)}$, $RSS_C^{(i)}$, and $RSC_O^{(i)}$ are the appropriate risk score components of the model's features for the specific IoT device i, which are defined as the sum of all risk scores assigned by M_{WRR} to elements of the device, as shown in Fig. 1. It should be noted that different sets of elements exist for each feature based on the type and functionality of the device.

4 Model Implementation and Operation

In this section, we present the implementation and the operation of the proposed Weighted Risk Ranking (WRR) model. First, we establish the risk mapping database (RMD) and define the weights of the WRR model's features by employing the domain expert questionnaire methodology along with an expert elimination process. Next, using the WRR model implementation results, we assign the final weighted risk scores for several IoT devices and define their risk ranking respectively. Noted that in the current model implementation the IoT domain and the context for the risk calculations we refer to is a typical enterprise network environment, and we used a binary-based logarithmic scale (where $W_0 = 0$ and $W_i = 2^{i-1}$) for the risk category weights.

4.1 Domain Expert Questionnaire Structure and Expert Analysis

In this study, we used a ranking methodology approach for the domain expert questionnaire. For each question, a set of alternatives/items was provided, and the experts were required to assign absolute weights (without repetition) from one to N, where one refers to the lowest risk assignment, and N refers to the highest risk assignment for a given question (N is the number of alternatives/items for the question). This approach guarantees that each alternative/item (for a given question) is ranked uniquely using an appropriate weight from a risk-oriented perspective. Moreover, we asked the experts to refer to "Risk" as a measure for quantifying how an item in the questionnaire could affect the security level of an organization (the risk context) compared to other items.

The questionnaire was composed of a total of 9 ranking questions, divided into three categories: (1) ranking the model's features, (2) ranking the elements of the service capabilities feature, and (3) ranking the elements of the operational contexts feature. Note that, the known vulnerabilities elements are defined for each IoT device under test using vulnerability scanners (such as Nessus [18]) and are not using the questionnaire.

In total, 23 experts answered the questionnaire, 18 of which are from the hi-tech industry, with a variety of expertise (31% SW/HW engineers, 17% IT/QA, and 30% in different areas, such as management and offensive cyber security); the rest of the experts are from academia (22% researchers). Most of the experts have an academic degree (22% BSc, 30% MSc/MBA, and 22% PhD) or are in the process of pursuing a degree. Most also have extensive experience in the cyber security domain (an average of 5 years of experience) and some experience in the IoT domain (78% have more than one year of IoT experience). In order to reduce the variance of the results used in our model, we eliminated a group/subset of experts that answered the questionnaire. For each question in the questionnaire, we applied the standard deviation statistical test considering the 2σ-rule [19] to select the group of experts to be eliminated. Using this approach, we referred only to the ranking results of the group of experts with maximum similarity/consensus. Namely, the expert elimination process is used to handle outlier experts answering the questionnaire and by that to reduce the variance of the experts' selection (the final ranking/weights).

4.2 Model Implementation

In this section, the final weights for the model's features as well as the final base risk scores for all elements of the model (except for known vulnerabilities elements), with respect to the appropriate category they belong to, are defined from the domain expert questionnaire, as follows.

Definition of Features' Weights First we asked the experts to rank the model's features (namely, known vulnerabilities, service capabilities, and operational contexts), with respect to the definition of risk in this paper (meaning, which feature is more risky when considering a typical enterprise network). We then calculated the weights of these features, which are the values we assigned to α, β, and γ as the weighted parameters of the WRR model. These weights are calculated as weighted averages, as follows:

$$\alpha = \frac{\bar{V}_K}{\bar{V}_K + \bar{S}_C + \bar{C}_O} = 0.384; \quad \beta = \frac{\bar{S}_C}{\bar{V}_K + \bar{S}_C + \bar{C}_O} = 0.341; \quad \gamma = \frac{\bar{C}_O}{\bar{V}_K + \bar{S}_C + \bar{C}_O} = 0.275;$$

where $\bar{V}_K$, $\bar{S}_C$, and $\bar{C}_O$, are the results obtained by averaging the weights assigned by the group of experts after employ the expert elimination process.

Definition of Elements' Base Risk Scores The next set of questions we asked in the questionnaire referred to the service capabilities and operational contexts elements of the model. Here as well, we averaged the ranking results, the weights assigned by the group of experts after employ the expert elimination process, and defined the final base risk scores for all the relevant elements with respect to the appropriate category they belong to. Namely, the element's base risk score for element i in category j of feature k, denoted as $EBRS_{i,j}^k$, is defined by the following:

$$EBRS_{i,j}^k = \frac{\bar{E}_i}{N_{C_j}} \times \frac{\bar{C}_j}{N_{F_k}} \times 10 \tag{2}$$

where $\bar{E}_i$ is the average ranking results (among all of the selected experts) of element i (in category j of feature k), N_{C_j} is the number of elements in category j (of feature k), $\bar{C}_j$ is the average ranking results (among all of the selected experts) of category j (of feature k), and N_{F_k} is the number of categories in feature k; all of which are multiplied by 10 in order to assign the final base risk score in the range [0.1÷10].

The final results for the list of the top 15 service capabilities of IoT devices are shown in Table 1, and the final results for the locations and time of operational contexts in enterprise environments are presented in Fig. 2 (as a heatmap representation). It should be noted that for operational contexts elements we referred to context as a combination between a specific location (server room; meeting room; CxO offices; IT department; internal locations, such as hallways, kitchen, etc.; and external locations, such as receptionist, parking, etc.) and time of operation (morning, afternoon, evening, and night) with respect to the appropriate weight categories. Note that all these elements and their base risk scores are stored in the RMD database of the proposed WRR model.

Table 1. List of top 15 IoT service capabilities and their base risk scores.

Capability	Category	Risk Score
Wi-Fi	Connectivity	9.5
Cellular	Connectivity	6.0
Camera	Audio and Video	5.8
Mic	Audio and Video	5.6
GPS	Movement and Position	5.4
BT/BLE	Connectivity	4.7
Ethernet	Connectivity	4.3
Gas Detector	Environmental	3.3
Smoke Detector	Environmental	3.3
Motion Detector	Movement and Position	3.1
Thermometer	Environmental	3.0
ECG	Health Monitoring	2.4
Infrared Sensor	Environmental	2.4
Proximity Sensor	Movement and Position	2.3
Lighting Sensor	Environmental	2.2

Server Room	8.1	7.2	8.0	8.2
Meeting Room	6.4	5.5	6.4	0.0
CxO Office	7.0	6.1	6.9	7.1
IT Department	7.4	6.5	7.3	7.5
Internal	4.8	3.9	4.7	4.9
External	3.5	2.6	3.4	3.6
Contexts	Morning	Afternoon	Evening	Night
	6:00-12:00	12:00-16:00	16:00-22:00	22:00-6:00

Fig. 2. Operational contexts and their base risk scores (heatmap representation).

4.3 Model Operation

In this section, we applied our proposed WRR model on several off the shelf IoT devices in the context of enterprise network environment and assign the weighted risk scores for these devices. We used these risk scores results for final ranking, namely higher risk score referred to high ranking. Using the results obtained we demonstrate the feasibility of the proposed model for device risk assessment task.

Risk Score Assignment – an Example. In this section, we illustrate the process of using our proposed WRR model to assign a risk score for a smartphone device (LG G4). First, we define all of the smartphone's elements and their base risk scores (using the RMD component), in terms of known vulnerabilities (only one CVE exists: CVE-2003-0001, with a base risk score of 3.3), service capabilities (Bluetooth, cellular, Wi-Fi, GPS, camera, mic, and infrared), and operational contexts (location: all, time: all). Note that for the elements' definition and base risk score assignment process, we used the following tools and information (also shown in Fig. 1): for known vulnerabilities, we employed the Nessus vulnerability scanner tool [18]; for the service capabilities, we used the specification of the device (based on the device type and model), and assign the base risk scores using Table 1; and for operational contexts, we referred to the maximum context (the worst-case scenario) among all possible contexts for the IoT device under test from Fig. 2. Therefore, since the smartphone is a mobile device (meaning it can be located anywhere on the network and operated at any time), we consider the maximum context possible; in our case this would be: {Location: Server Room, Time: Night}, with a base risk score of 8.2. Next, we applied our WRR method, where for each element we assign its appropriate weighted risk score according to Fig. 1 with respect to a binary-based logarithmic scale (namely, $W_0 = 0$, $W_1 = 2^0$, $W_2 = 2^1$, $W_3 = 2^2$, and $W_4 = 2^3$). Finally, using the device risk score formulas, we assign the final weighted risk score for the smartphone device under test as follows: $RSV_K^{(Smartphone)} = 3.3$; $RSS_C^{(Smartphone)} = 133.4$; and $RSC_O^{(Smartphone)} = 32.8$, such that $D_{RS}^{(Smartphone)} = 0.384 RSV_K^{(Smartphone)} + 0.341 RSS_C^{(Smartphone)} + 0.275 RSC_O^{(Smartphone)} = 55.8$ (as also shown in Table 2 in the next subsection).

Analysis of Results. In this section, we provide an analysis of the results obtained after applying the proposed WRR model, in order to assign risk scores for several IoT devices, and ranking these devices from a risk perspective (meaning, determined which of the devices is more risky to an organization), as shown in Table 2. Recall that we

Table 2. Risk scores and ranking assignment for IoT devices using the weighted risk score (WRS), base risk score (BRS), and standard NVD metrics used in the proof of concept.

Device type	Model	WRS		BRS		NVD	
		Risk score	Rank	Risk score	Rank	Risk score	Rank
Smartphone	LG G4	55.8	13	17.0	13	3.3	2
Smartphone	HTC One E9 PLUS	54.5	10	15.7	10	0	1
Smartphone	Samsung Galaxy Edge 7	55.3	12	16.5	12	0	1
SmartWatch	ZGPAX S8	55.0	11	16.1	11	3.3	2
SmartWatch	Sony 3 SWR50	45.6	8	10.8	6	0	1
IP Camera	GeoVision GV-AVD2700	25.9	3	13.9	8	13.8	5
IP Camera	Edimax IC 3116 W	41.8	7	12.1	7	5.8	3
WI-Fi Printer	HP Officejet Pro 6830	35.5	5	8.0	4	0	1
Smart TV	Samsung UE40K6000	53.8	9	15.1	9	16.8	7
Smart Fridge	Samsung RS757LhQESR/ML	5.6	1	2.8	1	0	1
Motion Sensor	SimpleHome XHS7-1001	36.8	6	7.4	3	0	1
Wireless Keyboard	Microsoft Wireless Keyboard 850	29.1	4	9.4	5	14.4	6
Wireless Keyboard	Logitech MK520	23.7	2	6.7	2	7.5	4

refer to the risk score assignment as a measure for ranking, i.e., assignment of a high risk score refers to a high ranking.

In Table 2, for each IoT device we list the type, manufacturer, and specific model, as well as the final weighted risk score, denoted as the WRS metric in the table, obtained using the proposed WRR model. We also present the final base risk score, denoted as the BRS metric in the table, obtained without applying the Weighted Risk Ranking method (shown in Fig. 1), and the results obtained by applying the standard NVD metric [17] which only considers known vulnerabilities elements without weights. For each metric, we ranked the IoT devices based on their risk scores (shown in the 'Rank' columns in the table). Note that the elements of known vulnerabilities are considered very sensitive information, as they expose real vulnerabilities that exist in the device; therefore, we do not present this information in the paper. Moreover, with respect to the elements of service capabilities, for each IoT device we refer only to the set of elements covered by our model (shown in Table 1). Due to space constraints, we also omit this information from the paper (for full details, see the online specs for each device presented in the table). From operational contexts elements point of view, we found that locations are the most important context, whereas the time context is less relevant (since all of the devices can be operated at any time of the day). However, as mentioned, for each IoT device under test we referred to the maximum operational context (the worst-case scenario) among all possible elements from Fig. 2.

Based on the results obtained for all of the metrics, it can be seen that the WRS and BRS metrics obtain very similar results (from a ranking perspective) with several minor differences, whereas the NVD metric presents much different results. This can be explained by the fact that in NVD metric only known vulnerabilities are considered; as shown in Table 2, six of the IoT devices under test have a risk score of 0.0 (i.e., these devices have no known vulnerabilities), and the most risky device based on this metric is the Samsung UE40K6000 smart TV with a risk score of 16.8 (since it has multiple known vulnerabilities with moderate base risk scores). Further examination of the results showed that although the known vulnerabilities feature is assigned the highest weight (of 0.384) by the experts, this feature is actually a less important factor when calculating the final weighted risk score for IoT devices than the other feature components. Namely, there are not a lot of known vulnerabilities associated with the devices presented in Table 2, and for those that do exist, the base risk score is quite low (as shown by the NVD metric). This explains the large gap in the ranking results between the WRS/BRS metrics and the NVD metric.

Another observation that can be made from the results is that the experts assigned a high weight (a weight of 9.5 as shown in Table 1) to Wi-Fi connectivity, a capability shared by most of the devices in Table 2. This specific capability has a lot of influence on the final weighted risk score for an IoT device (assigned with a weighted element risk score of 29.2), which explains the difference between the WRS and BRS ranking results for the Sony 3 SWR50 smartwatch device, the SimpleHome XHS7-1001 motion sensor device, and specifically the GeoVision GV-AVD2700 IP camera device which does not have Wi-Fi connectivity. Further examination of the ranking results obtained by these metrics, showed that the smartphone devices are assigned the highest risk scores (and thus are ranked the highest in both the WRS and BRS metrics), along with one of the smartwatch devices (the ZGPAX S8 model which ranked eleven); by examining its capabilities we found that this specific model is defined as a smartwatch phone device, which can be operated as a smartphone, and thus it was ranked quite high. This means that these devices are the riskiest devices (with respect to the list of devices tested in our evaluation) operating in enterprise environments according to the WRR model (in both versions, with and without assigning the weights to the elements, meaning the WRS and BRS metrics respectively). This can be explained by the fact that although these devices have a low risk of known vulnerabilities elements (with minimum base risk scores), they have the most risky service capabilities elements (including several connectivity means, such as Wi-Fi, cellular and Bluetooth, video and audio, GPS, and other capabilities) according to Table 1, and since these devices are mobile devices, they can be operated at any time and in any place in the network, and thus have the most risky operational context element (of {Location: Server room, Time: Night}).

Unexpected ranking results were obtained for the smart TV device in that it ranked quite high (ranked as nine with respect to the list of devices shown in Table 2) in both metrics, thus it is considered quite risky by our WRR model. This can be explained by the fact that the specific smart TV model that we tested has multiple known vulnerabilities elements, several service capabilities elements (Wi-Fi, Ethernet, and a microphone), and although it is a stationary device, it can be operated in quite risky operational contexts (meeting rooms, IT departments, etc., and at any time). Another reasonable result is shown for the Edimax IC 3116 W IP camera device which was ranked as a moderate risk (ranked as seven in both the WRS and BRS metrics), since it has only a single known vulnerability element (with base and weighted feature risk scores of 5.8 and 11.6 respectively), several service capabilities (25.1 and 101.7 feature risks scores) and quite low operational context (from risk perspective, with base and weighted feature risk scores of 4.9 and 9.8 respectively). The HP Officejet Pro 6830 Wi-Fi printer device is also ranked as a moderate risk, since no vulnerabilities exist for the specific device model we tested, it has just a few capabilities (Wi-Fi, Ethernet, and scanner which we consider it as a camera-like capability), and it can be operated in different locations and at any time in the organization. Both of the wireless keyboards that were tested were ranked with moderate and low risks (in both the WRS and BRS cases); each of these devices has known vulnerabilities, short-range wireless connectivity (we refer to it as Bluetooth-like connectivity), and these devices can be operated at any place and at any time in the network. As can be seen in Table 2, the Microsoft Wireless Keyboard and the Wi-Fi printer are ranked the opposite, with a risk ranking of four and five in the WRS and BRS columns. Finally, in both metrics the smart fridge device was ranked the lowest, meaning this specific device type and model is the least risky device operated in the network (with respect to the list of devices tested in our evaluation).

To conclude, both versions of our proposed WRR model (demonstrated by the WRS and BRS results in Table 2), reflect situations more accurately (than, for example, the standard NVD calculator), because the model has greater granularity, considering known vulnerabilities, service capabilities, and operational contexts together when calculating the final risk score for IoT devices. However, when using the risk category weight approach, the trade-off is that more calculations are needed (to assign weights to all of the device's elements, each according to its ranking category in Fig. 1), but using this approach guarantees a higher risk score for devices that have elements with a high risk ranking category. Moreover, our model achieves nearly the same ranking results of the group of experts, thus it can be used as a benchmark for the device risk assessment task.

5 Conclusions

The Internet of Things (IoT) poses new security and privacy risks, specifically in enterprise environments, where smart connected IoT devices deployed in the network increase the attack surface of the organization. In this paper, a weighted risk score model, denoted as the Weighted Risk Ranking (WRR) model, for IoT devices is presented. The proposed model assigns a risk score for a device under test based on the device's set of elements, by assigning weights for these elements according to the risk category and the model's features they belong to.

Assessing the security level of IoT devices and analyzing the risk and impact these devices can pose to the environment they are deployed in are considered very complex tasks. This is due to the heterogeneous nature of IoT devices (there are different types of devices which are developed by different vendors, and each device has its own set of capabilities, etc.) and the fact that these devices are used in a variety of contexts and states (for example, an IoT device that operates in an enterprise network is exposed to different environments than an IoT device that is part of a smart home deployment). From our perspective, current risk scoring models lack the ability to assign an appropriate risk score for IoT devices; these scoring systems do not comprehensively address all of the main aspects of IoT security considerations (particularly with respect to known vulnerabilities, service capabilities, and operational contexts) when assigning a risk score. Each of these aspects impact differently on the security risk level, and thus there is a need for a model that considers all of these security features together.

The suggested features and elements included in the model are incorporated into a final weighted risk score according to the model's definition. Namely, for a given IoT device, first, its elements are defined from the model's database according to the model's features (e.g., the software vulnerability element is part of the known vulnerabilities feature, the physical sensor element is part of the service capabilities feature, and the specific location the device is operated in is part of the operational contexts feature). For each element, a base risk score is assigned using the model's implementation (this information is stored in the model's database). It should be noted that the model's database is created prior to the model's use, and it is part of an ongoing implementation process of the model, meaning that the database can be enhanced with additional elements and their base risk scores based on the set of features in use, the relevant IoT domain, the scenario in which the device is being tested, the types of devices examined, and so on. Next, based on the suggested Weighted Risk Ranking method, the base risk score of each element is multiplied by the appropriate weight, resulting in a weighted risk score for each element. Finally, the final weighted risk score for a device is calculated as a weighted sum of all of the elements that exist in the device, based on the features' weights (α, β, γ parameters).

The suggested WRR model is implemented using a domain expert questionnaire in which the experts were asked to rank a list of alternatives for each category of questions. Using this information, the model's components (weights for features and base risk scores for elements) were defined after employing an expert elimination process. It should be noted that several challenges and limitations exist when using a domain expert questionnaire approach as a tool for research, including selecting the type of questionnaire to use (ranking, rating, Yes/No or open questions, etc.), the definition of an expert (level of expertise, seniority, knowledge, etc.), the amount and variety of experts answering the questionnaire, and more. Specifically, for the risk assessment task, each expert has his/her own perspective, based on their previous experience and current role. For example, the main considerations of the experts for this work included: known attacks executed by IoT devices, motivation to exploit these devices (i.e., what can be gained by exploiting IoT devices), the type and capabilities of IoT devices, the number of devices of the same type and the locations of the devices deployed in the network. These challenges and limitations can lead to inaccuracy and inconsistency of the data and misleading conclusions when using a domain expert questionnaire approach. In order to tackle this problem, we used different types of experts, from several domains (industry and academia), and with very extensive experience in the cyber security and IoT domains. Furthermore, in order to reduce the variance between the experts answering the questionnaire (and in so doing reduce the variance in the final results), we applied the expert elimination process which aims to handle possible outliers.

The application of the model to assign risk scores and rank devices (from a risk perspective) was demonstrated on several IoT devices in the context of a typical enterprise network environment. Based on the results obtained, we found that our proposed WRR model can be used as a risk assessment tool for IoT devices, particularly because the model reflects situations more accurately as it has greater granularity and considers all of the features together when assigning a risk score for devices under test (compared to other approaches such as the standard NVD calculator which considers only known vulnerabilities elements without weights). Given this, we believe that the proposed model could be used to prioritize (based on the device risk scores and ranking assignment) which IoT devices should be updated or patched first, as well as which devices require additional security analysis using a security testbed for the IoT domain [20, 21]. Moreover, the proposed model could also be used as part of a context-based network access control solution for IoT environments, providing decision making functionality, in order to determine whether and in what context(s) (e.g., specific location, time of operation, etc.) to connect a specific IoT device to the network. It should be noted that although the definition of the model is broadly defined, and it can be implemented for any IoT domain, the model is currently targeted for a specific use case scenario, and the proof of concept conducted in this work proves the feasibility of the proposed model to properly assign risk scores to IoT devices and rank them based on the security risk they pose in that context. However, new IoT devices can be assessed using the model with minor modifications, e.g., an IoT device that has elements that do not appear in the model; in this case, these elements can be considered as capability-like or context-like elements of the model, as shown in the model operation section. Therefore, although further implementation is required, our suggested WRR model can be used as a benchmark for the device risk assessment task.

The main goal of this research was to present the concept of a model for assigning a risk score for IoT devices using a weighted version of the main features that specifically characterize the IoT security domain. In future research, additional device specific and domain related features and elements will be used to enhance the model's capabilities (and specifically, the database, which is a crucial component of the model); this will allow us to generate a more accurate risk score for an IoT device, as well as to adjust the model with respect to different IoT application domains. For example, an important factor that should be considered in the model is whether the device is secured by design, including whether it uses TLS/SSL for data in transit or uses an encryption mechanism for data at rest, and whether the device is physically secured. This issue, along with other parameters (features and elements), will be considered in the future. In addition, the risk category weights will be considered as hyperparameters of the model which can be calibrated using trial and error according to model assignment (i.e., the final ranking of IoT devices based on risk score assignment). With regard to the domain expert questionnaire, questions will address different contexts (e.g., specific attacks, etc.), and additional experts will be included in order to minimize possible bias of the model's assignment. Furthermore, additional devices and device types should be evaluated in order to test and verify the model's assignment in different contexts and states (from both the device and IoT domain level perspectives). In addition to the comparison with the standard NVD approach, the suggested WRR model will also be compared against other similar models in the literature, e.g., the analytic hierarchy process (AHP), in order to further assess the strengths and weaknesses of the model. Finally, one of the main disadvantages of using a domain expert questionnaire is that the model is static (e.g., in order to add a new element to the model, all of the experts must answer another set of questions or complete the questionnaire again). Thus, we would like to consider other approaches for the problem at hand, including employing machine learning approaches and applying the model with big data (a large number of devices and contexts).

References

1. Atzori, L., Iera, A., Morabito, G.: The Internet of Things: a survey. Comput. Netw. **54**(15), 2787–2805 (2010)
2. Sicari, S., Rizzardi, A., Grieco, L.A., Coen-Porisini, A.: Security, privacy and trust in Internet of Things: the road ahead. Comput. Netw. **76**, 146–164 (2015)
3. Weber, R.H.: Internet of Things-New security and privacy challenges. Comput. Law Secur. Rev. **26**(1), 23–30 (2010)
4. Roman, R., Zhou, J., Lopez, J.: On the features and challenges of security and privacy in distributed Internet of Things. Comput. Netw. **57**(10), 2266–2279 (2013)
5. Abomhara, M. Køien, G.M.: Security and privacy in the Internet of Things: current status and open issues. In: 2014 International Conference on Privacy and Security in Mobile Systems (PRISMS), pp. 1–8. IEEE, May 2014
6. Chang, S.I., Huang, A., Chang, L.M., Liao, J.C.: Risk factors of enterprise internal control: Governance refers to Internet of Things (IoT) environment, RISK (2016)
7. Bi, Z., Da Xu, L., Wang, C.: Internet of Things for enterprise systems of modern manufacturing. IEEE Trans. Ind. Inf. **10**(2), 1537–1546 (2014)
8. Nurse, J.R., Creese, S., De Roure, D.: Security risk assessment in Internet of Things systems. IT Prof. **19**(5), 20–26 (2017)
9. NIST: IoT security and privacy risk considerations (2017). https://www.nist.gov/sites/default/files/documents/2017/12/20/nist_iot_security_and_privacy_risk_considerations_discussion_draft.pdf. Accessed 10 Mar 2019
10. Stine, I., Rice, M., Dunlap, S., Pecarina, J.: A cyber risk scoring system for medical devices. Int. J. Crit. Infrastruct. Prot. **19**, 32–46 (2017)
11. Watkins, L.A., Hurley, J.S.: Cyber maturity as measured by scientific-based risk metrics. J. Inf. Warfare **14**(3), 57–65 (2015)
12. Rapid7: Nexpose, a weighted model for risk calculation (2018). https://help.rapid7.com/nexpose/en-us/Files/Risk_scoring_FAQ.html. Accessed 10 Mar 2019
13. Mohajerani, Z., et al.: Cyber-related risk assessment and critical asset identification within the power grid. In: IEEE PES on Transmission and Distribution Conference and Exposition (2010)
14. Abie, H., Balasingham, I.: Risk-based adaptive security for smart IoT in eHealth. In: Proceedings of the 7th International Conference on Body Area Networks, pp. 269–275. Institute for Computer Sciences, Social-Informatics and Telecommunications Engineering (2012)

15. Jacobsson, A., Boldt, M., Carlsson, B.: A risk analysis of a smart home automation system. Future Gener. Comput. Syst. **56**, 719–733 (2016)
16. Rahmati, A., Fernandes, E., Eykholt, K., Prakash, A.: Tyche: a risk-based permission model for smart homes. In: 2018 IEEE Cybersecurity Development (SecDev), pp. 29–36. IEEE, September 2018
17. NIST: NVD vulnerability metrics and severity ratings for CVSS v3.0 (2019). https://nvd.nist.gov/vuln-metrics/cvss. Accessed 10 Mar 2019
18. Tenable: Nessus vulnerability scanner tool for network security (2018). https://www.tenable.com/products/nessus-home. Accessed 10 Mar 2019
19. Kdnuggets: Removing outliers using standard deviation in Python (2017). https://www.kdnuggets.com/2017/02/removing-outliers-standard-deviation-python.html. Accessed 10 Mar 2019
20. Siboni, S., Shabtai, A., Tippenhauer, N.O., Lee, J., Elovici, Y.: Advanced security testbed framework for wearable IoT devices. ACM Trans. Internet Technol. (TOIT) **16**(4), 26 (2016)
21. Siboni, S., et al.: Security testbed for Internet-of-Things Devices. IEEE Trans. Reliab. **68**(1), 23–44 (2018)

Connected Vehicles: A Privacy Analysis

Mark Quinlan$^{(\boxtimes)}$, Jun Zhao, and Andrew Simpson

Department of Computer Science, University of Oxford,
Wolfson Building, Parks Road, Oxford OX1 3QD, UK
{mark.quinlan,jun.zhao,andrew.simpson}@cs.ox.ac.uk

Abstract. Just as the world of consumer devices was forever changed by the introduction of computer controlled solutions, the introduction of the engine control unit (ECU) gave rise to the automobile's transformation from a transportation product to a technology platform. A modern car is capable of processing, analysing and transmitting data in ways that could not have been foreseen only a few years ago. These cars often incorporate telematics systems, which are used to provide navigation and internet connectivity over cellular networks, as well as data-recording devices for insurance and product development purposes. We examine the telematics system of a production vehicle, and aim to ascertain some of the associated privacy-related threats. We also consider how this analysis might underpin further research.

Keywords: Connected vehicles · Connected cars · Privacy ·
Privacy assessment · Data privacy · Security

1 Introduction

A modern automobile equipped with systems for navigation and communication, such as a wireless modem, is generally called a *connected car*. Such cars also have various systems connected to an in-vehicle network (often called the Controller Area Network bus, or CAN-Bus—a message protocol that allows multiple micro-controllers on a network to communicate without a single host computer) that collect data on their usage.

Naturally, connected vehicles bring with them worries relating to the privacy of personal data. A recent example of a connected vehicle privacy issue is the illegal tracking of leased vehicles in France[1]. In that case, it was found that the company was installing an additional tracking unit onto the CAN-Bus, which would relay not only GPS coordinates, but also vehicle usage statistics—without the user's knowledge or consent. Furthermore, connected cars present a significant opportunity for data misuse. For example, users might fabricate their location or usage data, or use the built-in applications maliciously [3], while,

---

[1] http://www.lepoint.fr/high-tech-internet/geolocalisation-la-cnil-rend-une-sanction-exemplaire-31-07-2014-1850400_47.php.

© Springer Nature Switzerland AG 2019
G. Wang et al. (Eds.): SpaCCS 2019 Workshops, LNCS 11637, pp. 35–44, 2019.
https://doi.org/10.1007/978-3-030-24900-7_3

on the manufacturer side, there are opportunities to share or sell data to third parties without appropriate consent.

Many of the systems currently in place do not allow for significant user control over what kinds of data are collected, nor do they have clear privacy policies in place [20]. In many cases, there may be users who are not aware of their data being collected and used by third parties [12], or even that a privacy policy for their vehicle exists [14].

We provide a high-level overview of the privacy risks affecting the current connected vehicle landscape. To this end, we provide a high-level assessment of the threat landscape based on an examination of a telematics unit, and extract sample data. We then make inferences to privacy issues surrounding the larger data transmission, handling and storage infrastructure.

2   Background

Within the Internet of Things (IoT) landscape, significant attention has been focused on privacy aspects relating to the use of connected objects. While continuously connected smartphones have been a consistent topic of interest [4,5], connected cars research has tended to focus on security (e.g. [17]).

Contributions such as [8] and [16] provide foundations with respect to security; they also provide a background for privacy concerns, without directly assessing a production telematics system for such threats. More pertinently: [6] provides an overview of the expectations and interests of the users and developers of connected vehicles; [13] expounds on the use of potentially nefarious use of location-based services as a privacy threat; and [10] illustrates how data generated by connected vehicles can be used for usage-based insurance purposes.

Our primary concern is privacy: we do not concern ourselves with security flaws (other than when such flaws lead to privacy compromises). A key concern has been an analysis of the data that these devices explicitly capture and return to their manufacturers. We gave consideration to an analysis of a popular telematics systems produced by a global manufacturer. A policy review was conducted, which yielded information pertaining to general areas of data collected.

3   Data Acquisition

3.1   Choice of Unit

We considered a connected vehicle telematics unit (by which we mean a head unit and/or a head unit with a TCU (Telematics Communications Unit, which we subsequently refer to as 'the sample-unit') featuring built-in internet connectivity that can be used without prior user set-up). With respect to our chosen manufacturer, any vehicle from 2009 onwards fitted with either a head unit and modem combination or a head unit with a built-in modem unit met the definition.

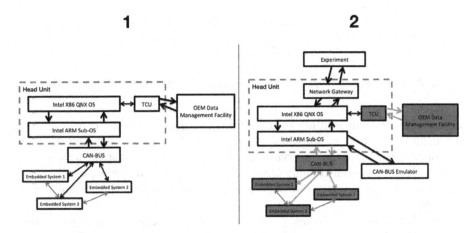

Fig. 1. The architecture as understood at a high-level is shown on the left-hand side. The right-hand side highlights the entry-method that was used. The sections of the original system that needed to be bypassed have been greyed out.

Our sample-unit was taken from a 2014 vehicle, of which the technology powering it can be found within production vehicles today, and chosen due to its similarity in terms of functionality with units provided by other manufacturers. The sample-unit was chosen on the basis of the following.

- A system built upon QNX[2] was a desirable feature, due to QNX being a commercial Unix-like real-time operating system developed by Blackberry that has been used in over 60 million cars (and other products, such as tablets and mobile phones)[3].
- The QNX system of our chosen manufacturer is open-source and enjoys the support of a relatively large third-party developer community. Currently, no other system is as well established within the automotive sector (although Automotive-Grade-Linux (AGL)[4] is increasing in popularity).
- Our chosen sample-unit allows for bench-testing functionality. Provided a vehicle can be emulated around the system, it is possible for an investigation to take place in a test environment, whereby only the telematics module (as opposed to the whole vehicle) is required.

3.2 System Overview

Our sample-unit functions identically to more advanced systems from the same manufacturer, but does not support functionality such as voice control or ges-

---

[2] http://www.qnx.com/news/events/japan-summit/en/presentations/Connectivity%20in%20automotive_en.pdf.

[3] http://www.osnews.com/story/28133/Ford_ditches_Microsoft_for_QNX_in_latest_in-vehicle_tech_platform.html.

[4] https://www.automotivelinux.org/announcements/2018/12/17/agl-grows-with-five-new-members.

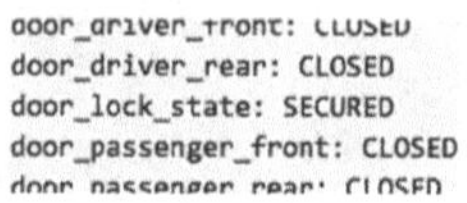

door_driver_front: CLOSED
door_driver_rear: CLOSED
door_lock_state: SECURED
door_passenger_front: CLOSED
door passenger rear: CLOSED

Fig. 2. An example of captured data containing sensor types and string values

tures. (However, code relating to these functions may be found on such units.) The architecture of the sample-unit (illustrated in Fig. 1) is divided into two main components: the multimedia service and connected services system, which runs on an X86-based system running QNX; and an ARM-based system, which manages the CAN-Bus interface that the car uses to communicate with its embedded controllers.

This design made it possible to build a test-bench environment in which the sample-unit's ARM-based module was connected to a vehicle CAN-Bus emulator, thus (to a certain extent) providing a 'complete vehicle' environment. We ensured that the emulator was coded with the Vehicle Identification Number (VIN) of the same car from which the sample-unit was taken.

The Intel element of the sample-unit unit is capable of acting as a network gateway with a fixed IP address (see Fig. 1). This system allows easy access (through a USB–Ethernet interface) to its internal systems and network. A configuration file allows for several USB interfaces (i.e. an Ethernet to USB converter with firmware matching that of what is presumably used by the manufacturer's technicians) to be used. Once a suitable USB interface was procured, it was possible to gain the root access password for the Intel system through injecting content into the navigation update service.

With root access enabled, the Intel component allowed execution of processes on both it and the ARM system. From there, an SSH server could be enabled from which we could login as root using the details procured from the navigation update service. From here, it became possible to clone the entire file system image of the unit for further analysis.

Using the data recovered, it was possible to build and execute a script containing API information, public and private keys, and login information in order to have the sample-unit send the message content to a local web server set-up on a laptop connected to the vehicle via the USB interface. The data recovered was sanitised and categorised, then used to analyse potential privacy implications.

3.3 Data Sanitation

To make better sense of the raw data collected, we went through a data-sanitation process. The data elements can be described thus.

– *Obfuscated data.* This is the raw data as procured through the experiment set-up. The data as it stands would not be usable for analytical purposes as it has been obfuscated by the manufacturer. In this case, it refers to a message ID of a proprietary value, sensor type and sensor data relating to a particular vehicle.

Table 1. Privacy policy unique data points

Information type	Unique data points	Information type	Unique data points
Speed	2	Steering inputs	2
Braking inputs	4	Accelerator input	3
Seat usage	2	Door/window usage	11
Interior climate	7	Exterior climate	3
Engine status	6	Fuel status	3
Lighting controls	2	Mileage	1
Vehicle coordinates	1	Date and time	2
Infotainment usage	7	Keyfob status	2
Vehicle identification	1		

- *Sensor types.* Of the returned datasets, these would be the first variable that is described. See, for example, Fig. 2, where door locks and hinge assemblies are shown to have their own sensors relaying data.
- *Sensor data.* This pertains to values associated with sensor type variables. Some values are straightforward (e.g. ON/OFF, OPEN/CLOSED, and TIME AND DATE), while some require more interpretation.
- *Informed descriptive data.* To provide relevant meaning to the data collected, a description was added to the variables and values that provided a non-numerical overview of what kind of data the variable pertained to (e.g. the brake positioning sensor indicates it collects data relating to the brake pedal and performance) and to provide meaning to the value that was being collected (e.g. ON/OFF means the ABS sensor is turned on or off). To ensure that the descriptions were as accurate as possible, we tried to use as many different sources as possible when analysing the data.

4   Analysis

The analysis of the sample-unit provided a plethora of information relating to the use of the vehicle, as well as some more personal features surrounding the use of a car. It also revealed the wider ecosystem in which the vehicle operates. The data was classified into a number of high-level categories (see Table 1). The *information types* represent parts of the core driving experience, such as steering, as well as other areas such as infotainment usage, and capturing time stamps. The *unique data points* represent specific, unique points of data about a category. For example, *door/window usage* has 11 unique data points, with separate messages covering opening status and how far the window is opened. Some data points contain more information than others. For example, *speed* can be broken down further into brake usage on each individual wheel. The experiment uncovered points of interest within the connected vehicle ecosystem that merit further discussion. The first topic (monetising sensor information) deals directly with the results in Table 1; the further topics representing a development of thoughts from both Table 1 and the data-acquisition process.

4.1 Monetising Sensor Information

The sensors from which our chosen sample-unit records data are capable of providing a detailed picture of vehicle usage that could give rise to excessive profiling. For example, individual wheel speed sensors can be used to determine the angle of a corner, and the speed and the forces being applied in that corner. This data can be combined with throttle positioning and brake force application to develop a driver profile. Also, the telematics can provide data relating to button presses on the in-vehicle system controller, from which it can be determined how often a user combines on-board infotainment use with driving.

In its privacy policy, our chosen manufacturer states that it shares its data with a newly formed subsidiary that essentially acts as a white-label data-storage service for around 8.5 million cars. This data is then stored on cloud-based servers and can be used to broker, for example, pay-as-you-drive insurance, whereby the customer pays a fee based on, for example, the amount of miles covered. This is a model already implemented in (for example) the UK under limited mileage policies via specialist providers [7].

Previously, a pay-how-you-drive model was not viable. However, such a model is now eminently possible. For example, if an individual often carries passengers, and often drives enthusiastically on busy roads where the potential for accidents may be significant, charges may rise. Previously, these were questions an insurance company might ask to help calculate the risk of a potential customer; now, however, there is the potential to acquire highly detailed driving reports [9].

It has been reported that, by 2025, the market for data types captured from connected cars could be worth almost 33 billion US dollars[5]. It can be assumed that the potential for significant abuse within these models exists. Looking beyond personal privacy interference, statistical inferences based on these datasets and form the basis of accident prediction and decision-making that could (in theory) serve to penalise users with specific driving habits.

4.2 Privacy Policies and Controls

Developing privacy policies becomes difficult when they need to be tailored to a wide range of potential specifications: the privacy information for the connected

---

[5] https://www.mckinsey.com/~/media/McKinsey/Industries/Automotive%20and%2 0Assembly/Our%20Insights/Monetizing%20car%20data/Monetizing-car-data.ashx.

services platform of one manufacturer is more akin to a 'If, Then' statement than a standard policy document[6]. In addition, policy documentation is not always available from the manufacturer, and in many countries such documentation is not explicitly agreed to upon purchase. When comparing privacy policies to our data, it becomes clear that users may not be aware of the amount of unique data points that are collected, as none of the policies have been that specific.

Typically, users are not made aware of the ways in which their data may be collected or used, and have no control over who can access their data, how their data is processed, or if it is shared with third parties. In many cases, the user is not made aware of the existence of the privacy policy, especially in cases where an owner purchases the vehicle via the second-hand market.

4.3 Third-Party Applications

Connected cars are often built upon platforms that allow for the installation and use of third-party applications and services. Our sample-unit is no different, collecting data on the use of and interaction with these applications (although this functionality was not explicitly tested). In many cases, these applications perform functions analogous to those one can download and use on any mobile device, such as a smartphone. As such, user privacy concerns in these areas mirror those found within mobile applications development and usage.

Many of these applications are designed to adapt to any given user's specific needs and context. However, these applications often do not provide mechanisms to provide users control over the kind of data that is collected and used by these applications, thereby giving rise to potential privacy violations [19]. These applications can also be developed and installed without the manufacturer's knowledge or consent, and therefore are not subject to any controls the manufacturer may have placed on vehicle system access.

It is, therefore, important to highlight the need to provide structural guarantees to users of connected cars in order to provide confidence that data confidentiality is ensured throughout the ecosystem. Of course, to do this, there is first a need to be aware of users' privacy expectations, as well as what constitutes a trustworthy ecosystem [1].

4.4 Data Confidentiality Within the Wider Ecosystem

In [15] Miorandi et al. define data confidentiality to be one of the defining issues faced by those designing and developing IoT systems. As a consequence of the large volumes of data generated by a connected car over its lifetime, together with the limitations of control over its data transmission systems, current approaches to preserving confidentiality may not be applicable to connected vehicles.

---

[6] https://myc-profile.bmwgroup.com/api/gateway/contentserver/staticcontent/Angular/gdpr/v2/?target=bmw-browser#/legal-docs-content?version=2018.05.15&fileName=Bmw_cd_pp_gb-en.json.

From our knowledge of the sample-unit (see Fig. 1), we can see that connected vehicles are highly reliant on continuous wireless connectivity from third-party service providers—which are known to be potentially vulnerable to various intrusions, including unauthorised network access, man-in-the-middle attacks, network jamming or interference, spoofing and denial-of-service attacks [2].

It is argued in [18] that information networks that support IoT applications need to be able to guarantee identification, integrity, confidentiality and undeniability. From a connected vehicle perspective, it is argued that network availability is the most important factor, followed by confidentiality [11]. Confidentiality issues arise due to the volume of data generated, as well as the effectiveness of control systems for access to these dynamic data streams [15]. There are also issues related to vehicle identity management (discussed further below). This makes cars as vulnerable to attack as any other IoT device. User privacy and security can become compounded by this lack of data integrity and confidentiality, and unauthorised access to or interference with systems within the car could hamper its ability to function safely [14].

4.5 The Automotive Lifecycle

With the lifecycle of an average car being approximately nine years[7], a connected car has a longer lifespan than the typical IoT device. In addition, it is significantly more likely to be re-sold over its lifetime. However, from our assessment of the data our chosen sample-unit collects, as well as the manner in which it does so, there does not appear to be an easy means of differentiating between users, so as to potentially generate data that could harm previous users when utilized for for the monetization of sensor data. Therefore, the vehicle continues to collect data as if it were being used by only one person. Furthermore, due to the fact that the vehicle is primarily identified by its VIN, within our system the possibility existed to continue monitoring the vehicle's use through applications that allow some remote information display or basic remote access. Further potential privacy infractions may occur at the disposal stage, where the vehicle may be recycled, or stripped for parts—another area where the connected car differs from many other IoT implementations.

4.6 A Lack of Standardisation

An issue that recurred within this study related to accurately defining telematics as a concept within the industry. A lack of standardisation within components used in automotive telematics systems means it is difficult to ascertain a single definition of telematics within connected cars.

As there are so many different platforms, components and systems, it becomes difficult to ensure that data confidentiality and long-term availability is maintained for users throughout the supply chain of these products. From the

---

[7] http://www.buckingham.ac.uk/wp-content/uploads/2014/11/pnc-2014-usedcar.pdf.

investigation of our sample-unit, it is by no means a certain prospect that the manufacturer will be able to maintain their infrastructure, nor that the systems built into the vehicles will be able to maintain their availability over the lifecycle of the car, which, on average, is significantly longer than the projected lifespan of many other IoT devices. This leads to complexities with regards to designing adequate privacy policies.

5   Conclusions

The current state-of-the-art within connected vehicles reveals that a significant amount of work still needs to take place in order to secure these vehicles. The technology within these vehicles has an exponential development rate accompanied by a long usage lifecycle: security, policy and the legality of what is being implemented in many cases needs to catch up with the technological changes. Furthermore, the academic literature reveals that there is significant scope for improvement in understanding exactly how these vehicles collect and use data.

We have provided an assessment of privacy-related threats associated with the connected vehicle landscape. This assessment was supported by an analysis of a popular telematics systems produced by a global manufacturer. As with any study of this nature, there are limitations to what has been done.

First, due to the available budget, only a single sample-unit has been procured. Such systems are designed to not function unless they are installed into a vehicle where all the sub-components have a matching VIN. In order to overcome this, a bench-testing environment was used, whereby an emulator took on most of the functions that the sample-unit was expected to interface with. However, this does not generate any simulated vehicle data. Second, the processes used to generate the messages arise out of a reverse-engineering process, which may have led to some functionality not being captured. Third, although great care was taken in ensuring that the procured telematics unit represented the largest possible group of connected vehicles, the results may not reflect other manufacturers' approaches

Planned future research activities include performing similar analyses on other types of telematics units, such as those based on AGL, and those from different manufacturers. Also, as this paper serves only as a high-level privacy analysis, there remains significant scope for a more in-depth analysis on the future business models that these datasets enable, as well as attempting to gain a better understanding of the end-users' perceptions of their privacy.

References

1. Albright, B.: Protecting connected cars. Aftermarket Bus. World **126**(2), 10–11 (2017)
2. Alheeti, A., Khattab, M., Mcdonald-Maier, K.: Intelligent intrusion detection in external communication systems for autonomous vehicles. Syst. Sci. Control Eng. **6**(1), 48–56 (2018)

3. Atzori, L., Iera, A., Morabito, G.: The Internet of Things: a survey. Comput. Netw. **54**(15), 2787–2805 (2010)
4. Benenson, Z., Gassmann, F., Reinfelder, L.: Android and iOS users' differences concerning security and privacy. In: CHI 2013 Extended Abstracts on Human Factors in Computing Systems, pp. 817–822. Communications of the ACM, New York (2013)
5. Camp, L.J.: Respecting people and respecting privacy. Commun. ACM **58**(7), 27–28 (2015)
6. Glancy, D.: Privacy in autonomous vehicles. Santa Clara Law Rev. **52**(4), 1171–1239 (2012)
7. Haberle, T., Charissis, L., Fehling, C., Nahm, J., Leymann, F.: The connected car in the cloud: a platform for prototyping telematics services. IEEE Softw. **32**(6), 11–17 (2015). https://doi.org/10.1109/MS.2015.137
8. Hubaux, J.P., Juels, A.: Privacy is dead, long live privacy. Commun. ACM **59**(6), 39–41 (2016). https://doi.org/10.1145/2834114
9. Joy, J., Gerla, M.: Internet of vehicles and autonomous connected car - privacy and security issues. In: 2017 26th International Conference on Computer Communication and Networks (ICCCN), pp. 1–9, July 2017. https://doi.org/10.1109/ICCCN.2017.8038391
10. Kaplun, V., Segal, M.: Breaching the privacy of connected vehicles network. Telecommun. Syst. **70**(4), 541–555 (2019)
11. Kasinathan, P., Pastrone, C., Spririto, M.A., Vinkovits, M.: Denial-of-service detection within the Internet of Things. In: Proceedings of the 9th IEEE International Conference on Wireless and Mobile Computing, Networking and Communications (WiMob 2013), pp. 600–607. IEEE (2013)
12. Larkin, J.: Mapping the legal framework for autonomous vehicles. Automot. Ind. **195**(2), 24–25 (2017)
13. Lim, J., Yu, H., Kim, K., Kim, M., Lee, S.: Preserving location privacy of connected vehicles with highly accurate location updates. IEEE Commun. Lett. **21**(3), 540–543 (2017). https://doi.org/10.1109/LCOMM.2016.2637902
14. Mena, D.M., Papanagiotou, I., Yang, B.: Internet of Things: survey on security. Inf. Secur. J.: Global Perspect. **27**(3), 162–182 (2018). https://doi.org/10.1080/19393555.2018.1458258
15. Miorandi, D., Sicari, S., Pellegrini, F.D., Chlamtac, I.: Internet of Things: vision, applications and research challenges. Ad Hoc Netw. **10**(7), 1497–1516 (2012). https://doi.org/10.1016/j.adhoc.2012.02.016
16. Othmane, L.B., Weffers, H., Mohamad, M.M., Wolf, M.: A survey of security and privacy in connected vehicles. In: Benhaddou, D., Al-Fuqaha, A. (eds.) Wireless Sensor and Mobile Ad-Hoc Networks, pp. 217–247. Springer, New York (2015). https://doi.org/10.1007/978-1-4939-2468-4_10
17. Ring, T.: Connected cars - the next target for hackers. Netw. Secur. **2015**(11), 11–16 (2015)
18. Suo, H., Wan, J., Zou, C., Liu, J.: Security in the Internet of Things: a review. In: 2012 International Conference on Computer Science and Electronics Engineering, vol. 3, pp. 648–651, March 2012
19. Wang, E.S.T., Lin, R.L.: Perceived quality factors of location-based apps on trust, perceived privacy risk, and continuous usage intention. Behav. Inf. Technol. **36**(1), 2–10 (2017)
20. Weber, R.H.: Internet of Things: new security and privacy challenges. Comput. Law Secur. Rev. **6**(1), 23–30 (2010)

Privacy-Preserving Big Data Analytics: From Theory to Practice

Mohammad G. Raeini$^{(\boxtimes)}$ and Mehrdad Nojoumian

Department of Computer and Electrical Engineering and Computer Science,
Florida Atlantic University, Boca Raton 33431, USA
mghasemineja2017@fau.edu

Abstract. In the last decade, with the advent of Internet of Things
(IoT) and Big Data phenomenons, data security and privacy have become
very crucial issues. A significant portion of the problem is due to not
utilizing appropriate security and privacy measures in data and computational infrastructures. Secure multiparty computation (secure MPC) is
a cryptographic tool that can be used to deal with the mentioned problems. This computational approach has attracted increasing attention,
and there has been significant amount of advancement in this domain.
In this paper, we review the important theoretical bases and practical
advancements of secure multiparty computation. In particular, we briefly
review three common cryptographic primitives used in secure MPC and
highlight the main arithmetic operations that are performed at the core
of secure MPC protocols. We also highlight the strengths and weaknesses
of different secure MPC approaches as well as the fundamental challenges
in this domain. Moreover, we review and compare the state-of-the-art
secure MPC tools that can be used for addressing security and privacy
challenges in the IoT and big data analytics. Using secure MPC in the
IoT and big data domains is a challenging task and requires significant
expert knowledge. This technical review aims at instilling in the reader
an enhanced understanding of different approaches in applying secure
MPC techniques to the IoT and big data analytics.

Keywords: Secure multiparty computation · Secure MPC ·
Internet of Things (IoT) · Big data analytics ·
Yao's garbled circuits · Yao's Millionaires problem · Secret sharing ·
Homomorphic encryption

1 Introduction

In recent years, data privacy has been a critical issue, e.g., the representatives of
companies such as Google and Facebook have recently been questioned on data
privacy concerns. A similar data privacy concern appeared recently in the news
about Sidewalk Labs, which is a smart-city company owned by Google. With
the unprecedented growth of the Internet in all aspects of life, the advent of

© Springer Nature Switzerland AG 2019
G. Wang et al. (Eds.): SpaCCS 2019 Workshops, LNCS 11637, pp. 45–59, 2019.
https://doi.org/10.1007/978-3-030-24900-7_4

phenomenons such as the Internet of Things (IoT) and big data, it is anticipated that more data privacy challenges will be raised in coming years.

To address the data privacy concerns, the root causes of the problem should first be understood. In the case of digital data in the information age, the problem starts when appropriate data privacy measures are not utilized in the data and computational infrastructures. In particular, the data owners store their data on the data centers or on the cloud owned by third parties. This data will then be used by the owners of the data centers for different purposes, e.g. advertisement, commercial and data analytics goals. It can be said that this is one of the primary sources of the problem.

Addressing data security and privacy concerns has been the focus of attention by many researchers from decades ago [30,37,38]. In [30], the pioneers of cryptography discussed how privacy-preserving computation using homomorphisms can be achieved. In [37] and [38], on the other hand, the idea of secure two-party computation was initiated. In particular, in [37], the *Yao's Millionaires problem* was introduced and in [38] the *Yao's garbled circuit* technique was developed to solve the Yao's Millionaires problem. The above seminal ideas led to the general idea of *secure multiparty computation* (secure MPC). Secure MPC is a cryptographic technique which enables a group of parties to evaluate a function based on the private data that each party provides, for instance in [26]. This technique can help us address data security and privacy issues to a good extent.

1.1 Our Contribution

There has been significant amount of theoretical and practical advancements in secure multiparty computation. Nowadays, there are various implementations and libraries of secure MPC frameworks for real-world applications. Each library is based on different theoretical approaches and works in certain settings. This is mainly because of the strengths and shortcomings of different MPC approaches. In spite of the amount of conducted research, the existing literature rarely pointed out the capabilities and incapabilities of different MPC solutions. For instance, in [23] the authors claimed that many existing MPC frameworks fail to work properly in practice, because of crashing or generating incorrect circuits [23]. A technical review comparing different approaches and highlighting both strengths and weaknesses of the MPC solutions is missing in the literature.

In this paper, we provide a technical review of secure MPC tools that can be used in the IoT and big data analytics. The contribution of this comparative and technical review is multi-fold. On the theoretical side, this paper highlights the strengths and weaknesses of different cryptographic techniques that are commonly used in MPC tools. It also delves into the main arithmetic operations that are carried out at the core of MPC protocols. On the practical side, this paper reviews the state-of-the-art MPC tools. We provide tables for summarizing and comparing the existing MPC tools, their security adversarial models, and the application domains in which each tool can be utilized. The paper also highlights potential approaches for the future secure MPC frameworks.

We would like to emphasize that in this paper we provide a very technical review of the secure MPC tools and libraries with an emphasis on the cryptographic primitives and mathematical/arithmetic operations that are performed at the core of secure MPC protocols. There are other comprehensive studies, including the recent ones [2] and [33], that have studied secure MPC tools from different perspectives. In [33], the authors studied the applications of privacy-preserving computation in fog computing. While in [2], a thorough analysis of secure MPC solutions and its relevance to other privacy-preserving computation areas, e.g. differential privacy, has been provided. In this technical review, our goal is to instill in the reader an enhanced understanding of different approaches in applying secure MPC solutions to the IoT and big data analytics.

2   Different Approaches for Secure Computation

There are different approaches to implement a secure multiparty computation scheme. These techniques are based on three cryptographic primitives, i.e., secret sharing [32], homomorphic encryption [25,30] and Yao's garbled circuits [38].

2.1   Secure Computation Based on Secret Sharing

Secret sharing is one of the dominant approaches used in secure multiparty computation. In this approach, the participating parties use a secret sharing scheme, e.g., Shamir's scheme [32], to share their secrets (private data). In order to emulate a secure MPC protocol, the parties then perform computations on the shares of their data, rather than directly on their data. Since the shares of the private data are random values, no information about that data is revealed.

An advantage of secure computation protocols based on secret sharing is that such protocols can provide information-theoretical security given that the underlying scheme is information-theoretically secure. Another advantage of MPC based on secret sharing is that there is no need for any encryption/decryption key. However, secret-sharing-based MPC protocols require significant amount of communication among the participating parties. In fact, privacy is achieved by distributing the computations among the parties.

2.2   Secure Computation Based on Homomorphic Encryption

Another commonly-used approach in secure multiparty computation protocols is homomorphic encryption. In this case, the parties utilize a homomorphic encryption scheme, e.g., the Paillier scheme [25], to encrypt their data. The parties then perform computations on the encrypted form of data. Homomorphic encryption has attracted significant attention in the last decade. In particular, by the appearance of fully homomorphic encryption (FHE) schemes [15], this research area has shown to be more promising.

Most of the cryptographic schemes are based on the difficulty of some computational problems, e.g., integer factorization or discrete logarithm. This can be considered as one of the drawbacks of homomorphic-encryption-based MPC protocols. This is due to the fact that if the underlying difficult problem is solved (e.g., by utilizing quantum computers), the encryption scheme would not be secure anymore. In addition, homomorphic-encryption-based MPC protocols are computationally intensive and supporting multi-key encryption is a challenging task in such schemes [1].

2.3 Secure Computation Based on Yao's Garbled Circuits

Yao's garbled circuits [38] is another dominant approach for secure two-party computation. A garbled circuit is an encrypted form of a function, which is supposed to be evaluated securely between two parties. More precisely, in this approach, one party encrypts the bits of their input and the intermediate state of the computation. This party then converts the computation into a circuit of binary gates, each represented as a garbled truth table. The other party, a.k.a., the evaluator, receives the circuit and the encrypted input bits. The evaluator then produces the encrypted output by evaluating each gate at the encrypted bits of the input and combining the results.

Yao's garbled circuit approach is the most efficient method for securely evaluating boolean circuits [20]. This approach does not require any communication between the parties during the evaluation. However, the intermediate state in the garbled circuits is far larger than the input data. This makes garbled circuits impractical for processing large data. Moreover, the garbled circuit approach provides computational security.

3   Building Blocks for Secure Computation

At the core of the three common approaches in secure computation, the main arithmetic operations, i.e., addition, multiplication, subtraction, division and comparison, are performed. These arithmetic operations, in fact, form the building blocks of secure computation.

3.1   Secure Comparison

Secure comparison is an important building block in secure computation [31]. The problem of secure comparison was initially introduced in [37], as the Yao's Millionaires problem. This problem is a well-studied, but challenging problem. Thus far, different solutions have been proposed to this problem. The proposed solutions are mostly based on homomorphic encryption techniques, secret sharing schemes and Yao's garbled circuits.

The current solutions to the secure comparison problem are very expensive, mostly in terms of the communication complexity. An inefficient secure comparison protocol can make a secure multiparty computation protocol even more inefficient. This is due to the fact that secure comparison may be used numerous times in a MPC protocol. For instance, secure comparison is frequently used in the secure argmax operation, which is another common operation in many privacy-preserving data mining algorithms [6]. Thus, efficient and practical solutions to the secure comparison problem result in improving secure computation protocols. There are different approaches for improving a secure comparison protocol. For example, reducing the number of interactions among the participating parties is a potential optimization technique.

3.2   Other Building Blocks for Secure Computation

For performing secure computation, the four main arithmetic operations need to be implemented in a secure fashion. These operations can be implemented securely using secret sharing schemes, homomorphic encryption techniques and Yao's garbled circuits. For instance, the Paillier homomorphic encryption scheme [25] allows us to calculate the addition of two encrypted values by multiplying their corresponding ciphertexts and without decrypting them. In the case of secret sharing schemes, two or more parties can calculate the addition of their secret values by adding the shares of the secret values locally and then conducting a Lagrange interpolation on their updated shares.

Depending on the application domain, the secure implementation of other operations may also be needed. For instance, in privacy-preserving data mining and machine learning, the secure version of three operations is needed. These operations include secure comparison, secure inner product of two vectors, and secure argmax [6]. In some cases, the secure version of natural logarithm, i.e. the $ln()$ function, the sign function, the sigmoid function is also required [9].

4   Security and Privacy Challenges in IoT and Big Data

Data security and privacy have been critical challenges both in the Internet of Things (IoT) and big data domains [4,34,40]. It is important to scrutinize major security and privacy issues in these domains. A good understanding of such issues helps us provide concrete solutions to the problems. The Cloud Security Alliance [4] has included secure computations and cryptographic solutions among the top ten challenges to big data security & privacy. Moreover, data privacy has been indentified as one of the major security concerns [4].

Addressing data security and privacy issues is a challenging task. Three primary challenges of using secure multiparty computation frameworks in the big data domain are as follows [36]:

1. MPC is not integrated well with current data processing and data analytic workflows
2. Significant expert knowledge is needed for implementing and running data analytics in the MPC frameworks
3. The MPC frameworks do not scale well for large data sets, because large-data processing systems do not support efficient parallel processing yet

In addition to the aforementioned challenges, there are still some limitations with secure multiparty computation schemes that preclude using them in the IoT and big data domains. First of all, providing a general-purpose efficient MPC framework for various applications in different domains has shown to be very difficult. There has been tremendous amount of research on secure computation for different applications, including privacy-preserving data mining, sealed-bid auctions, privacy-preserving face recognition, and private information retrieval, to name a few. Secure multiparty computation protocols have been used in different application domains with specific settings and assumptions depending on the suitability and efficiency criteria. Combining these solutions to have an integrated framework is quite challenging. The challenges that IoT and big data analytics bring will be added and will make the scenario even more complicated [19]. Nonetheless, a careful combination of different solutions might be a plausible approach in the near future.

5   Tools for Privacy-Preserving Big Data Analytics

In this section, we compare the state-of-the-art secure multiparty computation tools (including libraries, implementations and frameworks). These tools can be used for secure computation in the IoT and big data domains [2,33].

Fairplay [22] is a secure function evaluation (SFE) tool that allows two parties to perform a joint computation without any trusted third party. This tool is based on Yao's garbled circuits and provides a high-level function description language called SFDL. The Fiarplay compiler compiles SFDL programs into a boolean circuit and evaluates the circuit using its runtime environment.

FairplayMP [3] is an extension of Fairplay [22] for multiple parties. This tool is based on Yao's garbled circuits and secret sharing schemes. FairplayMP uses an emulated trusted third party. The emulated trusted third party receives the inputs from the parties, does the desired computations and privately informs the parties of their outputs.

Sharemind [5] is a secure multiparty computation framework consisting of three parties. It is one of the most developed and efficient MPC tools and supports 32-bit integer arithmetic. However, it uses a non-standard secret sharing technique and does not extend to more than three parties [41].

VIFF [10] is a compiler for secure multiparty computation based on standard secret sharing schemes. It uses parallelization and multi-threading to provide faster computations. This framework supports computations consisting of basic primitives, e.g. addition and multiplication, on secret-shared values.

SEPIA [8] is a Java library based on linear secret sharing schemes. It separates the parties into computational parties and the parties who provide inputs and obtain outputs. SEPIA is used for secure distributed computation on network data, e.g., for privacy-preserving network intrusion detection.

TASTY [17] is a tool (with a compiler) for two-party secure computation (2PC) based on Yao's garbled circuits and homomorphic encryption. This tool can be used for describing, generating, executing, benchmarking and comparing secure 2PC protocols. It allows a user to provide a description of the computations to be performed and transforms the description into a 2PC protocol.

SPDZ [11] is a secure multiparty computation protocol based on secret sharing and homomorphic encryption. SPDZ consists of an offline (preprocessing) phase and an online phase. In the offline phase, the required shared random data is generated and in the online phase, the actual secure computation is carried out.

SCAPI [13] is an open-source library for developing MPC frameworks and secure computation implementations. It comes with two instantiations of the Yao's garbled circuits. One instantiation is secure against active adversaries and the other is secure against passive adversaries. SCAPI is implemented in Java and uses the JNI framework for calling native codes, to make the library efficient.

Wysteria [27] is a high-level programming language for writing MPC programs. It supports mixed-mode programs consisting of private computations with multiparty computations. Wysteria compiles the MPC programs to circuits and then executes the circuits by its underlying MPC engine.

Obliv-C [39] is a language for secure computation programming based on the garbled circuits. It is an extension of the C programming language that provides data-oblivious programming constructs. The Obliv-C compiler, implemented as a modified version of CIL, transforms Obliv-C codes to plain C codes.

Enigma [42] is a decentralized computation framework which combines MPC and Blockchain technology to provide guaranteed privacy. It allows different parties to jointly store and perform computations on their data without exposing the privacy of the data. Enigma also removes the need for trusted third parties.

Frigate [23] is a validated compiler and fast circuit interpreter for secure computation. It introduces a C-style language for secure function evaluation based on garbled circuits. Frigate has been developed with an emphasis on the principles of compiler design. It addresses the limitations of many previous MPC frameworks and produces correct and functioning circuits [23].

Chameleon [29] is a hybrid framework for privacy-preserving machine learning. This framework is based on the ABY framwork [12], which implements a combination of secret sharing, garbled circuits and the GMW protocol [16]. Chameleon has an offline and an online phase and most of the computation is performed in the offline phase. It uses a semi-honest third party (STP) in the offline phase, for generating the required correlated random values.

WYS* [28] is a domain-specific language (DSL) for writing mixed-mode secure MPC programs. It is based on the the idea of Wysteria [27] and embedded/hosted in F* programming language. For running a MPC program in WYS*, the program is first compiled using the F* compiler. Then each party runs the compiled codes using the WYS* interpreter. The result, which is a boolean circuit, is evaluated using the GMW protocol [16] on the parties' secret shares.

Conclave [35] is a query compiler that makes secure computation on big data efficient. Conclave generates codes for cleartext processing in Python and Spark and codes for secure computation using Sharemind [5] and Obliv-C [39]. The idea behind Conclave is to minimize the computations under MPC as much as possible. Conclave can support only two or three parties and withstands a passive semi-honest adversary.

We summarized the reviewed secure MPC tools in Table 1. The table illustrates the main details and characteristics of the tools. Note that, due to the space constraints, we used some abbreviations in Table 1. The meaning of the abbreviations is provided in Table 2.

The first column of Table 1 shows the name of the MPC tools, the year in which each tool was developed, and the reference related to each tool. The second column determines the number of parties that each tool supports. The third column specifies the cryptographic primitives that have been used in the development of each tool. The fourth column defines the type of security, i.e. computational or information-theoretical, that each tool provides. The fifth column shows whether each tool uses some trusted third party (TTP) or such a party is simulated in the tool. The idea of doing secure multiparty computation without relying on any trusted third party is an interesting one. However, realizing such a computational model seems to be a challenging task; as the fifth column of Table 1 shows, the majority of the listed tools either need trusted third parties or simulate them. The last column of the table shows the programming languages that were used for the development of each tool.

We also provided a table that illustrates the adversarial model for each MPC tool; see Table 3. The table specifies the number of corrupted parties that each tool can tolerate. Note that in secure multiparty computation, the participating parties might be corrupted by some adversaries. The parties may also collude with each other. Therefore, it is important to consider such scenarios in the implementation. Finally, Table 4 shows some applications for each MPC tool.

Table 1. Secure MPC tools for big data computation (based on [33])

Tool/Library	Parties	Based on	Security	TTP	Prog. Lang.
Fairplay 2004 [22]	2	GC	Computational	Yes	SFDL (Java)
FairplayMP 2008 [3]	≥ 3	GC and SS	Computational	Em. TTP	SFDL (Java)
Sharemind 2008 [5]	3	Additive SS	Info. Theortic	Yes	SecreC (C++)
VIFF 2009 [10]	≥ 3	SS	Info. Theortic	No	Python
VIFF 2009 [10]	2	Paillier HE scheme	Computational	No	Python
SEPIA 2009 [8]	≥ 3	Shamir's SS	Computational	Sim. TTP	Java
TASTY 2010 [17]	2	HE and GC	Computational	No	Python
SPDZ 2012 [11]	≥ 2	SS and HE	Computational	Yes	C++/Python
SCAPI 2012 [13]	≥ 2	GC	Computational	No	Java
Wysteria 2014 [27]	≥ 2	GMW protocol	Info. Theortic	Sim. TTP	OCaml
Obliv-C 2015 [39]	2	GC	Computational	No	C
Enigma 2015 [42]	≥ 2	VSS and Blockchain	Info. Theortic	No	WebAssembly
Frigate 2016 [23]	2	GC	Computational	No	C++
Chameleon 2018 [29]	2	SS, GMW, GC	Computational	STP	C++
WYS* 2019 [28]	≥ 2	[27]	Info. Theortic	Sim. TTP	F*
Conclave 2019 [35]	2 or 3	[5] and [39]	Computational	Yes	Python/Spark

Table 2. Abbreviations used in Table 1

Notation	Meaning
HE	Homomorphic Encryption
GC	Yao's Garbled Circuits
GMW	The Goldreich, Micali, and Wigderson (GMW) protocol [16]
SFDL	Secure Function Definition Language
SS	Secret Sharing
VSS	Verifiable Secret Sharing
STP	Semi-honest Third Party
TTP	Trusted Third Party
Em. TTP	Emulated Trusted Third Party
Sim. TTP	Simulated Trusted Third Party

Table 3. Table of adversarial model

Tool/Library	Secure against
Fairplay 2004 [22]	Not mentioned
FairplayMP 2008 [3]	A collection of $\lfloor \frac{n}{2} \rfloor$ corrupt computation players, as long as they operate in a semi-honest way
Sharemind 2008 [5]	A passive adversary able to corrupt at most one party
VIFF 2009 [10]	Not mentioned
SEPIA 2009 [8]	$t < \frac{m}{2}$ colluding privacy peers. Note that the systems has n input peers and m privacy peers
TASTY 2010 [17]	Not mentioned
SPDZ 2012 [11]	An active adversary capable of corrupting up to $(n-1)$ parties
SCAPI 2012 [13]	Both active and passive adversaries
Wysteria 2014 [27]	A semi-honest adversary capable of corrupting up to $(n-1)$ parties
Obliv-C 2015 [39]	Semi-honest adversaries
Enigma 2015 [42]	Not mentioned
Frigate 2016 [23]	Semi-honest model
Chameleon 2018 [29]	Semi-honest (honest-but-curious) model
WYS* 2019 [28]	Semi-honest (honest-but-curious) model
Conclave 2019 [35]	A passive semi-honest adversary

Table 4. Table of applications

Tool/Library	Applications
Fairplay 2004 [22]	Secure two-party computation
FairplayMP 2008 [3]	Secure multiparty computation
Sharemind 2008 [5]	Tax fraud detection system
VIFF 2009 [10]	Sugar beet auction, decision tree learning, privacy-preserving verifiable computation
SEPIA 2009 [8]	Private information aggregation, network security and monitoring
TASTY 2010 [17]	Set intersection, face recognition
SPDZ 2012 [11]	Oblivious RAM schemes and oblivious data structures for MPC
SCAPI 2012 [13]	Privacy-preserving impersenation detection systems and fair exchange protocols
Wysteria 2014 [27]	DStress (a framework for privacy-preserving and distributed graph analytics)
Obliv-C 2015 [39]	secure computation and data-oblivious computation
Enigma 2015 [42]	6 decentralized computation, IoT, crypto bank, blind e-voting, n-factor authentication
Chameleon 2018 [29]	privacy-preserving machine learning, e.g. SVM and deep learning
WYS* 2019 [28]	Joint median, card dealing, private set intersection (PSI)
Conclave 2019 [35]	Secure MPC on big data, e.g. credit card regulation and market concentration

6   Technical Discussion and Future Works

6.1   Technical Discussion

There are three common approaches for implementing secure MPC protocols. These approaches include: secret sharing schemes, Yao's garbled circuits, and homomorphic encryption techniques. The approaches that work based on secret sharing and homomorphic encryption schemes usually use the so-called arithmetic gates, i.e. *Addition* and *Multiplication* gates. While, the approaches that work based on Yao's garbled circuits usually encrypt the inputs and garble the circuit of the function which is supposed to be securely computed. Although the three MPC approaches determine the overall schema for secure computation, sometimes it is preferred to securely implement certain functionalities. For instance, in the case of privacy-preserving data mining and machine learning, the three commonly-used operations [6], include secure comparison, secure inner product of two vectors, and secure argmax. Other common functions that may need to be implemented securely include the sigmoid function, the sign function and the floor function [9] and [7].

Secure comparison is an arithmetic operation which commonly appears in almost any secure computation protocol. Secure comparison is in fact the Yao's Millionaires problem [37], which is a well-studied problem. However, most of the secure comparison solutions are expensive in terms of the communication complexity, i.e., interaction among the parties. According to [31], secure comparison protocols based on additive homomorphic encryption schemes require significant amount of interaction among the parties. This is because additive homomorphic encryption schemes allow linear operations (i.e., addition or multiplication by a constant) on the encrypted values; whereas comparison is a non-linear arithmetic operation. The inefficiency of secure comparison protocols makes the secure argmax operation inefficient as well; and thus, the secure multiparty computation protocols. Therefore, providing an efficient solution to secure comparison can bring in a significant improvement for secure MPC protocols.

An advantage of secure MPC tools based on Yao's garbled circuits is that they are fast. However, such tools do not provide information-theoretical security and they are mostly used for secure two-party computations. Whereas, MPC tools based on secret sharing schemes provide information-theoretical security given that the underlying scheme is information-theoretically secure. MPC solutions based on secret sharing schemes do not need any cryptographic key. However, such tools require significant amounts of interactions among the parties. MPC tools based on homomorphic encryption techniques provide computational security. Early homomorphic encryption schemes, e.g., Paillier homomorphic encryption scheme [25], cannot support both addition and multiplication operations, which are required for secure multiparty computation. This reduces their applicability in secure MPC tools. Recent homomorphic encryption techniques, e.g., fully homomorphic encryption (FHE) [15], can support a limited number of addition and multiplication gates. In addition, an overlooked drawback of the FHE schemes is that they rarely support multi-key encryption [1].

MPC protocols based on secret sharing and those based on homomorphic encryption schemes work based on arithmetic gates, i.e. *Addition* and *Multiplication* gates. The multiplication gate in such protocols has shown to make the computations inefficient. For instance, for doing a multiplication in a MPC protocol based on Shamir's secret sharing, the participating parties must regularly perform a process called degree reduction. Similarly, in MPC protocols based on fully homomorphic encryption (FHE) schemes, the parties must regularly carry out a noise reduction process (i.e. bootstrapping) in order for the FHE schemes to work properly. In both cases, the degree reduction and the noise reduction processes deteriorate the performance of MPC protocols drastically.

6.2   Future Works

There are different interesting avenues for further research. One line of research is to evaluate and test the existing MPC solutions in different application domains, with the purpose of improving such solutions. For instance, one can perform experimental research using the recent MPC prototypes, e.g., Enigma [42], which is decentralized thanks to the Blockchain technology. Another direction is to focus on the main arithmetic operations which are run at the core of MPC protocols. For instance, providing efficient solutions for secure comparison can improve the efficiency of the MPC solutions. Improving the multiplication gate of MPC solutions based on homomorphic encryption or secret sharing schemes can also result in more efficient and practical MPC solutions.

Another very interesting line of research is to integrate social mechanisms, e.g., trust and reputation, in secure MPC protocols. Utilizing social mechanisms alongside secure MPC protocols can help us achieve more secure and trustworthy data and computation frameworks [18,43]. This is because trust and reputation are considered as soft security measures that compliment hard security measures, e.g. cryptography and secure MPC protocols. In particular, secure MPC solutions combined with trust and reputation machanisms can be helpful in trustworthy machine learning. It is worth mentioning that trustworthiness in data analytics and machine learning techniques is becoming more important as we rely more on such techniques [21,24]. Integrating secure MPC protocols into emerging decentralized computation technologies, e.g., the Blockchain technology, can also be another potential line of research [42].

One may also do further research on more efficient secure solutions to the commonly-used operations/functions in data mining and machine learning techniques. However, for achieving such solutions it may be needed to accept a trade-off between approximation and efficiency. In [9], for instance, the authors faced some challenges for implementing logistic regression over encrypted data. According to [9], the homomorphic implementation of the sign function, which is closely related to the comparison operator, is very difficult. Implementing the sigmoid function using homomorphic encryption seems also to be very difficult. Note that the sigmoid function is commonly used in neural networks' activation functions and in logistic regression models. Even more challenging seems to be the floor function [9]. The authors [9] dealt with these challenges using polynomial approximation, e.g., Taylor polynomials and minimax approximation [14]. An interesting line of research is to see how such approximation methods will perform for the functions that are commonly used in the secure MPC protocols. For instance, one may further study the approximation solutions for the secure comparison and secure argmax operations.

7   Conclusion

Data security and privacy have been crucial issues in recent years. It can be said that these issues will become even more crucial as we are going well into the Internet of Things (IoT) and big data eras. One of the main causes of data privacy violation is due to not utilizing appropriate data privacy measures in the data and computational infrastructures. Secure multiparty computation (secure MPC) is a powerful cryptographic tool that can help us address data security and privacy issues. In this paper, we provided a technical review to the cryptographic techniques commonly used in MPC protocols. We delved into the arithmetic operations that are run at the core of secure MPC protocols. In addition, we highlighted the strengths and weaknesses of different approaches used in secure MPC, and the challenges we face for designing practical MPC solutions. We also compared the state-of-the-art MPC tools that can be used for addressing security and privacy issues in the IoT and big data domains.

Considering all aspects and challenges of secure computation, solutions based on secret sharing schemes integrated into decentralized computation frameworks seem to be more promising for the future. Such solutions are decentralized, provide information-theoretical security and do not need any cryptographic key. Enigma [42] might be considered as a sample proof-of-work and a prototype for potential practical solutions. In addition, integrating social mechanisms, such as trust and reputation, into secure multiparty computation protocols provides more reliable and trustworthy data and computation frameworks. Our technical review and comparative study of different secure MPC approaches and developed MPC tools will have significant contributions to applying secure MPC solutions to the IoT and big data domains.

References

1. Acar, A., Aksu, H., Uluagac, A.S., Conti, M.: A survey on homomorphic encryption schemes: theory and implementation. ACM Comput. Surv. (CSUR) **51**(4), 79 (2018)
2. Alx, P.S.N., Alx, N.V., Au, P.F., Au, C.O., Au, P.S., Au, M.S., Phi, M.V., Tue, N.B., Tue, B.S.: D1. 1 state of the art analysis of MPC techniques and frameworks (2017)
3. Ben-David, A., Nisan, N., Pinkas, B.: FairplayMP: a system for secure multi-party computation. In: Proceedings of the 15th ACM Conference on Computer and Communications Security, pp. 257–266. ACM (2008)
4. BigDataWorkingGroup: Expanded top ten big data security and privacy challenges (2013). https://downloads.cloudsecurityalliance.org/initiatives/bdwg/Expanded_Top_Ten_Big_Data_Security_and_Privacy_Challenges.pdf
5. Bogdanov, D., Laur, S., Willemson, J.: Sharemind: a framework for fast privacy-preserving computations. In: Jajodia, S., Lopez, J. (eds.) ESORICS 2008. LNCS, vol. 5283, pp. 192–206. Springer, Heidelberg (2008). https://doi.org/10.1007/978-3-540-88313-5_13
6. Bost, R., Popa, R.A., Tu, S., Goldwasser, S.: Machine learning classification over encrypted data. In: NDSS, vol. 4324, p. 4325 (2015)
7. Bourse, F., Minelli, M., Minihold, M., Paillier, P.: Fast homomorphic evaluation of deep discretized neural networks. In: Shacham, H., Boldyreva, A. (eds.) CRYPTO 2018. LNCS, vol. 10993, pp. 483–512. Springer, Cham (2018). https://doi.org/10.1007/978-3-319-96878-0_17
8. Burkhart, M., Strasser, M., Many, D., Dimitropoulos, X.: SEPIA: privacy-preserving aggregation of multi-domain network events and statistics. In: USENIX Security Symposium, Washington, DC, USA, pp. 223–239 (2010)
9. Chen, H., et al.: Logistic regression over encrypted data from fully homomorphic encryption. BMC Med. Genomics **11**(4), 81 (2018)

10. Damgård, I., Geisler, M., Krøigaard, M., Nielsen, J.B.: Asynchronous multiparty computation: theory and implementation. In: Jarecki, S., Tsudik, G. (eds.) PKC 2009. LNCS, vol. 5443, pp. 160–179. Springer, Heidelberg (2009). https://doi.org/10.1007/978-3-642-00468-1_10

11. Damgård, I., Pastro, V., Smart, N., Zakarias, S.: Multiparty computation from somewhat homomorphic encryption. In: Safavi-Naini, R., Canetti, R. (eds.) CRYPTO 2012. LNCS, vol. 7417, pp. 643–662. Springer, Heidelberg (2012). https://doi.org/10.1007/978-3-642-32009-5_38

12. Demmler, D., Schneider, T., Zohner, M.: ABY-a framework for efficient mixed-protocol secure two-party computation. In: NDSS (2015)

13. Ejgenberg, Y., Farbstein, M., Levy, M., Lindell, Y.: SCAPI: the secure computation application programming interface. IACR Cryptology EPrint Archive 2012, 629 (2012)

14. Fraser, W.: A survey of methods of computing minimax and near-minimax polynomial approximations for functions of a single independent variable. J. ACM (JACM) 12(3), 295–314 (1965)

15. Gentry, C., et al.: Fully homomorphic encryption using ideal lattices. In: STOC vol. 9, pp. 169–178 (2009)

16. Goldreich, O., Micali, S., Wigderson, A.: How to play any mental game. In: Proceedings of the Nineteenth Annual ACM Symposium on Theory of Computing, pp. 218–229. ACM (1987)

17. Henecka, W., Sadeghi, A.R., Schneider, T., Wehrenberg, I., et al.: TASTY: tool for automating secure two-party computations. In: Proceedings of the 17th ACM Conference on Computer and Communications Security, pp. 451–462. ACM (2010)

18. Jøsang, A., Ismail, R., Boyd, C.: A survey of trust and reputation systems for online service provision. Decis. Support Syst. 43(2), 618–644 (2007)

19. Kaisler, S., Armour, F., Espinosa, J.A., Money, W.: Big data: issues and challenges moving forward. In: 2013 46th Hawaii International Conference on System Sciences, pp. 995–1004. IEEE (2013)

20. Kolesnikov, V., Sadeghi, A.-R., Schneider, T.: Improved garbled circuit building blocks and applications to auctions and computing minima. In: Garay, J.A., Miyaji, A., Otsuka, A. (eds.) CANS 2009. LNCS, vol. 5888, pp. 1–20. Springer, Heidelberg (2009). https://doi.org/10.1007/978-3-642-10433-6_1

21. LaValle, S., Lesser, E., Shockley, R., Hopkins, M.S., Kruschwitz, N.: Big data, analytics and the path from insights to value. MIT Sloan Manag. Rev. 52(2), 21 (2011)

22. Malkhi, D., Nisan, N., Pinkas, B., Sella, Y., et al.: Fairplay-secure two-party computation system. In: USENIX Security Symposium, vol. 4, p. 9. San Diego (2004)

23. Mood, B., Gupta, D., Carter, H., Butler, K., Traynor, P.: Frigate: a validated, extensible, and efficient compiler and interpreter for secure computation. In: 2016 IEEE European Symposium on Security and Privacy (EuroS&P), pp. 112–127. IEEE (2016)

24. Najafabadi, M.M., Villanustre, F., Khoshgoftaar, T.M., Seliya, N., Wald, R., Muharemagic, E.: Deep learning applications and challenges in big data analytics. J. Big Data 2(1), 1 (2015)

25. Paillier, P.: Public-key cryptosystems based on composite degree residuosity classes. In: Stern, J. (ed.) EUROCRYPT 1999. LNCS, vol. 1592, pp. 223–238. Springer, Heidelberg (1999). https://doi.org/10.1007/3-540-48910-X_16

26. Raeini, M.G., Nojoumian, M.: Secure error correction using multiparty computation. In: 2018 IEEE 8th Annual Computing and Communication Workshop and Conference (CCWC), pp. 468–473. IEEE (2018)

27. Rastogi, A., Hammer, M.A., Hicks, M.: Wysteria: a programming language for generic, mixed-mode multiparty computations. In: 2014 IEEE Symposium on Security and Privacy, pp. 655–670. IEEE (2014)
28. Rastogi, A., Swamy, N., Hicks, M.: Wys*: a DSL for verified secure multi-party computations. In: Nielson, F., Sands, D. (eds.) POST 2019. LNCS, vol. 11426, pp. 99–122. Springer, Cham (2019). https://doi.org/10.1007/978-3-030-17138-4_5
29. Riazi, M.S., Weinert, C., Tkachenko, O., Songhori, E.M., Schneider, T., Koushanfar, F.: Chameleon: a hybrid secure computation framework for machine learning applications. In: Proceedings of the 2018 on Asia Conference on Computer and Communications Security, pp. 707–721. ACM (2018)
30. Rivest, R.L., Adleman, L., Dertouzos, M.L., et al.: On data banks and privacy homomorphisms. Found. Secure Comput. 4(11), 169–180 (1978)
31. Schneider, M., Schneider, T.: Notes on non-interactive secure comparison in image feature extraction in the encrypted domain with privacy-preserving sift. In: Proceedings of the 2nd ACM workshop on Information hiding and multimedia security, pp. 135–140. ACM (2014)
32. Shamir, A.: How to share a secret. Commun. ACM 22(11), 612–613 (1979)
33. Sousa, P.R., Antunes, L., Martins, R.: The present and future of privacy-preserving computation in fog computing. In: Rahmani, A.M., Liljeberg, P., Preden, J.-S., Jantsch, A. (eds.) Fog Computing in the Internet of Things, pp. 51–69. Springer, Cham (2018). https://doi.org/10.1007/978-3-319-57639-8_4
34. Tonyali, S., Akkaya, K., Saputro, N., Uluagac, A.S., Nojoumian, M.: Privacy-preserving protocols for secure and reliable data aggregation in IOT-enabled smart metering systems. Future Gener. Comput. Syst. 78, 547–557 (2018)
35. Volgushev, N., Schwarzkopf, M., Getchell, B., Varia, M., Lapets, A., Bestavros, A.: Conclave: secure multi-party computation on big data. In: Proceedings of the Fourteenth EuroSys Conference 2019, p. 3. ACM (2019)
36. Volgushev, N., Schwarzkopf, M., Lapets, A., Varia, M., Bestavros, A.: Integrating MPC in big data workflows. In: Proceedings of the 2016 ACM SIGSAC Conference on Computer and Communications Security. pp. 1844–1846. ACM (2016)
37. Yao, A.C.C.: Protocols for secure computations. In: FOCS, vol. 82, pp. 160–164 (1982)
38. Yao, A.C.C.: How to generate and exchange secrets. In: 27th Annual Symposium on Foundations of Computer Science (SFCS 1986), pp. 162–167. IEEE (1986)
39. Zahur, S., Evans, D.: Obliv-c: a language for extensible data-oblivious computation. IACR Cryptology ePrint Archive (2015)
40. Zarpelao, B.B., Miani, R.S., Kawakani, C.T., de Alvarenga, S.C.: A survey of intrusion detection in Internet of Things. J. Netw. Comput. Appl. 84, 25–37 (2017)
41. Zhang, Y., Steele, A., Blanton, M.: PICCO: a general-purpose compiler for private distributed computation. In: Proceedings of the 2013 ACM SIGSAC Conference on Computer and communications security, pp. 813–826. ACM (2013)
42. Zyskind, G., Nathan, O., Pentland, A.: Enigma: Decentralized computation platform with guaranteed privacy. arXiv preprint arXiv:1506.03471 (2015)
43. Zyskind, G., Nathan, O., et al.: Decentralizing privacy: using blockchain to protect personal data. In: Security and Privacy Workshops (SPW), 2015 IEEE, pp. 180–184. IEEE (2015)

The 9th International Symposium on Trust, Security and Privacy for Emerging Applications (TSP 2019)

TSP 2019 Organizing and Program Committees

General Chairs

Xiaodong Lin   University of Ontario Institute of Technology, Canada
Khalid Alharbi   Northern Border University, Saudi Arabia

Program Chairs

Imad Jawhar   United Arab Emirates University, UAE
Deqing Zou   Huazhong University of Science of Technology, China
Xiaohui Liang   University of Massachusetts at Boston, USA

Program Committee

Ying Dai   Temple University, USA
Toon De Pessemier   Ghent University, Belgium
Xiaofeng Ding   Huazhong University of Science and Technology, China
Ed Fernandez   Florida Atlantic University, USA
Xiaojun Hei   Huazhong University of Science and Technology, China
Abdessamad Imine   Lorraine University, France
Ricky J. Sethi   Fitchburg State University, USA
Haitao Lang   Department Physics and Electronics, China
Xin Li   Nanjing University of Aeronautics and Astronautics, China
Chi Lin   Dalian University of Technology, China
Pouya Ostovari   Temple University, USA
Filipa Peleja   Yahoo Research Barcelona, Spain
Chao Song   University of Electronic Science and Technology of China, China
Guangzhong Sun   University of Science and Technology of China, China
Yunsheng Wang   Kettering University, USA
Yanghua Xiao   Fudan University, China
Xuanxia Yao   University of Science and Technology Beijing, China
Lin Ye   Harbin Institute of Technology, China
Mingwu Zhang   Hubei University of Technology, China
Yaxiong Zhao   Google Inc., USA
Huan Zhou   China Three Gorges University, China
Youwen Zhu   Nanjing University of Aeronautics and Astronautics, China

Publicity Chairs

Can Wang	Griffith University, Australia
David Zheng	Frostburg State University, USA
Dawei Li	Montclair State University, USA
Wei Chen	Interdigital Communications Inc., USA

Web Chair

Mingmin Shao	Hunan University, China

Steering Chairs

Wenjun Jiang	Hunan University, China
Guojun Wang	Guangzhou University, China

Steering Committee

Laurence T. Yang	St. Francis Xavier University, Canada
Minyi Guo	Shanghai Jiao Tong University, China
Jie Li	Shanghai Jiao Tong University, China
Jianhua Ma	Hosei University, Japan
Peter Mueller	IBM Zurich Research Laboratory, Switzerland
Indrakshi Ray	Colorado State University, USA
Kouichi Sakurai	Kyushu University, Japan
Bhavani Thuraisingham	The University of Texas at Dallas, USA
Jie Wu	Temple University, USA
Yang Xiang	University of Technology Sydney, Australia
Kun Yang	University of Essex, UK
Wanlei Zhou	University of Technology Sydney, Australia

A Framework to Identify People in Unstructured Environments Incorporating Biometrics

Janelle Mason$^{(\boxtimes)}$, Prosenjit Chatterjee, Kaushik Roy,
and Albert Esterline

North Carolina A&T State University, Greensboro, NC 27411, USA
{jcmason, pchatterjee}@aggies.ncat.edu,
{kroy, esterlin}@ncat.edu

Abstract. We outline our computational framework for identity. We have a prototype web application, but this paper is a conceptual level. The interest is in identity as an equivalence relation and how information can be evidence for identity hypotheses. Our account is based on the situation theory of Barwise and Perry. We consider a (legal) identity case to be a constellation of situations, and we indicate how the structure of such a case facilitates discounting and combining evidence using Dempster-Shafer theory. Semantic Web resources are used to capture the structure of evidence as it relates to situations. We have developed OWL ontologies and use the concepts therein defined in RDF triple stores to capture case data. URIs (as used in the Semantic Web) are used for unambiguous references to individuals. We sketch a scenario that uses two biometric modalities in an uncontrolled environment and show how our framework applies. Recently, biometrics has gained the limelight as a means to identify individuals, but much else may be available for this task, including sensor data, witness reports, and data on file. To our knowledge, this is the only framework that in principle can accommodate any kind of evidence for identity. It is not an alternative to biometrics, but rather provides a way to incorporate biometrics into a larger context.

Keywords: Biometrics · Identity · Dempster-Shafer theory · Semantic Web · Evidence · Argumentation schemes

1 Introduction

Identifying an individual in an unstructured environment is a challenge, particularly if results are required in near real time. (By an "unstructured," or "uncontrolled," "environment" we mean an environment that arises spontaneously, beyond the control of those monitoring agents in it, for example, what we encounter in walking down a street as opposed to a studio where portraits are taken.) In such cases, there is strong motivation to make use of multiple sources of evidence. The question then arises of how the evidence should be combined and when some evidence should be discounted because it is unreliable or inappropriate. We here present our computational framework for identity, which structures a case for identity into a constellation of situations. Most

© Springer Nature Switzerland AG 2019
G. Wang et al. (Eds.): SpaCCS 2019 Workshops, LNCS 11637, pp. 65–75, 2019.
https://doi.org/10.1007/978-3-030-24900-7_5

work in computer science on identity is concerned with descriptions or profiles of individuals or their behaviors that are unique to the individuals. Our framework is unique in that it puts the use of these profiles into a larger context and accommodates other ways of picking out agents. We here describe the components of our framework and how they go together. The components proved well established computational techniques. Our focus is on identity as an equivalence relation and equational reasoning is a well-established field in computer science.

The rest of this paper is organized as follows. The next section discusses related work, and Sect. 3 presents our framework. Section 4 analyzes an example scenario per our framework, showing how an identity-related scenario may be structured, and showing how the various threads of our framework conspire to support identity hypotheses. Section 5 concludes.

2 Related Work

Interpretation of video footage and images can have a significant impact for identifying an agent in a situation. Identifying a person through a biometric recognition system involves sensor cameras that can capture images and video clips of an individual. The goal is to recognize a person through their facial and gait features using suitable classification techniques. The introduction of a facial recognition system generally brings high-end accuracy for the classification of individuals through neural networks when training has been done appropriately. Such a system, however, has problems with un-controlled environment, limited light, or when the images captured were blurry. At the same time, if we include gait enrollment, then the identification process becomes more authentic and reliable. Gait enrollment through an appearance-based model, however, also has limitations when the clients' appearance unpredictably changes over time. In contrast, model-based gait enrollment with optimized feature extraction and recognition has a striking impact on biometric recognitions (i.e. periocular) [18, 23, 24]. Zhou and Bhanu focused on the side-face and gait features and their optimal integration and utilization of information for identification [22, 25]. The continuous identification process through real-time machine learning techniques using a light net can outperform state-of-the-art conventional classification techniques.

Our framework [8, 26] can take, for example, information from facial and gait recognition systems, put the information in context, and combine the level of evidence these two sources provide to come up with numerical measures of belief for various identity hypotheses that allow one to rank these hypotheses. To put the information in context means to structure a (legal) case (as for the identity of the culprit in some incident) as a constellation of situations. The key situation in a criminal case is the crime scene, but there are also situations where information is collected (perhaps for matching purposes, as with biometrics), and situations where information is integrated to help decide among candidate hypotheses. The information involved here can be from many kinds of sources, not just biometric.

Note that an agent can be picked out not only via a description or profile but also by an expression that references an individual by virtue of a causal chain beginning with someone directly acquainted with the individual and passed on to others by a (causal) chain of conversations in which the individual is referred to [14, 17]. (See Subsect. 3.1 below.) The machine-learning community has worked with causal frameworks in rather different settings (see, e.g., [1]), some state-of-the-art results in machine translation [2], speech recognition [4], and attention mechanisms [2] may have aspects that transfer to causal chains of references, but our framework is the only approach to directly address this phenomenon.

3 Our Framework

An element of identity, such as a singular denoting expression, on its own generally does not convey enough information to provide evidence to confirm one's identity. For example, a first name on its own is not always enough evidence to determine the identity of someone. Questions can be raised, such as is this the given name, which is a name given to a person at birth [20], of the person or is this their nickname? Our framework is a computational framework for identity partially implemented as a web application. The focus is on evaluating identity hypotheses. Identity is an equivalence relation, and identity hypotheses are of the form "a is the same as b". We do not directly address identity from a profiling perspective, which is the act or process of extrapolating information about a person based on known traits or tendencies [16].

Our framework has three foundations, which are situation theory, Dempster-Shafer (DS) theory, and the Semantic Web standards. Regarding situation theory, we base our research on Barwise and Perry's situation theory [3] and we refer to Devlin's formalization of situation semantics [6]. We use DS theory to combine and discount evidence. This theory uses justification to distribute evidence [12]. In our framework, the Semantic Web standards are used to maintain the structure of information and to denote individuals unambiguously. The Semantic Web standards include the Resource Description Framework (RDF) and the Web Ontology Language (OWL).

In general, situation theory allows us to characterize the structure of information. Information about the world is always situated, and we say that a situation supports information. As Devlin explains, an infon is a basic item of information. It involves an n-place relation, R, and n objects appropriate for the corresponding argument places of R, as well as a location and time. There is also a 0-or-1 polarity, 1 indicating that things are thus related at the time and location, and 0 indicating otherwise. This allows for negative information. It is possible for a situation to carry information about another situation by virtue of constraints. Constraints can be derived from language, nature, or conventions of society. For example, a situation where there is smoke carries information about a situation where there is fire by virtue of the natural constraint that smoke is produced by combustion. Again, a situation in which a reliable adult shouts "Fire!" also carries information about a situation where there is fire, in this case by virtue of constraints that are conventions of natural language. An utterance (a speech act) is performed in what is called an utterance situation. It carries information about a corresponding described situation. The described situation is the topic of the speech act. A central idea of situation semantics (situation theory applied to meaning) is that the meaning of an expression is a relation between an utterance situation and a described situation. A resource situation fills out references needed for a successful utterance. For example, Jane says to Bill, "The deer that I saw yesterday is in the yard." Here the utterance situation includes Jane and Bill, and Jane is making this utterance. The described situation is the yard as it currently exists, containing a certain deer. There is one resource situation, in which Jane sees the deer that is currently in the yard. We are interested in situations that require judgments of identity hypotheses for some agent.

An identity judgment (as in a CSI) is made in an utterance situation. We make use of a generalization of such a situation, where an investigator has a suite of evidence implicating various suspects (or, more generally, has a suite of evidence for various identity hypotheses). The investigator can utter corresponding judgments supported at various levels by the available evidence. Such a potential utterance situation is what we call an id-situation. It is part of a constellation of situations that forms a case, with the crime scene (in a criminal investigation) the described situation. Resource situations include such things as where a fingerprint was taken and filed. With machine learning, there could be a huge number of resource situations; we use summary metadata in such cases for levels of evidence.

We consider how information can be evidence for identity hypotheses and how such evidence can be discounted and combined. Many of our examples are taken from criminal justice, which focuses on identifying individuals and is general: any area of human activity is subject to criminal behavior. And criminal investigations, like computation, have limits on time and other resources [10]. (See [27] for more information.)

DS theory is used in our framework to provide numerical values for evidence-based confidence in our identity hypotheses [12]. The frame of discernment contains the set of all possible candidates for our identity hypotheses. The strength of the evidence is captured by what is called mass. A mass function assigns values to subsets of the frame of discernment such that the sum of all masses is 1.0. The mass assigned to the frame of discernment itself represents ignorance. A set that has non-zero mass is a focal element. A refinement involves an analysis of the frame of discernment to restructure it so that the mass function may more accurately capture the distribution of evidence. This does not mean the set will grow or diminish in this process. Based on the mass function, the value of the belief function for a subset θ of the frame of discernment is the lower bound of likelihood for θ. This value is the summation of all the masses of the sets that are subsets of θ. The value of the plausibility function for θ is the upper bound of likelihood for θ, calculated as the sum of the masses of the sets that overlap θ. Note that $0.0 \leq$ belief $(\theta) \leq$ plausibility $(\theta) \leq 1.0$ for any subset θ of the frame of discernment.

Using DS theory, new mass functions can be created through the combination of several mass functions for evidence from several sources. As evidence is collected, the focal elements generally become clearer. The aggregation of evidence must be addressed as more evidence is introduced to provide a summary of the information in a meaningful and simple way. In DS theory, combination rules provide distinctive ways to aggregate information from multiple sources. For example, Dempster's Combination Rule permits the combination of two independent mass functions. Using it, the assigned mass values get redistributed, and we may end up with conflicting hypotheses. Where there is conflict, the evidence is considered disjoint. Mass gets normalized with

Dempster's Rule. See [5] for additional information. The reliability and strength in the evidence is considered when redistributing the mass values.

In our framework, we are exploring argumentation schemes when combining evidence using DS theory. Argumentation schemes provide a more generalized method to combine evidence. We refer to Dung's study of argumentation [7], Woolridge's analysis of argumentation from the perspective of inconsistencies amongst the belief of multiple agents [21], and the analysis of [21] to determine the appropriate combination rule using DS theory for argumentation schemes. A series of questions are asked, if the response to the question concerning the evidence is negative, a different combination rule is considered that offers a generic method to assess the combination of the evidence.

Lastly, we consider the Semantic Web resources in our framework to capture the structure of evidence as it relates to constellation of situations. OWL ontologies are used encode evidence in the form of RDF triple stores [15]. Uniform Resource Identifiers (URIs) are a method to identify classes, properties, and individuals. We are interested in using the OWL property **owl:sameAs** to denote sameness in identity.

The Semantic Web has an open-world assumption: a statement that does not follow from what has been asserted is not assumed false. This assumption allows ontologies to evolve in a decentralized way, being aligned as needed, and triple stores from different sources may be federated. According to situation theory, a situation is a partial theory; this is essentially the open world assumption. Simple DS theory, however, has a closed-world assumption (the frame of discernment recognizes all possible candidates), but there are at least two ways to handle open-world aspects (see [11, 19]).

Objects that provide evidence (e.g., photos or written documents) are threads that stitch together the situations that make up an id-case. In a legal setting, if these objects are to serve as evidence, we need guarantees that they are genuine all along the chain. Chain of Custody theory addresses what is needed "to ensure the integrity of evidence" [9].

A chain of custody involves a sequence of what we call information-relevant actions. Barwise emphasized one kind of information-relevant action, utterances. Implicit in his work and explicit in Devlin's in another such action, perception. We, however, recognize a multitude of kinds, for example, taking and duplicating a fingerprint. While a legal perspective emphasizes what authority was in control, a more general perspective adds the existence of a causal chain from a physical feature to where the information is used. Information-relevant actions include taking and filing a fingerprint and recording situations on closed-circuit TV as well as matching fingerprints, mugshots, or DNA, where chains converge. Among information-relevant actions are information-propagating actions, which form links in the chains, e.g., taking a fingerprint but also uttering a true statement.

Computational methods are inherent in the components that contribute to our framework. Information is structured by means of situations as formalized by Devlin [6]. Information and the relations and operations by which it propagates are represented formally in RDF using ontologies expressed in OWL. The ontologies are supplemented with SWRL rules. The RDF triple stores are queried with SPARQL, and the Pellet reasoner is used to derive new RDF triples. Identity is a well-studied equivalence relation, and equational reasoning is well established in computer science. As a relevant example, we might have the person identified by gait in the doorway as is the person who left the package, the person who left the package is the same person who bought the clock in the shop (as we know from receipts), and the person who bought the clock is the person identified by face in the shop. From this, by the transitivity of identity (equality), we may conclude that the person identified in the doorway is the same as the person identified in the shop. Note that OWL has identity in the form of the **owl:sameAs** property, and OWL reasoners support equational reasoning. OWL also supports inverse functional properties. (If R denotes an inverse functional property and a, b, and c denote individuals, then from $a\ R\ c$ and $b\ R\ c$ we may infer $a = b$.) We overlay this logical machinery with DS theory, whose rich variations we adapt in our very novel setting.

3.1   URIs

URIs are the fundamental singular denoting expressions ("names") on the Semantic Web, and an account of identity using Semantic-Web resources must be clear on what is required for a URI to denote something. Halpin [13] identifies three positions regarding how agents can determine what a URI denotes; two of these positions are relevant here. The 'logical position' on the meaning of a URI is that it is given by whatever satisfies the model(s) given by the formal semantics of the documents where that URI occurs. In philosophy (see, e.g., [14, 17]), this is the descriptivist theory of meaning and was challenged by the 'causal theory of reference', according to which an agent fixes a name to a referent known through direct acquaintance, and a causal chain to a current user of the name from past users allows its referent to be known across time. (The causality here is in the communicative acts.) This is the same as Halpin's 'direct reference position' on the meaning of a URI, that the meaning is whatever was intended by the owner of the URI. Basically, the referent of a URI is established by fiat by the owner and is then communicated to others in a causal chain by creating web pages and Semantic-Web statements containing the URI.

Virtually all work in computer science addressing identity takes a descriptivist position on denoting individuals. Profiles are descriptive devices that denote individuals. Generally overlooked are expressions that denote individuals by virtue of a causal chain, but in fact it is natural to use URIs in this fashion in RDF encodings. For example, we assume that legal professionals assign URIs to suspects, equipment, fingerprints, and other things. If the professional did not have direct acquaintance with, for example, a suspect, then they are on a causal chain leading back to, say, a detective thus acquainted. Once the URI is associated via a causal chain to an individual, it retains this meaning as it is communicated across the Web, where the causality now is the technologies and conventions of the Web. (There are clearly hybrid cases, where a partial description disambiguates among individuals known by direct acquaintance.) URIs in the Semantic Web are ideal for supporting this causal-chain reference since each person can define URIs in a domain they control, thus avoiding clashes with URIs introduced by others, and the non-unique name assumption of the Semantic Web allows us later to assert that two URIs in fact denote the same individual if we discover that this indeed is the case. An example is when we hypothesize that the person who accessed Fred's workstation Tuesday is the same person who accessed Tom's

Thursday. (Note that the individual is picked out via situations and no other properties of the person are known.)

4   Scenario

This section presents a scenario to illustrate how situations may structure the information in a case. The scenario presents a hypothetical customer-assistance system that recognizes individuals by face and gait. We point out situations where information is acquired and classifiers are trained. Causal chains propagating information about individuals are noted. And we note an id-situation and the situations tied to it. We make remarks about how DS theory might apply. The focus is on how the situations structure a case. Space constraints prohibit discussion of computation or inference except for some equational reasoning and remarks on DS theory.

A retail home-improvement company runs a voluntary program to make shopping more convenient for regular clients. A client who volunteers for the program has their face photographed from several angles (see the bottom of the left side of Fig. 1) and has a video made of them walking (see the top of the left side of Fig. 1). Machine learning is used with this data to train classifiers to recognize the client's face and to recognize their gait. The system also keeps contact information on the client and keeps track of their purchases. It also records the name of the salesperson who serviced them. The company has surveillance cameras at the entrances to the store (see the top of the right side of Fig. 1). When a client enters, software attempts to find a classifier with a good match with the facial image from the camera and a classifier with a good match with the gait recorded by the camera. If the client has enrolled in the program, in normal conditions, the system would identify the person and notify the salesperson who helped them in the past. The salesperson can pull up on their smart phone descriptions for the client's previous purchases and inquiries. If the entering client has not registered with the program, then the matches should be below the threshold for

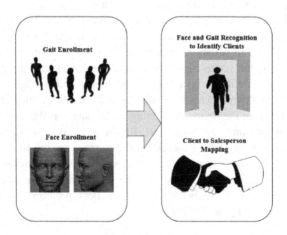

Fig. 1. Lumberyard customer assistance identifier system.

signaling a valid match. It is not a problem if by chance someone not registered is found to match the classifiers for some enrolled person. Then the assigned salesperson simply apologizes for the misidentification. Nor is it a problem if the entering client has enrolled in the program but is not recognized. In that case, they simply miss the convenience of having a known sales person come to their assistance.

The situations involved in the enrollment phase here start with where the client meets with the representative. Next are two situations, where (1) photos are taken of the face and (2) where the video is taken for the gait. Next, there another two situations, where (1) a classifier is trained for facial recognition and (2) a classifier is trained for gait recognition. The photo situation has an information-relevant action by which information regarding the face ends up on photos, and the facial-training situation has an information-relevant action by which the facial information on the photos is aggregated in the classifier. There is a casual chain here, from the person (or their face) to the photos to the classier. Implicitly, this chain supports identities: the person (with the face) is the same as the person in the photos is the same as the person described by the classifier. By the transitivity of identity, the person (with the face) is the same as the person described by the classifier. Similarly, the video situation has an information-relevant action by which information about the gait ends up on a video, and the gait-training situation has an information-relevant action by which the gait information on the video is aggregated in the classifier. There is a causal chain here as well, from the person (or their gait) to the video to the classifier. Again, this chain implicitly supports identities: the person (with the gait) is the same as the person in the video is the same as the person described by the classifier. By the transitivity of identity, the person (with the gait is the same as the person described by the classifier.

The situations involved in the recognition phase begin with the one where the client comes through the entrance in the presence of the surveillance camera; call this situation *SD*. The next situation is where the software attempts to find matches for the face and gait. This is the id-situation, with all the evidence at hand, and where an identity judgment (formally the utterance of an identity statement) could be made. The corresponding described situation is *SD*. Assuming that a good match is found, the next situation is where the appropriate salesperson is found and alerted. Finally, there is the situation where the client and salesperson meet and pursue their business. In *SD*, there are information-relevant actions from the person entering the store to the facial image and gait footage. In the id-situation, there is an information-relevant action from this image and footage to the name (or other unique identifier) of the client. There is a causal chain here, from client who enters to the image and footage to the (implicit) utterance of the client's name. And this chain supports identities: the person entering is the same as the person in the image and footage is the same as the person named (who is described by the face and gait classifiers). By the transitivity of identity, the person entering is the same as the person named (and described by the face and gait classifiers). By this and the long-range identity we have from the enrollment phase, the transitivity of identity allows us to conclude that the person whose face and gait were recorded in the enrollment phase is the same as the person named (by virtue of being described by the face and gait classifiers).

Regarding the application of DS theory here, for identifying the person at the entrance: we have evidence from two sources. Sometimes either on its own is sufficient, but sometimes we need both to do a reasonable job. We would use argumentation schemes to determine the most appropriate combination rule. There could be several reasons for discounting some evidence. Suppose, for example, the person responsible for enrolling participants is off for a day and someone with much less training and experience takes over. The photos and video would be of lower quality and the machine learning would be done with little thought. We might then discount the evidence from our matches for clients enrolled in that unfortunate day. Possibly a clearer case would be if the substitute employee did, say, the photos and the expert did the video. We then might discount the facial match compared to the gait match.

5 Conclusion

This paper presents a computational framework for identity at a conceptual level. Based on Barwise and Perry's situation theory, we consider a legal case to be a constellation of situations that supports identity judgments. A situation supports information and may carry information about another situation. We have developed OWL ontologies and use the concepts defined in them for RDF triple stores that capture the structure of evidence based on situations. We are interested in various types of situations, such as utterance, described, and resource situations. The situations of greatest interest are ones that make identity judgments, including those using biometric information and meta-data. As far as we know, this is the only framework that accommodates any kind of evidence for identity. It is not an alternative to biometrics, but rather provides a way to incorporate biometrics into a larger context.

We present a scenario where the identity of an individual is assessed through our framework; the focus is on the situation that structures the information. The scenario is concerned with identifying customers through their biometric information (gait and facial) upon entry into a home improvement company. The identity of customers who volunteer for enrollment in the system are recorded as URIs. If the identity judgment meets or exceeds a threshold, the identity of the customer is revealed to employees in the store. The combination of facial recognition and gait recognition provides the evidence used to determine the identity of the customer. Using DS theory in our computational framework for identity enables us to combine and discount the evidence.

We plan to continue to enhance our web application. This application will be used as a teaching tool by the Department of Criminal Justice (with whom we collaborate) at our university. We are expanding our framework into cyberspace, where identity is a growing issue.

Acknowledgments. This research is based upon work supported by the Army Research Office (Contract No. W911NF-15-1-0524).

References

1. Alvarez-Melis, D., Jaakkola, T.S.: A causal framework for explaining the predictions of black-box sequence-to-sequence models. arXiv preprint arXiv:1707.01943 (2017)
2. Bahdanau, D., Cho, K., Bengio, Y.: Neural machine translation by jointly learning to align and translate. arXiv preprint arXiv:1409.0473 (2014)
3. Barwise, J., Perry, J.: Situations and Attitudes (new ed.). Center for the Study of Language and Information, New York (1998)
4. Chan, W., Jaitly, N., Le, Q.V., Vinyals, O.: Listen, attend and spell. arXiv preprint arXiv: 1508.01211 1(2), 3 (2015)
5. Curley, S.P.: The application of Dempster-Shafer theory demonstrated with justification provided by legal evidence. Judgment Decis. Mak. **2**(5), 257 (2007)
6. Devlin, K.: Logic and Information. Cambridge University Press, Cambridge (1995)
7. Dung, P.M.: On the acceptability of arguments and its fundamental role in nonmonotonic reasoning, logic programming and n-person games. Artif. Intell. **77**(2), 321–357 (1995)
8. Esterline, A., Nick, W., Mason, J.: Situations, information, and evidence (late breaking report). In: 2018 IEEE Conference on Cognitive and Computational Aspects of Situation Management (CogSIMA), pp. 171–173. IEEE (2018)
9. Giannelli, P.C.: Chain of custody. In: Faculty Publications, School of Law, Case Western Reserve University, p. 309 (1993)
10. Haack, S.: Evidence Matters: Science, Proof, and Truth in the Law. Cambridge University Press, Cambridge (2014)
11. Haenni, R.: Uncover Dempster's Rule Where it is Hidden. In: FUSION, pp. 1–8 (2006)
12. Halpern, J.Y.: Reasoning About Uncertainty. MIT Press, Cambridge (2005)
13. Halpin, H.: Sense and reference on the web. Minds Mach. **21**(2), 153–178 (2011)
14. Kripke, S.: Naming and Necessity. Harvard University Press, Cambridge (1980)
15. McDaniel, M., Sloan, E., Day, S., et al.: Situation-based ontologies for a computational framework for identity focusing on crime scenes. In: 2017 IEEE Conference on Cognitive and Computational Aspects of Situation Management (CogSIMA), pp. 1–7, March 2017
16. Merriam-Webster Online. Merriam-Webster Online Dictionary entry: Profiling. https://www.merriamwebster.com/dictionary/profiling. Accessed 02 Jan 2019
17. Putnam, H.: The meaning of 'meaning'. Minn. Stud. Philos. Sci. **7**, 131–193 (1975)
18. Rani, M.P., Arumugam, G.: An efficient gait recognition system for human identification using modified ica. Int. J. Comput. Sci. Inf. Technol. **2**(1), 55–67 (2010)
19. Smets, P., Kennes, R.: The transferable belief model. Artif. Intell. **66**(2), 191–234 (1994)
20. The American Heritage Dictionary. The American heritage dictionary entry: given name. https://ahdictionary.com/word/search.html?q=given+name. Accessed 02 Jan 2019
21. Wooldridge, M.: An Introduction to Multiagent Systems. Wiley, Hoboken (2009)
22. Zhou, X., Bhanu, B.: Feature fusion of side face and gait for video-based human identification. Pattern Recognit. **41**(3), 778–795 (2008)
23. Alonso-Fernandez, F., Bigun, J.: A survey on periocular biometrics research. Pattern Recognit. Lett. **82**, 92–105 (2018). https://arxiv.org/abs/1810.03360
24. Bartuzi, E., Roszczewska, K., Czajka, A., Pacut, A.: Unconstrained biometric recognition based on thermal hand images. In: 2018 International Workshop on Biometrics and Forensics (IWBF), pp. 1–8. IEEE (2018)
25. Gonzalez-Sosa, E., Fierrez, J., Vera-Rodriguez, R., Alonso-Fernandez, F.: Facial soft biometrics for recognition in the wild: Recent works, annotation, and COTS evaluation. IEEE Trans. Inf. Forensics Secur. **13**(8), 2001–2014 (2018)

26. Mason, J., Kyei, K., Foster, H., Esterline, A.: A framework for identity: Dempster-Shafer theory the flow and combination of evidence. In: 2018 IEEE Symposium Series on Computational Intelligence (SSCI), pp. 1700–1706. IEEE (2018)
27. Mason, J., et al.: A computational framework for identity based on situation theory. In: International Symposium on Affective Science and Engineering, pp. 1–7. Japan Society of Kansei Engineering (2018)

Continuous Authentication Using Mouse Clickstream Data Analysis

Sultan Almalki$^{(\boxtimes)}$, Prosenjit Chatterjee$^{(\boxtimes)}$, and Kaushik Roy$^{(\boxtimes)}$

Department of Computer Science, North Carolina A&T State University,
Greensboro, USA
{ssalmalki,pchatterjee}@aggies.ncat.edu,
kroy@ncat.edu

Abstract. Biometrics is used to authenticate an individual based on physiological or behavioral traits. Mouse dynamics is an example of a behavioral
biometric that can be used to perform continuous authentication as protection
against security breaches. Recent research on mouse dynamics has shown
promising results in identifying users; however, it has not yet reached an
acceptable level of accuracy. In this paper, an empirical evaluation of different
classification techniques is conducted on a mouse dynamics dataset, the Balabit
Mouse Challenge dataset. User identification is carried out using three mouse
actions: mouse move, point and click, and drag and drop. Verification and
authentication methods are conducted using three machine-learning classifiers:
the Decision Tree classifier, the K-Nearest Neighbors classifier, and the Random
Forest classifier. The results show that the three classifiers can distinguish
between a genuine user and an impostor with a relatively high degree of
accuracy. In the verification mode, all the classifiers achieve a perfect accuracy
of 100%. In authentication mode, all three classifiers achieved the highest
accuracy (ACC) and Area Under Curve (AUC) from scenario B using the point
and click action data: (Decision Tree - ACC: 87.6%, AUC: 90.3%), (K-Nearest
Neighbors - ACC: 99.3%, AUC: 99.9%), and (Random Forest - ACC: 89.9%,
AUC: 92.5%).

Keywords: Mouse dynamics · Biometric · Continuous authentication ·
Behavioral biometric · Machine learning

1 Introduction

User authentication is a method that is used to determine whether a user is genuine
("allowed to access the system") or an impostor ("prohibited from access to the system") [1]. User authentication has three types of classes: knowledge based, object or
token based, and biometric based. Knowledge-based user authentication is characterized by confidentiality; it is something that only the user would know. Object-based
user authentication is characterized by control; it is something that the user has.
Biometric-based user authentication relies on the user's physiological or behavioral
characteristics; it is something the user is. While the weaknesses of knowledge-based
and object-based approaches are that the user may lose or forget passwords and tokens,

© Springer Nature Switzerland AG 2019
G. Wang et al. (Eds.): SpaCCS 2019 Workshops, LNCS 11637, pp. 76–85, 2019.
https://doi.org/10.1007/978-3-030-24900-7_6

the advantage of a biometric-based approach is that it can uniquely identify an individual by using the individual's biological characteristics.

Although using biometric makes the authentication stronger and determines a user's identity uniquely, verification based on physiological biometrics such as iris, face, or fingerprint offers mainly a one-time static authentication [2, 3]. To avoid this drawback, behavioral biometrics such as mouse clickstream data can be used to continuously authenticate a user by monitoring the user's behavior [4]. In this work, an empirical evaluation of three classifiers is conducted on the Balabit dataset [5], which contains data for 10 users with a set of 39 behavioral features per user [6].

The rest of the paper is organized in four sections. Section 2 summarizes some previous research in this area. Section 3 describes the Balabit dataset and the feature extraction method. Section 4 describes the model and the experiments, followed by a discussion of the test results. Section 5 has concluding remarks and suggestions for future work.

2   Related Work

User behavioral analysis has been a focus of research for more than a decade. This section briefly presents some of the research on mouse-based authentication.

Antal et al. [6] applied a Random Forest (RF) classifier for each user using mouse movements for verifying impostor detection. They used the Balabit dataset [5], which includes 10 users. Each user has many sections and mouse actions. They segmented each session's data into three types of mouse actions: Mouse Movement (MM), Point Click (PC), and Drag and Drop (DD). The researchers extracted 39 features and obtained results of 80.17% average accuracy (ACC) and 0.87 average Area Under Curve (AUC). The highest accuracies achieved for users (7 and 9) were 93% and 0.97 AUC. The lowest accuracy achieved for a user (8) was 72% and 0.80 AUC.

Nakkabi et al. [7] proposed a user authentication scheme based on mouse dynamics. They collected mouse behavior data from 48 users and applied a fuzzy classification that relied on a learning algorithm for multivariate data analysis. They conducted an evaluation and achieved a False Acceptance Rate (FAR) of 0% and a False Rejection Rate (FRR) of 0.36%. Their experiments required more than 2000 mouse events in order to classify a user as legitimate.

Feher et al. [8] introduced a framework for user verification using mouse activities. The framework was divided into three parts: acquisition, learning, and verification. The first step is to capture user actions from the users' mouse activities. Then, classify each event type and store them in a database. The third phase is to send each event to the favorite classifier based on action type. The classifier has two layers: a prediction layer and a decision layer. The researchers conducted tests of multi-class classifier using a RF classifier. They collected the data from 25 volunteers. They obtained an Equal Error Rate (EER) of 1.01% based on 30 actions.

Gamboa et al. [9] developed a data acquisition system for collecting users' mouse activities. The system records all user interaction throughout the world wide web. The dataset was collected from 50 participants; each user has 400 strokes. A stroke is defined as a group of points between two actions. The authors proposed 58 behavioral features extracted from the raw data using some mathematical operations. These features were used to identify a user based on how they interact with the system. Furthermore, Gamboa et al. developed a sequential classifier using statistical pattern recognition techniques in order to distinguish between users. The authors achieved an equal error rate of 0.7% per 100 mouse strokes.

Another biometric authentication approach based on mouse dynamics was introduced by Shen et al. [10]. They collected user behavioral data under a controlled environment using the software tool they developed. The software collected the events of "mouse move" or "mouse click" for about thirty minutes in each session. The dataset obtained had 15 sessions for each of 28 subjects. Based on a mining method, the researchers focused on using frequent and fixed actions as behavioral patterns for extracting user characteristics through pattern growth. They used an SVM and achieved an FAR of 0.37% and an FRR of 1.12%.

Schulz [11] collected a dataset from 72 volunteers using a software tool on their personal machines. The software tool presented a continuous authentication system using mouse events; it segmented a user's events into length of a movement, curvature, inflection, and curve straightness features, and then computed a user's behavioral signature using histograms based on curve characteristics. For the verification stage, the researcher used Euclidean distance for classification and computed the distance between a user's login and the mouse activities. An EER of 24.3% from a group of 60 mouse curves is obtained. In contrast, by using groups of 3600 mouse curves, the performance increased to an EER of 11.2%.

Bours et al. in [12] proposed a login system based on mouse dynamics. They collected data from 28 participants of different age groups. They used a technique called "follow the maze" in which the participants performed a task by following the tracks on their own computer. This task was performed five times per session in order to acquire sufficient data on mouse movements. The maze contained 18 tracks, divided into 9 horizontal and 9 vertical tracks. They measured the various distances using Euclidean distance, Manhattan distance, and edit distance algorithms. The results that they obtained were an EER of 26.8% in the case of the horizontal direction and an EER of 27.0% in the case of the vertical direction.

Hashia et al. [13] worked on mouse movement as a biometric. They proposed two authentication methods: the first method is for initial login of users (enrollment), and the second one is to monitor a computer for suspicious activities (verification). It required from the user about 20 s to complete each of two methods. For the enrollment phase, a user must be using the mouse and following a series of dots that showed one at a time on the user's screen. The purpose of this step is to record the coordinates of the mouse every 50 ms and then calculate the speed, deviation from a straight line, and angles. They used the data collected from the enrollment phase for the verification phase by comparing a user's credentials and the data collected in the enrollment phase. They tested their approach using 15 participants of age 22–30. They achieved an error rate of 20% when using 1.5 standard deviations of the average from the corresponding enrollment value, and an error rate of 15% using 1 standard deviation of the average from the corresponding enrollment value.

3   Description of Mouse Raw Data

This research used the Balabit Mouse Challenge dataset [5], obtained at the Budapest office of the Balabit company. The dataset contains raw data obtained from 10 users using remote desktop clients connected to remote servers. It has many sessions with characteristics of how a person uses a mouse. Each session includes a set of rows, where each row recorded a user action as (rtime, ctime, button, state, x, y): "rtime" is the elapsed time recorded since the start of the session using the network monitoring device, "ctime" is the elapsed time through the client computer, "button" is a mouse button, "state" is information about the button, and "x" and "y" are the Cartesian coordinates of the mouse location [6].

3.1   Extraction of Features

A mouse action is a set of sequential user actions that represent a movement of the mouse between two points. This study uses the user features extracted from the Balabit Mouse Challenge dataset [5]. This dataset divides the raw data into three types of actions: MM, PC, and DD. MM describes a movement between two screen positions; PC is a Point Click or Mouse click; DD is a drag-and-drop event. The dataset presents 39 features extracted from an individual's mouse actions. A detailed description of features is found in [6].

4   Mouse Dynamics Model and Experimental Results

In this research, supervised machine-learning techniques were utilized to monitor the behavior of users in order to distinguish legal users from illegal users [14]. Three machine-learning algorithms were evaluated: Decision Tree Learning (DT), k-Nearest Neighbors (k-NN), and Random Forest (RF). The Scikit-learn software tools were used for the analysis of mouse clickstream data [15]. A significant step in the classification was to prepare the training data in CSV format, so that it could be interpreted by the classifiers. In the model, if a user's mouse dynamics are the same as the characteristics stored in the system's database, then the system lets the user continue working on the device; otherwise, the system must log out the user (see Fig. 1). Specifically, the following steps describe how the model works:

- Data Collection Phase: Raw data of the users are collected.
- Features Extraction Phase: Meaningful features, such MM, PC, and DD, were extracted using the method reported in Antal et al. [6].
- Data Preparation Phase: For the training phase, all the users' data was aggregated and put in random order. The training dataset was then split into two parts: the first part (70% of the data) was used for training, and the second part (30% of the data) was used for testing the model's performance. For every experiment, the balance of training sets and evaluation sets remained the same in order to avoid classifier bias.

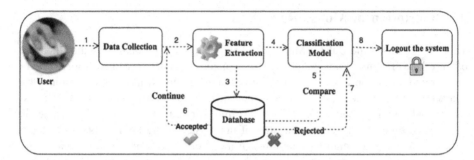

Fig. 1. User behavioral biometrics model

- Select a Classifier Phase: DT, RF, and KNN were utilized to show the ability of the proposed model to determine whether a user was genuine or an impostor from a user's mouse clickstream data.
- Training Data Phase: The training process began by reading the characteristics of all the users from the training dataset and then loading them into the three classifiers to train the model. This step was a significant step, since the training data contained the user behavior itself and a class label.
- Testing Data Phase: After completion of the training step, the model was tested on the new data that was never used for training, to categorize whether the user as a genuine user or an impostor.

The experiment was conducted in two stages: (i) a verification stage, and (ii) an authentication stage. The evaluations were measured using classifier accuracy (ACC) and area under curve (AUC). Another important evaluation to examine the classifiers is to plot the receiver operating characteristic (ROC). The ROC curve plots the True Positive Rate (TPR) against the False Positive Rate (FPR) [16].

4.1 Verification Stage

In this stage, all three classifiers were first trained using the data that only contained the genuine user's actions (positive). Each user has many sessions; all users' sessions data were placed in one Excel file. Then, the experiment was conducted by doing training and testing for each user using the DT, K-NN, and RF classifiers. The goal of the verification stage was to verify whether the mouse data was related to a given user. After testing all the users using three classifiers, a perfect score of 100% verification rate was achieved.

4.2 Authentication Stage

In this stage, each user is in one of two classes: genuine (positive) and impostor (negative). The impostor actions were selected from the other users. Then, we assigned the positive action as {1} and the negative action as {0}. The classifiers are responsible for determining the probability that the user belongs to the genuine class or imposter class. Therefore, all classifiers were tested based on these two scenarios:

A. A single user's data with all actions (MM, PC, DD)
B. All the users' data with a single action (MM, PC, DD)

Scenario A: A Single User's Data with All Actions. In scenario (A), an experiment was conducted for a single user (35, 7, 9, 12, 15, 16, 20, 21, 23, and 29) with all actions (MM, PC, and DD), using the three classifiers. The DT, K-NN, and RF classifiers achieved average accuracies of 91.9%, 94.4%, and 79.7%, respectively. The highest average accuracies were achieved for user (9): (ACC: 91.8%), DT 96.2%, KNN 99.2%, and RF 80.1%. The lowest average accuracies were achieved for user (12): (ACC: 85.6%), DT 90.1%, KNN 91.5%, and RF 75.2%. Table 1 reports the results in detail for each user. The AUC value is computed based on the FPR and the TPR. ROC curves are given in Figs. 2, 3, and 4.

Table 1. Scenario A: single user, all actions (MM, PC, DD)

User	Decision tree		K-nearest neighbors		Random forest	
	ACC%	AUC	ACC%	AUC	ACC%	AUC
35	84.9	92.1	96.6	99.4	88.3	91.2
7	92.4	93.8	88.7	92.2	85.8	88.1
9	96.2	97.1	99.2	99.1	80.1	81.0
12	90.1	97.5	91.5	99.2	75.2	79.7
15	92.6	98.1	99.7	99.3	80.5	82.5
16	88.6	91.0	97.3	99.4	84.9	86.7
20	93.8	97.2	90.1	99.0	75.6	80.5
21	95.6	97.9	92.4	99.3	72.8	77.3
23	91.1	96.4	95.2	99.3	82.2	84.9
29	94.5	96.5	93.5	99.8	71.7	74.4
Avg	91.9	95.7	94.4	98.6	79.7	82.6

Scenario B: All Users' Data with a Single Action. In scenario (B), the dataset was initially separated into three groups of mouse actions: MM, PC, and DD. Each group contained all users (35, 7, 9, 12, 15, 16, 20, 21, 23, and 29). Training and testing of the three classifiers were then conducted on each group based on the single action. The results are reported in Table 2 (MM), Table 3 (PC), and Table 4 (DD). The highest accuracies were achieved with the PC action compared to MM and DD, as shown in Table 3 (PC): (DT: ACC: 87.6%, AUC: 90.3%), (KNN: ACC: 99.3%, AUC: 99.9%), and (RF: ACC: 89.9%, AUC: 92.5%). Also, ROC curves are given in Figs. 5, 6 and 7 for (MM), Figs. 8, 9, and 10 for (PC), Figs. 11, 12 and 13 for (DD).

82   S. Almalki et al.

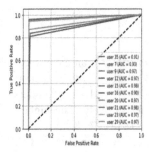 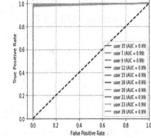 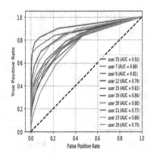

Fig. 2. ROC curve for DT, single user, all actions

Fig. 3. ROC curve for KNN, single user, all actions

Fig. 4. ROC curve for RF, single user, all actions

Table 2. Scenario B: all users, single action (MM action)

User	Decision tree		K-nearest neighbors		Random forest	
	ACC%	AUC	ACC%	AUC	ACC%	AUC
35	92.9	95.8	99.5	100	97.3	99.0
7	95.4	98.1	99.7	100	98.8	99.8
9	83.2	86.7	99.2	99.9	85.1	87.6
12	81.1	84.0	99.5	99.6	86.2	89.9
15	80.6	83.0	99.7	99.9	88.5	91.9
16	93.6	96.3	99.3	99.8	93.9	95.2
20	80.8	84.4	99.1	100	87.6	90.7
21	78.6	80.6	99.4	99.6	80.8	84.5
23	75.7	78.1	99.2	99.7	85.2	89.6
29	79.5	81.2	99.5	99.4	82.7	85.3
Avg	84.1	86.8	99.4	99.8	88.6	91.3

Table 3. Scenario B: all users, single action (PC action)

User	Decision tree		K-nearest neighbors		Random forest	
	ACC%	AUC	ACC%	AUC	ACC%	AUC
35	93.9	95.7	98.6	99.9	91.3	94.4
7	95.4	97.6	99.7	100	98.8	99.7
9	85.2	88.7	99.2	100	89.1	92.4
12	90.1	93.4	99.5	99.9	86.2	89.9
15	84.6	86.5	99.7	99.9	88.5	91.0
16	91.6	94.8	99.3	100	95.9	97.1
20	86.8	89.1	99.1	99.9	88.6	91.4
21	82.6	85.0	99.9	99.9	89.1	91.0
23	83.1	87.8	99.2	99.8	89.2	92.3
29	82.5	84.7	98.9	99.8	82.7	85.5
Avg	87.6	90.3	99.3	99.9	89.9	92.5

Table 4. Scenario B: all users, single action (DD action)

User	Decision tree		K-nearest neighbors		Random forest	
	ACC%	AUC	ACC%	AUC	ACC%	AUC
35	92.3	94.5	98.6	99.4	98.3	99.0
7	93.9	95.5	95.7	97.9	95.8	97.8
9	82.5	86.9	98.2	99.7	87.1	91.8
12	85.3	89.3	98.5	99.5	89.2	93.5
15	88.1	90.5	99.7	100	90.5	93.1
16	87.6	89.6	98.3	99.6	91.9	94.4
20	85.8	88.2	98.1	99.5	89.6	92.1
21	85.6	89.2	96.4	98.2	79.8	82.8
23	85.2	87.8	98.2	99.5	93.2	96.0
29	82.8	85.0	98.5	99.6	80.7	84.4
Avg	86.9	89.7	98.0	99.3	89.6	92.5

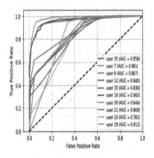

Fig. 5. ROC curve for DT, all users, MM action

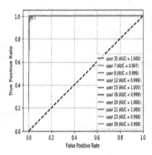

Fig. 6. ROC curve for KNN, all users, MM action

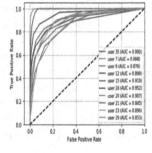

Fig. 7. ROC curve for RF, all users, MM action

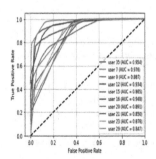

Fig. 8. ROC curve for DT, all users, PC action

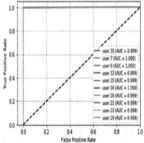

Fig. 9. ROC curve for KNN, all users, PC action

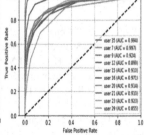

Fig. 10. ROC curve for RF, all users, PC action

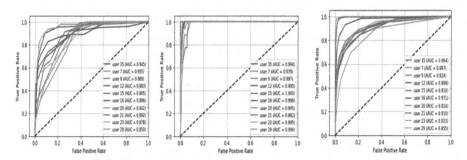

Fig. 11. ROC curve for DT, all users, DD action

Fig. 12. ROC curve for KNN, all users, DD action

Fig. 13. ROC curve for RF, all users, DD action

5 Conclusion

This paper provides a continuous user authentication model based on mouse click-stream data analysis. Each of three machine-learning classifiers used 39 features of mouse actions MM, PC, and DD. The classifiers were able to determine a genuine user from an impostor with reasonable accuracies and AUC.

In the verification phase, the model was able to recognize the user with an accuracy of 100%. In the authentication phase, data containing genuine and impostor actions were examined using two scenarios: (A) a single user with all actions, and (B) a single action with all users. The best results were obtained from scenario B using the PC action: (DT - ACC: 87.6%, AUC: 90.3%), (KNN - ACC: 99.3%, AUC: 99.9%), and (RF - ACC: 89.9%, AUC: 92.5%). In the future, a deep learning model will be constructed using the MM, PC, and DD actions, and its performance will be compared with the traditional classifiers.

Acknowledgment. This research is partially supported by the Army Research Office (Contract No. W911NF-15-1-0524).

References

1. Pisani, P.H., Lorena, A.C., de Carvalho, A.C.: Adaptive biometric systems using ensembles. IEEE Intell. Syst. **33**(2), 19–28 (2018)
2. Hameed, S.M., Hobi, M.M.: User authentication based on keystroke dynamics using backpropagation network. Int. J. Adv. Res. Comput. Sci. **3**(4), 35–40 (2012)
3. Gorad, B.J., Kodavade, D.V.: User identity verification using mouse signature. IOSR J. Comput. Eng. (IOSR-JCE) **12**(4), 33–36 (2013)
4. Shen, C., Cai, Z., Guan, X., Du, Y., Maxion, R.A.: User authentication through mouse dynamics. IEEE Trans. Inf. Forensics Secur. **8**(1), 16–30 (2013)
5. Fülöp, Á., Kovács, L., Kurics, T., Windhager-Pokol, E.: Balabit Mouse Dynamics Challenge data set (2016). https://github.com/balabit/Mouse-Dynamics-Challenge
6. Antal, M., Egyed-Zsigmond, E.: Intrusion detection using mouse dynamics. arXiv preprint arXiv:1810.04668 (2018)

7. Nakkabi, Y., Traoré, I., Ahmed, A.A.E.: Improving mouse dynamics biometric performance using variance reduction via extractors with separate features. IEEE Trans. Syst. Man Cybern.-Part A: Syst. Hum. **40**(6), 1345–1353 (2010)
8. Feher, C., Elovici, Y., Moskovitch, R., Rokach, L., Schclar, A.: User identity verification via mouse dynamics. Inf. Sci. **201**, 19–36 (2012)
9. Gamboa, H., Fred, A.: A behavioral biometric system based on human-computer interaction. Biom. Technol. Hum. Identif. **5404**, 381–393 (2004)
10. Shen, C., Cai, Z., Guan, X.: Continuous authentication for mouse dynamics: a pattern-growth approach. In: 2012 42nd Annual IEEE/IFIP International Conference on Dependable Systems and Networks (DSN), pp. 1–12, June 2012
11. Schulz, D. A.: Mouse curve biometrics. In: 2006 Biometrics Symposium: Special Session on Research at the Biometric Consortium Conference, pp. 1–6, September 2006
12. Bours, P., Fullu, C.J.: A login system using mouse dynamics. In: Fifth International Conference on Intelligent Information Hiding and Multimedia Signal Processing, IIH-MSP 2009, pp. 1072–1077, September 2009
13. Hashia, S., Pollett, C., Stamp, M.: On using mouse movements as a biometric. Proceeding Int. Conf. Comput. Sci. Its Appl. **1**, 5 (2004)
14. Luzbashev, V., Filippov, A.I., Kogos, Konstantin, A.G.: Continuous user authentication in mobile phone browser based on gesture characteristics, pp. 90–95 (2018). https://doi.org/10.1109/WorldS4.2018.8611589
15. Jovic, A., Brkic, K., Bogunovic, N.: An overview of free software tools for general data mining. In: 2014 37th International Convention on Information and Communication Technology, Electronics and Microelectronics (MIPRO), pp. 1112–1117, May 2014
16. Salman, O.A., Hameed, S.M.: Using mouse dynamics for continuous user authentication. In: Proceedings of the Future Technologies Conference, November, pp. 776–787 (2018)

Presentation Attack Detection Using Wavelet Transform and Deep Residual Neural Net

Prosenjit Chatterjee[1](✉), Alex Yalchin[2](✉), Joseph Shelton[3](✉),
Kaushik Roy[1](✉), Xiaohong Yuan[1](✉), and Kossi D. Edoh[4](✉)

[1] Department of Computer Science, North Carolina A&T State University,
Greensbor, USA
pchatterjee@aggies.ncat.edu, {kroy,xhyuan}@ncat.edu
[2] Department of Computer Science, Elon University, Elon, NC, USA
ayalcin@elon.edu
[3] Department of Engineering and Computer Science, Virginia State University,
Petersburg, VA, USA
jshelton@vsu.edu
[4] Department of Mathematics, North Carolina A&T State University,
Greensbor, USA
kdedoh@ncat.edu

Abstract. Biometric authentication is becoming more prevalent for secured authentication systems. However, the biometric systems can be deceived by the imposters in several ways. Among other imposter attacks, print attacks, mask-attacks, and replay-attacks fall under the presentation attack category. The biometric images, especially iris and face, are vulnerable to different presentation attacks. This research applies deep learning approaches to mitigate the presentation attacks in a biometric access control system. Our contribution in this paper is two-fold: first, we applied the wavelet transform to extract the features from the biometric images. Second, we modified the deep residual neural net and applied it on the spoof datasets in an attempt to detect the presentation attacks. This research applied deep learning technique on three biometric spoof datasets: ATVS, CASIA two class, and CASIA cropped image sets. The datasets used in this research contain images that are captured both in a controlled and uncontrolled environment along with different resolution and sizes. We obtained the best accuracy of 93% on the ATVS Iris dataset. For CASIA two class and CASIA cropped datasets, we achieved test accuracies of 91% and 82%, respectively.

Keywords: Biometrics · Wavelet transform · Deep residual neural network · Presentation attack detection

1 Introduction

Biometric authentication uses an individual's identity for access control and has been widely implemented for controlling the secured gateway of the member's login [1, 2]. Several organizations validate their members' access through biometric-enabled

© Springer Nature Switzerland AG 2019
G. Wang et al. (Eds.): SpaCCS 2019 Workshops, LNCS 11637, pp. 86–94, 2019.
https://doi.org/10.1007/978-3-030-24900-7_7

surveillance and security systems. The earlier biometric authentication techniques utilized physiological traits such as fingerprint, face, iris, periocular region, voice, heart rate, and body mass. Biometric authentication systems have evolved to make use of individual behavioral patterns such as touch pattern, keystroke dynamics, etc., to distinguish real and fake identity. It is evident that the human iris and facial biometric image samples are vulnerable to different types of presentation attacks [1, 2]. Though the presentation attack falls under the 'hacking attack' category, it is also referred to as a replay attack. There are several other vulnerable points that the hackers exploit to compromise a biometric-based authentication system. Fake human faces can be created through 3D printing devices, by the use of 3D Mask, or presenting an identical twin, or similar looking individual, to deceive an authentication system. Additionally, the human iris can be copied using textured contact lenses to deceive an iris-based authentication system. A key research focus is to build a robust classification technique that can identify the smallest deviation on real and fake iris and facial images in order to detect presentation attacks.

Recently, deep convolutional neural networks have been used to mitigate presentation attacks [3–5]; however, most of them require huge computational time to train and classify real and fake image samples. To counter the presentation attacks, a high-resolution image set is required. However, high-quality images increase computational complexity during training, validation, and classification. To address this issue, we apply a deep learning approach that can detect spoofing attacks with less computational effort and time.

In this paper, we apply the Wavelet Transform [6] on image datasets to extract features. Once the feature extraction is done, we feed the extracted features to a modified Residual Neural Net, denoted as 'modified-ResNet' inspired by the Residual Neural Net (ResNet) reported in [7], for accurate classification. The ResNet has superior features such as batch normalization, parameter optimization, and reduced error through skip layer connection techniques, with surprisingly less computational complexity. We observe a significant improvement in classification time with high accuracy, to distinguish real and fake images.

The rest of the paper is organized as follows. Section 2 discusses our related work. Section 3 describes the proposed methodology. Section 4 discusses the datasets used for this research effort, Sect. 5 shows the experimental results and discussion, and Sect. 6 provides us with conclusions.

2 Related Work

A reliable biometric recognition system has long been a prominent goal to mitigate presentation attacks in a wide range. Recently, deep learning techniques have been used for presentation attack detection (PAD) and have become instrumental to many secured organizations where biometric authentication is mandatory [4]. Some specific well-known spoofing instruments, like silicon masks, are widely used by attackers. Yang et al. [3] used numerous testing protocols and implemented facial localization, spatial augmentation, and temporal augmentation, to diverse feature learning for the deep convolutional neural network (deep CNN). They also experimented with texture based, motion-based, 3D Shape-based detection techniques to identify genuine and fake individuals [6]. Menotti et al. [4] performed research on deep representation for detecting presentation attacks in different biometric substances. Manjani et al. [5] proposed a multilevel deep dictionary learning-based PAD algorithm that can discriminate among different types of attacks. However, the biometric recognition system using the deep CNN technique is completely dependent on recognizing the pattern of test objects with the previously learned training objects. A successful match includes accurate pattern matching of the feature-sets from the test object to the already learned training object. The vital biometric information of an individual, such as faces and iris, are essential for the training. For "mug shot" images of faces taken at least one year apart, even the best current algorithms can have error rates of 43%–50% [8–12]. Henceforth, face and iris images of an individual, when implemented altogether on a biometric recognition system, is proven to be authentic amongst other biometric modalities and many researchers agreed on that.

Several researchers worked on the face and iris recognition system and proposed diverse methods to extract features in detail [13]. Feature extraction through Wavelet involves losses at the edges after the Label 1 decomposition. We investigated the Biorthogonal wavelet transform [6], the Discrete Wavelet Transform (DWT) [6] and 2D-Gabor wavelets [14] and their inverse form. From the experiment, we found that DWT [6] works better with images in the matrix format (n x m) and can convolve in either direction, which facilitates feature augmentation including spatial and temporal augmentation during the deep learning training phase.

In our previous work [15, 16], we applied convolutional neural network (CNN) to mitigate the spoofing attacks and obtained a reasonable performance. After extensive experimental analysis, we found that Residual Neural Network (RNN), especially ResNet [7], is the most effective deep learning approach for training and validation process. RNN utilizes single layer skip connection techniques during learning on the internal convolutional layers and avoids the vanishing gradients issues and optimize the huge parameters efficiently. Additionally, the effective single layer skipping makes the network less complex during the initial training phase, and towards the end of the training, all layers get expanded for detailed level learning.

3 Proposed Methodology

In this research, we used the DWT [6] and its inverse form to elicit features from the face and iris images. We then implemented a 'modified ResNet', inspired by the ResNet [7], in an attempt to mitigate the presentation attacks. We trained, validated and tested the ResNet model for the images captured under controlled and uncontrolled environment. The DWT [6] and its inverse form (IDWT) [6] were used to extract the features from the face and iris images. The extracted features are then fed into 'modified ResNet' for accurate classification. The high-level flow diagram of our methodology is shown in Fig. 1. In this effort, we used DWT for feature extraction and decomposition, and then applied the inverse form of DWT for reconstruction.

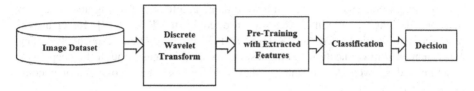

Fig. 1. High level architecture of the proposed methodology

The discrete function is represented as a weighted sum in the space spanned by the bases φ and ψ:

$$x|m| = \frac{1}{\sqrt{N}} \sum_k W_\varphi[j_0, k]\varphi_{j_0,k}[m] + \frac{1}{N} \sum_{j=j_0}^{\infty} \sum_k W_\psi[j, k]\psi_{j,k}[m], \quad (m = 0, \cdots, N-1)$$

. . ..

$$(1)$$

The inverse wavelet transform, where the summation over j is used for different scale levels and the sum over k is used for different conversions in each scale level:

$$W_\varphi[j_0, k] = (\mathbf{x}, \varphi_{j_0}, k) = \frac{1}{\sqrt{N}} \sum_{m=0}^{N-1} x[m]\varphi_{j_0,k} \quad - \forall(k) \quad \cdots \quad (2)$$

$$W_\psi[j, k] = (\mathbf{x}, \psi_{j,k}) = \frac{1}{\sqrt{N}} \sum_{m=0}^{N-1} x[m]\psi_{j,k}[m] \quad - \forall(k)\&\forall(j > j_0) \quad \cdots \quad (3)$$

where W_φ $[j, k]$ is called the *approximation coefficient* and W_ψ $[j, k]$ is called the *detail coefficient*.

We limit our wavelet decomposition to label-1, in order to prevent data loss at edges. The feature extraction, decomposition, and reconstruction mechanism, which we implemented for our research, is shown in Fig. 2.

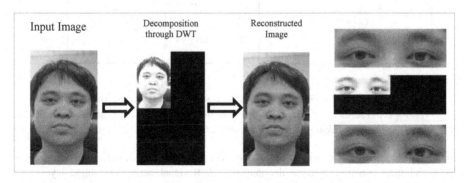

Fig. 2. DWT applied on CASIA [8, 9] sample face antispoofing image.

To prevent presentation attack in a wide range and to save training and execution time, we designed a 'modified ResNet' inspired by the ResNet [7]. He et al. [7] proposed and implemented an 18 layer and 34-layer ResNet, respectively. They experimented skip connection techniques and handled images through the deep CNN structure and showed the advantages they achieved based on computational complexities and low error rate.

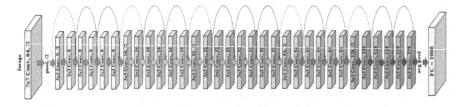

(a). Modified ResNet Framework Structure.

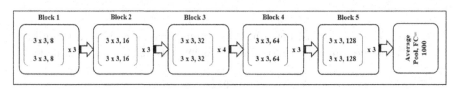

(b). Modified ResNet Framework Structure in blocks and their convolution layer distribution.

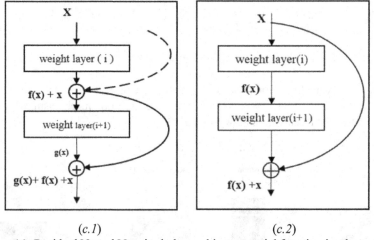

(c.1)   (c.2)

(c). Residual Neural Net single layer skip sequential function implemented.
(c.1) – represents single layer skip connection techniques implemented.
(c.2) – represents double layer skip connection techniques implemented.

Fig. 3. (a) Modified ResNet framework structure. (b). Modified ResNet framework structure in blocks and their convolution layer distribution. (c). Residual neural net single layer skip sequential function implemented. *(c.1) – represents single layer skip connection techniques implemented. (c.2) – represents double layer skip connection techniques implemented.*

In comparison, our 'modified ResNet' is quite lighter than the ResNet [7], as our 'modified ResNet' has a total of 32 discrete convolution 2D layers, 2 Max Pooling 2D layers and 1 Fully Connected (FC) dense layer, shown in Fig. 3(a) and (b). Our 'modified ResNet' has 5 building blocks of convolution layers and their distribution maintaining the single layer skip-connection techniques as shown in Fig. 3(c).

4 Datasets Used

Our research methodology is evaluated based on the three different categories of image datasets: ATVS [1, 2], CASIA [8, 9], and CASIA-cropped [8, 9]. ATVS [1, 2] contains the real and fake images of periocular regions. The datasets contain fifty subjects. Subjects had both eyes photographed four times per session, with two different sessions. Each image was then undertaken through gray-scaled printing and successive scanning for fake image generation. Each user contains 32 images, 800 per class (real and fake), and a total of 1600 with a uniform resolution of 640 × 480.

CASIA [8, 9] dataset contains both the high resolution still images and video clips. There are fifty subjects and four classes within the dataset. Every class contains one landscape-style video and one portrait-style video. The four classes are real subjects, "cut photo" attacks (printed photo of subject with eyeholes cut out, real user positioned behind photo to fool blinking detection systems), "wrap photo" (printed photo of subject held up to the camera, photo is moved back and forth to fool liveness detection systems), and video replay attacks (tablet or screen held up to the camera while playing a video of subject).

CASIA cropped is the customized image datasets that were created from the original CASIA images [8, 9] by using OpenCV Haar cascades [17]. Furthermore, we created custom resized CASIA image sets with different resolutions and lower dimensions. In our work, we considered high resolution image as 720 × 1280 (portrait style), and standard-resolution image as 640 × 480 (landscape style) and 480 × 640 (portrait style). We also experimented on custom resized image datasets. For custom resized image datasets, we modified images on different resolutions and dimensions, such as 240 × 320, and 225 × 225. Overall, there are approximately 127,000 images that were used for this work.

5 Results and Discussions

The training pattern of the CNNs varies depending on time and memory availability of CPU/GPUs. To achieve the realistic performances, we ran different implementations of CNNs, including the 'modified ResNet', on all the datasets separately for multiple times and observed their performances and minute variations. In Table 1, we compare the test accuracies of the 'modified ResNet' with the DWT and 'modified ResNet' on ATVS Iris [1, 2], CASIA Two Class [8, 9], and CASIA cropped [8, 9] datasets.

In addition, we compared the test accuracies on our previously implemented 'modified VGGNet' [16], and with DWT and the 'modified VGG Net' [16]. We achieved highest accuracies when we use the DWT with the 'modified ResNet'. The proposed approach takes the lowest computational time compared to the other approaches as given in Table 1.

Table 1. Classification accuracies and average execution time of different classification techniques implemented

Classification techniques used	Datasets used			Average execution time for ATVS Iris (in seconds)
	ATVS Iris	CASIA Two Class	CASIA Cropped	
Modified ResNet [34 layers]	94.40	91.0	85.70	1,962
DWT + 'Modified ResNet' [34 layers]	92.57	90.80	82.4	1311
Modified VGG Net' [19 layers] [16]	97.00	96.00	95.00	1459
DWT + 'Modified VGG Net' [19 layers] [16]	89.00	86.00	78.00	3045

The Receiver Operating Characteristic curve (ROC) for the ATVS Iris datasets shows a True Positive Rate (TPR) of 98%, as shown in Fig. 4(a). The average error rate for our proposed model is in the range of (3.6%–5.2%).

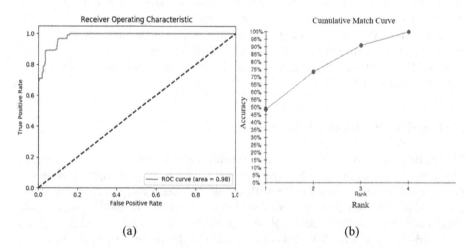

(a)   (b)

Fig. 4. (a). ROC curve and (b). Cumulative match characteristics (CMC) curve on binary classification on ATVS dataset using DWT + 'Modified ResNet' classification technique.

The test accuracy reported of the 'modified ResNet' was significant, irrespective of its deep network architecture. The training and validation process is reasonably faster due to the skip connection techniques at initial stages of training and the 32 convolution layers towards the end of training for fast training. Our 'modified ResNet' uses optimum CPU/GPU memory. The 'modified ResNet' efficiently handled standard black and white ATVS iris image and CASIA two-class, cropped, and custom resized face images datasets with precision.

The ROC curve in Fig. 4(a) plots the TPR versus the False Positive Rate (FPR) for our proposed 'modified ResNet' on different image datasets. In the best-case scenario, TPR should be as close as possible to 1.0, meaning that during training and validation none of the images were rejected by mistake.

The FPR should be as close to 0.0 as possible, meaning that all presentation attacks were rejected, and none were mistakenly accepted as real users. In all cases, the Area Under the Curve (AUC) remains in the range of 0.96 to 1.00, which is close to the ideal value of 1.0. However, the TPR is generally higher for the controlled grayscale ATVS image datasets compared to less controlled CASIA color image datasets and CASIA cropped datasets.

We achieved the 90.1% rank 3 identification and recognition accuracy with precision as shown in Fig. 4(b) in the Cumulative Match Characteristics (CMC) curve.

6 Conclusion

In this paper, we applied the 'modified ResNet' in combination with DWT to mitigate the presanction attacks on iris and face images. The modified ResNet architecture used here takes less computational time compared to other deep nets, without compromising the accuracy. Our future work will focus on testing our framework with other popular biometric datasets and observing stability and performance. Our future plan includes an extensive focus on the test accuracy and improving the overall performance of our proposed architecture.

Acknowledgment. This research is based upon work supported by the Science & Technology Center: Bio/Computational Evolution in Action Consortium (BEACON) and the Army Research Office (Contract No. W911NF-15-1-0524).

References

1. Fierrez, J., Ortega-Garcia, J., Torre-Toledano, D., Gonzalez-Rodriguez, J.: BioSec baseline corpus: a multimodal biometric database. Pattern Recognit. **40**(4), 1389–1392 (2007)
2. Galbally, J., Ortiz-Lopez, J., Fierrez, J., Ortega-Garcia, J.: Iris liveness detection based on quality related features. In Proceedings of the International Conference on Biometrics, New Delhi, India, ICB, pp. 271–276, March 2012
3. Yang, J., Lei, Z., Li, S.: Learn convolutional neural network for face anti-spoofing. arXiv: 1408.5601v2 [cs.CV], August 2014

4. Menotti, D., et al.: Deep representations for iris, face, and fingerprint spoofing detection, arXiv:1410.1980v3 [cs.CV], Pre-print of article that will appear in IEEE Transactions on Information Forensics and Security (T.IFS), 29 January 2015
5. Manjani, I., Tariyal, S., Vatsa, M., Singh, R., Majumdar, A.: Detecting silicone mask-based presentation attack via deep dictionary learning. IEEE Trans. Inf. Forensics Secur. **12**(7), 1713–1723 (2017)
6. Rao, R.: Wavelet Transforms. Encyclopedia of Imaging Science and Technology. Wiley, January 2002. https://doi.org/10.1002/0471443395.img112
7. He, K., Zhang, X., Ren, S., Sun, J.: Deep Residual Learning for Image Recognition. arXiv: 1512.03385v1 [cs.CV] 10 December 2015
8. Zhiwei, Z., Yan, J., Liu, S., Lei, Z., Yi, D., Li, S.Z.: A face antispoofing database with diverse attacks. In: Proceedings of IAPR International Conference on Biometrics (ICB), Beijing, China, pp. 26–31 (2012)
9. Chinese Academy of Sciences (CASIA), Institute of Automation, Face antispoofing dataset. http://www.cbsr.ia.ac.cn/english/FASDB_Agreement/Agreement.pdf
10. Pentland, A., Choudhury, T.: Face recognition for smart environments. Computer **33**(2), 50–55 (2000)
11. Phillips, P.J., Martin, A., Wilson, C.L., Przybocki, M.: An introduction to evaluating biometric systems. Computer **33**(2), 56–63 (2000)
12. Phillips, P.J., Moon, H., Rizvi, S.A., Rauss, P.J.: The FERET evaluation methodology for face-recognition algorithms. IEEE Trans. Pattern Anal. Mach. Intell. **22**(10), 1090–1104 (2000)
13. Daugman, J.: How iris recognition works. IEEE Trans. Circuits Syst. Video Technol. **14**(1), 21–30 (2004)
14. Lee, T.S.: Image representation using 2D Gabor wavelets. IEEE Trans. Pattern Anal. Mach. Intell. **18**(10), 959–971 (1996)
15. Spencer, J., Lawrence, D., Roy, K., Chatterjee, P., Esterline, A., Kim, J.: Presentation attack detection using convolutional neural networks and local binary patterns. In: First International Conference on Pattern Recognition and Artificial Intelligence, Montreal, Canada, 14–17 May 2018, pp. 529–534 (2018)
16. Chatterjee, P., Roy, K.: Anti-spoofing approach using deep convolutional neural network. In: Recent Trends and Future Technology in Applied Intelligence, January 2018. https://doi.org/10.1007/978-3-319-92058-0_72
17. Mordvintsev, A., Abid, K.: Face Detection using Haar Cascades. [online] OpenCV Tutorial (2013). https://opencv-python-tutroals.readthedocs.io/en/latest/py_tutorials/py_objdetect/py_face_detection/py_face_detection.html. Accessed 2018

Cost-Efficient Task Scheduling
for Geo-distributed Data Analytics

Linfeng Xie[1], Yang Dai[1], Yongjin Zhu[1], Xin Li[2,3($\boxtimes$)], Xiangbo Li[3],
and Zhuzhong Qian[3]

[1] JiangSu Frontier Electric Technology Co., LTD, Nanjing 210000, China
[2] CCST, Nanjing University of Aeronautics and Astronautics,
Nanjing 210000, China
lics@nuaa.edu.cn
[3] State Key Laboratory for Novel Software Technology, Nanjing University,
Nanjing 210000, China

Abstract. Geo-distributed data processing is affected by many factors,
some countries or regions prohibit the transmission of original user data
abroad. Therefore, it is necessary to adopt a non-centralized processing method for these data, but at the same time, many problems will
arise. Firstly, it is unavoidable to transfer job's intermediate data across
regions, which will result in data transmission cost. Secondly, the WAN
bandwidth is often much smaller than the bandwidth within clusters,
which makes it easier to become the bottleneck of geo-distributed job.
In addition, because the idle computing resources in the cluster may
change with time, it will also cause some difficulties in task scheduling.
Therefore, this paper considers the problem of task scheduling for big
data jobs on geo-distributed data, considering the budget constraints
on intermediate data trans-regional transmission, and without moving
the original data. we design a budget-constrained task scheduling strategy CETS. Through the experimental analysis of different scenarios, the
effectiveness of the proposed algorithm strategy is verified.

Keywords: Big data · Cloud computing · Cost efficient ·
Geo-distributed data processing · Task scheduling

1 Introduction

Geo-distributed data processing has attracted more and more attention. Many
companies or organizations set up clusters in different regions to handle corresponding business. Jobs in these clusters generate a large amount of data every
day, and the analysis of these data is required every day. On the other hand, more
and more small and medium-sized companies and organizations choose to buy
cloud servers on public cloud platform to build their clusters. There are many
problems we need to deal with geo-distributed data processing. Many existing
big data processing systems are centralized processing style, the data of each

© Springer Nature Switzerland AG 2019
G. Wang et al. (Eds.): SpaCCS 2019 Workshops, LNCS 11637, pp. 95–104, 2019.
https://doi.org/10.1007/978-3-030-24900-7_8

cluster must be centralized into one cluster first [1]. But this will result in a lot of time and money costs, and the costs of data transmission will increase with the increase of data volume. Even without considering the time and cost factors, this centralized method may encounter more thorny legal and regulatory problems. Nowadays, in order to protect data privacy, many countries or regions prohibit such cross-border data transmission [2].

Although a lot of work [1–3] has pointed out that it is better to transfer computing tasks than to transmit data, that is, transfer computing tasks to the cluster where the data is located. This way can avoid the transmission of original data, but for existing big data processing systems, the trans-domain transmission of intermediate data is unavoidable. Therefore, for a geo-distributed data processing job, there are two important concerns: data transmission cost and job completion time.

The cost of data transmission is related to the amount of data transmitted between clusters and the charging standards on the corresponding links, reasonable selection of data transmission links is conducive to reducing the cost of data transmission. Job's completion time is mainly affected by data transmission time and task completion time, data transmission time is affected by bandwidth, while tasks' computing time is related to the amount of idle resources in the cluster and the configuration of cloud servers. Because bandwidth of WAN is often much smaller than that of cluster, it is easier to become the bottleneck of geo-distributed data processing job. Some work [1] optimizes the data transmission of bottleneck links between clusters, which can reduce data transmission time, but it can not minimize job completion time because it does not consider tasks' computing time. And minimizing data transmission time does not necessarily meet the user's data transmission budget, because it only considers the data transmission of bottleneck links, and in order to limit the total amount of data transmission, all links must be taken into account. Some work [4] considers the computing time of tasks, but it assumes that computing capacity of different clusters is same and the number of available computing nodes is stable, but in practice, the company will rent different type and number of cloud servers for each cluster according to its business. Therefore, the number of computing resources and heterogeneity of clusters are also the issues we need to consider. In addition, for geo-distributed data processing jobs, jobs in a single cluster are background loads, and background loads change dynamically over time, so the number of idle resources in each cluster will also change dynamically. We also need to consider this factor when calculating the tasks' computing time for geo-distributed data processing jobs.

This paper considers the problem of task scheduling for big data jobs on geo-distributed data, considering the budget constraints on intermediate data trans-regional transmission, and without moving the original data. A cost-constrained task scheduling strategy CETS for multi-stage Spark-type jobs is proposed. It includes: a budget allocation strategy which can adjust the data transmission budget of each stage adaptively, a estimation method of stage completion time, and a task scheduling strategy with data transmission cost constraints.

Table 1. Ali cloud bandwidth charge standard (Yuan/GB)

	North China	Hong Kong	USA
Price	0.8	1.0	0.5

Table 2. Ali cloud WAN bandwidth (Mbps)

	NC-3	NC-5	EC-1	SC-1
NC-3	821	79	78	79
NC-5	–	820	103	71
EC-1	–	–	848	103
SC-1	–	–	–	821

2   Background and Motivation

Geo-distributed data processing jobs are affected by many factors. Laws and regulations make it impossible for us to move the original data, and the trans-domain transmission of data also generates costs. As shown in Table 1, the charging standards of different links may be different, so for some users who are sensitive to it, data transmission cost is a problem that must be considered.

In addition, trans-domain data transmission makes the job completion time affected by bandwidth heterogeneity. We tested the WAN bandwidth between cloud servers in different regions on Ali cloud. As shown in Table 2, WAN bandwidth is much lower than that within the same cluster, and the gap can be more than ten times. Therefore, the bandwidth of WAN links is more likely to become the bottleneck of large data processing operations across regions. Moreover, the bandwidth of different links are also very different, such as the bandwidth between EC-1 and SC-1 is 103 Mbps, while the bandwidth between NC-5 and SC-1 is only 71 Mbps. It will directly affect the data transmission time of geo-distributed data processing jobs.

The heterogeneity of servers between clusters will directly affect the computing time of tasks. There are differences in computing performance between servers in different clusters, which makes the same task run in different clusters with different completion times.

Previous work [1,2] usually did not consider the limitation of computing resources, but for small and medium-sized companies using public cloud servers, the cluster size is generally small, so the computing resources must also be considered limited. The computing resources in the cluster will change dynamically because of the background load. In this case, the task scheduling will be more complex. On the one hand, due to the dynamic change of the amount of idle computing resources, in order to more accurately estimate the completion time, it is necessary to make a prediction of the amount of idle computing resources in each cluster. On the other hand, the dynamic change of cluster environment will make the one-time task allocation strategy no longer applicable, so it is necessary to design a new task scheduling strategy.

3 Cost-Efficient Task Scheduling

In Spark [5], the system divides a job into several stages according to its directed acyclic graph, each stage corresponds to a batch of tasks that can be submitted for operation. There is a barrier between the adjacent stages: shuffle. According to spark's processing logic, we can transform the minimization of job completion time into the minimization of completion time of each stage.

Without considering data skew, we assume that each task has same amount of input data. In this way, we only need to determine the number of tasks allocated to each cluster, rather then elaborating on each specific task. We adopt the concepts of map and reduce task of MapReduce model [6]. The tasks that need to be scheduled at the current stage are equivalent to reduce tasks, and the tasks that are run at last stage are equivalent to map tasks. We call the task scheduling strategy designed in this section CETS.

Considering the constraints of data transmission budget and the optimization of completion time, for n cluster environments, the allocation of reduce tasks in a stage needs to satisfy the following conditions:

$$
\begin{aligned}
&\min\ z \\
&st.\quad N_{ri} \geq 0, \qquad\qquad i = 1, 2, ..., n \\
&\quad\ \ \sum_{i=1}^{n} N_{ri} = N_r \\
&\quad\ \ T_i(N_{ri}) \leq z, \qquad i = 1, 2, ..., n \\
&\quad\ \ \sum_{i=1}^{n} F_i(N_{ri}) \leq s
\end{aligned}
\qquad\text{(LP1)}
$$

Where i denotes cluster i, N_{ri} denotes the number of reduce tasks allocated to cluster i, N_r denotes the total number of reduce tasks, T_i denotes the expected completion time of cluster i, F_i denotes the data transfer cost of cluster i,and s denotes the data transfer budget for current stage (shuffle). To solve the linear programming LP1, we need to calculate the expected completion time T_i and data transmission cost F_i of each cluster i.

Let's say: D_u is the amount of data transferred between a map task and reduce task, D_{ji} is the total amount of data transferred from cluster j to cluster i, B_{ji} is the bandwidth size from cluster j to cluster i, N_{ri} is the number of reduce tasks allocated to cluster i, and N_{mj} is the number of map tasks in the previous stage within cluster j.

Then the shuffle time T_d of cluster i can be derived from the following formula:

$$
\begin{aligned}
T_d &= \sum_{j \in J_i} D_{ji}/B_{ji} \\
&= \sum_{j \in J_i} N_{mj} * N_{ri} * D_u/B_{ji}
\end{aligned}
\qquad (1)
$$

Where $J_i = \{j \mid j \in \mathbb{N}, 1 \leq j \leq n, j \neq i\}$, denotes the collection of $n-1$ clusters except cluster i.

If the computing time of a task is T_t and the number of waves is R, then the total task processing time is $T_s = T_t * R$. In Spark, the number of waves R can be calculated from the number of reduce tasks N_{ri} and the number of CPU cores of all task executors: $R = N_{ri}/E_i$.

Let D_t be the amount of input data of a reduce task, N_m be the number of map tasks in the previous stage, then $D_t = N_m * D_u$. Suppose that nodes in the same cluster are not heterogeneous, we introduce a concept of node computing ability C_i, which is used to express the time that a task takes to process unit data on a node, which can be obtained from history data. Then the computing time of a task can be obtained: $T_t = D_t * C_i$.

In summary, we can get the completion time T_i of a stage within cluster i:

$$
\begin{aligned}
T_i &= T_d + T_s \\
&= \sum_{j \in J_i} D_{ji}/B_{ji} + T_t * R \\
&= \sum_{j \in J_i} N_{mj} * N_{ri} * D_u/B_{ji} + (D_t * C_i) * (N_{ri}/E_i) \\
&= \sum_{j \in J_i} N_{mj} * N_{ri} * D_u/B_{ji} + (N_m * D_u * C_i) * (N_{ri}/E_i) \\
&= \left[\sum_{j \in J_i} N_{mj} * N_{ri}/B_{ji} + (N_m * C_i) * (N_{ri}/E_i) \right] * D_u
\end{aligned}
\tag{2}
$$

D_u is unknown, but it has no effect on solving linear programming LP1.

Set P_{ji} as the price of data transmission from cluster j to cluster i, then the cost of pulling data from other clusters by the cluster i is:

$$
\begin{aligned}
F_i &= \sum_{j \in J_i} D_{ji} * P_{ji} \\
&= \sum_{j \in J_i} N_{mj} * N_{ri} * D_u * P_{ji}
\end{aligned}
\tag{3}
$$

Since we transform the minimization of job completion time into the minimization of stage completion time, and the data transmission budget given by users is for the whole job rather than a single phase, we need to design corresponding strategies to divide the corresponding data transmission budget for each stage. Assume user's budget M can enable the job to run successfully, the budget assigned to each shuffle is $\{s_1, s_2, ..., s_k\}$, initialized as $\{M/k, M/k, ..., M/k\}$. Let the algorithm for solving linear programming LP1 be ResolveLP(budget), where budget is the given budget of the current shuffle. Run the budget allocation algorithm before each shuffle.

Algorithm 1. budget allocation algorithm

Input: shuffle id: i, current allocation: $\{s_1, s_2, ..., s_k\}$, stop flag: $STOP$ (initialized as $False$)

   Output: updated allocation: $\{s_1, s_2, ..., s_k\}$

1: **while** $STOP = false$ or $ResolveLP(s_i)$ has not feasible solution **do**
2:    **if** $ResolveLP(s_i)$ has feasible solution *and* $STOP = True$ **then**
3:       **return** $\{s_1, s_2, ..., s_k\}$;
4:    **else if** $ResolveLP(s_i)$ has not feasible solution *and* $STOP = False$ **then**
5:       **if** $i = k$ **then**
6:          $STOP \leftarrow True$;
7:       **else**
8:          $s_i \leftarrow s_i - s_i/2$;
9:          **for** s_j in $\{s_{i+1}, ..., s_k\}$ **do**
10:             $s_j \leftarrow s_j + (s_i/2) / (k - i)$;
11:    **else**
12:       $s_i \leftarrow s_i + s_i/2$;
13:       **for** s_j in $\{s_{i+1}, ..., s_k\}$ **do**
14:          $s_j \leftarrow s_j - (s_i/2) / (k - i)$;
15:       $STOP \leftarrow True$;

---

4 Evaluation

To verify the effectiveness of the proposed algorithm, simulation experiments are carried out to compare CETS with Iridium [1] and Spark's Naive strategy for Reduce tasks. We simulate three clusters. Bandwidth charges for cluster A, B and C are 0.8 yuan/GB, 1.0 yuan/GB and 0.5 yuan/GB respectively. Bandwidth parameters are set as shown in Table 3. We set up three types of job, small, medium and large, which contain 100, 500 and 1000 tasks respectively. The total amount of shuffle data is 1 GB, 5 GB and 10 GB, respectively.

Table 3. Bandwidth setting (Mbps)

	Cluster A	Cluster B	Cluster C
Cluster A	800	50	50
Cluster B	70	800	70
Cluster C	10	50	800

Figure 1 shows the results of three types of jobs using CETS algorithm, Iridium and Naive strategy under different cluster nodes size. Because the main comparison is job completion time, there is no data transmission budget constraint in this experiment. We run 10 groups of experiments with different initial data distribution for each cluster size, and the average completion time of the job as follows.

The experimental results show that the CETS algorithm outperforms Iridium and Naive for different cluster sizes and job types. The average job completion time of CETS is 44.5%, 32.7% and 23.1% lower than that of Iridium under the four cluster node sizes. This is because Iridium only considers the optimization of data transmission time, but does not consider the computing time of tasks. Because of this, when the cluster size is small, CETS has better optimization effect than Iridium. Spark's scheduling mechanism does not consider bandwidth and only considers computing resources. Compared with CETS and Iridium, when the cluster size is large and computing resources are no longer the bottleneck of jobs, the performance disadvantages of Naive are more obvious.

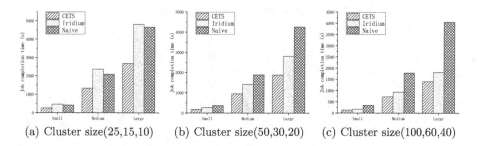

(a) Cluster size(25,15,10)   (b) Cluster size(50,30,20)   (c) Cluster size(100,60,40)

Fig. 1. Job's completion time under different cluster sizes

Figure 2 shows the minimum data transmission cost and corresponding data size for three different types of jobs when the cluster size is 100, 60 and 40. The experimental results show that both Iridium and CETS can reduce the data transmission cost, but CETS has better effect. Compared with Iridium and Naive, CETS's data transmission cost reduced by 38.5% and 42.4% on average, data transmission size decreased by 34.2% and 39.8%. CETS reduces the data transmission cost more than size, because CETS choose the link with lower cost to transmit data. The reason why CETS reduces more data transmission than Iridium is that when the data transmission budget is very small, CETS will choose to sacrifice time in exchange for the reduction of the budget, and the budget is closely related to the amount of data transmission, which will result in the reduction of data transmission.

According to the distribution proportion of the initial data in the three clusters, we set four cases: average distribution (avg), 80% in cluster A (A_Heavy), 80% in cluster B (B_Heavy) and 80% in cluster C (C_Heavy).

· Figure 3 shows the completion time and data transmission cost and size of large jobs under different initial data distribution, without data transmission budget constraints. The results show that CETS algorithm can reduce job completion time under different data distribution. When the data are evenly distributed, the data transmission cost and size of the three scheduling strategies are very close. This is because no matter which cluster a reduce task is assigned to, it needs to pull the same amount of data from the other two clusters, so

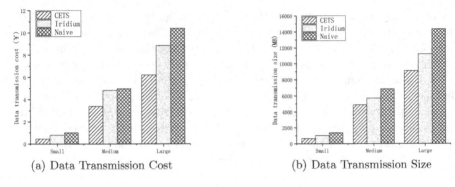

Fig. 2. Minimum data transmission cost and size

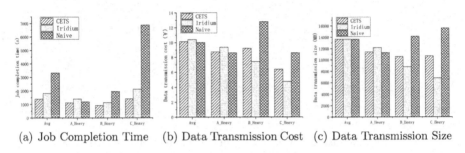

Fig. 3. Job under different initial data distributions

the data transmission size is similar. However, the completion time of CETS is significantly shorter than that of other strategies, which is 23.3% and 58.0% lower than that of Iridium and Naive, respectively. This is because although the data transmission size is almost the same, CETS will take into account the transmission link and resources to minimize job completion time. When the data is concentrated in a cluster, the bandwidth between clusters is the main consideration of Iridium, while the Naive strategy mainly considers the computing resources. Because of the bottleneck in the uplink of cluster C, Iridium will choose to allocate tasks in cluster C to reduce data transmission in the case of C_heavy. However, due to the least computing resources in cluster C, job completion time is longer than that of B_heavy and C_heavy. Naive strategy is more likely to assign tasks to cluster A which has more computing resources, so when C_heavy, job completion time increases dramatically due to the impact of bottleneck links of cluster C. In the case of B_heavy and C_heavy, although CETS's data transmission cost and size are higher than Iridium's, it also has a 25% decrease compared with Native, and the job completion time of CETS is also significantly reduced. The job completion time of CETS is 18.5% and 33.27% lower than Iridium's.

5   Related Work

Kloudas et al. [3] proposed Pixida for large data jobs with complex directed acyclic graphs. Its optimization objective is the data transmission on resource-constrained links between clusters. They proposed a topological concept called SILO to simplify job's directed acyclic graphs. It is considered that data transmission between computing nodes within the same SILO node is better than data transmission to another SILO node. Pixida transforms the task allocation problem into a graph cutting problem, and designs a deformed graph cutting algorithm for task allocation. Jayalath and Eugster et al. [7] extended Pig Latin [8] and designed Rout to support geo-distributed data and operation. They believe that it is necessary to pre-analyze a geo-distributed job before it is executed in order to reduce the amount of data transmission between clusters. Like Pig Latin, Rout generates a MapReduce data flow graph for a job and analyze it to find key nodes. Based on the marked data flow graph, Rout generates the corresponding execution plan to avoid data transmission to overloaded clusters. Meta-MapReduce [9], designed by Afrati et al., considers reducing data transmission between clusters by transferring only intermediate data necessary to obtain the final results of jobs. On the one hand, Meta-MapReduce considers the location of data and tasks to avoid data movement. On the other hand, they designed an algorithm that can use metadata to calculate the required output data to avoid uploading all data. Pu et al. [1] designed Iridium to shorten the response time of jobs by optimizing the placement of data and tasks. By optimizing the placement of data and tasks, the author reduces the transmission time of data in the bottleneck link. Gadre et al. [10] designed a global Reduce task allocation algorithm to minimize data transmission. The algorithm solves the problems of when to start a job's reduce phase, the placement of global reduce task, the placement of intermediate data and the time consumption of data transmission.

6   Conclusion

We have a deep research on the background and significance of geo-distributed data processing jobs. Considering data transmission budget, bandwidth and cluster heterogeneity, we design a task scheduling strategy CETS. We carried out simulation experiments, and through the experimental analysis of different scenarios, the effectiveness of the algorithm strategy proposed in this paper is verified.

References

1. Pu, Q., et al.: Low latency geo-distributed data analytics. ACM SIGCOMM Comput. Commun. Rev. **45**(4), 421–434 (2015)
2. Vulimiri, A., Curino, C., Godfrey, P.B., Jungblut, T., Padhye, J., Varghese, G.: Global analytics in the face of bandwidth and regulatory constraints (2017)
3. Preguiça, K., Rodrigues, R.: Pixida: optimizing data parallel jobs in bandwidth-skewed environments. In: Proceedings of VLDB Endowment (2015)
4. Hu, Z., Li, B., Luo, J.: Flutter: scheduling tasks closer to data across geo-distributed datacenters. In: IEEE INFOCOM 2016-The 35th Annual IEEE International Conference on Computer Communications, pp. 1–9. IEEE (2016)
5. Zaharia, M., Chowdhury, M., Franklin, M.J., Shenker, S., Stoica, I.: Spark: cluster computing with working sets. HotCloud **10**(10–10), 95 (2010)
6. Dean, J., Ghemawat, S.: MapReduce: simplified data processing on large clusters. Commun. ACM **51**(1), 107–113 (2008)
7. Jayalath, C., Eugster, P.: Efficient geo-distributed data processing with rout. In: 2013 IEEE 33rd International Conference on Distributed Computing Systems, pp. 470–480. IEEE (2013)
8. Olston, C., Reed, B., Srivastava, U., Kumar, R., Tomkins, A.: Pig Latin: a not-so-foreign language for data processing. In: Proceedings of the 2008 ACM SIGMOD International Conference on Management of Data, pp. 1099–1110. ACM (2008)
9. Afrati, F., Dolev, S., Sharma, S., Ullman, J.D.: Meta-MapReduce: a technique for reducing communication in MapReduce computations arXiv preprint arXiv:1508.01171 (2015)
10. Gadre, H., Rodero, I., Parashar, M.: Investigating MapReduce framework extensions for efficient processing of geographically scattered datasets. ACM SIGMETRICS Perform. Eval. Rev. **39**(3), 116–118 (2011)

Task Scheduling for Streaming Applications in a Cloud-Edge System

Fei Yin[1], Xinjia Li[1], Xin Li[2,3(✉)], and Yize Li[3]

[1] JiangSu Frontier Electric Technology Co., LTD, Nanjing 210000, China
[2] CCST, Nanjing University of Aeronautics and Astronautics,
Nanjing 210000, China
lics@nuaa.edu.cn
[3] State Key Laboratory for Novel Software Technology, Nanjing University,
Nanjing 210000, China

Abstract. With the increasing popularity of ubiquitous smart devices, more and more IoT (Internet of Things) data processing applications are deployed. Due to the inherent defects of traditional data transmission networks and the low latency requirement of applications, effective use of bandwidth computing resources to support the efficient deployment of applications has become a very important issue. In this paper, we focus on how to deploy multi-source streaming data processing applications in a cloud-edge collaborative computing network and pay attention to make the overall application data processing delay lower. We abstract the application into a form of streaming data processing, formalize it as a *Stream Processing Task Scheduling Problem*. We present an efficient algorithm to solve the above problem. Simulation experiments show that our approach can significantly reduce the end-to-end latency of applications compared to commonly used greedy algorithms.

Keywords: Edge computing · End to end delay · Internet of Things · Stream data processing · Task scheduling

1 Introduction

With the development of the Internet of Things, the active market and the popularity of edge smart devices [1], more and more IoT applications are deployed. IoT devices often generate a large amount of real-time data, such as videos, system monitoring and acquisition information, radar information, and so on. These applications include network monitoring and control, device network intrusion detection, weather and earthquake-related weather activity data monitoring, user web access data analysis and large field ecosystem monitoring. These data are transmitted and processed in the form of data streams in a data processing system. Due to the large number of devices across the network, the number of data streams transmitted in the WAN is huge. The bandwidth capacity of the WAN network is limited, and the geographical distribution of the device makes

© Springer Nature Switzerland AG 2019
G. Wang et al. (Eds.): SpaCCS 2019 Workshops, LNCS 11637, pp. 105–114, 2019.
https://doi.org/10.1007/978-3-030-24900-7_9

the data transmission load of the entire network huge, which is likely to cause delay increase or even data loss.

In order to achieve the purpose of being lightweight and easy to deploy, smart devices are often limited in size, and the computing power and energy reserves of the devices themselves are also limited. Simply deploying application tasks on these smart devices can often deplete computing and storage power, resulting in reduced battery life, severe device fever, and worse user experience. In response to this situation, researchers have proposed data center-based solutions [2, 3]. Since the data center is far away from the geographical area where the application is located, it will cause a considerable impact on the delay of the users, which will affect the user experience. The ever-increasing amount of data scattered across geographic regions makes it impractical to transfer all of the data to the data center over the already crowded backbone network.

Currently, researchers in related fields have proposed the concept of Edge Computing (Fog Computing). The edge cloud is a distributed cloud platform structure. The idea is to send the data that the application needs to process to the small service cloud at the edge of the network for processing. The data calculation and processing request of the application is satisfied by deploying a small computing server at the edge of the network close to the user, such as a wireless base station, an edge local area network, or the like. Processing the data stream at the edge compute node saves time in data transfer to the data center. And because the raw data of many devices can be filtered and merged at the edge computing node first, the amount of data transmitted in the WAN will be greatly reduced.

Deploying streaming data processing tasks under the edge computing network framework, the ensuing question is which strategy to use to deploy data processing tasks. Due to cost issues, the widespread deployment of edge computing nodes is still unrealistic [4]. There are many types of IoT applications, and the number of applications is relatively large, while the WAN bandwidth resources are limited. In a multi-input streaming data processing application, the data streams that the task needs to process are widely distributed in different edge network regions. Due to the delay difference of multiple input data streams and the bandwidth resource competition between multiple applications, the task deployment strategy will affect end-to-end latency and bandwidth resource usage of data streams. At the same time, when there are multiple task copies in a task in the system to process the data stream of the application, it is necessary to take into consideration both the placement problem of multiple task copies in the system and the data flow routing problem that the data stream should be distributed to which computing task to process.

In order to solve the above problems, this paper studies the *Stream Processing Task Scheduling Problem*. Since an application has parallel processing tasks, we decompose the problem into two key processes: *task deployment with fixed stream routing (TDWFSR)* and *stream routing with fixed tasks location (SRWFTL)*. The two process are depended on each other to get a better performance. In the process of *SRWFTL*, we design a stream routing method to minimized delay with random fixed task replicas' location on nodes which are the source of the stream.

Tn the process of *TDWFSR*, we design a task deploy and re-deploy method which consider the bandwidth competition and is delay incremental sensing. We call the hole above process DHG algorithm. In this paper, the efficiency of the proposed method is verified by simulation experiments. Compared with the algorithm that can not perceive the multi-edge node bandwidth resource competition and the delay difference between edge nodes, the proposed algorithm can achieve lower data stream processing delay and higher bandwidth utilization efficiency.

2 Background and Related Work

The data processing mode of streaming data processing is a computational framework model proposed to cope with the need to process streaming data quickly [5]. The idea of streaming data processing is that the current data arrives in real time and the system gives the results in real time. At present, many systems related to streaming data processing in a single data center have become excellent popular computing frameworks, such as Flink [6], Storm [7], Spark Streaming [8] and so on. These task-based frameworks based on streaming computing models can handle high throughput and low latency tasks in the data center [9].

Some research work has investigated the issue of streaming data processing deployed in edge network environments. Article [10] describes a stream data model based overlay network (SBON), which is based on the cost space, the abstract representation of the network and the ongoing stream, and the method of deploying the streaming data processing node by minimizing the system energy cost. Article [11] describes a method for similarity query of data input and processing in a streaming DAG task deployment system. Through the job DAG input and shared lookup, the network minimum usage-aware deployment of two processes to the task Deploy to reduce the network overhead of the current system. In the work [12–14], a two-stage data collection and transmission and final data processing streaming data processing tasks are described in detail, and the problems of network usage and delay accuracy are discussed. the study. In work [15], in order to deal with WAN instability, fast and highly available stream processing is implemented on the WAN. The paper proposes a replication-based streaming data processing method. The paper sends the same data stream to multiple task copies in order to get the fastest delay in the completion of the transfer of all task copies.

The data processing tasks considered in this paper are completely different in the multi-edge node-data center collaborative deployment scenario and the scenario assumptions in the above research work. Deploying streaming data processing tasks in traditional data centers, network bandwidth limitations are often not important resource constraints. However, in the scenario considered in this paper, multi-source input often means that the bandwidth limitation of the network becomes the main resource limitation bottleneck.

3 System and Problem Statement

3.1 Infrastructure Model

We consider a cloud-edge network consisting of multiple edge compute nodes and a data center node, denoted by D. Each node has a certain ability to transmit data to the network. The bandwidth of node d is B_d. For each edge computing node, their bandwidth is limited. The bandwidth capability of the data center node is much larger than that of the edge node. It can be considered that there is no limit to the bandwidth capability during the task deployment.

Based on the above process, we can describe the process of application deployment as a streaming data processing task that needs to be deployed in the system. A computing task needs to process data streams distributed across different compute nodes. The set of computing tasks that need to be deployed in the system is S. The set of all pending data streams is Q. A s processing a data stream q data, you need to maintain a data transmission channel between the compute node where s is located and the compute node where q is located, the bandwidth is r_q. The task s that can be used to process data for an application has T_s. The set of data streams that an application needs to process is $q \in Q_s$. At this time, s can be arbitrarily routed to one of the task replica belong to s.

3.2 Task Placement and Stream Routing Decision

One of the data processing tasks has no more than one copy of the task deployed on each node. We use the variable $x_{std} = \{0, 1\}$ to indicate whether the t copy of the data processing task s is deployed on the d compute node. We have the tasks placement decision variable equations:

$$\forall s \in S, \sum_{d \in D} \sum_{t \in T_s} x_{std} = |T_s| \tag{1}$$

$$\forall s \in S, \forall t \in T_s, \forall d \in D, x_{std} = \{0, 1\} \tag{2}$$

Each data stream is routed to a copy of one of the types of data processing tasks for processing. We use the variable $y_{qst} = \{0, 1\}$ to indicate whether $q \in Q$ is routed to the t copy of the data processing task s, we have the streams routing decision variable equations:

$$\forall s \in S, \forall q \in Q_s, \sum_{t \in T_s} y_{qst} = 1 \tag{3}$$

$$\forall s \in S, \forall q \in Q_s, \forall t \in T_s, y_{qst} = \{0, 1\} \tag{4}$$

After the discussion in Sects. 3.1, 3.2, and 3.3 above, we can clearly see the abstract deployment process of the streaming data processing application in the cloud-edge environment, as shown in Fig. 1.

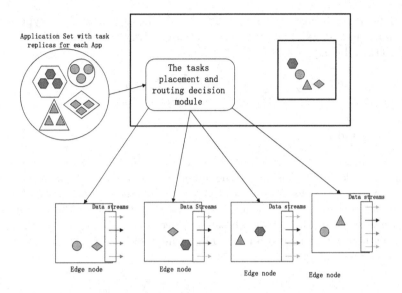

Application Set with task
replicas for each App

The tasks
placement and
routing decision
module

Data streams

Data Streams

Data streams

Data streams

Edge node

Edge node

Edge node

Edge node

Fig. 1. Task deployment and data stream routing.

3.3 Bandwidth Consumption

Each data processing task deployed in the system consumes a certain amount of bandwidth resources to support the inflow and outflow of data streams. When a copy of a current data processing task s is deployed on a compute node d, the bandwidth resource consuming node d is related to the data stream from which it is selected for data processing. It is necessary to decide on the route of each $q \in Q_s$. $\forall s \in S$, $\forall d \in D$, $\forall t \in T_s$, when the copy t of the task s is deployed at the node d', we let the P_{std} represents the bandwidth resource consumed by the task copy on the node $\forall d \in D \wedge d \neq d'$. Because of the routing problem of the current data stream, so we need to decide the participation calculation of y_{qst}. Then P_{std} is expressed as:

$$\forall s \in S, \forall t \in T_s, \forall d \in D, d \neq d', P_{std} = \sum_{q \in \{Q_s \cap Q_d\}} r_{qs} y_{qst} \tag{5}$$

Let $K_{std'}$ denote the d' bandwidth resource consumed by the data processing task s after being deployed in the d' node. For the node d' where the task is located, then we have $K_{std'}$ is expressed as:

$$\forall s \in S, \forall t \in T_s, d \neq d', K_std = \sum_{q \in \{Q_s - Q_s \cap Q_d\}} \tag{6}$$

The upper limit of the bandwidth resource of any computing node is U_d. At this time, the sum of the bandwidth resource consumption of the data stream transmission on one node to support all related computing tasks cannot exceed the bandwidth capacity of the computing node. Let S_d denote the type set of the computing task existing on the current computing node d, and the resource limitation can be expressed as:

$$\forall d \in D, \sum_{s \in S_d} \sum_{t \in T_s} x_{std} K_{std} + \sum_{s \notin S_d} \sum_{t \in T_s} x_{std} P_{std} \leq U_d \qquad (7)$$

3.4 Delay Cost

When the data stream is transmitted to the compute node where the data processing task is located, considering the impact of the delay between the compute nodes on the current system, the overall delay of the flow service request is still considered to describe the efficiency of the current system. Since the current data stream needs to be routed through the y_{std} decision variable, a copy of a data processing task s is deployed after a computing node, and the resulting system delay is written as follows:

$$\forall s \in S, \forall t \in T_s, \forall d \in D, H_{std} = \sum_{q \in \{Q - Q_d\}} y_{qst} L_{d_q d} \qquad (8)$$

The L is the latency matrix between the nodes D. d_q is the stream q's location node. Data processing tasks can have deployment problems with replicas. It is necessary to decide whether all copies of a current data processing task are deployed in a data center or a service area in an edge cloud. Our goal is to make the latency of all data stream requests in the current system less expensive. Let V denote the current system overall delay cost, then V can be expressed as:

$$V = \sum_{s \in S, t \in T_s, d \in D} x_{std} H_{std} = \sum_{s \in S, t \in T_s, d \in D} x_{std} \sum_{q \in \{Q - Q_d\}} y_{qst} L_{d_q d} \qquad (9)$$

3.5 Tasks Placement Problem and Complexity Analysis

Tasks Placement Problem. According to the above analysis process, $\forall s \in S$, selecting different deployment locations d causes the system nodes to consume different bandwidth resources and the delay cost caused in the system. Then the current problem is expressed as: $\forall s \in S, \forall t \in T_s$, selecting the position $d \in D$ makes the current V minimum, and satisfies the constraint conditions (1)(2)(3)(4)(5)(6)(7)(8)(9). From this we get a formal description of the multi-copy data processing task deployment problem. We have:

$$\min_{XY} \quad V, \quad s.t. \quad (1)(2)(3)(4)(5)(6)(7)(8)(9). \qquad (10)$$

4   Application Scheduling Solution

Our algorithm is based on the following key ideas. The system's task deployment process is split into three processes, (a) data localization that does not consider bandwidth load, and greedy task placement, and (b) end-to-end short-est delay routing decision without considering data inflow bandwidth load, called *SRWFTL* (c) Consider the minimum cost of the system bandwidth load limit to increase the greedy task deployment location re-adjustment, called *TDWFSR*. In the above three processes, only one of the variables in X and Y is involved. In (a) process, since the bandwidth limitation is not considered, the deployment of the task only considers deploying the task to those data streams to other Nodes that cost a lot of money are equivalent to initializing a feasible solution for X without bandwidth constraints. In the process of (b), due to the limitation of the number of task copies, all the data streams that an application needs to process at this time cannot be processed by the task copy of the application at its local node, and the bandwidth resource limitation of the node is not consid-ered at this time. The Y value is determined by a method that does not have a data stream capable of obtaining a local data processing service in a greedy manner with a minimum delay cost. In the process of (c), the conditions of the bandwidth limitation are added. The (c) process has two core points. The X and Y values are obtained during the (a) process and (b) are used to calculate the bandwidth resource limits and the delay cost of the system on each node. In the problem of dealing with insufficient bandwidth resource constraints, the data stream deletion is selected from the nodes that violate the bandwidth resource limitation by using the option to delete the minimum cost increment.

The above idea is to be able to separate the decisions of X and Y, and to obtain locally superior results in each basic process, and then add restrictions, greedy punishment to delete to meet the system limitations. The details is shown in Algorithm 1.

5   Performance Evaluation

5.1   Setup

The simulation experiment platform was carried out using Matlab 2018b on a computer with a CPU of CORE I7 and a memory of 16 GB. Set the delay to reach the data center to be 0.75 s. The delay distribution between edge computing nodes is subject to a random distribution between [0.1, 0.4]S. The bandwidth capability of each edge computing node to transfer data to the WAN is the same as the bandwidth of 50 MB/s. In order to simulate the effect of the algorithm under different edge calculation node scales, we set the number of edge nodes to be 50, 100, 150, 200, 250, 300, 350, 400, 450, 500, respectively. In order to simulate the effect of multiple types of application data streams competing for bandwidth resources, we set the size of each data stream to be randomly distributed between [1, 3] MB/S. We make the bandwidth consumption of the data stream generated on all computing nodes about 60% of the computing node's bandwidth, and one node generates 16 data streams. Set the total number of data streams that need to be processed for all task copies of each task type to be 6, 7, 8, 9, 10 evenly distributed.

Algorithm 1. *DHG* Divided Handle X and Y Greed algorithm

Input: The physical substrate network (D, L, U), the application tasks and
      stream data information (S, T, Q)
Output: the tasks placement decision matrix X and the stream routing
      decision matrix Y
for $s \in S$ do
   | Deploy the $|T_s|$ copy of task s in nodes random choose from D_s; for
   | $q \in Q_s$ do
   | | Route q to the node d which can be find by (12);
   | end
end
Update the X and Y;
Calculate the bandwidth usage matrix RU, V;
while $\exists RU(d) > U(d)$ do
   | for $d \in D$ do
   | | if $RU(d) > U(d)$ then
   | | | Delete the s_t find by (13);
   | | | Re-routing the $q \in Q_{s_t}$ by the method show by step (3);
   | | | Calculate the ΔV_d;
   | | end
   | end
   | delete the s_t in node d which make the ΔV_d minimum;
   | update the X, Y;
end
return X and Y;

In order to verify the validity of our algorithm, we use the methods in Table 1 to compare with our algorithm.

5.2 Result

We analyze the performance of V values of different methods under different number of edge nodes. We use the V-means of other methods minus the V-means of our method and then divide by the V-means of the other methods. As shown in Fig. 2), in the case of two task copies, the method is reduced by 80% compared to the ODC method, 36% less than the Hash method, and 20% less than the closest method. In the case of 4 task copies, the method is reduced by 86% compared to the ODC method, 15% less than the Hash method, and the Closest method is reduced by 7%.

Since the data transmission on the network consumes both the bandwidth resources of the sender and the receiver, the Closest method with localized execution and our method have improved. It is worth noting that as the number of task copies increases, the Closest method has a certain effect of localization of task data. At this time, our method compares the Closest method with less optimization. The reason is that with the increase of replicas, the Closest method gets most of the delay reduction due to data localization processing, and the

Table 1. The edge nodes and applications' setup number

Algorithms	Description
ODC	The ODC (only data center available) method deploys all tasks to the data center
$HASH$	$HASH$ random method, randomly assigns a data stream that a task needs to process to any copy of the corresponding task, and then randomly deploys the task copy in the edge computing node. If the edge node bandwidth resource is not satisfied, then the task is deployed in the data. In the center
$CLOSEST$	The $CLOSEST$ method randomly assigns a data stream that a task needs to process to any one of the corresponding tasks, and then deploys the task copy to the computing node closest to the data stream and capable of meeting the bandwidth resource requirements. Otherwise, the task copy is deployed in the data. center

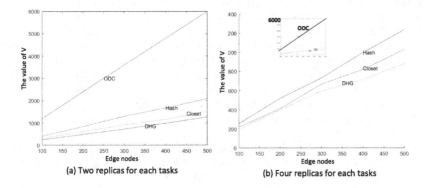

(a) Two replicas for each tasks

(b) Four replicas for each tasks

Fig. 2. V value change under different edge nodes.

data transmitted through the network is reduced. At this time, the influence of the network delay difference between the edge nodes is weakened, so our method In this case the effect is weakened.

6 Conclusion

This paper studies the problem of streaming task placement. We discussed the problem of data flow routing and multitasking placement in multi-copy streaming task placement problems. By formalizing the resource consumption model of data routing and task deployment in the edge system, the delay cost model caused by the system is established. We present a greedy algorithm to solve this problem. The experimental results show that our algorithm can well find the available bandwidth resources in the edge computing network and can sense the delay difference between the edge nodes, thus reducing the average delay of the system application request.

References

1. L. Columbus Internet Of Things Market To Reach \$267B By 2020. https://www.forbes.com/sites/louiscolumbus/2017/01/29/%0Ainternet-of-things-market-to-reach-267b-by-2020/. Accessed 1 May 2019
2. Yang, L., Cao, J., Yuan, Y., Li, T., Han, A., Chan, C.: A framework for partitioning and execution of data stream applications in mobile cloud computing. In: International Conference on Cloud Computing 2012, vol. 40, pp. 23–32. https://doi.org/10.1145/2479942.2479946
3. Yang, L., Cao, J., Cheng, H., Ji, Y.: Multi-user computation partitioning for latency sensitive mobile cloud applications. IEEE Trans. Comput. 8(64), 2253–2266 (2015)
4. Soyata T., et al.: COMBAT: mobile-Cloud-based cOmpute/coMmunications infrastructure for BATtlefield applications. In: Proceedings of SPIE, vol. 8403, pp. 1–13. https://doi.org/10.1117/12.919146
5. Akidau, T., et al.: The dataflow model: a practical approach to balancing correctness, latency, and cost in massive-scale, unbounded, out-of-order data processing. In: Very Large Data Bases 2015, vol. 8, pp. 1792–1803 (2015)
6. Flink Home page. https://flink.apache.org/. Accessed 1 May 2019
7. Storm Home page. https://storm.apache.org/. Accessed 1 May 2019
8. Spark Home page. https://spark.apache.org/. Accessed 1 May 2019
9. Chintapalli, S., et al.: Benchmarking streaming computation engines: storm, flink and spark streaming. In: International Parallel and Distributed Processing Symposium 2016, pp. 1789–1792 (2016). https://doi.org/10.1109/IPDPSW.2016.138
10. Pietzuch, P.R., Ledlie, J., Shneidman, J., Roussopoulos, M., Welsh, M., Seltzer, M.I.: Network-aware operator placement for stream-processing systems. In: International Conference on Data Engineering 2006, p. 49 (2006). https://doi.org/10.1109/ICDE.2006.105
11. Jonathan, A., Chandra, A., Weissman, J.B.: Multi-query optimization in wide-area streaming analytics. In: Symposium on Cloud Computing 2018, pp. 412–425 (2018). https://doi.org/10.1145/3267809.3267842
12. Heintz, B.: Optimizing Timeliness, Accuracy, and Cost in Geo-Distributed Data-Intensive Computing Systems (2016)
13. Heintz, B., Chandra, A., Sitaraman, R.K.: Optimizing grouped aggregation in geo-distributed streaming analytics. In: High Performance Distributed Computing 2015, pp. 133–144 (2015). https://doi.org/10.1145/2749246.2749276
14. Heintz, B., Chandra, A., Sitaraman, R.K.: Trading timeliness and accuracy in geo-distributed streaming analytics. In: Symposium on Cloud Computing 2016, pp. 361–373 (2016). https://doi.org/10.1145/2987550.2987580
15. Hwang, J., Cetintemel, U., Zdonik, S.B.: Fast and highly-available stream processing over wide area networks. In: International Conference on Data Engineering 2008, pp. 804–813 (2008). https://doi.org/10.1109/ICDE.2008.4497489

The 5th International Symposium on Sensor-Cloud Systems (SCS 2019)

SCS 2019 Organizing and Program Committees

Steering Chairs

Jiannong Cao   The Hong Kong Polytechnic University, SAR China
Weijia Jia   University of Macau, SAR China

Advisory Chairs

Guojun Wang   Guangzhou University, China
Qing Li   City University of Hong Kong, SAR China

Steering Committee

Xiaojiang Chen   Northwest University, China
Kim-Kwang Raymond Choo   The University of Texas at San Antonio, USA
Mianxiong Dong   Muroran Institute of Technology, Japan
Wei Dong   Zhejiang University, China
Xiao-Jiang (James) Du   Temple University, USA
Guangjie Han   Hohai University, China
Kuan-Ching Li   Providence University, Taiwan
Limin Sun   Institute of Information Engineering,
     Chinese Academy of Sciences, China

Hongyi Wu   Old Dominion University (ODU), USA
Yang Xiao   The University of Alabama, USA

General Chairs

Tian Wang   Huaqiao University, China
Md Zakirul Alam Bhuiyan   Fordham University, USA

Program Chairs

Chunsheng Zhu   The University of British Columbia, Canada
Zhangbing Zhou   China University of Geosciences, TELECOM
     SudParis, China, France

Program Committee

Bashar, A. M. A. Elman   Plymouth State University, USA
Yonghong Chen   Huaqiao University, China

Siyao Cheng	Harbin Institute of Technology, China
Lin Cui	Jinan University, China
Haipeng Dai	Nanjing University, China
Weiwei Fang	Beijing Jiaotong University, China
Zhitao Guan	North China Electric Power University, China
Xiali (Sharon) Hei	Delaware State University, USA
Qiangsheng Hua	Huazhong University of Science and Technology, China
Patrick Hung	University of Ontario Institute of Technology, Canada
Yongxuan Lai	Xiamen University, China
Feng Li	Shandong University, China
Guanghui Li	Jiangnan University, China
Jianxin Li	University of West Australia, Australia
Junbin Liang	Guangxi University, China
Wanyu Lin	University of Toronto, Canada
Zhen Ling	Southeast University, China
Anfeng Liu	Central South University, China
Chi (Harold) Liu	Beijing Institute of Technology, China
Kai Liu	Chongqing University, China
Liang Liu	Beijing University of Posts and Telecommunications, China
Peng Liu	Hangzhou Dianzi University, China
Xiao Liu	Deakin University, Australia
Xuxun Liu	South China University of Technology, China
Kai Peng	Huaqiao University, China
Zhen Peng	College of William and Mary, USA
Rajesh Prasad	Saint Anselm College, USA
Yiran Shen	Data61 CSIRO, Australia
Rui Tan	Nanyang Technological University, Singapore
Shaolei Teng	Howard University, USA
Jiliang Wang	Tsinghua University, China
Weigang Wu	Sun Yat-Sen University, China
Yong Xie	Xiamen University of Technology, China
Wenzheng Xu	Sichuan University, China
Guisong Yang	University of Shanghai for Science and Technology, China
Dongxiao Yu	Huazhong University of Science and Technology, China
Yong Yu	Shanxi Normal University, China
Dong Yuan	Sydney University, Australia
Shigeng Zhang	Central South University, China
Chunsheng Zhu	The University of British Columbia, Canada
Yanmin Zhu	Shanghai Jiao Tong University, China

Journal Special Issue Chairs

Kim-Kwang Raymond Choo   University of Texas at San Antonio, USA
James Xi Zheng   Macquarie University, Australia

Publicity Chairs

Zeyu Sun   Luoyang Institute of Science and Technology, China
Xiaofei Xing   Guangzhou University, China
Zenghua Zhao   Tianjin University, China

Coordination Chairs

Zhen Peng   College of William and Mary, USA
Yang Liu   Beijing University of Posts and Telecommunications,
             China

Web Chair

Yuzhu Liang   Huaqiao University, China

Limited Memory Eigenvector Recursive Principal Component Analysis in Sensor-Cloud Based Adaptive Operational Modal Online Identification

Cheng Wang[1,2]([⊠]), Haiyang Huang[1], Tianshu Zhang[1],
and Jianwei Chen[3]

[1] College of Computer Science and Technology, Huaqiao University,
Xiamen 361021, China
wangcheng@hqu.edu.cn
[2] State Key Laboratory for Strength and Vibration of Mechanical Structures,
Xi'an Jiaotong University, Xi'an 710049, China
[3] Department of Mathematics and Statistics, San Diego State University,
San Diego, CA 92182, USA

Abstract. Time-varying operational modal analysis (OMA) can identify the transient modal parameters for the linear time-varying (LTV) structures only from the time domain nonstationary vibration response signal measured by vibration response sensors. However, because large-scale sensors data poses significant problems for data processing and storage, methods with excessive computation time and memory requirements are unsuitable for online, real-time health monitoring and fault diagnosis. Recently, the emergence of sensor-cloud greatly improves the computing power and storage capacity of traditional wireless sensor networks by combining cloud computing. Therefore, sensor-cloud can be used to deal with data problems in OMA: the wireless sensor networks layer is used to collect data and the calculations are performed on the cloud computing platform. Furthermore, a limited memory eigenvector recursive principal component analysis (LMERPCA) based OMA method is designed to reduce the runtime and memory requirements and facilitate online process in conjunction with the cloud computing. This approach combines moving window technology and eigenvector recursive principal component analysis method and can identify the transient natural frequencies and modal shapes of slow LTV structures online and in real time. Finally, modal identification results from a cantilever beam with weakly damped and slowly time-varying density show that the LMERPCA-based OMA can identify the transient modal parameters online. Compared with limited memory principal component analysis (LMPCA)-based OMA, the LMERPCA-based approach has a faster runtime, lower memory space requirements, higher identification accuracy, and greater stability.

Keywords: Operational modal analysis · Slow linear time-varying ·
Sensor-cloud · Principal component analysis · Moving window ·
Eigenvector recursive

© Springer Nature Switzerland AG 2019
G. Wang et al. (Eds.): SpaCCS 2019 Workshops, LNCS 11637, pp. 119–129, 2019.
https://doi.org/10.1007/978-3-030-24900-7_10

1 Introduction

OMA refers to extracting modal parameters (modal shapes, natural frequencies and modal ratios) from the vibration response signal measured by vibration response sensors [1]. In recent years, OMA has been widely used in large-scale structures under operating conditions or environmental excitation, because it does not require to measure input which is often expensive or unmeasurable. OMA can be applied in structural health monitoring, fault detection and diagnosis, structural design, etc. [2].

As practical mechanical structures are often LTV, which mass, stiffness or damping will change over time, such as the vibration of continuous bridges under moving vehicles [3]. The identification methods should have the ability to adapt to track system changes [4]. Moreover, the vibration response signal measured by vibration response sensors will be nonstationary and increase over time. These data should be stored properly and processed quickly by algorithm.

In recent years, LTV OMA methods are mainly divided into time domain and time-frequency analysis methods [1]. Time domain approach includes time-dependent state space (TSS) and time-dependent autoregressive moving average (TARMA) types. Liu et al. proposed an improved subspace-based identification algorithm to enhance the anti-noise ability [5]. TSS methods cannot be operated recursively by using aggregate data from multiple experiments [6]. In other words, TSS method has high computational complexity. Ma et al. considered an exponentially weighted kernel recursive extended least squares TARMA [6]. The time and memory complexities still have $O(N^2)$. For the time-frequency analysis methods, Dziedziech et al. [7] utilized the wavelet-based frequency response method to estimate time-varying parameters. These methods process data offline and batch-wise rather than online and in real time. Wang et al. proposed the application of moving window and PCA to slow linear time-varying (SLTV) structures and developed a limited memory principal component analysis (LMPCA)-based OMA algorithm to identify the transient natural frequencies and transient modal shapes of a linear time-varying continuous cantilever beam [8]. In short, these existing methods still have high runtime and memory requirements and are unsuitable for online, real-time health monitoring and fault diagnosis.

Sensor-cloud is the integration of sensor networks and cloud computing [9]. Recently, there are many studies on sensor-cloud, such as trust evaluation [10], security and privacy [11], and storage [12]. Sensor-cloud enable data collection [13] and have been applied to structural health monitoring [14]. The emergence of smart city [15], vehicular Networks [16, 17] and Internet of things [18] has led to an increase in the number of sensors and the amount of sensor data. With the support of cloud computing platforms, sensor-cloud can manage these data [19]. Coincidentally, OMA also needs vibration response sensor data and then processes it. Therefore, a combination of sensor cloud and OMA is feasible.

In this paper, we propose to combine sensor-cloud with OMA. To address the runtime and memory problem, a limited memory eigenvector recursive principal component analysis (LMERPCA) based OMA method is proposed. This approach applies the moving window and eigenvector recursive principal component analysis (ERPCA), a rank-1 matrix is used to correct the errors, and new principal components

(PCs) and eigenvectors are updated recursively. Because the time and space complexity of LMERPCA-based OMA method is $O(N)$, combining sensor-cloud with LMERPCA-based OMA can track change of modal parameters for SLTV structures.

2   Combining Sensor-Cloud with LMERPCA-Based OMA

2.1   The Process of LMERPCA Algorithm

Traditionally, the sample matrix is updated via a limited memory method, with the latest sample added and the oldest sample removed from the data matrix. ERPCA directly updates the principal components (PCs) and eigenvectors via the previously obtained eigenvectors. The newest models are calculated by a recursive approach rather than the recalculation of the entire sample matrix. The ERPCA algorithm sharply reduces the time and space complexity than LMPCA. LMERPCA integrates ERPCA and moving window approach, updating the selected portion of data recursively for each sample (the oldest sample is removed and the newly acquired one is added). The process of LMERPCA is illustrated in Fig. 1 for a data window length of L. LMERPCA removes the oldest sample $\vec{x}_1^{(i)} \in \mathbb{R}^{N \times 1}$ in the window before updating and adding the latest sample $\vec{x}_1^{(i+L)} \in \mathbb{R}^{N \times 1}$ to the window, while the intermediate window is used as the transitional matrix. The deviations, PCs, and eigenvectors of the window after updating the matrix and the intermediate window matrix are derived as follows.

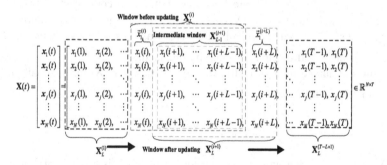

Fig. 1. The process of combining moving window with ERPCA

2.2   The Derivation of LMERPCA Algorithm

ERPCA has been proposed [20], we have adapted it to work with moving window technology. For a limited memory length L, the data matrix $\mathbf{X}_L^{(i)} \in \mathbb{R}^{N \times L}$ at time $t(i)$ and $\mathbf{X}_L^{(i+1)} \in \mathbb{R}^{N \times L}$ at time $t(i+1)$ are considered. The common data matrix of the two matrices is $\mathbf{X}_{L-1}^{(i+1)} \in \mathbb{R}^{N \times (L-1)}$. Let $\vec{b}_{\mathbf{X}_L^{(i)}} \in \mathbb{R}^{N \times 1}$ and $\mathbf{C}_{\mathbf{X}_L^{(i)} \mathbf{X}_L^{(i)}} \in \mathbb{R}^{N \times N}$ be the mean vector and autocorrelation matrix, respectively, of $\mathbf{X}_L^{(i)} \in \mathbb{R}^{N \times L}$. After removing sample

$\vec{x}_1^{(i)} \in \mathbb{R}^{N \times 1}$, the mean vector $\vec{b}_{\mathbf{X}_{L-1}^{(i+1)}} \in \mathbb{R}^{N \times 1}$ and autocorrelation matrix $\mathbf{C}_{\mathbf{X}_{L-1}^{(i+1)} \mathbf{X}_{L-1}^{(i+1)}} \in \mathbb{R}^{N \times N}$ of the intermediate matrix $\mathbf{X}_{L-1}^{(i+1)} \in \mathbb{R}^{N \times (L-1)}$ are derived as follows:

$$\vec{b}_{\mathbf{X}_{L-1}^{(i+1)}} = \frac{1}{L-1}\left(L\vec{b}_{\mathbf{X}_L^{(i)}} - (\vec{x}_1^{(i)})\right) \tag{1}$$

$$\mathbf{C}_{\mathbf{X}_L^{(i)} \mathbf{X}_L^{(i)}} = \frac{L-1}{(L-1)-1} \Sigma_{\mathbf{X}_L^{(i)}}^{-1} \Sigma_{\mathbf{X}_{L-1}^{(i+1)}} \mathbf{C}_{\mathbf{X}_{L-1}^{(i+1)} \mathbf{X}_{L-1}^{(i+1)}} \Sigma_{\mathbf{X}_{L-1}^{(i+1)}} \Sigma_{\mathbf{X}_L^{(i)}}^{-1} + \Sigma_{\mathbf{X}_L^{(i)}}^{-1} \Delta \mathbf{b}_{\mathbf{X}_L^{(i)}} \Delta \mathbf{b}_{\mathbf{X}_L^{(i)}}^T \Sigma_{\mathbf{X}_L^{(i)}}^{-1} + \frac{1}{L-1}\vec{x}_1^{(i)}\vec{x}_1^{(i)T} \tag{2}$$

where $\Delta\vec{b}_{\mathbf{X}_L^{(i)}} = \vec{b}_{\mathbf{X}_L^{(i)}} - \vec{b}_{\mathbf{X}_{L-1}^{(i+1)}} \in \mathbb{R}^{N \times 1}$, $\Sigma_{\mathbf{X}_L^{(i)}} \in \mathbb{R}^{N \times N}$ represents the diagonal matrix of the standard deviation in the window before updating $\mathbf{X}_L^{(i)} \in \mathbb{R}^{N \times L}$, and $\Sigma_{\mathbf{X}_{L-1}^{(i+1)}} \in \mathbb{R}^{N \times N}$ represents the diagonal matrix of the standard deviation in the intermediate data window $\mathbf{X}_{L-1}^{(i+1)} \in \mathbb{R}^{N \times (L-1)}$.

In LMERPCA, the model is updated when a new data point is added, so the overall variance and mean values change gradually. Hence, we use the original model to simplify Eq. (2) as:

$$\mathbf{C}_{\mathbf{X}_L^{(i+1)} \mathbf{X}_L^{(i+1)T}} \approx \mathbf{C}_{\mathbf{X}_L^{(i)} \mathbf{X}_L^{(i)T}} + \frac{1}{L-1}\vec{x}_1^{(i+1)}\vec{x}_1^{(i+1)T} - \frac{1}{L-1}\vec{x}_1^{(i)}\vec{x}_1^{(i)T} \tag{3}$$

where $\vec{x}_1^{(i+1)}\vec{x}_1^{(i+1)T}$ and $\vec{x}_1^{(i)}\vec{x}_1^{(i)T}$ are both rank-1 matrices composed of two vectors. Based on the definition of rank-1 correction [21], the autocorrelation matrix $\mathbf{C}_{\mathbf{X}_L^{(i+1)} \mathbf{X}_L^{(i+1)T}}$ at step $i+1$ can be calculated by applying rank-1 correction twice, and the updated PC vectors and eigenvectors can be obtained.

Suppose the autocorrelation matrix of step i is $\mathbf{C}_{\mathbf{X}_L^{(i)} \mathbf{X}_L^{(i)T}}$. We orthogonally decompose this matrix as follows:

$$\mathbf{C}_{\mathbf{X}_L^{(i)} \mathbf{X}_L^{(i)T}} = \mathbf{V}^{(i)} \mathbf{\Lambda}^{(i)} \mathbf{V}^{(i)T} \tag{4}$$

where $\mathbf{V}^{(i)} \in \mathbb{R}^{N \times N}$ is the unit orthogonal matrix and $\mathbf{\Lambda}^{(i)}$ is a diagonal matrix composed of the eigenvalues of the autocorrelation matrix. Equation (3) is reformulated as:

$$\begin{aligned}\mathbf{C}_{\mathbf{X}_L^{(i+1)} \mathbf{X}_L^{(i+1)T}} &= \mathbf{V}^{(i)}\left[\mathbf{\Lambda}^{(i)} + \left(-\frac{1}{L-1}\right)(\mathbf{V}^{(i)T}\vec{x}_1^{(i)})(\mathbf{V}^{(i)T}\vec{x}_1^{(i)})^T\right]\mathbf{V}^{(i)T} + \frac{1}{L-1}\vec{x}_1^{(i+1)}\vec{x}_1^{(i+1)T} \\ &= \mathbf{V}^{(i)}(\mathbf{D} + \varepsilon\vec{u}\vec{u}^T)\mathbf{V}^{(i)T} + \frac{1}{L-1}\vec{x}_1^{(i+1)}\vec{x}_1^{(i+1)T}\end{aligned} \tag{5}$$

Setting $\mathbf{D} = \mathbf{\Lambda}^{(i)} \in \mathbb{R}^{N \times N}$, $\varepsilon = -\frac{1}{L-1}$, and $\vec{u} = (\mathbf{p}^{(i)T}\vec{x}_1^{(i)}) \in \mathbb{R}^{N \times 1}$, the result after the first rank-1 correction is:

$$\mathbf{\Lambda}^{(i)} + (-\frac{1}{L-1})(\mathbf{V}^{(i)T}\vec{x}_1^{(i)})(\mathbf{V}^{(i)T}\vec{x}_1^{(i)})^T = \mathbf{V}^{(i)'}\mathbf{\Lambda}^{(i)'}\mathbf{V}^{(i)'T} \tag{6}$$

Modifying Eq. (4) as:

$$\mathbf{C}_{\mathbf{X}_L^{(i+1)}\mathbf{X}_L^{(i+1)T}} = \mathbf{V}^{(i)}(\mathbf{V}^{(i)'}\mathbf{\Lambda}^{(i)'}\mathbf{V}^{(i)'T})\mathbf{V}^{(i)T} + \frac{1}{L-1}\vec{x}_1^{(i)}\vec{x}_1^{(i)T} \tag{7}$$

we can further transform Eq. (6) into:

$$\begin{aligned}\mathbf{C}_{\mathbf{X}_L^{(i+1)}\mathbf{X}_L^{(i+1)T}} &= \mathbf{V}^{(i)}\mathbf{V}^{(i)'}[\mathbf{\Lambda}^{(i)'} + \frac{1}{L-1}(\mathbf{V}^{(i)'T}\mathbf{V}^{(i)T}\vec{x}_1^{(i+1)})(\mathbf{V}^{(i)'T}\mathbf{V}^{(i)T}\vec{x}_1^{(i+1)})^T](\mathbf{V}^{(i)}\mathbf{V}^{(i)'})^T \\ &= \mathbf{V}^{(i)}\mathbf{V}^{(i)'}(\mathbf{D}' + \varepsilon'\vec{u}'\vec{u}'^T)(\mathbf{V}^{(i)}\mathbf{V}^{(i)'})^T\end{aligned} \tag{8}$$

Setting $\mathbf{D}' = \mathbf{\Lambda}^{(i)'} \in \mathbb{R}^{N \times N}$, $\varepsilon' = -\frac{1}{L-1}$, and $\vec{u}' = (\mathbf{V}^{(i)'T}\mathbf{V}^{(i)T}\vec{x}_1^{(i+1)}) \in \mathbb{R}^{N \times 1}$, the result after the second rank-1 correction is:

$$\mathbf{\Lambda}^{(i)'} + (-\frac{1}{L-1})(\mathbf{V}^{(i)'T}\vec{x}_1^{(i+1)})(\mathbf{V}^{(i)'T}\vec{x}_1^{(i+1)})^T = \mathbf{V}^{(i)''}\mathbf{\Lambda}^{(i)''}\mathbf{V}^{(i)''T} \tag{9}$$

After applying rank-1 correction twice, we can decompose the autocorrelation matrix as:

$$\mathbf{C}_{\mathbf{X}_L^{(i+1)}\mathbf{X}_L^{(i+1)T}} = (\mathbf{V}^{(i)}\mathbf{V}^{(i)'}\mathbf{V}^{(i)''})\mathbf{\Lambda}^{(i)''}(\mathbf{V}^{(i)}\mathbf{V}^{(i)'}\mathbf{V}^{(i)''})^T \tag{10}$$

Finally, $\mathbf{\Lambda}^{(i)''}$ is the diagonal matrix composed of the updated eigenvalues, and the updated eigenvectors $\mathbf{V}^{(i+1)}$ and PCs $\mathbf{Y}_L^{(i+1)}$ can be calculated by:

$$\mathbf{V}^{(i+1)} = \mathbf{V}^{(i)}\mathbf{V}^{(i)'}\mathbf{V}^{(i)''} \tag{11}$$

$$\mathbf{Y}_L^{(i+1)} = \mathbf{V}^{(i+1)T}\mathbf{X}_L^{(i+1)} \tag{12}$$

The PCs and eigenvectors are recursively updated by the above equations. It is easy to see, the eigenvectors and PCs at time $t(i + 1)$ are only related to eigenvalues at time $t(i)$ and data matrix and eigenvalues at time $t(i + 1)$. Thus, the incident characteristics of SLTV structures are tracked.

2.3   The LMERPCA-Based OMA Algorithm for SLTV Structures

The process of LMERPCA-based online transient modal parameter identification method is shown in Fig. 2. In short, ERPCA is used to update eigenvectors and eigenvalues to calculate modal shapes and natural frequencies. Moving window enables online and real-time identification. The performance comparison between LMPCA and LMERPCA is shown in the Table 1.

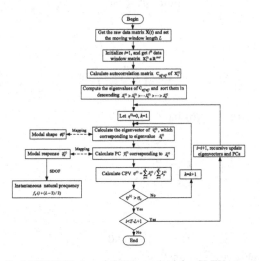

Fig. 2. LMERPCA-based OMA method for SLTV structures

Table 1. Comparison of the two time-varying OMA algorithms

Method	Time complexity	Space complexity	Time of matrix decomposition	Accuracy comparison
LMPCA-based OMA	$O(N^2L)$, $(L \gg N)$	$O(NL)$, $(L \gg N)$	T-L + 1	Meet the demand
LMERPCA-based OMA	$O(N)$	$O(N)$	1	Better than LMPCA-based OMA

2.4   Framework of Combining Sensor-Cloud with LMERPCA-Based OMA

For large buildings or mechanical structure, the input is usually not measurable or expensive. OMA can identify the modal parameters (modal shapes, natural frequencies and modal ratios), which can describe the dynamic characteristics of the structure. The LMERPCA-based OMA sensor-cloud system can be divided into three layers, the vibration response sensors layer, the cloud layer and the user layer. It is worth noting that the lower the complexity of the algorithm, the smaller the delay and the less computational power required in the cloud layer, LMERPCA-based OMA method is conducted in this layer then, as shown in Fig. 3.

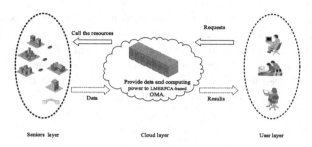

Fig. 3. The process of combining sensor-cloud with OMA

3 Simulation Verification of LMERPCA-Based OMA on SLTV

3.1 Parameters of SLTV Cantilever Beam

A cantilever beam model [8] with dimensions of 1 m × 0.02 m × 0.02 m (*length × height × width*), cross-sectional area $A = W \times H = 4 \times 10^{-4}$ m², density $\rho_0 = 7860$ kg/m³, inertia time $I = WH^3/12$, and Young's modulus $E = 0.03$ *Pa* is considered. The time-varying mass property is simulated by changing the density of the beam according to:

$$\rho = \begin{cases} \rho_0, \ 0 \le t \le 0.5s \\ \rho_0[1 - 0.08(t - 0.5)], \ 0.5s < t \le 4s \end{cases} \tag{13}$$

For a simulation time of 4 s, the time-varying transient natural frequencies of the first ten modes at the start and finish times are listed in Fig. 4.

Order t/s	1	2	3	4	5	6	7	8	9	10
0s	16.9997	104.6552	293.038	574.2391	949.2649	1418.0561	1980.6357	2637.0355	3387.3056	4231.5200
4s	19.6807	123.3374	345.3485	676.7473	1118.7194	1671.1952	2334.2016	3107.7761	3991.9779	4986.8942

Fig. 4. Change in transient natural frequencies (0–4 s)

3.2 Simulation Parameters Setting

The forced response signals were acquired using the *Newmark-β* method. The proportional coefficients were set to $\beta_M = 4 \times 10^{-4}$, $\beta_K = 1 \times 10^{-7}$. The initial velocities and displacement were set to zero. From Fig. 4, it is clear that the transient natural frequencies increase with time. For the frequency of 4986.8942 Hz at the finish time, the sampling frequency was set to 10000 Hz based on sampling theory, as a sampling frequency very close to the highest resonant frequency could result in errors. However, setting higher sampling frequencies will increase the computational load. The simulation time was set to 4 s, and the integration step for *Newmark-β* was set to 1/10000 s; the limited memory length L was set to 4096 data points and the threshold η_0 was set to 95%. We added 2.0% Gaussian measurement noise to the displacement response signals in the time domain. Independent noise components of different magnitudes were added to both the transfer function and response signals for the load identification. The noise was calculated as follows:

$$\widehat{X}_i = (1 + r \cdot e)X_i \tag{14}$$

where e is a normal random vector with a mean value of 0 and standard deviation of 1; r is the noise level, set to 2.0% in our experiments.

3.3   Transient Modal Parameter Identification Results

Figure 5 shows the Fast Fourier Transformation (FFT) results of the PCs at after 1.7028 s and 2.2547 s. Because of the SLTV nature of the structures, it is not easy to describe the transient modal shapes for the whole process. Figure 6 compares the first three transient modal shapes and Pareto charts after 1.7028 s and 2.2547 s. Figure 7(a)–(c) compares the first three transient frequencies given by LMPCA-based OMA, the theoretical calculation, and LMERPCA-based OMA. The theoretical values were calculated from the analytical solution. Finally, to reflect the accuracy of the transient modal shapes, the modal assurance criterion (MAC) values are compared in Fig. 8. Table 2 compares the time and space complexity of LMPCA- and LMERPCA-based OMA.

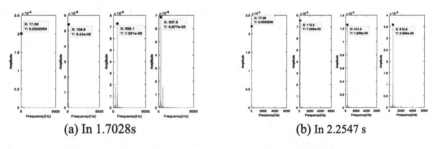

(a) In 1.7028s   (b) In 2.2547 s

Fig. 5.   FFT results for the first four PCs of LMERPCA

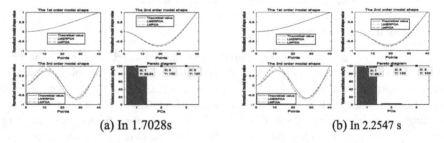

(a) In 1.7028s   (b) In 2.2547 s

Fig. 6.   Transient modal shape comparison between LMPCA and LMERPCA

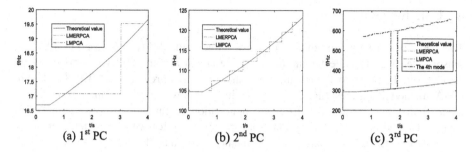

Fig. 7. Frequency comparison between LMPCA and LMERPCA

Table 2. Absolute time and memory requirements comparison between LMERPCA- and LMPCA-based OMA

Method	Time (s)	Memory (MB)
LMPCA	361.754	3519.4
LMERPCA	158.988	1939.3

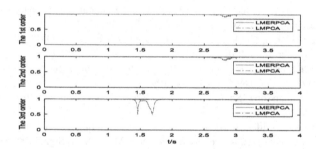

Fig. 8. MAC values comparison between LMERPCA- and LMPCA-based OMA

3.4 Analysis of Operational Modal Identification Results

(1) Figures 5, 6, 7 and 8 show that LMERPCA-based OMA can accurately track and identify the time-varying transient modal frequencies and mode shapes of an SLTV continuous cantilever beam using only non-stationary response signals. Additionally, the accuracy of LMERPCA-based OMA is insensitive to Gaussian measurement noise.

(2) In the Pareto charts (Fig. 6(a) and Fig. (b)), which show the variance contribution for each PC, when the threshold is $\eta_0 = 99.999\%$, the first three modes capture the main contribution of the whole vibration.

(3) Table 2 indicates LMERPCA-based OMA requires less time and memory than LMPCA-based OMA. In other words, LMERPCA-based OMA is more suitable for integration into devices in sensor-cloud and can be applied to online health monitoring and fault diagnosis.

4 Conclusions

This paper proposed a combination of sensor-cloud and LMERPCA-based OMA. The sensor layer used to collect vibration response signal and the OMA is carried out in cloud layer. In order to reduce the time and space requirements, LMERPCA-based OMA method integrates ERPCA and moving window technique, and the transient mode shapes and frequencies from the non-stationary random response signals for weakly damped and SLTV vibration structures can be effectively extracted then.

However, LMERPCA-based OMA method also has the drawback of moving window. The moving window length should be selected adaptively. In addition, the proposed method is also limited to weakly damped and SLTV structures. To identify modal parameters of fast LTV structures will be addressed in subsequent studies.

Acknowledgments. This work has been financially supported by the National Natural Science Foundation of China (Grant Nos. 51305142, 51305143).

References

1. Brandt, A.: A signal processing framework for operational modal analysis in time and frequency domain. Mech. Syst. Signal Process. **115**, 380–393 (2019)
2. Kedadouche, M., Liu, Z., Vu, V.H.: A new approach based on OMA-empirical wavelet transforms for bearing fault diagnosis. Measurement **90**, 292–308 (2016)
3. Chatterjee, P.K., Datta, T.K., Surana, C.S.: Vibration of continuous bridges under moving vehicles. J. Sound Vib. **169**(5), 619–632 (1994)
4. Ljunga, L., Gunnarssona, S.: Adaptation and tracking in system identification—a survey. Automatica **26**(1), 7–21 (1990)
5. Liu, K., Deng, L.: Identification of pseudo-natural frequencies of an axially moving cantilever beam using a subspace-based algorithm. Mech. Syst. Signal Process. **20**(1), 94–113 (2006)
6. Ma, Z.S., Liu, L., et al.: Parametric output-only identification of time-varying structures using a kernel recursive extended least squares TARMA approach. Mech. Syst. Signal Process. **98**, 684–701 (2018)
7. Dziedziech, K., Staszewski, W.J., Uhl, T.: Wavelet-based modal analysis for time-variant systems. Mech. Syst. Signal Process. **50–51**, 323–337 (2015)
8. Wang, C., Guan, W., et al.: Adaptive operational modal identification for slow linear time-varying structures based on frozen-in coefficient method and limited memory recursive principal component analysis. Mech. Syst. Signal Process. **100**, 899–925 (2018)
9. Wang, T., Zhang, G., et al.: A novel trust mechanism based on fog computing in sensor-cloud system. Future Gener. Comput. Syst. (2018). https://doi.org/10.1016/j.future.2018.05.049
10. Zhang, G., Wang, T., et al.: Detection of hidden data attacks combined fog computing and trust evaluation method in sensor-cloud system. Concur. Comput. Pract. Exp. e5109 (2018). https://doi.org/10.1002/cpe.5109
11. Wang, T., Zhang, G., et al.: A secure IoT service architecture with an efficient balance dynamics based on cloud and edge computing. IEEE Internet Things J. (2018). https://doi.org/10.1109/jiot.2018.2870288

12. Wang, T., Zhou, J., et al.: Fog-based computing and storage offloading for data synchronization in IoT. IEEE Internet Things J. (2018). https://doi.org/10.1109/jiot.2018. 2875915

13. Wang, T., Zeng, J., et al.: Data collection from WSNs to the cloud based on mobile Fog elements. Future Gener. Comput. Syst. (2017). https://doi.org/10.1016/j.future.2017.07.031

14. Bhuiyan, M.Z.A., Wang, G., et al.: Dependable structural health monitoring using wireless sensor networks. IEEE Trans. Dependable Secure Comput. **14**(4), 363–376 (2017)

15. Ren, Y., Liu, W., et al.: A collaboration platform for effective task and data reporter selection in crowdsourcing network. IEEE Access **7**, 19238–19257 (2019)

16. Teng, H., Liu, W., et al.: A cost-efficient greedy code dissemination scheme through vehicle to sensing devices (V2SD) communication in smart city. IEEE Access **7**, 16675–16694 (2019)

17. Huang, B., Liu, W., et al.: Deployment optimization of data centers in vehicular networks. IEEE Access **7**, 20644–20663 (2019)

18. Li, J., Liu, W., et al.: Battery-friendly relay selection scheme for prolonging the lifetimes of sensor nodes in the internet of things. IEEE Access (2019). https://doi.org/10.1109/access. 2019.2904079

19. Wang, T., Liang, Y., et al.: Coupling resource management based on fog computing in smart city systems. J. Netw. Comput. Appl. (2019). https://doi.org/10.1016/j.jnca.2019.02.021

20. Erdogmus, D., Rao, Y.N., et al.: Recursive principal components analysis using eigenvector matrix perturbation. EURASIP J. Appl. Signal Process. **2004**, 2034–2041 (2004)

21. Gandhi, R., Rajgor, A.: Updating singular value decomposition for rank one matrix perturbation. arXiv preprint arXiv:1707.08369 (2017)

Optimization of Optical Imaging MIMO-OFDM Precoding Matrix for Underwater VLC

Yanlong Li[1,2], Hongbing Qiu[1,2], Xiao Chen[1], Jielin Fu[1,2(✉)], Junyi Wang[1], and Yitao Zhang[1]

[1] Department of Information and Communication,
Guilin University of Electronic Technology, Guilin 541004, China
{lylong,qiuhb,hmfjl,wangjy}@guet.edu.cn
[2] Ministry of Education Key Laboratory of Cognitive Radio and Information Processing, Guilin University of Electronic Technology, Guilin 541004, China

Abstract. The absorption and scattering are the main problems affecting high-speed data transmission in underwater visible light communication system (UVLC). To address these problems, we propose the imaging multiple input multiple output (MIMO) system for the underwater communication in this paper. Furthermore, the proposed system uses imaging lens to separate the light signal resulting in that decreasing disturbance of the proposed system is better than that of non-imaging MIMO. In this paper, aiming at the problem of high bit error rate (BER) caused by channel correlation in underwater imaging optical MIMO communication system, a precoding algorithm based on received signal Euclidean distance of imaging multiple input multiple output-orthogonal frequency division multiplexing (MIMO-OFDM) is proposed. In order to maximize the minimum Euclidean distance of the received signal set, the precoding matrix is solved under the constraints of the non-negative optical signal and the total power. The system uses the precoding matrix to precode the signals and the receiver detects signals through the maximum likelihood algorithm with the channel matrix and the optimal precoding matrix. The simulation results show that the imaging MIMO system achieves 12 dB gain at the same bit error rate (BER) compared to non-imaging MIMO. Furthermore, the proposed algorithm based on received signal Euclidean distance achieves about 5 dB gain under the same channel compared to the SVD-based precoding algorithm in imaging MIMO system, it greatly improve the BER performance of the imaging optical MIMO-OFDM system in UVLC.

Keywords: Underwater LED communication · Imaging MIMO · Spatial correlation · Euclidean distance · Precoding matrix

1 Introduction

With the deepening of human exploration of the ocean, a new underwater short-range wireless high-speed communication technology is urgently needed to meet

G. Wang et al. (Eds.): SpaCCS 2019 Workshops, LNCS 11637, pp. 130–148, 2019.
https://doi.org/10.1007/978-3-030-24900-7_11

the increasing underwater communication needs [1]. Underwater wireless optical communication (UWOC) has become a mainstream solution for high-speed and short-distance underwater wireless communication with its unique advantages. Compared with the more mature underwater acoustic communication system, there is a low-loss transmission window of blue-green light-emitting diode (LED) light with a wavelength of 450–570 nm [2], making visible light communication (VLC) to be a possible way of underwater short-distance high-speed data transmission. VLC has the advantages of low power consumption, miniaturization, high speed, and cannot easily be intercepted [3]. Thus, it is suitable for underwater real-time video transmission, high throughput wireless sensor network and other scenarios.

However, the modulation bandwidth of LED for visible light communication is limited, and the visible light signal will reduce the power due to the expansion of the beam surface during the propagation process. The availability of a large number of high signal-to-noise ratio (SNR) sub-channels with limited bandwidth makes MIMO techniques an attractive option for achieving high data rates. Therefore, the multi-path spatial multiplexing based on LED visible light communication underwater has important research significance for greatly improving the underwater short-distance high-speed data transmission efficiency. When the transmission distance is relatively long, it will be affected by seawater absorption, scattering, turbulence disturbance, natural light noise seriously, etc. At the same time, MIMO-OFDM systems utilize the diversity or multiplexing of space, time, and frequency to enhance the additional channel capacity [4], and increase the tolerance of this communication system to interference, noise, multipath, etc. The path separation and equalization at the receiving end are effective to extract the original signal [5]. In the visible light communication system, the intensity modulation and direct detection (IM/DD) methods are mainly used, it causes sub-channel correlated, so a decorrelation operation is needed to reduce the spatial correlation of the sub-channels, which can decrease interference between each sub-channel and improve the transmission rate and BER performance of the system.

To solve the problem of spatial correlation, there are three main solutions at present. Optical imaging technology is used to improve the quality of received images, receive field angle and reduce the size of imaging at the receiving end. Through spatial separation, PD array can distinguish the signals sent by different leds and reduce the interference between signals [6–10]. Imaging MIMO has obvious advantages in improving channel correlation. PD array size is small, and imaging of different LED emitters on PD array is often separated from each other [6]. In [8], the imaging MIMO (I-MIMO) system is proposed, and the mathematical model of I-MIMO channel under the direct channel is given. The initial electrical signal is intensity modulated and emitted by the LED, and the imaging lens projects the LED transmitting source onto the PD detection array. Each PD or pixel point becomes a receiving unit to realize the separation between different channels [7]. The second is the use of non-imaging solution to decrease spatial correlation, through the optimization of the array structure or the addition of non-imaging devices to reduce the correlation between sub-channels. The more typical means are normal array vector tilt technology and other methods to adjust the space position [11–13]. In the third category, the channel correlation is reduced by means of constellation design, precoding and spatial light modulation from the perspective of signal processing by decreasing the correlation in the electrical signal phase [14–17].

In the spatial light modulation method, the author of [16, 17] makes only one LED or part of the LED emit light in each time slot through spatial modulation, thus reducing the interference between LED beams and the BER of the system. However, because there is only one or part of LED in each time slot of spatial modulation, its communication rate and spectral efficiency are lower than that of spatial multiplexed MIMO system, and it is difficult to meet the requirement of underwater short-range high-speed communication in the future. [14] proposes an optical MIMO precoding scheme based on singular value decomposition (SVD), the precoding matrix based on channel state information is designed to match the channel characteristic, and then MIMO channel is decomposed into parallel sub-channels by SVD. So the interference between the sub-channels is eliminated by spatial isolation. The authors of [14] build optimal model to minimize the BER of the system under limited total power, to get the optimal power allocation matrix of sub-channels, lead to the agreement with the performance of sub-channels.

In [18, 19], the precoding method that maximizes the minimum Euclidean distance of the received signal is adopted, which solves the optimal precoding matrix with the maximum Euclidean distance of the received signal as the optimization objective under the premise of satisfying the non-negative nature of the transmitted signal, and improves the BER performance of the imaging optical MIMO system. However, compared with the OFDM system, the current precoding of received signal Euclidean distance based on the single carrier OOK or PAM communication system is not only difficult to adapt to the muddy underwater scene, but also has a low channel capacity. Therefore, the suitable precoding method for underwater imaging MIMO remains to be studied.

In this paper, an underwater optical precoding scheme based on the minimum Euclidean distance of optical MIMO receiving signal set is proposed. Its design idea is to maximize the minimum Euclidean distance of the received signal set by optimizing the transmitting power of different LEDs on the transmitting array under the condition of non-negative signal and optical power constraint, so as to alleviate the BER performance degradation caused by channel correlation. The simulation results show that the BER of the proposed Euclidean distance-based precoding algorithm is better than that of SVD-based precoding in the case of different correlated channels. With the enhancement of channel correlation, BER performance is still kept at a relatively low level, and higher spatial multiplexing gain can be achieved when channel correlation is strong. We summarize the main contribution of this paper as follows:

(1) We give the I-MIMO underwater channel model, system model, and analyze the influence of BER performance on different spatial correlation.

(2) We study the BER performance of I-MIMO and non-imaging MIMO under different channel states, we show that the imaging MIMO system achieves obviously performance gain at the same bit error rate (BER) compared to non-imaging MIMO.

(3) We propose an underwater optical precoding scheme based on the Euclidean distance of optical MIMO receiving signal set to maximize the minimum Euclidean distance. And, the precoding matrix is solved under the constraints of the non-negative optical signal and the total power to decrease spatial correlation, it improves the BER performance of imaging MIMO system obviously compared to SVD-based precoding algorithm.

The rest of the paper is structured as follows. In Sect. 2, we firstly introduce the model of imaging MIMO communication system in UVLC system and calculate channel matrix in imaging MIMO system. In Sect. 3, we give the I-MIMO channel model underwater, then, calculate the channel condition number under different I-MIMO system spatial position. In Sect. 4, we describe the precoding algorithm based on the maximized Euclidean distance of receiving signal set. In Sect. 5, we present the simulation results and BER performance under different channel condition number and the proposed precoding algorithm. In Sect. 6, we draw the conclusions.

Notation: Throughout this paper, vectors and matrices will be represented by boldfaced lower-case and upper-case letters (e.g. $\mathbf{x}$ and $\mathbf{X}$), respectively. Variables and constants are denoted in lower-case and upper-case letters (e.g. x and X), respectively. Let $\mathbf{I}_N \in \mathbb{R}^{N \times N}$ denote an $N \times N$ identity matrix. Superscript T represents the transpose of a matrix. We give the definition of matrix condition number in the following. Let $\mathbb{E}\{x\}$ represent the mean of x. Let $\mathrm{diag}[x_1 x_2, ..., x_N]$ denote the diagonal matrix of N dimension matrix, $x_1 x_2, ..., x_N$ are diagonal elements.

Definition 1 (The matrix condition number in [20]). Let $Cond(\mathbf{H})$ indicate the matrix condition number. Let λ_k denote the k-th singular value of $\mathbf{H}$. The ratio of the largest and smallest singular values of the matrix $\mathbf{H}$ is defined as the matrix condition number of $\mathbf{H}$, i.e.,

$$Cond(\mathbf{H}) = \max(\lambda_k)/\min(\lambda_k). \tag{1}$$

2 Imaging MIMO System Modeling

In this paper, we consider a 2×2 imaging MIMO VLC system, as shown in Fig. 1, which consists of two LEDs (two LEDs are defined as LED1 and LED2, respectively) at the transmitter and two PDs (two PDs are defined as PD1 and PD2, respectively) at the receiver. The LED1 and LED2 are received by the receiving arrays PD1 and PD2 through the imaging lens, respectively.

Furthermore, Fig. 2 shows a block diagram of an 2×2 imaging MIMO system. The serial bit stream is converted to parallel and modulated by Quadrature Amplitude Modulation (QAM) into the sign of OFDM sub-carriers. The

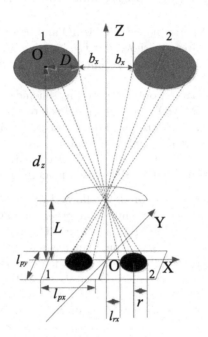

Fig. 1. The title of figure

bit streams are mapped onto the asymmetrically clipped optical OFDM (ACO-OFDM). In order to keep the optical OFDM signal non-negative, the ACO-OFDM system only transmits data through the odd sub-carriers, and the even sub-carriers do not contain information data. And then make the data symbol on the latter half of the sub-carriers to be the conjugate of the first half, so as to make Hermitian symmetry operation. After that, inverse fast fourier transform (IFFT) is performed, and the cyclic prefix (CP) is inserted. The negative part of the signal is clipped so that it can be modulated by light intensity. Then the transmitting signal is $\mathbf{s} = [s_1, s_2, ..., s_{N_T}]^{\mathsf{T}} \in \mathbb{R}^{N_T \times 1}$. By optical IM/DD modulation, the transmitted signal is $\mathbf{x} = [x_1, x_2, ..., x_{N_T}]^{\mathsf{T}} \in \mathbb{R}^{N_T \times 1}$. The receiving algorithm is adopted in the imaging diversity optical MIMO model [21,22], which is a system model proposed to improve the imaging MIMO channel matrix acquisition based on non-imaging MIMO. In the receiver, the zero-forcing (ZF) detection algorithm is adopted to recover signals, and the received signal is defined as $\mathbf{r} = [r_1, r_2, ..., r_{N_R}]^{\mathsf{T}} \in \mathbb{R}^{N_R \times 1}$. Each element h_{ij} in the channel matrix $\mathbf{H}_{N_T N_R}$ can be written as

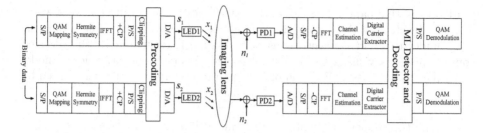

Fig. 2. Block diagram of imaging MIMO-ACO-OFDM communication system.

$$h_{ij} = a_{ij}h'_i, \tag{2}$$

where h'_i is the normalized power at the i-th LED imaging of the imaging prism aperture when the receiver is in a particular position, and a_{ij} quantifies the amount of power that falls on the j-th receiver, and it represents the proportion of the imaged area of the i-th emitter LED that falls on the j-th detector point in the array, and can be written as

$$a_{ij} = \frac{b_{is(s=j)}}{\sum\limits_{s=1}^{s=N_R} b_{is}}, \tag{3}$$

where b_{is} is the imaging area of the i-th transmitter emitted light fall on the s-th detector element. The size of the imaged position is determined by the geometric light calculation, and different spatial positions also bring different spatial correlations.

Furthermore, h'_i in underwater can be rewritten as [23]

$$h'_i = \begin{cases} H(0)\eta_t\eta_c\eta_r l_{ch}, 0 \le \psi \le \psi_c \\ 0, \psi > \psi_c \end{cases}, \tag{4}$$

where ψ is the angle of incidence of light at the receiver, and ψ_c is the emission angle, η_t, η_c, η_r are transmitter efficiency, channel propagating efficiency and receiver efficiency, respectively. All the key parameters mentioned above are listed in Table 2, in this paper, the configuration of the typical parameters is taken based on the literature [23].

In UVLC, the optical signal propagation under water is also severely affected by the spatiotemporal variation of underwater medium, especially in special transmission environment and receiver mobility [24–26], such as absorption, scattering, turbulence-induced fading, delay spread (temporal dispersion) of highly scattering and multipath, etc. However, we use multiple parallel link diversity multiplexing for the imaging MIMO system to overcome the underwater transmission environment impact, in which the first problem is deal with imaging signal formation, i.e., how to separate signal from different transmitters to decrease disturbance. Thus, for the sake of simplicity, both absorption and scattering contribute to the loss of optical intensity depending on the wavelength and water turbidity in this paper. The aggregated attenuation coefficient $c(\mu)$, μ is wavelength, denoted by the sum of absorption coefficient and scattering coefficient [26], under different concentrations of hydroxide is estimated by the received optical power. By using the widely recognized Beers exponential decay model [27], the channel loss as function of link span in underwater channel is given by

$$l_{ch} = \exp(-c(\mu)d). \tag{5}$$

So in this paper, a point-to-point direct link is considered and precise Transmit-Receive alignment is assumed. Thus, we can obtain the channel direct current (DC) gain by

$$H(0) = \frac{m+1}{2\pi}\cos^m(\phi).a_{eff}(d,\psi), \tag{6}$$

where ϕ and ψ are the deviation angles of transmitter and receiver relative to the optical axis, which can be called irradiance angle and incidence angle, respectively [28,29]. In our experiment, both angles of ϕ and ψ are considered to be 0 degree. m represents the Lambertian order, which is a characteristic constant by $m = -\ln(2)/\ln(\cos(\phi_{1/2}))$ with $\phi_{1/2}$ being the half-power semi-angle of the LED. a_{eff} changes only with the link distance d, thus we have

$$a_{eff}(d,\psi) = \frac{\pi D_r^2.\cos(\psi)/4}{\pi(d.\tan(\phi_{1/2}) + D_t/2)^2}, \tag{7}$$

where D_t and D_r represent the optical emitter and receiver focusing lens aperture, respectively. The link span threshold d is the link distance when the half-power illuminance area from light source equals to the receiver lens section area.

The elements of channel matrix $\mathbf{H}_{N_T N_R}$ are composed of a DC gain between each transmitter and receiver for underwater channel, and they are given in (2). $\mathbf{n}$ is a combination of thermal noise and shot noise and obeys a zero-mean Gaussian distribution, i.e., $\mathcal{N}\left(0, \sigma_{N_t}^2 \mathbf{I}_N\right)$, where $\sigma_{N_T}^2$ is the noise variance corresponding to each detector. So for the I-MIMO system with N_T transmitting antenna and N_R receiving antenna $\mathbf{r}$ can be modeled as

$$\mathbf{r} = \mathbf{Hx} + \mathbf{n}, \tag{8}$$

where $\mathbf{H}_{N_T N_R}$ is

$$\mathbf{H}_{N_T N_R} = \begin{bmatrix} h_{11} & h_{12} & \cdots & h_{1N_R} \\ h_{21} & h_{22} & \cdots & h_{2N_R} \\ \vdots & \vdots & \ddots & \cdots \\ h_{N_T 1} & h_{N_T 2} & \cdots & h_{N_T N_R} \end{bmatrix}. \tag{9}$$

3 Spatial Correlation Analysis

3.1 The Special Location Spatial Correlation of Calculating

In the underwater visible light communication(UVLC) MIMO communication scenario, the ratio of LED spacing to the vertical distance and the ratio of PD spacing to the vertical distance cannot be arbitrarily increased due to the limitation of the short-distance VLC communication environment size and the field of view of the receiver, meanwhile the LED is symmetrically distributed about the imaging lens. The spatial correlation of the MIMO channel is often reduced by changing parameters, such as LED spacing, PD spacing, and vertical distance from the LED to the PD within a certain range to improve system performance. In order to verify the spatial correlation of MIMO channel and the relationship between these parameters, underwater visible MIMO communication scenario is simulated in this paper. The simulation parameters are shown in Table 2, and the configuration of the parameters is taken based on the literature [23].

For the typical 2×2 MIMO communication scenario of UVLC, we can use the correlation function to describe channel spatial correlation, i.e., each row and column of the channel matrix correlation function can be calculated to indicate spatial correlation. In communication system, channel matrix usually can be used to estimate the transmitted data. As the value of channel matrix element is growing closer, the spatial correlation of sub-channel is becoming more and more stronger naturally. The matrix condition number of this channel matrix is bigger. It means sub-channel has bigger interference. And the noise or small disturbances will have an effect on demodulation, and the BER performance will be worse, i.e., the matrix is sicker. Actually, the correlation function of sub-channel is approximately equal to the condition number [30]. So the condition number of the channel matrix is used as an indicator to measure the spatial correlation of the channel [20].

$Cond(\mathbf{H})$ is defined in (1) as the ratio of the largest and smallest singular values of the matrix $\mathbf{H}$. The average $Cond(\mathbf{H})$ of different channel matrix $\mathbf{H}$ is a measure of the MIMO channel multiplex gain size. The average multiplexing gain is growing larger and larger as the average condition number of channel matrix is becoming smaller and smaller. In a communication system, when the conditional number of channel matrix is large, it means that the finally recovered signal is affected by noise badly, and the performance of this communication system is poor; when the conditional number of matrix is small, the finally recovered signal is affected by noise slightly, and the performance of this communication system is good.

In this paper, the 2×2 imaging MIMO system is taken as an example for analysis. In fact, the number of detection units at the receiving end is more than the number of transmitting ends to ensure complete reception. Imaging MIMO detection arrays generally take into account cost savings, so it is assumed that there is no spacing between the PD arrays, and the number of detection units is sufficient. As we all know, every lens has its magnification. Let m denote magnification, and $m = L/d_z$, which L is the focal length of lens, d_z is the vertical distance between LED and PD. When the focal length of lens is 10 cm, the vertical distance between the PD and the LED is about 2.2 m and LED diameter is 20 cm [23], the imaging diameter is $l_d = D/m - 1$ cm based on the magnification of imaging lens. Thus, in an actual imaging MIMO VLC system whose parameters can be changed is the LED spacing and the vertical distance from LED to PD. Moreover, imaging diameter and imaging spacing determine whether the images intersect together. So we discuss this two parameters in this section.

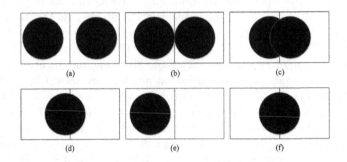

Fig. 3. The different signals of imaging with different spatial positions for transmission and reception by in I-MIMO communication system.

If the detector area is too large and the received signal falls on a detector, the signal can not be recovered. But if each signal area is larger than the size of one detector, the signal can be recovered. As Fig. 1 shows. Therefore, the use of similar techniques for a large number of transmitters and receivers can estimate the size of the smallest pixel. Noted that in order to ensure the matrix $\mathbf{H}_{2 \times 2}$ be full rank, the number of receiver (detector) is always more than the number of transmitter so that the pseudo-inverse transformation can be used to estimate the transmitted data. The imaging position and size formed by different spatial positions and the corresponding correlation can be discussed in six cases as Fig. 3 shows. And in Table 1, we give channel matrix and condition number under six cases.

Table 1. The channel matrix and condition number under different spatial location.

Type	h_{11}	h_{12}	h_{21}	h_{22}	$Cond(h)$
a	7.5334×10^{-5}	0	0	7.5334×10^{-5}	1
b	7.5334×10^{-5}	0	0	7.5334×10^{-5}	1
c1	9.8059×10^{-6}	8.7265×10^{-6}	8.7265×10^{-6}	9.8059×10^{-6}	17.1692
c2	5.3947×10^{-6}	4.1871×10^{-6}	4.1871×10^{-6}	5.3947×10^{-6}	7.9346
c3	2.5838×10^{-5}	4.1235×10^{-4}	4.1235×10^{-4}	2.5838×10^{-5}	1.1337
d	5.0354×10^{-6}	4.5220×10^{-6}	5.0354×10^{-6}	4.5220×10^{-6}	1.5469×10^{17}
e	0.9989×10^{-5}	0	0.9989×10^{-5}	0	∞
f	4.9947×10^{-6}	4.56×10^{-6}	4.56×10^{-6}	4.9947×10^{-6}	21.9798

As shown in Fig. 3(a), when the image is formed by the LED pitch and the object distance does not intersect, i.e. the imaging spacing is longer than imaging diameter, we can give the channel $\mathbf{H}_{2 \times 2}$ on the basis of channel model of (2).

When exactly intersecting, in Fig. 3(b) the channel $\mathbf{H}_{2\times2}$ can be exactly the same as Fig. 3(a).

The case of Fig. 3(d) occurs when the LED space is asymmetrical. Such a situation can occur when the position of transmitting light source and receiving PD is symmetric, but the irradiation angle is different. Spatial correlation is too strong under the circumstances, the rank of channel matrix is 1, i.e., non-full rank, the location of LED, lens and PD are not good spatial positions.

The case of Fig. 3(e) can not be detected, because the area falls into the same detection unit. If the detector pixel size is larger than the imaged spacing, all signals will fall on one detector and the signal will not be recovered. But if each imaging space is greater than the detector pixel space, the signal can be recovered. The detector area is too large and the received signal falls on a detector and the signal cannot be recovered. However, if each signal area is larger than the size of one detector, the signal can be recovered. Therefore, similar techniques can be used for a large number of transmitters and receivers to estimate the minimum pixel size. At the same time, noted that in order to make the rank of matrix $\mathbf{H}_{2\times2}$ be full, the receiver (detector) is always more than the transmitter, so the pseudo-inverse transform can be used to estimate the transmitted data.

In the case of Fig. 3(f), the left and right sides of the area are completely symmetrical, moreover, the imaging spacing is equal to imaging diameter, which can be detected. The imaging a_{ij} is 0.5, the rank is 2, and truly full rank.

3.2   The Ordinary Location Spatial Correlation of Calculating

As shown in Fig. 3(c), when the formed imaging signal intersect, it can be divided into two conditions to form this intersecting imaging, the first case is that d_z is fixed, the other case is that the object distance b_x is fixed.

When the object distance d_z is fixed, i.e., the magnification is invariant. The imaging spacing (the distance between the two center of a circle) is $l_{rx} \approx \frac{2b_x}{m}$, so the intersecting images are formed. b_x is calculated according to the relation between imaging spacing and imaging diameter, i.e. $0 < l_{rx} < l_d$, this condition makes the imaging spacing value ranges from 0 to l_d (imaging diameter) or $2r$ (imaging radius), i.e. $b_x \in [0, 0.1]$. Furthermore, we analyse the spatial correlation under the distance between LEDs from far to near.

As shown in Fig. 4, the distance between LEDs is from far to near at first, the red circle represents image by LED2, the black circle represents image by LED1, the square 1 represents PD1, the square 2 represents PD2. The imaging distance is greater than r (imaging radius) and less than l_d (imaging diameter), i.e, $b_x \in [0.05, 0.1]$. By exploiting the knowledge of the circle and the triangle, we can obtain the height x of triangle and the sector arc length y of circle, which is given by

$$\frac{r}{r - \frac{b_x}{2m}} = \frac{\pi r}{y} = \frac{l_d}{x}. \tag{10}$$

Thus, the overlapping area of the two images can be obtained as a fan-shaped minus triangle. So a_{ij} is the ratio of overlapping area and total area of transmitter, i.e.

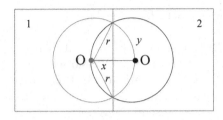
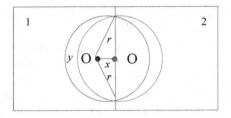

Fig. 4. Intersection imaging diagram.   **Fig. 5.** Intersection imaging diagram.

$$a_{ij} = \frac{a_{is(s=j)}}{\sum\limits_{s=1}^{s=N_R} a_{is}} = \frac{\pi r^2 - (0.5ry - 0.5(\frac{b_x}{2m})x)}{\pi r^2}. \tag{11}$$

The distance between LEDs is from far to near further, it means the image is much closer from each other since the distance between LEDs source become smaller as shown in Fig. 5. The imaging distance is greater than 0 and less than r (imaging radius), i.e, $b_x \in [0, 0.05]$. And the ratio of overlapping area and total area of transmitter a_{ij} is similar to that when $b_x \in [0.05, 0.1]$.

When the object distance b_x is fixed and d_z is changed, the formed imaging signal intersect. And the overlapping imaging is like Fig. 4 when the distance is from far to near. In order to keep imaging intersect, the imaging spacing is larger than r and less than $2r$, i.e, $0 < l_{rx} < l_d$, b_x can be calculated, such as $b_x = 0.075$ m.

By exploiting the knowledge of the circle, the triangle height x and the sector arc length y can be obtained by

$$\frac{r}{r - \frac{b_x}{2m}} = \frac{\pi r}{y} = \frac{l_d}{x}. \tag{12}$$

Thus, in this case, the overlapping area of the two images can be obtained as a fan-shaped minus triangle. So a_{ij} is the ratio of overlapping area and total area of transmitter, i.e.

$$a_{ij} = \frac{a_{is(s=j)}}{\sum\limits_{s=1}^{s=N_R} a_{is}} = \frac{0.5ry - 0.5(\frac{b_x}{2m})x}{\pi r^2}. \tag{13}$$

So we can use the ratio of overlapping area a_{ij} to get channel matrix under different spatial location. Furthermore, the different channel matrix shows different spatial correlation of sub-channel, i.e., different interference of sub-channel.

4   A Precoding Algorithm Based on Received Signal Euclidean Distance for Imaging MIMO System

In an imaging MIMO VLC system, the N_T dimensional precoding square matrix $\mathbf{W}$ is used to precode the N_T dimensional time domain MIMO-ACO-OFDM signal vector **s** in the time domain, and the signal **x** to be sent is obtained as

$$\mathbf{x} = \mathbf{W}\mathbf{s}. \tag{14}$$

In this optical MIMO system, serial binary bit information is mapped into $Nt \times 1$ signal vector $\mathbf{s} \in \mathbf{S}_{M \times N_t}$, where $\mathbf{S}_{M \times N_t}$ is the signal set of the modulation scheme, M is modulation order, and **s** is the signal vector of MIMO-OFDM after clipping. Under the condition of high SNR, BER performance mainly depends on the minimum Euclidean distance $d_{\min}$ of the received signal set [18], which is given as

$$d_{\min} = \min_{\substack{i,j \in [1,2\ldots,M \times M], \\ \forall i \neq j, \mathbf{s} \in \mathbf{S}_{M \times N_T}}} \|\mathbf{H}\mathbf{W}(\mathbf{s}_i - \mathbf{s}_j)\|_2. \tag{15}$$

The BER performance of optical MIMO system can be improved by assigning different power to different transmitting antennas, which is equivalent to multiplying the signal vector **s** by N_T dimension diagonal precoding square matrix before transmitting the signal. At the same time, the optimal precoding matrix of MIMO for imaging MIMO system is diagonal matrix [19], therefore, a precoding method based on diagonal matrix is proposed. Let **W** denotes the diagonal matrix pre-encoder, and the elements on its main diagonal are all greater than zero, while the non-diagonal elements are all zero. The minimum Euclidean distance between the received signal vectors is maximized by multiplying the transmitting signal vector **s** by the diagonal precoding matrix. The optimal precoding matrix **W** can be obtained by solving the following optimization problems, which is given as

$$\begin{aligned}
&\max_{W} \quad d_{\min} \\
&s.t. \quad tr(\mathbf{W}) \leq P_{\max} \\
&\quad w_{k,l} \geq 0, k \in [1,2,...,N_T], l \in [1,2,...,N_R], \forall k \neq l \\
&\quad w_{k,l} = 0, k \in [1,2,...,N_T], l \in [1,2,...,N_R], \forall k = l,
\end{aligned} \tag{16}$$

where $P_{\max}$ is the total emission power of the LED array, $w(k,l)$ is the element of the k-th row and l-th column in the matrix **W**.

At the receiving end, when the maximum likelihood (ML) detection algorithm is adopted, the channel matrix **H** and precoding matrix **W** are used for MIMO detection and decoding. Thus, the original signal **s** at the sending end is recovered, which can be obtained as

$$\hat{\mathbf{s}} = \arg \min_{\mathbf{s} \in \mathbf{S}_{M,N_T}} \|y - \mathbf{H}\mathbf{W}\mathbf{s}\|^2, \tag{17}$$

where **W** represents the optimal diagonal precoding matrix. Furthermore, we can use the detected signal vector $\hat{\mathbf{s}}$ to modulate the original information bits, respectively.

Since OFDM system is a multi-carrier modulation system, the set of time-domain signal is becoming bigger and bigger in geometric orders of magnitude with the increase of the number of sub-carriers. So it is a huge amount of computation to directly use time-domain OFDM symbols to solve the precoding matrix.

Table 2. The system simulation parameters.

Simulation parameters	Value
LED Diameter (cm) (D)	20
Receiving FOV ($^{\circ}$)	100
Angle of irradiance ($^{\circ}$) (ϕ)	100
Angle of incidence ($^{\circ}$) (ψ)	100
Half power angle ($^{\circ}$) ($\phi_{1/2}$)	60
Lambert radiation order (m)	1
Lens focal length (cm) (L)	10
PD detection area (cm^2)	1
Array size	2×2
PD photoelectric conversion efficiency (A/W)	0.6
Transmitter aperture (mm) (D_t)	50
Receiver aperture (mm) (D_r)	100
Transmission distance (m) (d)	2.2
Transmit efficiency (η_t)	0.1289
Receiving efficiency (η_r)	0.9500
Channel efficiency (η_c)	0.1289
Aggregated attenuation coefficient (μ)	0.15

This paper use linear precoding method, and IFFT also have linear properties, in addition, the ACO-OFDM time-domain clipping treatment will not lead to any information loss [31,32]. So in order to reduce the computational complexity, precoding of time-domain OFDM signal can be equivalent to precoding of the frequency domain signal before IFFT. We use the QAM symbols of different LEDs on the same sub-carrier to build signal vector **s**, thus, we can solve the optimal precoding matrix **W**.

By introducing genetic algorithm (GA) [33], so as to solve the optimal precoding matrix. For the sake of generality, we set $P_{\max}$ as 1, each LED by a power allocation factor $\rho_i, (0 < \rho_i < 1, i \in N_T)$, satisfy the constraint condition $\sum_{(i \in N_T)} \rho_i = 1$, and use ρ_i to make up precoding matrix $\mathbf{W} = diag(\rho_1, \rho_2, ..., \rho_{N_T})$. A set of optimal allocation factors can be found by the search of genetic algorithm, so that the minimum Euclidean distance of the received signal set can be the maximum after the LED power distribution value is optimized and adjusted. In this paper, we think each power optimization factor as a chromosome for the encoding of a gene use to finish the real coding [34], the chromosome of the gene array is $\mathbf{p}_i = (\rho_{i,1}, \rho_{i,2}, ..., \rho_{i,N_T})$ for the i-th individual.

The optimization goal of the optimal problem Eq. (16) is to make the minimum Euclidean distance maximum of receiving signal. Therefore, the fitness value of an individual should be positively correlated with the minimum

Euclidean distance corresponding to the received signal, the minimum Euclidean distance is bigger and bigger with the fitness value increasing. We take the considering that the fitness should be greater than zero, so we directly use the minimum Euclidean distance as fitness function, which can be given as

$$Fit(\mathbf{p}_i) = \min_{\substack{i,j \in [1,2\ldots,M \times M], \\ \forall i \neq j, \mathbf{s} \in \mathbf{S}_{M \times N_T}}} \|\mathbf{H} \cdot diag(\mathbf{p}_i) \cdot (\mathbf{s}_i - \mathbf{s}_j)\|_2. \tag{18}$$

It is not difficult to conclude from the above equation that the larger the minimum Euclidean distance of the received signal set is, the larger the individual fitness value will be, thus ensuring that the individual that can provide a larger minimum Euclidean distance in the population, which has a greater probability of entering the next generation population. Through selection, crossover and mutation, the population is constantly updated until the population converges to the optimal solution. So in our simulations, in an 2×2 imaging MIMO system as shown in Fig. 2, when the crossover ratio is 0.4, the mutation ratio is 0.005, the population size is 1000, we take the channel state of c1, c2, f as an example, the searching optimal precoding matrix of c1, c2, f is $\mathbf{W} = $ diag[0.3342 0.6658], diag[0.6596 0.3404], diag[0.6661 0.3339] by GA algorithm with 1000 times iteration. After a large number of experiments, the genetic algorithm adopted in this paper converges to the optimal solution after 50 iterations, it has fast convergence and low computational complexity by using the algorithm to calculate the $\mathbf{W}$.

5   System Simulation Results

In our simulations, we adopted MIMO-ACO-OFDM modulation, and considered the receiving method adopted in the imaging diversity optical MIMO model. The receiver uses zero-forcing (ZF) detection algorithm without special emphasis in this paper. The simulation parameters are shown in Table 2. The comparison of BER performance in the same imaging state under different channel condition number is analyzed by taking the case of the Fig. 6 image intersection. The Fig. 7 shows that BER performance in the same imaging state and compared to non-imaging MIMO system. The comparison of BER performance in the different imaging state is analyzed by taking the case of the Fig. 8 image intersection.

As shown in Fig. 6, as the channel condition number decreases, i.e., the channel spatial correlation weakens, the BER of the imaging system gradually decreases. When the channel condition number drops to about 1, i.e., the channel spatial correlation is the weakest, the BER of the imaging system reaches 10^{-6} at 20 dB; and when the channel condition number is about 1, the BER is basically close, the curve of every channel condition number basically overlaps. As shown in Fig. 7, compared to non-imaging MIMO systems, the imaging MIMO system achieves 12 dB gain at the same BER. It can be seen that the imaging MIMO system has a weaker spatial correlation and a lower SNR at the same BER due to signal-separated and energy harvesting based on area of photoelectric converter.

Furthermore, we also show BER versus SNR using different spreading states with a, b, c1, c2, c3, and f in Table 1 as shown in Fig. 8. We can see that the performances of I-MIMO system is much bétter than that of the non-imaging MIMO system. In addition, the system adopting ZF can work properly. Thus, it further validates the availability of the proposed I-MIMO system scheme underwater.

Based on the simulation results in Fig. 9, we can see that I-MIMO based on ZF can provide guarantee for the recovery of transmitted signal underwater. In addition, the proposed system achieves a relatively high SNR when the channel is relatively bad, which indicates that the system scheme uses imaging lens can significantly reduce the disturbance between each other and separate signal.

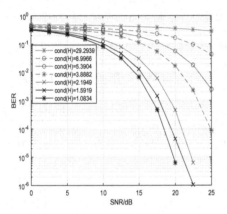

Fig. 6. BER performance of different channel conditions in intersecting imaging MIMO system.

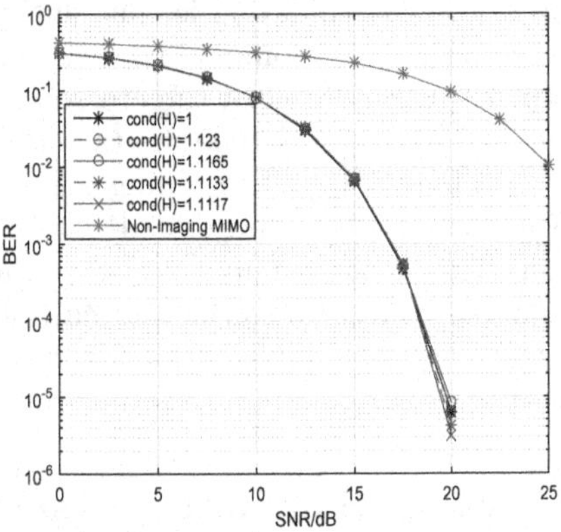

Fig. 7. BER performance of different channel conditions in intersecting imaging MIMO and non-imaging MIMO system.

As shown in Fig. 9, we compared the BER performance of the ZF, ML, SVD-based precoding algorithms under state f, c1, c2. When the channel state information is known to the transmitter, the channel characteristics can be matched by using precoding technology to improve the system performance. [14] combines the characteristics of indoor VLC channel and proposed the method based on SVD precoding scheme to decrease spatial correlation. In this method, the information data is transmitted through symbols mapping of a particular set of symbols, to ensure that the precoded signal is non-negative signal. Then, make the VLC MIMO system finish SVD to get independent parallel sub-channels in order to eliminate inter-channel interference. After that, the paper considers the minimum BER of the system as the goal and the limited power as the constraint condition, and solves the optimal power allocation matrix. And then each signal of sub-channel after symbol mapping is precoded by the optimal power allocation matrix, so that BER performance of each sub-channel are trend to be

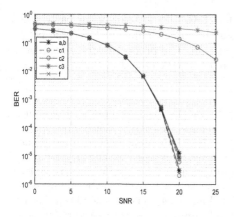 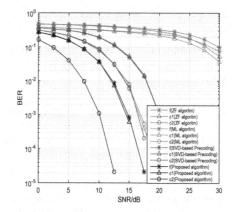

Fig. 8. BER performance of channel conditions for different imaging states in imaging MIMO system.

Fig. 9. BER performance of different uncoded and precoding algorithms in imaging MIMO system.

the same. The encoding algorithm to recover the transmitted symbol is adopted after being shaped, finally obtain the transmitting information data by symbolic inverse mapping.

All BER performances of ML algorithm are better than that of ZF when spatial correlation of sub-channels are strong as Fig. 9 shows, i.e., channel condition number is bigger, since ML algorithm is optimal detection algorithm. And when the spatial is becoming weaker and weaker, nearly close to 1, the BER performance of ML algorithm is the same with ZF. Thus, we use power allocation based on SVD to get average gain. We can see the performance of SVD algorithm are better than ML when the spatial is bigger, but when the spatial become weaker, the SVD-based procoding is worse, the spatial correlation is about 1 at this moment. Furthermore, to decrease the spatial correlation of sub-channels, we use the proposed precoding algorithm based on the receiving end Euclidean distance to allocate power, since it do not make signal go through clipping, the BER performance is better than SVD-based precoding algorithm. The results show that the proposed algorithm improve the BER performance about 5 dB under channel of c1, c2, f.

6   Conclusion

In this paper, the spatial correlation of underwater visible light imaging MIMO communication under different LED positions was calculated. The BER performance of underwater imaging MIMO-OFDM were studied. The BER performance of non-imaging and imaging MIMO decreases as channel condition number o decreases, and compared to non-imaging MIMO systems, the BER of imaging MIMO system achieves 12 dB gain at the same BER under the same channel. Furthermore, we used the proposed precoding matrix based on the Euclidean distance of receiving signal set to allocate power on each sub-channel and achieves about 5 dB gain under the same channel at the same BER compared to the SVD-based procoding algorithm. The proposed precoding algorithm improve the BER performance of imaging MIMO system in underwater VLC substantially.

Acknowledgments. This work is supported by the National Natural Science Foundation of China under grant (61761014), Guangxi Natural Science Foundation (2018GXNSFBA281131), Ministry of Education Key Laboratory of Cognitive Radio and Information Processing (CRKL170106), Guangxi key research and development plan(Guike AB18126030), Innovation Project of Guangxi Graduate Education (YCBZ 2017050), Guangxi University Young and Middle-aged Teachers Basic Ability Improvement Plan (2018KY0208), Guangxi Cooperative Innovation Center of cloud computing and Big Data (No1716) and Guangxi Colleges and Universities Key Laboratory of cloud computing and complex systems.

References

1. Han, S., Noh, Y., Liang, R., Chen, R., Cheng, Y.-J., Gerla, M.: Evaluation of underwater optical-acoustic hybrid network. China Commun. **11**(5), 49–59 (2014)
2. Zeng, Z., Fu, S., Zhang, H., Dong, Y., Cheng, J.: A survey of underwater optical wireless communications. IEEE Commun. Surv. Tutor. **19**(1), 204–238 (2017)
3. Arnon, S.: Underwater optical wireless communication network. Opt. Eng. **49**(1), 015001 (2010)
4. Priyanjali, K.S., Nageswaramma, O., Dikshit, A.K., Mrudula, S.: Threshold based soft partial parallel interference cancellation for MIMO-OFDM system. In: IEEE International Conference on Recent Trends in Electronics, Information & Communication Technology (RTEICT), pp. 861–865. IEEE (2016)
5. Jamali, M.V., Salehi, J.A.: On the BER of multiple-input multiple-output underwater wireless optical communication systems. In: 2015 4th International Workshop on Optical Wireless Communications (IWOW), pp. 26–30. IEEE (2015)
6. Tsonev, D., Sinanovic, S., Haas, H.: Practical MIMO capacity for indoor optical wireless communication with white LEDs. In: 2013 IEEE 77th Vehicular Technology Conference (VTC Spring), pp. 1–5. IEEE (2013)
7. Azhar, A.H., Tran, T., OBrien, D.: A gigabit/s indoor wireless transmission using MIMO-OFDM visible-light communications. IEEE Photonics Technol. Lett. **25**(2), 171–174 (2013)
8. Zeng, L., et al.: High data rate multiple input multiple output (MIMO) optical wireless communications using white led lighting. IEEE J. Sel. Areas Commun. **27**(9), 1654–1662 (2009)
9. Wang, T.Q., Sekercioglu, Y.A., Armstrong, J.: Analysis of an optical wireless receiver using a hemispherical lens with application in MIMO visible light communications. J. Lightwave Technol. **31**(11), 1744–1754 (2013)
10. Chen, T., Liu, L., Tu, B., Zheng, Z., Hu, W.: High-spatial-diversity imaging receiver using fisheye lens for indoor MIMO VLCs. IEEE Photonics Technol. Lett. **26**(22), 2260–2263 (2014)
11. Nuwanpriya, A., Ho, S.-W., Chen, C.S.: Indoor MIMO visible light communications: novel angle diversity receivers for mobile users. IEEE J. Sel. Areas Commun. **33**(9), 1780–1792 (2015)

12. Nuwanpriya, A., Ho, S.-W., Chen, C.S.: Angle diversity receiver for indoor MIMO visible light communications. In: 2014 IEEE Globecom Workshops (GC Wkshps), pp. 444–449. IEEE (2014)
13. He, C., Wang, T.Q., Armstrong, J.: MIMO optical wireless receiver using photodetectors with different fields of view. In: 2015 IEEE 81st Vehicular Technology Conference (VTC Spring), pp. 1–5. IEEE (2015)
14. Liu, Q.-F., Xiao, S.-F., Huang, K.-Z., Zhong, Z.: A svd-based optical MIMO precoding scheme in indoor visible light communication. Int. J. Future Comput. Commun. **3**(6), 421 (2014)
15. Serafimovski, N., et al.: Practical implementation of spatial modulation. IEEE Trans. Veh. Technol. **62**(9), 4511–4523 (2013)
16. Zhu, H.-Y., Zhu, Y.-J., Zhang, J.-K., Zhang, Y.-Y.: A double-layer VLC system with low-complexity ML detection and binary constellation designs. IEEE Commun. Lett. **19**(4), 561–564 (2015)
17. Wang, W.-Y., Zhu, Y.-J., Zhang, Y.-Y., Zhang, J.-K.: An optimal power allocation for multi-LED phase-shifted-based MISO VLC systems. IEEE Photonics Technol. Lett. **27**(22), 2391–2394 (2015)
18. Srinivas, V.A., Naresh, Y., Chockalingam, A.: Optimal precoder for MIMO schemes in indoor wireless VLC systems. In: 2018 IEEE 87th Vehicular Technology Conference (VTC Spring), pp. 1–5. IEEE (2018)
19. Kadampot, I.A., Park, K.-H., Alouini, M.-S.: Precoded generalized space shift keying for indoor visible light communications. In: 2014 3rd International Workshop in Optical Wireless Communications (IWOW), pp. 85–89. IEEE (2014)
20. Tran, T.-A., O'Brien, D.C.: Performance metrics for multi-input multi-output (MIMO) visible light communications. In: 2012 International Workshop on Optical Wireless Communications (IWOW), pp. 1–3. IEEE (2012)
21. Mobley, C.D.: Light and Water: Radiative Transfer in Natural Waters. Academic Press, California (1994)
22. Fath, T., Haas, H.: Performance comparison of MIMO techniques for optical wireless communications in indoor environments. IEEE Trans. Commun. **61**(2), 733–742 (2013)
23. Wang, P., Li, C., Xu, Z.: A cost-efficient real-time 25 Mb/s system for LED-UOWC: design, channel coding, FPGA implementation, and characterization. J. Lightwave Technol. **36**(13), 2627–2637 (2018)
24. Haltrin, V.I.: Chlorophyll-based model of seawater optical properties. Appl. Opt. **38**(33), 6826–6832 (1999)
25. Smith, R.C., Baker, K.S.: Optical properties of the clearest natural waters (200–800 nm). Appl. Opt. **20**(2), 177–184 (1981)
26. Kopelevich, O.: Small-parameter model of optical properties of sea water. Ocean Opt. **1**, 208–234 (1983)
27. Kerker, M.: Physical optics of ocean water. J. Colloid Interface Sci. **126**, 386 (1988)
28. Hamza, T., Khalighi, M.-A., Bourennane, S., Léon, P., Opderbecke, J.: Investigation of solar noise impact on the performance of underwater wireless optical communication links. Opt. Exp. **24**(22), 25832–25845 (2016)
29. Zeng, Y., Wang, J., Ling, X., Liang, X., Zhao, C.: Joint precoder and DC bias design for MIMO VLC systems. In: 2017 IEEE 17th International Conference on Communication Technology (ICCT), pp. 1180–1185. IEEE (2017)
30. Van Hufel, S., Vandewalle, J.: Iterative speed improvement for solving slowly varying total least squares problems. Mech. Syst. Signal Process. **2**(4), 327–348 (1988)
31. Dissanayake, S.D., Armstrong, J.: Comparison of ACO-OFDM, DCO-OFDM and ADO-OFDM in IM/DD systems. J. Lightwave Technol. **31**(7), 1063–1072 (2013)

32. Armstrong, J., Lowery, A.: Power efficient optical OFDM. Electron. Lett. **42**(6), 1 (2006)
33. Ding, J., Ji, Y.: Evolutionary algorithm-based optimisation of the signal-to-noise ratio for indoor visible-light communication utilising white light-emitting diode. IET Optoelectron. **6**(6), 307–317 (2012)
34. Shuaifang, X., Kaizhi, H., Zhou, Z., et al.: Spatial correlation analysis of MIMO channel in indoor visible light communication. J. Electron. Inf. Technol. **36**(9), 2117–2123 (2014)

Data Collection Scheme for Underwater Sensor Cloud System Based on Fog Computing

Haitao Yu[1]([⊠]), Jiansheng Yao[1], Xianhao Shen[1], Yanling Huang[1],
and Meijuan Jia[2]

[1] College of Tourism, Guilin University of Technology, Guilin 541004, China
albertyht@163.com
[2] College of Computer Science and Information Technology,
Daqing Normal University, Daqing 163712, China

Abstract. The scheme design of data collection for Underwater Acoustic Sensor Networks (UASNs) poses many challenges due to long propagation, high mobility, limited bandwidth, multi-path and Doppler Effect. In this paper, unlike the traditional underwater sensor network architecture (single sink or multi-sink), we proposed a novel underwater sensor cloud system based on fog computing in view of time-critical underwater applications. In such an architecture, fog nodes with great computation and storage capacity are responsible for computing, dimension reduction and redundant removal for data collected from physical sensor nodes, and then transfer the processed and compressed data to surface center sink node. After that, the center sink sends the received data from fog nodes to cloud computing center. In addition, in this paper we present distance difference and waiting area-based routing protocol, called DDWA. Finally, in comparison with RDBF, naive flooding and HH-VBF, we conduct extensive simulations using NS-3 simulator to verify the effectiveness and validity of the proposed data collection scheme in the context of the proposed architecture.

Keywords: Underwater sensor network · Sensor cloud · Fog computing · Routing protocol · NS-3 simulator

1 Introduction

Currently, underwater acoustic sensor networks (UASN) are widely used in coastline surveillance and protection, ocean disaster prevention, pollution monitoring, military defense, assisted navigation, marine aquatic environment monitoring, and resource exploration, underwater multi-media applications, etc. However, underwater acoustic sensor networks using acoustic signals as transmission media pose grand challenges, such as slow propagation speed of acoustic signals, multi-path effect, noise, path loss and Doppler spread, which result in high bit error rate, low data rate, energy constraint and high mobility. Therefore, the data collection of terrestrial Ad hoc sensor networks cannot be applied in underwater environments directly.

Contributions: firstly, we presented a novel fog computing based underwater sensor cloud system architecture, and then we proposed data collection scheme in the context

© Springer Nature Switzerland AG 2019
G. Wang et al. (Eds.): SpaCCS 2019 Workshops, LNCS 11637, pp. 149–159, 2019.
https://doi.org/10.1007/978-3-030-24900-7_12

of the proposed underwater sensor cloud system; secondly, on the basis of the architecture of underwater sensor cloud, we design an efficient transmission protocol for UASNs, DDWA, which makes routing decisions according to the difference between the expected residual distance to fog nodes and the advancement distance of packets. Finally, we conduct extensive simulations in comparison with RDBF, naive flooding and HH-VBF routing protocol to verify the effectiveness and validity of the proposed data scheme.

The rest of this paper is organized as follows: in Sect. 2, we review the related works about data collection and routing protocols in UASNs. The architecture of underwater sensor cloud system based on fog computing is presented in Sect. 3. DDWA routing protocol is described in Sect. 4. Finally, we present the simulation results in Sect. 5, followed by our conclusions in Sect. 6.

2   Related Works

The researches on sensor cloud mainly focus on terrestrial sensor network and IOT, such as literatures [1–3]. Few researches on underwater sensor cloud is carried out. In [4], the authors proposed an underwater sensor cloud architecture for underwater sensor motes to collect, store and retrieve environmental data.

2.1   Data Collection Schemes for Underwater Sensor Networks

In [5], the authors proposed an underwater data collection scheme by means of autonomous underwater vehicle, and an extend algorithm of variants of traveling salesperson problem is designed to minimize travel time and fuel expenditure. In [6], the authors proposed two mechanisms of selective relay cooperation and dynamic network coded cooperation for underwater data collection to improve the data transmission reliability. However, in the protocols, because destination node selects relay node of the retransmission, the extra delay will inevitably be increased correspondingly. In [7], the authors present an underwater application model for collecting data from USNs with multiple mobile actors to get high temporal resolution capability. DP Williams proposed an adaptive strategy for performing data collection with a sonar-equipped autonomous underwater vehicle [8], where AUV route is adapted to prevent portions of the mission area from being either characterized by poor image quality or obscured by shadows caused by sand ripples. I Vasilescu, etc. proposed an underwater data collection scheme by the cooperation between mobile nodes and static nodes [9], the mobile nodes collect data from static nodes using high-speed optical communication. However, the underwater optical communication is applicable for short range transmission. N Ilyas, etc. proposed an AUV-aided efficient data gathering scheme where AUV gathers data from gateways for reliable data delivery, and a shortest path tree algorithm is used to minimize energy consumption [10]. Ghoreyshi S M, ect. proposed Cluster-based AUV-aided Data Collection scheme (CADC) for large-scale UWSNs, where AUV gather data from cluster head according to the planed path [11].

2.2   Underwater Routing

The routing protocols designed for terrestrial sensor networks can not work properly in underwater acoustic sensor networks due to the long propagation delay, high mobility, limited bandwidth, energy-constraint and high manufacture and deployment costs. In UASNs, routing protocols can mainly be classified into location-based routing, location-free routing, auxiliary equipment-based routing and cross-layer design routing. Location based routing can be classified into three-dimension based routing and depth-based routing. Three-dimension location-based includes HHVBF [12], RDBF [13] and so on. Depth-based routing includes VARP [14], WDFAD-DBR [15], GEDAR [16] and so on. Location-free routing is classified into clustering routing and beacon-based routing.

3   Data Collection Scheme for Underwater Sensor Cloud System

3.1   Architecture of Underwater Sensor Cloud System Based on Fog Computing

We design an architecture of underwater sensor cloud system based on fog computing, as shown in Fig. 1. The architecture consists of four layers: physical sensor layer, fog layer, sink layer and cloud layer. The communication process of the architecture is as follows: the nodes in the physical layer which are equipped with acoustic antenna has limited storage and computation capacity. Such nodes are usually fixed at the bottom of ocean by anchored mode or float at certain depth position by buoys. They only sense underwater data and are responsible for sending the collected information to the corresponding fog node by means of acoustic link according to the certain routing policy. Fog nodes in fog layer are provided with strong computation and storage capacity compared with nodes in the physical layer, which are usually AUVs or mobile nodes. There are some fog nodes in an underwater sensor network, each of which is responsible for the local data processing of a designated area based on principle of proximity. Fog nodes implement local computation over the received data from the physical nodes to discard useless data, dimension reduction or extract key information and so on. According to the final computing results, fog nodes decide the data delivery mode of delay requirements. For delay-insensitive data or application, the computing results are carried by mobile fog nodes. When fog nodes reach surface, they deliver the data to surface sink node in sink layer. For delay-sensitive data, the data computed by fog nodes shall be transmitted to the surface sink nodes by other above-level fog nodes in multi-hop mode. For example, environment pollution event is found after data analysis is made. This is due to the fact that the movement speed of AUVs cannot guarantee the delay requirement. AUVs or other mobile nodes are equipped with both acoustic antenna and radio antenna. Acoustic antenna is responsible for underwater communication with physical nodes or other fog nodes and radio antenna is responsible for the land communication with surface sink nodes. Nodes in sink layer receive the processed data from fog node. After data fusion operation, sink node transmit the fused data to cloud computing center by radio signals. In traditional underwater sensor network architecture, the surface sinks are responsible for not only all the raw data reception but also data transmission to control center. In this case, the loss of some packet maybe take place because sink node cannot receive many packets at the same time due to the reception delay. However, in the proposed architecture of sensor cloud system based on fog computing, the surface sink nodes only received the processed data from AUVs, which can relieve the burden of data reception. Most of important, fog nodes can coordinate each other to schedule the data transmission of each fog nodes. When AUVs rise to surface, they can negotiate the detailed schedule policy by radio communication. The detailed schedule algorithm is out of the limit of this paper. Such the scheduling mechanism can avoid data reception loss. Cloud computing center in cloud layer is responsible for data storage or the complicated computation of data.

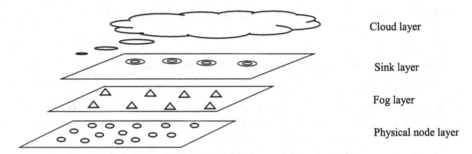

Fig. 1. Architecture of underwater sensor cloud system based on fog computing.

3.2 Management Area of Fog Node

Each fog node is responsible for data collection, local computation and local storage. Let the three-dimension size of underwater sensor network deployment area be $L * L * L$ and the number of fog node be M. The underwater network deployment area is divided into M sub-areas, and each sub-area is managed by a designated fog node. Let FN_i be the ith fog node and $Area_i$ be the ith sub-area. FN_i is responsible for the management of $Area_i$, including data collection, local storage and storage computation and so on. The range of the ith sub-area is confined to $[0, 0, (i-1) * L/M] \times [L, L, i * L/M]$. Each of fog node moves along a circle trajectory and make certain sojourn at designated location for some time to collect data from nodes in the corresponding sub-area. Let the center of the lowest plane of deployment area be coordinate origin (0, 0), and then the equation of circle trajectory of the fog node in the ith sub-area is as followed:

$$(x - L/2)^2 + (y - L/2)^2 = (\sqrt{2}L/2)^2$$
$$Z = L * 2/M + (i-1) * L/M \tag{1}$$

By the partition mode, the trajectory curve is divided into two parts equally in the horizontal and vertical directions so that all the nodes in the sub-area can transmit data to the corresponding fog in the least hop number.

4 DDWA Routing Protocol

In this section, we present DDWA routing protocol. For convenience, we define some symbols used in this paper. Symbol R denotes the transmission range of nodes if not specified. Symbol $\|\cdot\|$ denotes Euclidean norm. Symbol ρ denotes node density and v_{sound} denotes the propagation speed of packets in water. L_{size} and v_{send} denote the size of a packet and the transmission rate of modems.

Definition 1 (expected residual distance, ERD for short in the paper) ERD of a packet is defined as follows: when a packet reaches node A, and the coordinates of node A and the designated fog node are $POS_A(x_A, y_A, z_A)$ and $POS_D(x_D, y_D, z_D)$, respectively, then ERD of the packet at POS_A is $\|POS_D - POS_A\|$.

Definition 2 (advancement distance, AD for short in the paper) AD of a packet is defined as follows: when a packet is forwarded from nodes A to B, and the coordinates of nodes A and B are $POS_A(x_A, y_A, z_A)$ and $POS_B(x_B, y_B, z_B)$, respectively, then AD of the packet from nodes A to B is $\|POS_B - POS_A\|$.

Definition 3 (valid forwarding region, VFR for short in the paper) VFR of a packet is defined as follows: node A receives a packet forwarded by last hop forwarding node, and the coordinates of node A and fog node are $POS_A(x_A, y_A, z_A)$ and $POS_D(x_D, y_D, z_D)$, respectively. VFR of the packet at POS_A is the area $\{s(x, y, z) \mid \|s - pos_A\| \leq R\} \cap \{t(x, y, z) \mid \|t - pos_D\| \leq \|pos_A - pos_D\|\}$.

Definition 4 (waiting area and suppressing area, WA and SA for short in the paper) WA of a node is defined as follows: when a node receives a packet forwarded by previous hop node, WA of the packet is the area where nodes have higher forwarding priority than the node. Contrary to **WA**, **SA** of the packet is the area where nodes have lower forwarding priority than the node.

4.1 Description of WA and SA

Here forwarding priority is related to the forwarding policy. In this paper, forwarding priorities are determined based on the difference between ERD and AD. The smaller the difference between ERD and AD is, the higher forwarding priority is. According to definitions 3 and 4, **WA** and **SA** are a part of **VFR** for the same node. As shown in Fig. 2, node S sends a packet to Fog node. Area S1 is the VFR of the packet. Because node A is within area S1, it becomes the next hop qualified forwarding node. When the packet reaches node A, node A gets the coordinate of previous hop forwarding node S, which is embedded in the packet. Node A judges whether it is located within **VFR** of the packet according to the coordinates of S, A and Fog node. Since A is closer to fog node than S, namely they are located in VFR of the packet, it considers itself as a qualified candidate to forward the packet. On the contrary, node E just simply discards the packet because it is not located within the VFR of the packet. Due to space constraints, the computation processes of WA and SA are not given in detail in this paper.

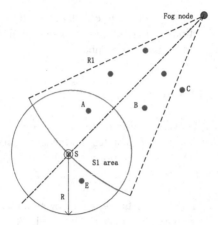

Fig. 2. Overview of DDWA.

4.2 Compute Holding Time

A node schedules the packet forwarding according to holding time so as to reduce the number of forwarding nodes. When a node receives a packet, it calculates the holding time of the packet based on **AD** and **ERD** of the packet.

When node S forward a packet for the Fog node, if node F within the VFR of the packet receives the packet. The coordinates of Nodes S, F and Fog node are $C_S = [x_S, y_S, z_S]$, $C_F = [x_F, y_F, z_F]$ and $C_D = [x_D, y_D, z_D]$, respectively. Node computes the holding time of the packet according to formula (2).

$$T_{holding} = \alpha T_{Delay} + \beta R/v_{sound} + (R - AD_F)/v_{sound} \qquad (2)$$

where α is expressed as $\alpha = \frac{(ERD_F - AD_F) - [(\|C_D - C_S\| - R) - R]}{\|C_D - C_S\| - [(\|C_D - C_S\| - R) - R]} = \frac{(ERD_F - AD_F) - (\|C_D - C_S\| - 2R)}{2R}$.
$\|C_D - C_S\|$ is the maximum value of the difference between ERD and AD; $(\|C_D - C_S\| - R) - R$ is the minimum value of the difference between ERD and AD. T_{Delay} is the predefined maximum waiting time, which is expressed as $Inf\{T_{Delay}\} = \lceil \rho \times V_{VFR} \rceil \times L_{size}/v_{send}$, where V_{VFR} denotes the volume of VFR of the packet. $\lceil \rho \times V_{VFR} \rceil$ denotes the expected number of nodes within VFR of a packet. $\lceil \rho \times V_{VFR} \rceil \times L_{size}/v_{send}$ denotes the sum of expected time which all nodes within VFR spend on forwarding the received packet from previous hop.

In the second item of the right-hand side in Eq. (2), v_{sound} is the propagation speed in the water. Because the propagation speed of underwater acoustic signal varies with underwater pressure, temperature and salinity, we make use of linear interpolation method to calculate the propagation speed according to the depths of the start point and end point of acoustic signal propagation. β is a coefficient within in [0, 1], which is expressed as Eq. (3):

$$\beta = \sum_{k=1}^{\infty} \frac{\left(\int_V \rho dV\right)^k}{k!} exp^{-\int_{V_{WA}} \rho dV} = 1 - exp^{-\int_{V_{WA}} \rho dV} \qquad (3)$$

where V_{WA} is the volume of **WA**. V is divided into a great number of small virtual cubes with Binomial probability distribution for the occupancy of a node. Assuming the number of the cube is large and Poisson distribution approximates to Binomial distribution. According to Eq. (3), β is the probability that at least one node exists in region V_{WA}.

The third item of the right-hand side in Eq. (2) is the maximum difference between the time when a packet reaches the current node and the time when the packet reaches the nodes in **WA** of the current node.

The first item of the right-hand side Eq. (2) is the delay caused by transmissions, and the second and third items are the waiting delay caused by propagation of acoustic signals in water.

5   Performance Evaluation

5.1   Simulation Setup

In simulation, we use NS-3 simulation tool, a discrete event simulator, to evaluate the performance of proposed data gather scheme, namely the DDWA routing protocol in the architecture of underwater sensor cloud system based on fog computing. For simplicity, Table 1 summarizes the main parameters setup in the simulation.

Table 1. Parameter setup

Parameter	Value
Sending energy	50 W, default in NS-3
Receiving energy or idle state	158 mW, default in NS-3
R	2 km
Data rate	16 kbps
Node number	200–500, randomly generate network topology
Deployment region	3D area of $(10 \text{ km})^3$
Fog node number	5
Movement model	RandomWalk 2D Mobility Model
Source node	Randomly deploy at the depth of 10 km
Sink location	At the center of the surface
Packet generation model	1 packet per 5 s, Poisson distribution,

Performance metrics include packet delivery ratio (PDR), **end-to-end delay** and **energy tax**.

5.2   Performance Comparison and Analysis

We evaluate DDWA routing algorithm in the context of the proposed fog computing based sensor cloud system architecture against HH-VBF [12], RDBF [13], Flooding in the single-sink network architecture in terms of average PDR, average energy tax, average end-to-end delay.

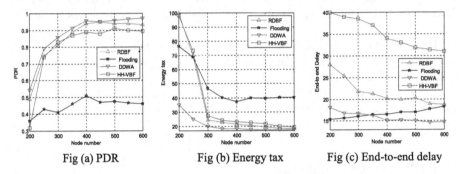

Fig (a) PDR   Fig (b) Energy tax   Fig (c) End-to-end delay

Fig. 3. Performance comparison among algorithms

5.2.1   PDR Comparison

PDR comparison is shown as Fig. 3(a). In the proposed fog computing based underwater sensor cloud system architecture, PDR outperforms the other routing protocol mainly due to the following reasons: the data collected by fog node make local processing so that the amount of transmission can be reduced effectively at the surface sink node. In the simulation process, we found that when more than one packet reach sink node in other three protocols, part of packets have to be lost due to the limited processing capacity. However, in the proposed architecture in this paper, in most cases the final delivery to surface sink node is completed by fog nodes visa task scheduling mode, thus avoiding packet loss. Finally, the characteristic of DDWA routing algorithm compared with other 3 routing protocols can also contribute to the PDR improvement, the detailed analysis is as below. On the one hand, DDWA can assign different forwarding priorities for node with the same distance to destination. Therefore, in dense networks, DDWA can reduce the number of forwarding nodes effectively compared with RDBF, thus decreasing the collision probability at receivers. On the other hand, the larger AD will result in the higher forwarding probability in next hop. This is because the larger AD will result in the larger valid forwarding area of next hop. The valid forwarding node is referred as to the area with no overlapping the previous hop forwarding area. In overlapping area, a part is **WA** and the rest part is the **SA**. According to forwarding policy of DDWA, a node can forward the received packets only when there are no forwarding nodes. And nodes in **SA** will never become qualified forwarding ones in the next hop. Therefore, using **AD** as a routing parameter to select nodes with the larger valid forwarding area as qualified forwarding nodes, DDWA can improve PDR, especially in sparse networks. In HH-VBF, nodes in routing pipe become qualified forwarding nodes, which results in the increase of forwarding nodes. The more forwarding nodes are, the higher the collision probability is, especially in dense networks. However, in DDWA, only nodes in VFR have qualification in forwarding packets, thus reducing the number of forwarding nodes.

5.2.2 Energy Tax Comparison

Energy tax comparison is shown as Fig. 3(b). In the proposed architecture, the fog node in each sub-area is responsible for local storage and local computation for collected data from the designated area. For delay-sensitive data, the processed data are transmitted to surface sink by multi-hop. For delay-insensitive data, the mobile fog node carries them to surface and then deliver to the sink node. Because the local processed data can be reduced in amount, the corresponding energy consumption can be decreased. Finally, the characteristic of DDWA routing algorithm compared with other 3 routing protocols can also contribute to the energy efficiency performance improvement, the detailed analysis is as below. It can be seen from Fig. 3(b) that DDWA and RDBF are lower in energy tax than HH-VBF. It is because the forwarding range of packets is confined within the routing pipe, which is larger than DDWA and RDBF. Therefore, the number of forwarding nodes in every hop will be more than that of the other two, thus increasing energy tax. DDWA considers not only ERD but also AD while making routing decision. However, RDBF only considers ERD. In this way, nodes with the same ERD in RDBF have the same priority for forwarding, which will be forwarded the same packet at the same time. But in DDWA, nodes with same ERD have not necessarily the same priority for forwarding since AD is also used as a parameter of holding time of packets except ERD.

5.2.3 End-to-End Delay Comparison

End-to-end delay comparison is shown as Fig. 3(c). In the proposed network architecture, the sensed data is processed by computation, redundant data removal and so on, therefore the amount of data is reduced so as to the decrease the end-to-end delay. In addition, the processed data with delay requirement are transmitted by AUVs directly from lower to upper instead of other relay nodes or AUV carrying modes, the holding time of packets and the movement delay of reaching surface are also avoided, which contribute to the reduction of end-to-end delay. Finally, the characteristic of DDWA routing algorithm compared with other 3 routing protocols can also contribute to the delay performance improvement, the detailed analysis is as below. In DDWA T_{Delay} is calculated according to the expected number of nodes in VFR and transmission rate of packets to guarantee that every node in VFR can complete the transmission of held packets. But in HH-VBF, T_{Delay} is a predefined waiting time which is commonly above a maximum point-to-point propagation delay, thus increasing the holding time of packets. It can be seen from Fig. 3(c) that DDWA is about 5 s lower than RDBF in end-to-end delay. It is due to the fact that RDBF only considers ERD in routing decision process. However, not only ERD but also AD are considered by DDWA at the same time.

6 Conclusions

This paper proposed a novel fog computing based underwater sensor cloud system architecture to relieve the burden of surface sink nodes and communication bandwidth overhead, thus reducing communication delay and network energy consumption. On the basis of the architecture, we present data collection scheme for time-critical and delay-insensitive application. In order to improve the routing performance of UASNs, we presented a reliable and energy-efficient routing protocol, DDWA. DDWA makes routing decision according to the expected residual distance to destination, advancement distance and node density, which make a tradeoff between waiting time and energy. Energy tax and end-to-end delay are reduced while guaranteeing the reliability of transmissions.

Acknowledgments. This work is supported by National Natural Science Foundation of China under Grant No. 41661031, Guangxi Natural Science Foundation under Grant No. 2018GXNSFAA138209 and 2018GXNSFAA294061; Foundation of Guilin University of Technology under Grant No. GUTQDJJ2017; Daqing Normal University Natural Science Fund Project under Grant No. 17zr04.

References

1. Wang, T., Zhang, G., Bhuiyan, M.D.Z.A., et al.: A novel trust mechanism based on Fog Computing in Sensor–Cloud System. Future Gener. Comput. Syst. (2018)
2. Wang, T., Zeng, J., Lai, Y., et al.: Data collection from WSNs to the cloud based on mobile Fog elements. Future Gener. Comput. Syst. (2017)
3. Wang, T., Zhou, J., Liu, A., et al.: Fog-based computing and storage offloading for data synchronization in IoT. IEEE Internet Things 6(3), 4272–4282 (2018)
4. Srimathi, C., Park, S.H., Rajesh, N.: Proposed framework for underwater sensor cloud for environmental monitoring. In: 2013 Fifth International Conference on Ubiquitous and Future Networks (ICUFN), pp. 104–109. IEEE (2013)
5. Hollinger, G.A., Choudhary, S., Qarabaqi, P., et al.: Underwater data collection using robotic sensor networks. IEEE J. Sel. Areas Commun. 30(5), 899–911 (2012)
6. Zhang, Y., Chen, Y., Zhou, S., et al.: Dynamic node cooperation in an underwater data collection network. IEEE Sens. J. 16(11), 4127–4136 (2016)
7. Wang, J., Li, D., Zhou, M., et al.: Data collection with multiple mobile actors in underwater sensor networks. In: 2008 the 28th International Conference on Distributed Computing Systems Workshops, pp. 216–221. IEEE (2008)
8. Williams, D.P.: AUV-enabled adaptive underwater surveying for optimal data collection. Intel. Serv. Robot. 5(1), 33–54 (2012)
9. Vasilescu, I., Kotay, K., Rus, D., et al.: Data collection, storage, and retrieval with an underwater sensor network. In: Proceedings of the 3rd International Conference on Embedded Networked Sensor Systems, pp. 154–165. ACM (2005)
10. Ilyas, N., Alghamdi, T.A., Farooq, M.N., et al.: AEDG: AUV-aided efficient data gathering routing protocol for underwater wireless sensor networks. Procedia Comput. Sci. 52, 568–575 (2015)

11. Ghoreyshi, S.M., Shahrabi, A., Boutaleb, T.: An efficient AUV-aided data collection in underwater sensor networks. In: 2018 IEEE 32nd International Conference on Advanced Information Networking and Applications (AINA), pp. 281–288. IEEE (2018)
12. Nicolaou, N., et al.: Improving the robustness of location-based routing for underwater sensor networks. In: OCEANS 2007-Europe. IEEE (2007)
13. Li, Z., Yao, N., Gao, Q.: Relative distance based forwarding protocol for underwater wireless networks. Int. J. Distrib. Sensor Netw. 10(2), 173089 (2014)
14. Noh, Y., Lee, U., et al.: VAPR: void-aware pressure routing for underwater sensor networks. IEEE Trans. Mob. Comput. 12(5), 895–908 (2013)
15. Haitao, Yu., Yao, Nianmin, et al.: WDFAD-DBR: weighting depth and forwarding area division DBR routing protocol for UASNs. Ad Hoc Netw. 37(2), 256–282 (2016)
16. Coutinho, R.W.L., Boukerche, A., et al.: Geographic and opportunistic routing for underwater sensor networks. IEEE Trans. Comput. 65(2), 548–561 (2016)

A Survey on Fog Computing

Rui Huang[1], Yu Sun[2], Chao Huang[3], Guang Zhao[3], and Ying Ma[1(✉)]

[1] Xiamen University of Technology, Xiamen 361024, China
{rhuang,maying}@xmut.edu.cn
[2] National Tsing Hua University, Hsinchu 30013, Taiwan
sunyu6336@163.com
[3] Xiamen Great Power GeoInformation Technology Co., Ltd., Xiamen 361008, China
{yunjielei,gzhao}@yeah.net

Abstract. Fog computing is a conceptual extension of cloud computing. This paper firstly compares the differences and connections between cloud computing and fog computing. Subsequently, a comprehensive analysis of the top journals and conferences related to fog computing in the past five years and 876 articles on WoS search were conducted. Finally, based on the basic structure of fog calculation, the current research status and challenges are also provided.

Keywords: Cloud computing · Fog computing

1 Introduction

According to a commission report from the Fog World Congress, by 2022, the global fog computing market will exceed \$180 billion. Fog computing related technologies will focus on agriculture, data centers, energy and utilities, health, industrial, military, retail, smart buildings, smart cities, smart homes, transportation and wearables, etc. [1]. Different from cloud computing, fog computing is a new generation of distributed computing, with better "decentralization" characteristics, which can be applied to networked cars, drones, autonomous driving, online games, video transmission, industrial control systems and Smart city management requires industries with low latency, high transmission rate, and high security.

As a data-generating infrastructure, the network sensor process has exploded. The International Data Corporation (IDC) report indicates that the number of sensors connected globally will exceed 30 billion in 2020, and the number of connected devices will increase from 50 billion to 1 trillion. These include 500 million sensors in the US factories, 212 billion available sensors, 110 million connected cars with 5.5 billion sensors, and 1.2 million connected homes with 200 million sensors [2]. The resulting demands include low latency, location awareness, a wider geographical distribution, adaptability to mobility applications, etc., and the development of fog computing technology supporting more edge nodes has unprecedented opportunities and challenges. Fog computing centralizes data to

G. Wang et al. (Eds.): SpaCCS 2019 Workshops, LNCS 11637, pp. 160–169, 2019.
https://doi.org/10.1007/978-3-030-24900-7_13

process data and apply on devices at the edge of the network, rather than keeping them almost entirely in the cloud like cloud computing. The storage and processing of data depends more on the local device than on the server.

The rest of this paper is organized as follows. Section 2 briefly reviews the related concepts of fog computing. Section 3 investigates relevant articles and analysis the state of the fog computing research. After describes a typical fog computing structure in Sect. 4, the research states and challenges are provided in Sect. 5. Section 6 finalizes the paper with conclusions and the future work.

2   Related Concepts of Fog Computing

2.1   Cloud Computing

When it comes to cloud computing, you have to say "cloud", witch is actually a group of computers. They are interconnected through network connections, and the number of these computers is usually large. There is no specific type device, and it can be a personal computer, which is a web server to provide services to a wide range of users [3].

In the big data era, almost everyone has a certain understanding of cloud computing. In our daily life, cloud computing is everywhere. So what is cloud computing? According to the National Institute of Standards and Technology (NIST) definition [4]: Cloud computing is a pay-as-you-go model that provides usable, convenient, and on-demand network access. These patterns go into a configurable pool of computing resources (including networks, applications, storage, services, servers, etc.), and they can be managed with little or no interaction with the service provider. Generally speaking, "cloud" is equivalent to the network, the Internet. We collect a lot of resources in the cloud, and then use these resources in the cloud to calculate is called cloud computing.

Cloud computing is mainly to solve computing problems and storage problems, while the storage of data resources is in the hands of individuals. Even if cloud computing implements a privacy policy for users other than data owners, it must be mentioned that these data are for private companies that have data. In this case, it is completely open. If a private enterprise disregards moral laws for its own sake, the consequences are unimaginable (Fig. 1).

2.2   Fog Computing

Fog computing provides computing, storage, and networking services between end devices and data centers, and is described as a highly virtualized platform. Similar to cloud computing, fog computing provides storage, computing, data, and application services to customers, who is to perform task processing at the end close to the data source [5,6]. The fog computing combines the advantages of cloud computing and client computing. It utilizes cloud services as the main real resource sharing aspect, and fully utilizes the computing functions of personal computer. The fog computing mainly has the following characteristics [7]:

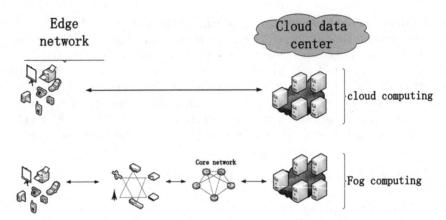

Fig. 1. Different deployments of cloud computing and fog computing

(1) Low delay at the edge of the net

At present, with the Internet of Things develops rapidly, the requirements of users are gradually increasing. For example, online games require system to update in real time, which has extremely high requirements for delay.

(2) Widely distributed geographical location

While cloud computing is calculated by bringing resources together, the fog computing is in stark contrast to that in geographical distribution, which is more effective in meeting our daily needs.

(3) Huge number of nodes

Fog computing has a large number of network nodes, which are widely used in daily life. For example, the camera monitoring environment around us needs to have a large number of network nodes, which can be realized through a large-scale sensor network.

(4) The leading role of wireless access

In cloud computing, our device signals need to be processed through the cloud, but this is not needed for fog computing. It allows our devices to communicate directly, so its mobile performance is very strong without computing through the cloud.

(5) Real-time analysis and near source control

Fog computing supports real-time interaction and online cloud analysis to meet user needs.

(6) Heterogeneity

In practical applications, fog computing supports a wide variety of heterogeneous hardware and software devices in a variety of environments with a variety of factors [6].

2.3   Differences Among Cloud Computing and Fog Computing

Fog computing is an extension of cloud computing so that they have many similarities in processing problems, and the methods used in the specific processing of data have their own advantages and disadvantages. Therefore, in actual application, it should be judged according to different situations.

From the Table 1, we can understand the distinction between the both more intuitively.

Table 1. Distinctions features of the cloud computing and fog computing.

Features	Fog computing	Cloud computing
Service node location	Between source and center	Cloud data center
Number of service nodes	Very large	Few
Amount of users	10,000,000-100,000,000	Tens of billions
Delay	Few	High
Bandwidth requirement	Less bandwidth	Larger bandwidth
Mobility support	Support	Limited
Service type	Limited local	Global
Target users	Mobile app	Ordinary internet application

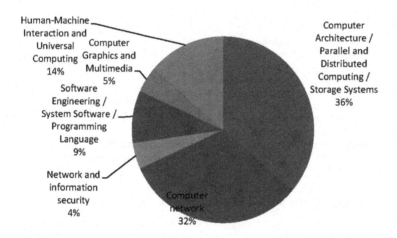

Fig. 2. Proportion of the articles in each direction in computer science

3   Relevant Articles Analysis

In order to investigate the existing research in fog computing, we analyse the top conferences and journals in every research directions of computer science as show in Table 2 and Fig. 2. We also conduct a further analysis on the 876 related articles querying from WoS. The result has been shown in Fig. 3.

Table 2. Top conference and Top journal articles related to Fog computing

Title	Type	#no.	Ratio
IEEE Transactions on Computers	Journal	1	4.5
International Symposium on Computer Architecture and High Performance Computing Workshops	Conference	3	13.6
International Symposium on Computer Architecture	Conference	3	13.6
Euromicro International Conference on Parallel	Conference	1	4.5
IEEE Transactions on Mobile Computing	Journal	4	18
IEEE International Conference on Computer Communications	Conference	3	13.6
IEEE Transactions on Dependable and Secure Computing	Journal	1	4.5
International Conference on Software Engineering	Conference	2	9
IEEE Transactions on Image Processing	Journal	1	4.5
ACM Conference on Human Factors in Computing Systems	Journal	2	9
ACM International Conference on Ubiquitous Computing	Conference	1	4.5

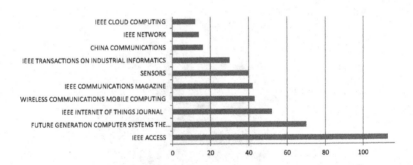

Fig. 3. The number of related articles indexed of WOS

From Table 2, we can see the top journal IEEE Transactions on Mobile Computing published the largest number of articles in the past 5 years. Twelve publications has published 22 articles. We also can see that the field of Computer Architecture/Parallel and Distributed Computing/Storage Systems has published 36% of the total top papers, as shown in Fig. 2. The IEEE ACCESS published more than 100 papers, which is the largest number of papers in this filed, as shown in Fig. 3.

4 Fog Computing Structure

The architecture of the fog computing can be divided into the following five layers [8], as shown in Fig. 4.

(1) End user layer

The so-called terminal refers to the terminal device composed of the user's mobile phone, computer, etc. This layer of equipment is not only similar to mobile devices such as mobile phones and computers, but also includes fixed devices such as street lights, cameras, and road sensors. In this layer, both the generation of the task and the return of the processing result are received.

(2) Access network layer

The network equipment of this layer is mainly a wireless network device, and some auxiliary devices are wired networks. After the terminal user layer generates a task, the next access layer operates to send the task information to the corresponding fog node through the access network layer. It also contains many corresponding rules. This layer includes wireless access networks such as Wi-Fi, 5G and wired LAN, because the underlying devices not only have wireless devices but also wired devices.

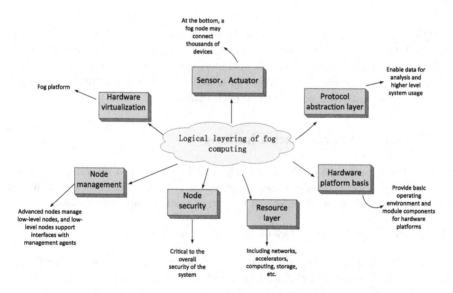

Fig. 4. The logical layers of the fog computing

(3) Fog layer

The core of the fog computing is the layer of fog layer, which is placed in the fog layer with high-intensity computing and storage devices close to the user. Because it is close to the user, the fog node can greatly reduce the delay of the traditional cloud computing, and can also support user mobility. According to the deployment location and function, fog nodes can be divided into three categories

    a. Fog edge node: The fog node closest to the end user layer is composed of an intelligent gateway, a border router, which has computing, storage, communication and other functions.
    b. Fog let: The micro-mist acts as an intermediate device, such as pre-processing, which is located between the fog edge node and the fog server.
    c. Fog server: Strong computing power and large storage space can enable it handle more requests and connect to the remote transport center.

(4) Core network layer

This layer is mostly a multi-hop wired network, which mainly sends some tasks beyond the fog layer computing and storage capabilities to the cloud data center.

(5) Cloud layer

The "cloud" is generally far from the ground. The cloud layer here is the remote data center, and the server in the cloud layer has more computing power and storage capacity than the server in the fog layer. In order to make the virtual machine move between cloud servers to achieve maximum execution efficiency, the servers here are also connected to each other.

5　Research States and Challenges

In 2011, Cisco proposed the fog computing, and then made a relevant definition. Since then, the fog computing has appeared in everyone's field of vision, which attracts more and more attention of industry, academe and government.

(1) Research on characteristics of the computing of fog

Since the concept of fog computing was proposed, many people are still very strange to it. The introduction and interpretation of fog computing is something that many scholars nowadays relish. Zhu introduced fog computing in [9], and describes its characteristics, and looks forward to its future development. And then, Peng et al. [10] proposed a scheme for wireless network access in fog computing, and introduced the F-RAN architecture in detail, mainly by reducing the burden on the front line by making full use of local radio signals. Interference problems are also described in this document and solutions are proposed. In

2018, Mahmud et al. [11] analyzed the challenges faced by fog computing, integrated the development data of current fog computing, summarized the current development characteristics. Finally, they pointed out the current development status of fog computing, and clarified the computing of fog.

(2) Research on the problem of time delay

Time delay is an important indicator to judge whether the network environment is excellent. The fog computing has the advantage of low latency compared with cloud computing. Researchers have also been exploring from the direction of reducing the delay. In 2016, Dastjerdi et al. [12] interpret the delay. Masri, W. et al. [13] pointed out in 2017 that the adjacent fogs communicate with each other to improve the processing speed (F2F), so that the overall operation delay is reduced. Smart cities require high computational delays and need real-time location refresh. Their research uses VFC models to reduce response time and latency.

(3) Research on fog computing framework

As a system-level architecture, fog computing can provide a series of services including computing and storage. Currently, fog computing has not developed for a long time, and the technology is not mature. It requires a common framework for development and mutual implementation of different platforms. In 2018, Sood et al. [14] proposed a comprehensive framework for student stress testing, which is mainly used to collect and analyze student stress information data in specific scenarios. Liu et al. introduced the related concepts of fog computing in 2017, explained the delayed resource allocation framework in detail, and proposed some related application extensions [15]. Due to the low delay, fog computing will be widely used in the medical field. The development of medical testing is in urgent need of a complete framework.

(4) Research on security of fog computing

The most important thing in the big data age is the security issue, which is the direction that many scholars are committed to research. The data in the fog computing does not need to be transmitted to the cloud, but it does not mean that the data can be secured. In this regard, Sood et al. [16] proposed a network security framework for identifying malicious edge devices in fog for data security of fog computing edge devices, and successfully verified that this framework can clearly identify malicious devices to reduce the risk of data.

6   Conclusion

Cloud computing technology has developed rapidly, but it has its shortcomings. Through simple understanding of fog computing, fog computing supplements some of the shortcomings of cloud computing. When faced with massive data, we should use fog computing properly, because the technology of fog computing is not mature. We need to ensure the efficiency of the algorithm, not only to ensure the robustness of the algorithm. Fog computing may provide an urgent solution to conquered problem of processing big data.

Acknowledgments. This work was supported in part by the National Natural Science Foundation of China (Grant No. 61502404), Natural Science Foundation of Fujian Province of China (Grant No. 2019J01851), Distinguished Young Scholars Foundation of Fujian Educational Committee (Grant No. DYS201707), Xiamen Science and Technology Program (Grant No. 3502Z20183059), and Open Fund of Key Laboratory of Data mining and Intelligent Recommendation, Fujian Province University. We thank the anonymous reviewers for their great helpful comments.

References

1. IDC, Worldwide Internet of Things Forecast Update, 2017–2021, document #US43304017, IDC, Framingham, MA, USA, February 2018
2. www.openfogconsortium.org/growth
3. Idehen, I., Wang, B., Shetye, K., Overbye, T., Weber, J.: Visualization of large-scale electric grid oscillation modes. In: 2018 IEEE North American Power Symposium (NAPS), pp. 1–6 (2018)
4. https://www.nist.gov/
5. Shi, W., Jie, C., Quan, Z., Li, Y., Xu, L.: Edge computing: vision and challenges. IEEE Internet Things J. **3**(5), 637–646 (2016)
6. Cartlidge, E.: The internet of things: from hype to reality. Opt. Photonics News **28**(9), 26 (2017)
7. Bonomi, F., Milito, R., Zhu, J., Addepalli, S.: Fog computing and its role in the internet of things. In: Proceedings of the First Edition of the MCC Workshop on Mobile Cloud Computing, pp. 13–16 (2012)
8. Vaquero, L.M., Rodero-Merino, L.: Finding your way in the fog: towards a comprehensive definition of fog computing. ACM SIGCOMM Comput. Commun. Rev. **44**(5), 27–32 (2014)
9. Zhu, J.: Improving web sites performance using edge servers in fog computing architecture. In: IEEE Seventh International Symposium on Service-Oriented System Engineering, pp. 320–323. IEEE Computer Society (2013)
10. Peng, M., Yan, S., Zhang, K., Wang, C.: Fog computing based radio access networks: issues and challenges. IEEE Netw. **30**(4), 46–53 (2015)
11. Mahmud, R., Kotagiri, R., Buyya, R.: Fog computing: a taxonomy, survey and future directions. In: Di Martino, B., Li, K.-C., Yang, L.T., Esposito, A. (eds.) Internet of Everything. IT, pp. 103–130. Springer, Singapore (2018). https://doi.org/10.1007/978-981-10-5861-5_5
12. Dastjerdi, A.V.: Fog computing: principles, architectures, and applications. In: Buyya, R., Dastjerdi, A.V. (eds.) Internet of Things: Principles and Paradigms, pp. 61–75 (2016)
13. Masri, W., Al Ridhawi, I., Mostafa, N., Pourghomi, P.: Minimizing delay in IoT systems through collaborative fog-to-fog (F2F) communication. In: 2017 Ninth International Conference on Ubiquitous and Future Networks (ICUFN), pp. 1005–1010 (2017)

14. Verma, P., Sood, S.K.: A comprehensive framework for student stress monitoring in fog-cloud IoT environment: m-health perspective. Med. Biol. Eng. Comput. **57**(1), 231–244 (2019)
15. Liu, Y., Fieldsend, J.E., Min, G.: A framework of fog computing: architecture, challenges, and optimization. IEEE Access **5**, 25445–25454 (2017)
16. Sohal, A.S., Sandhu, R., Sood, S.K., Chang, V.: A cybersecurity framework to identify malicious edge device in fog computing and cloud-of-things environments. Comput. Secur. **74**, 340–354 (2018)

An Approximate Data Collection Algorithm in Space-Based Internet of Things

Changjiang Fei[(⊠)], Baokang Zhao, Wanrong Yu, and Chunqing Wu

College of Computer, National University of Defense Technology,
Changsha 410073, China
feichangjiang.hi@163.com,
{bkzhao,wlyu,wuchunqing}@nudt.edu.cn

Abstract. Space-based Internet of Things (S-IoT) is an important way to realize the real interconnection of all things because of its global coverage, infrastructure independence and strong resistance to destruction. In the S-IoT, a large amount of sensory data needs to be transmitted through a space-based information network with severely limited resources, which poses a great challenge to data collection. Therefore, this paper proposes an approximate data collection algorithm for the S-IoT, namely the sampling-reconstruction (SR) algorithm. The SR algorithm only collects the sensory data of some nodes, and then reconstructs the unacquired sensory data by leveraging the spatio-temporal correlation between sensory data, thereby reducing the amount of data that needs to be transmitted. We evaluated the performance of SR algorithm using real weather data set. The experimental results show that the SR algorithm can effectively reduce the amount of data collected under the condition of satisfying required data collection accuracy.

Keywords: Sensory data collection · Space-based Internet of Things ·
Internet of Things · Spectral clustering · Spatio-temporal compressive sensing

1 Introduction

The goal of the Internet of Things (IoTs) is to connect everything. The ground IoT mainly transmits information through terrestrial networks such as the Internet, mobile communication networks, and private networks. In this case, the range of the IoT applications is limited due to the limitation of the coverage area of terrestrial networks. For example, a large number of nodes are difficult to deploy and apply effectively in areas without sufficient terrestrial infrastructures such as oceans, forests, and polar regions. Space-based information networks have broad advantages such as global coverage, infrastructure independence and strong resistance to destruction. Using space-based information network as the network for IoT information transmission, building a space-based Internet of Things (S-IoT) is an effective way to realize the real interconnection of all things [1–4]. S-IoT has attracted lots of attention from industrials, including Iridium, Orbcomm, Globalstar, Inmarsat, etc. Moreover, according to NSR's report, the revenues of S-IoT are expected to reach 1.7 billion dollars by 2020 [5].

G. Wang et al. (Eds.): SpaCCS 2019 Workshops, LNCS 11637, pp. 170–184, 2019.
https://doi.org/10.1007/978-3-030-24900-7_14

Data collection is the basis for S-IoT to implement various application services. However, data collection in S-IoT faces huge challenges. On the one hand, the S-IoT has a large amount of sensory data that needs to be transmitted. The space-based information network covers a wide range, and a single satellite can usually cover thousands of kilometers, providing data transmission services for a large number of ground nodes. It is estimated that by 2025, the number of M2 M/IoT networks connected by space-based information network will reach 5.96 million [6]. A large number of nodes will generate a large amount of sensory data. On the other hand, although space-based information networks are constantly evolving, compared with terrestrial networks, there are still very few network nodes, and resources such as computing, storage, communication, and energy are severely limited. In particular, due to the asymmetric uplink and downlink bandwidth, massive sensory data will compete for very limited uplink resources.

As shown in Fig. 1, the S-IoT needs to carry a large amount of sensory data of the perception layer through the network layer where resources are severely restricted, and provides support for the various application services in application layer, presenting an obvious "slender waist" structure. Therefore, the S-IoT is difficult to achieve complete and accurate data collection.

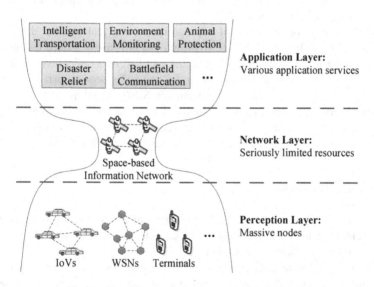

Fig. 1. The "slender waist" structure of the S-IoT.

Although the amount of data that the S-IoT needs to collect is very large, there is a strong correlation between the sensory data in both time and space dimensions, so there is redundancy. This inspires us to design a data collection algorithm and reduce the amount of data collected on the basis of satisfying users' requirements for data precision.

At present, we have not seen research related to approximate data collection in the S-IoT. A large number of approximate data collection algorithms have been proposed in terrestrial IoT and WSN [7]. These algorithms can be divided into three categories: model-based algorithms [8, 9], compressed-sensing based algorithms [10, 11] and query-driven algorithms [12, 13]. However, model-based algorithms and compressed-sensing based algorithms have high requirements for the processing power of ground nodes; query-driven algorithms are usually designed for specific types of queries, not general data collection algorithms.

In this paper, we propose an approximate data collection algorithm for the S-IoT, namely the sampling-reconstruction (SR) algorithm. The SR algorithm only collects the sensory data of some nodes in each data collection cycle, and then reconstructs the unacquired sensory data by using the spatio-temporal correlation between the data. The SR algorithm mainly includes three stages: clustering, sampling and reconstruction. In each data collection cycle, the SR algorithm first clusters the ground nodes into a series of clusters with strong spatial correlation. Subsequent sampling and reconstruction are performed separately in each cluster. In the sampling phase, the SR algorithm determines the sampling probability of the node based on the curvature characteristics of historical sensory data in the time and space dimensions, and randomly selects some nodes to collect data. In the reconstruction phase, the SR algorithm uses the historical values of sensory data and the collected partial sensory data to reconstruct the sensory data of unacquired nodes through the spatio-temporal compressive sensing (ST-CS) technology.

We evaluated the performance of SR algorithm using real weather data set. The experimental results show that the SR algorithm can effectively reduce the amount of data collected under the condition of satisfying required data collection accuracy.

The rest of this paper is organized as follows: The second part describes the problem scenario of approximate data collection in S-IoT. The third part elaborates the SR algorithm proposed in this paper, including the overall framework of SR algorithm and the process of clustering, sampling and reconstruction. The fourth part evaluates the performance of SR algorithm and the fifth part gives the conclusion.

2   Problem Scenario

As shown in Fig. 2, in the sensory data collection of the S-IoT, a ground node first transmits sensory data to a satellite node. The satellite node then sends the sensory data to the data center via the ground station.

In a data collection task, ground nodes are distributed within a certain geographic area. As shown in Fig. 3, the ground nodes in a data collection task are distributed in a rectangular area, and the number of nodes is N. We establish a two-dimensional coordinate system xOy with the lower left corner of the rectangular area as the origin. Using the positioning device on the node, we can get the coordinate of each node. At the moment t, the coordinate of node n_i ($i = 1, \cdots, N$) can be expressed as $(x_i(t), y_i(t))$ $(x_i(t) \in [0, x_m], y_i(t) \in [0, y_m])$, in which x_m, y_m are the maximum values of the horizontal and vertical coordinates of the rectangular area.

At the moment of data collection t_0, the sensory data of node n_i can be expressed as $d_i(t_0)$ and sensory data in different data collection cycles can be represented as a series

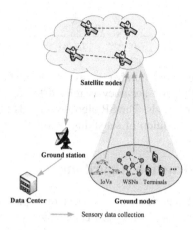

Fig. 2. The data collection of S-IoT.

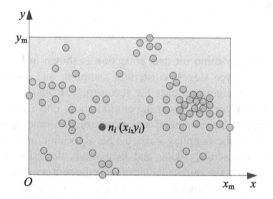

Fig. 3. Ground nodes in a data collection task.

$$d_i(0), d_i(T), d_i(2T), \cdots,$$

in which T is the data collection period. At t_0, the collection of sensory data of all nodes is $\{d_1(t_0), \cdots, d_N(t_0)\}$.

In order to reduce the amount of data collected, the SR algorithm collects only the sensory data of some nodes in each data collection cycle, and then reconstructs the sensory data of unacquired nodes. At the moment of data collection t_0, the number of nodes collecting sensory data is $M(M \leq N)$, the reconstructed sensory data is $\{d'_1(t_0), \cdots, d'_N(t_0)\}$. Therefore, the sensory data collection ratio is M/N. We define the data collection accuracy as

$$A = 1 - \frac{1}{N} \sum_{n=1}^{N} \frac{|d'_n(t_0) - d_n(t_0)|}{|d_n(t_0)| + \alpha},$$

in which α is a small positive number to avoid calculation error occurred when $|d_n(t_0)| = 0$. The data collection accuracy is related to sampling methods, sampling ratios, and reconstruction methods. The SR algorithm needs to reduce the sensory data collection ratio under the condition of satisfying required data collection accuracy.

3   Sampling-Reconstruction Algorithm

The basic idea of the SR algorithm is to collect only part of the sensory data and reconstruct the uncollected data in the data center by leveraging the spatio-temporal correlation of sensory data. In this section, we first give the overall framework of SR algorithm, and then elaborate the basic process of clustering, sampling and reconstruction in SR algorithm.

3.1   Overview

The framework of SR algorithm for data collection is shown in Fig. 4. The SR algorithm mainly includes three stages: clustering, sampling and reconstruction. In the clustering stage, the SR algorithm uses the reconstructed sensory data from the historical sensory data repository to cluster the ground nodes into a series of clusters with strong spatial correlation. The sampling and reconstruction process is performed separately in each cluster. In the sampling stage, the SR algorithm first determines the node that needs to report the sensory data, and then sends the sampling notices to the sampled nodes, and finally the sampled nodes report the sensory data to the data center. The transmission of sampling notices can make full use of the advantages of satellite network broadcasting. In the reconstruction stage, the SR algorithm reconstructs the

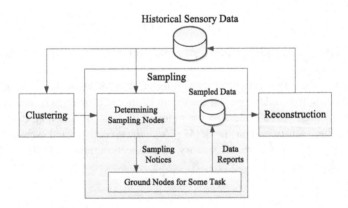

Fig. 4. The framework of SR algorithm.

sensory data of unacquired nodes based on the acquired sensory data by using the temporal and spatial correlation between sensory data. The reconstructed sensory data is stored in the historical sensory data repository for subsequent data collection and application services.

3.2 Clustering

In the time dimension, the sensory data of a node is strongly correlated in a neighboring time period T_C. The value of T_C is related to the type of sensory data. In the spatial dimension, intuitively, there is a stronger correlation between the sensory data of neighboring nodes than that of the distant nodes. However, it is not accurate to judge the correlation of sensory data only through the distance between nodes, i.e. the geographical position of nodes. For example, if one of two neighboring nodes is located in the lawn and the other is in the woods, there will be a significant difference in light intensity between them. Therefore, when we perform spatial correlation division, in addition to the locations of nodes, we also consider the sensory data of nodes.

In order to divide the nodes into a series of clusters with strong spatial correlation, we first cluster the nodes by using the reconstructed sensory data in the previous cycle. The clustering algorithm is spectral clustering algorithm. At a certain data collection moment t_0, the clustering sample set is $P = \{\mathbf{p}_1, \cdots, \mathbf{p}_N\}$, in which the sample points $\mathbf{p}_i = (x_i(t_0 - T), y_i(t_0 - T), d'_i(t_0 - T))$ $(i = 1, \cdots, N)$. The process of node clustering is shown in Algorithm 1, where K' is the dimension after dimensionality reduction, K is the dimension after clustering, σ is Gaussian kernel function; $C_1, \cdots, C_K$ are the clusters after clustering, C_k $(k = 1, \cdots, K)$ is the subset of P, $C_{k_i} \cap C_{k_j} = \emptyset$ $(k_i, k_j = 1, \cdots, K$ and $k_i \neq k_j)$, and $C_1 \cup C_2 \cup \cdots \cup C_K = P$. The algorithm uses the Ncut method.

Firstly, we construct adjacency matrix $\mathbf{W}$ using the full join method. The Gaussian radial kernel RBF is used to calculate the weights between the sample points (line 2–7). Secondly, the degree matrix $\mathbf{D}$ (line 9–12) and Laplacian matrix $\mathbf{L}$ (line 13) are constructed. Thirdly, we calculate the eigenvectors $\mathbf{f}_1, \cdots, \mathbf{f}_{K'}$ corresponding to the K' smallest eigenvalues of $\mathbf{D}^{-1/2}\mathbf{L}\mathbf{D}^{-1/2}$ (line 14). Eigenvectors $\mathbf{f}_1, \cdots, \mathbf{f}_{K'}$ constitute matrix $\mathbf{F}$(line 15) and feature matrix $\mathbf{F}^*$ is produced through standardizing $\mathbf{F}$ by row (line 17–22). Finally, we build a new sample set P' after dimensionality reduction (line 24–27). P' is further clustered by K-Means clustering algorithm to obtain the final clusters $C_1, \cdots, C_K$ (line 28).

Assuming the number of nodes in cluster C_k is N_k, then the sensory data of all nodes in C_k at t_0 and previous T_C can be expressed as a $L \times N_k$ matrix

$$\mathbf{D}_k(t_0) = \begin{bmatrix} d_{k_1}(t_0) & d_{k_2}(t_0) & \cdots & d_{k_{N_k}}(t_0) \\ d_{k_1}(t_0 - T) & d_{k_2}(t_0 - T) & \cdots & d_{k_{N_k}}(t_0 - T) \\ \vdots & \vdots & \ddots & \vdots \\ d_{k_1}(t_0 - (L-1)T) & d_{k_2}(t_0 - (L-1)T) & \cdots & d_{k_{N_k}}(t_0 - (L-1)T) \end{bmatrix},$$

in which, $L = \lfloor T_C/T \rfloor + 1$ is the number of data collection; $k_1, \cdots, k_{N_k}$ are the serial numbers of the nodes in C_k. We call $\mathbf{D}_k(t_0)$ as the sensory data matrix of C_k at t_0.

Algorithm 1 Node Clustering

Input: P, K', K, N, σ

Output: $C_1, \cdots, C_K$

1: /* *Constructs adjacency matrix* **W** */

2: **for each** $i \in \{1, \cdots, N\}$ **do**

3: **for each** $j \in \{1, \cdots, N\}$ **do**

4:   $w_{ij} = \exp\left(-\left\|\mathbf{p}_i - \mathbf{p}_j\right\|_2^2 / 2\sigma^2\right)$

5: **end for**

6: **end for**

7: $\mathbf{W} = (w_{ij})_{N \times N}$

8: /* *Constructs degree matrix* **D** */

9: **for each** $i \in \{1, \cdots, N\}$ **do**

10: $d_i = \sum_{j=1}^{N} w_{ij}$

11: **end for**

12: $\mathbf{D} = \mathrm{diag}(d_1, d_2, \cdots, d_N)$

13: $\mathbf{L} = \mathbf{D} - \mathbf{W}$

14: $\{\mathbf{f}_1, \cdots, \mathbf{f}_{K'}\} = Eigenvector(\mathbf{D}^{-1/2}\mathbf{L}\mathbf{D}^{-1/2}, K')$

15: $\mathbf{F} = (\mathbf{f}_1, \cdots, \mathbf{f}_{K'})$

16: /* *Standardizes* **F** *by row and generates* $\mathbf{F}^*$ */

17: **for each** $i \in \{1, \cdots, N\}$ **do**

18: **for each** $j \in \{1, \cdots, K'\}$ **do**

19:   $f_{ij}^* = f_{ij} / \sqrt{\sum_{k'=1}^{K'} f_{ik'}^2}$

20: **end for**

21: **end for**

22: $\mathbf{F}^* = (f_{ij}^*)_{N \times K'}$

23: /* *Constructs new samples after reducing dimensionality* */

24: **for each** $i \in \{1, \cdots, N\}$ **do**

25: $\mathbf{p}_i' = (f_{i1}^*, \cdots, f_{iK'}^*)^{\mathrm{T}}$

26: **end for**

27: $P' = \{\mathbf{p}_1', \cdots, \mathbf{p}_N'\}$

28: $\{C_1, \cdots, C_K\} = Kmeans(P', K)$

29: **return** $C_1, \cdots, C_K$

3.3 Sampling

When selecting the nodes that report sensory data, we use random sampling to ensure that each node has the opportunity to report the data. In order to obtain higher data collection accuracy under a certain number of sampling nodes, we assign different sampling probability to each node.

Intuitively, if the sensory data of a node changes greatly in the recent period, or the sensory data of a node is significantly different with neighboring nodes, the more the sensory data needs to be reported and the sampling probability should be larger. We use the curvature characteristics of sensory data in time and space dimensions to characterize the above two features. Next we calculate the curvature of sensory data in the time dimension and the spatial dimension respectively.

Time Dimension Curvature. In the time dimension, we firstly produce a interpolation curve using the reconstructed sensory data at $t_0 - T$ and previous T_C. We use the mean value of curvatures of interpolation curve at each interpolation point (except for the two endpoints) as the time dimension curvature. The reconstructed sensory data of $n_i(i = k_1, \cdots, k_{N_k})$ in C_k at $t_0 - T$ and previous T_C is shown in Table 1.

Table 1. The reconstructed sensory data of n_i at $t_0 - T$ and previous T_C

t	$t_0 - (L-1)T$	$t_0 - (L-2)T$	...	$t_0 - T$
$d_i'(t)$	$d_i'(t_0 - (L-1)T)$	$d_i'(t_0 - (L-2)T)$	...	$d_i'(t_0 - T)$

We perform interpolation in $[t_0 - (L-1)T, t_0 - T]$ using the data in Table 1. The interpolation method is cubic spline interpolation and natural boundary conditions are adopted. The segmentation expression of the cubic spline interpolation function is

$$s(t) = d_i'(t_0 - lT) + \left\{ d_i'[t_0 - lT, t_0 - (l-1)T] - \left(\frac{1}{3}M_l + \frac{1}{6}M_{l-1} \right)h_l \right\}(t - t_0 + lT)$$
$$+ \frac{1}{2}M_l(t - t_0 + lT)^2 + \frac{1}{6h_l}(M_{l-1} - M_l)(t - t_0 + lT)^3,$$
$$(t \in [t_0 - lT, t_0 - (l-1)T], l = L-1, \cdots, 2)$$

in which

$$d_i'[t_0 - lT, t_0 - (l-1)T] = \frac{d_i'(t_0-lT)-d_i'(t_0-(l-1)T)}{(t_0-lT)-(t_0-(l-1)T)} = \frac{d_i'(t_0-(l-1)T)-d_i'(t_0-lT)}{T};$$
$$h_l = (t_0 - (l-1)T) - (t_0 - lT) = T;$$
$$M_l = s''(t_0 - lT)(l = L-1, \cdots, 1).$$

According to natural boundary conditions, $M_{L-1} = 0$, $M_1 = 0$. $M_{L-2}, \cdots, M_2$ can be obtained through the following formula:

$$\begin{bmatrix} 2 & \lambda_{L-2} & & & & \\ \mu_{L-3} & 2 & \lambda_{L-3} & & & \\ & \ddots & \ddots & \ddots & & \\ & & \mu_3 & 2 & \lambda_3 & \\ & & & \mu_2 & 2 \end{bmatrix} \begin{bmatrix} M_{L-2} \\ M_{L-3} \\ \vdots \\ M_3 \\ M_2 \end{bmatrix} = \begin{bmatrix} d_{L-2} \\ d_{L-3} \\ \vdots \\ d_3 \\ d_2 \end{bmatrix},$$

in which

$$\lambda_l = 1 - \mu_l,$$

$$\mu_l = \frac{h_{l+1}}{h_{l+1} + h_l} = \frac{1}{2},$$

$$\begin{aligned} d_l &= 6d_i'[t_0 - (l+1)T, t_0 - lT, t_0 - (l-1)T] \\ &= 6\frac{d_i'[t_0 - (l+1)T, t_0 - lT] - d_i'[t_0 - lT, t_0 - (l-1)T]}{(t_0 - (l+1)T) - (t_0 - (l-1)T)} \\ &= 3\frac{d_i'[t_0 - lT, t_0 - (l-1)T] - d_i'[t_0 - (l+1)T, t_0 - lT]}{T} \end{aligned}$$

The curvature of interpolation curve $s(t)$ at $t_0 - lT$ ($l = L-2, \cdots, 2$) is

$$c_i(t_0 - lT) = \frac{|M_l|}{\left(1 + (s'(t_0 - lT))^2\right)^{\frac{3}{2}}},$$

in which

$$s'(t_0 - lT) = d_i'[t_0 - lT, t_0 - (l-1)T] - \left(\frac{1}{3}M_l + \frac{1}{6}M_{l-1}\right)h_l.$$

Therefore, the mean value of curvatures of $s(t)$ at $t_0 - (L-2)T, \cdots, t_0 - 2T$ is

$$\bar{c}_i = \frac{1}{L-3}\sum_{l=2}^{L-2} c_i(t_0 - lT).$$

Spatial Dimension Curvature. In the spatial dimension, we use the Gaussian curvature of interpolation surface at each node at $t_0 - T$ as spatial dimension curvature. When the number of nodes is large, the overhead of two-dimensional interpolation is large. Moreover, we only need to obtain the curvature characteristics. Therefore, we estimate the curvature directly, which is similar to the curvature estimation of point-based surface. We use a simple estimation method proposed in [14], namely the Voronoi element method. Any other method that can accurately estimate the curvature and meet the cost requirements can also be used. Data points in C_k can be represented as $P_k = \left\{ \mathbf{p}_{k_1}, \cdots, \mathbf{p}_{k_{N_k}} \right\}$, where the data points $\mathbf{p}_i = (x_i(t_0 - T), y_i(t_0 - T), d_i'(t_0 - T))$ $(i = k_1, \cdots, k_{N_k})$. For data point $\mathbf{p}_i$, the process of curvature estimation using the Voronoi element method is as follows.

Estimating the Normal Vector. Firstly, we collect a possible neighbor set $\tilde{N}_i = \left\{ \mathbf{p}_j \middle| \|\mathbf{p}_i - \mathbf{p}_j\| < r_i \right\}$ for $\mathbf{p}_i$, where $r_i > 0$ is a distance threshold. Assuming the elements of $\tilde{N}_i$ is $\mathbf{p}_{i_1}, \cdots, \mathbf{p}_{i_m}$ except for $\mathbf{p}_i$, then the covariance matrix of the neighbors of $\mathbf{p}_i$ can be expressed as

$$C = \begin{bmatrix} \mathbf{p}_{i_1} - \bar{\mathbf{p}}_i \\ \cdots \\ \mathbf{p}_{i_m} - \bar{\mathbf{p}}_i \end{bmatrix}^T \begin{bmatrix} \mathbf{p}_{i_1} - \bar{\mathbf{p}}_i \\ \cdots \\ \mathbf{p}_{i_m} - \bar{\mathbf{p}}_i \end{bmatrix},$$

in which $\bar{\mathbf{p}}_i$ is the center of $\mathbf{p}_{i_1}, \cdots, \mathbf{p}_{i_m}$. The eigenvector $\mathbf{v}_{\min}$ corresponding to the minimum eigenvalue $\lambda_{\min}$ of C can be used as a valid estimation of the normal vector of $\mathbf{p}_i$.

Determine the Set of Neighbors. We project the points in $\tilde{N}_i$ to the tangent plane of $\mathbf{p}_i$ and produce $P(\mathbf{p}_i)$. Then, we perform Delaunay triangulation for $P(\mathbf{p}_i)$ and get a graph T_i. The neighbor set of $\mathbf{p}_i$ is $N_i = \{\mathbf{p}_j | \mathbf{p}_j$ is the neighbor of $\mathbf{p}_i$ in $T_i\}$.

Calculate Gaussian Curvature. Figure 5(a) is a triangular grid diagram composed by $\mathbf{p}_i$ and its neighbors. According to [15], the Gaussian curvature at $\mathbf{p}_i$ can be estimated by

$$k_G(\mathbf{p}_i) = \frac{2\pi - \sum_{j=1}^{\#f} \theta_j}{A_{\mathrm{mixed}}}$$

where $\#f$ is the number of triangles including $\mathbf{p}_i$, θ_j is shown in Fig. 5(a), A_{mixed} is the area of the shaded portion in Fig. 5(a) and can be calculated according to the method in Fig. 5(b).

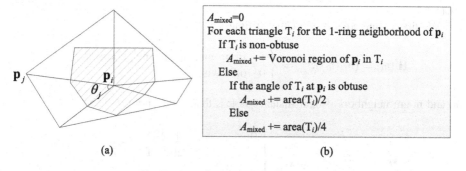

(a)   (b)

Fig. 5. Gaussian curvature calculation.

Therefore, the sampling probability of n_i is

$$p_i = \beta(\bar{c}_i + k_G(\mathbf{p}_i))$$

in which β is the sampling probability adjust parameter.

3.4   Reconstruction

If the sensory data exhibits an obvious low-rank structure (i.e. redundancy) and spatiotemporal stability [16, 17], the ST-CS technology can effectively reconstruct the sensory data.

For sensory data matrix $\mathbf{D}_k(t_0)$ of C_k at t_0, we define a $L \times N_k$ sampling indicator matrix

$$\mathbf{S}_k(t_0) = (s_i(t))_{L \times N_k} = \begin{cases} 1 & \text{if } d_i(t) \text{ in } \mathbf{D}_k(t_0) \text{ been sampled} \\ 0 & \text{otherwise} \end{cases},$$

which indicates whether a sensory data in $\mathbf{D}_k(t_0)$ is sampled.

Assuming the reconstructed sensory data matrix is $\hat{\mathbf{D}}_k(t_0)$, then $\hat{\mathbf{D}}_k(t_0)$ can be expressed as the following form through singular value decomposition:

$$\hat{\mathbf{D}}_k(t_0) = \mathbf{L}\mathbf{R}^*.$$

Through theoretical derivations [16], the sensory data reconstruction problem is translated into the following optimization problem:

$$\min\left\{ \|\mathbf{S}_k(t_0) \cdot (\mathbf{L}\mathbf{R}^*) - \mathbf{D}_k(t_0)\|_F^2 + \lambda\left(\|\mathbf{L}\|_F^2 + \|\mathbf{R}^*\|_F^2\right) + \|\mathbf{H}(t_0)\mathbf{L}\mathbf{R}^*\|_F^2 + \|\mathbf{L}\mathbf{R}^*\mathbf{T}\|_F^2 \right\},$$

where λ is the Lagrange multiplier, $\|\cdot\|_F^2$ is the Frobenius (Euclidean) paradigm. $\mathbf{H}(t_0)$ and $\mathbf{T}$ are space and time constraint matrices respectively, which are described later. By adjusting λ, $\mathbf{L}$ and $\mathbf{R}^*$ can be estimated through this optimization problem, and then get $\hat{\mathbf{D}}_k(t_0)$.

We first define adjacency matrix at time t_0:

$$\mathbf{H}'(t_0) = (h'_{i,j}(t_0))_{N \times N} = \begin{cases} 1 & \text{if } n_i \text{ and } n_j \text{ are neighbors at } t_0 \\ 0 & \text{otherwise} \end{cases}.$$

n_i and n_j are neighbors if their distance is less than a threshold d. Then

$$\mathbf{H}(t_0) = (h_{i,j}(t_0))_{N \times N} = \begin{cases} 0 & \text{if } \sum_{j=1}^{N} h'_{i,j}(t_0) = 0 \\ 1 & \text{else if } i = j \\ -\dfrac{h'_{i,j}(t_0)}{\sum_{j=1}^{N} h'_{i,j}(t_0)} & \text{otherwise} \end{cases}.$$

According to [18], we set $\mathbf{T} = Toeplitz(0, 1, -2, 1)_{L \times L}$, i.e.

$$T = \begin{bmatrix} 1 & -2 & 1 & 0 & \cdots \\ 0 & 1 & -2 & 1 & \vdots \\ 0 & 0 & 1 & -2 & \vdots \\ \vdots & \ddots & \ddots & \ddots & \ddots \end{bmatrix}_{L \times L}.$$

4 Performance Evaluation

4.1 Experimental Scenario

In order to analyze the performance of the proposed SR algorithm, we tested SR algorithm on a real data set. The data set used in the experiment is the hourly observation data of China ground meteorological station acquired from National Meteorological Information Center. We used temperature data of 145 meteorological stations in Sichuan Province from 0:00 on March 21, 2019 to 13:00 on March 27, 2019. We emulated collecting these data through SR algorithm.

4.2 Experimental Results and Analysis

The purpose of the SR algorithm is to obtain the high data collection accuracy by collecting a small amount of data, so we mainly evaluate the data collection accuracy and data collection ratio.

In SR algorithm, the number of clusters K will affect the performance of the algorithm. We analyzed the influence of the number of clusters under different sampling probability adjustment parameters β, as shown in Fig. 6. When $K = 1$, it means that clustering is not performed. It can be seen that number of clusters will greatly

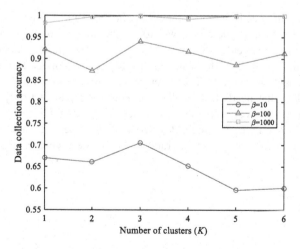

Fig. 6. The impact of the number of clusters on the data collection accuracy.

impact data collection accuracy. When $K = 3$, the data collection accuracies are the highest overall, which are 70.53%, 94.06% and 99.96% respectively. When $K = 5$, the data collection accuracy was 59.61%, 88.66% and 99.95% respectively, which are even worse than not clustering (66.99%, 92.15 and 98.25% respectively). Therefore, in this data collection task, it is appropriate to set the number of clusters as 3. In addition, when β is small, the sampled nodes are less, then the number of clusters has a great influence on the data collection accuracy; when β is large (for example $\beta = 1000$), there are many sampled nodes, the number of clusters has less influence on the data collection accuracy.

When $K = 3$, the clustering result is shown in Fig. 7. The different colors of the points in the figure indicate that the points belong to different clusters. Figure 7(a) is 3D view and Fig. 7(b) is 2D view of x–y plane.

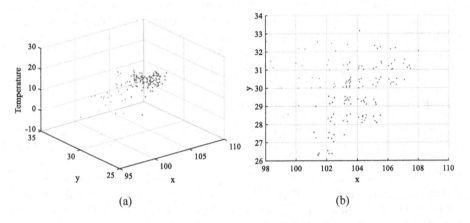

(a)   (b)

Fig. 7. Clustering result ($K = 3$).

The SR algorithm needs to reduce the data collection ratio while satisfying required data collection accuracy. Therefore, we count the minimum data collection ratio required for different data collection accuracy under several cluster numbers, as shown in Fig. 8. In general, SR algorithm can significantly reduce data collection ratio under different data collection accuracy. The lower the data collection accuracy, the lower the proportion of data that needs to be collected. This is because we only need a small amount of data to achieve the required accuracy. Corresponding to Fig. 6, since the data collection accuracy is the highest when $K = 3$, under the same required data collection accuracy, the data collection ratio is the smallest when $K = 3$.

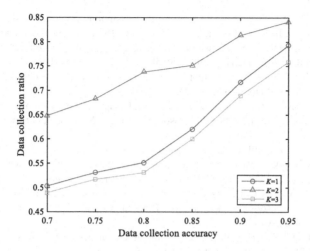

Fig. 8. Data collection ratio required for different data collection accuracy.

5   Conclusion

In S-IoT, massive sensory data and severely limited resources make the complete and accurate data collection difficult to achieve. In this paper, an approximate data collection algorithm, namely the SR algorithm, is proposed. By leveraging the spatio-temporal correlation between sensory data, the SR algorithm only collects the sensory data of some nodes in each data collection cycle, and then reconstructs the unacquired sensory data in the data center, thereby reducing the data collection ratio. The experimental results show that SR algorithm can greatly reduce the amount of data collected under the condition of satisfying required data collection accuracy.

References

1. Hu, D., He, L., Wu, J.: A novel forward-link multiplexed scheme in satellite-based Internet of Things. IEEE Internet Things J. **5**(2), 1265–1274 (2018)
2. Kak, A., Guven, E., Ergin, U.E., Akyildiz, I.F.: Performance evaluation of SDN-based Internet of Space Things. In: 2018 IEEE Globecom Workshops (GC Wkshps), pp. 1–6. IEEE Press, Piscataway (2018)
3. Akyildiz, I.F., Kak, A.: The Internet of Space Things/CubeSats: a ubiquitous cyber-physical system for the connected world. Comput. Netw. **150**, 134–149 (2019)
4. Bacco, M., et al.: IoT applications and services in space information networks. IEEE Wirel. Commun. **26**(2), 31–37 (2019)
5. M2M and IoT via Satellite, 9th edn. https://www.nsr.com/research/m2m-and-iot-via-satellite-9th-edition/. Accessed 28 May 2019
6. M2M and IoT via Satellite, 7th edn. http://www.nsr.com/research-reports/satellite-communications-1/m2m-and-iot-via-satellite-7th-edition/. Accessed 28 Feb 2017
7. Cheng, S., Cai, Z., Li, J.: Approximate sensory data collection: a survey. Sensors **17**(3), 564 (2017)

8. Gedik, B., Liu, L., Yu, P.S.: ASAP: an adaptive sampling approach to data collection in sensor networks. IEEE Trans. Parallel Distrib. Syst. **18**(12), 1766–1783 (2007)
9. Wang, C., Ma, H., He, Y., Xiong, S.: Adaptive approximate data collection for wireless sensor networks. IEEE Trans. Parallel Distrib. Syst. **23**(6), 1004–1016 (2012)
10. Nguyen, M.T., Teague, K.A.: Compressive sensing based random walk routing in wireless sensor networks. Ad Hoc Netw. **54**, 99–110 (2017)
11. Chen, S., Zhang, S., Zheng, X., Ruan, X.: Layered adaptive compression design for efficient data collection in industrial wireless sensor networks. J. Netw. Comput. Appl. **129**, 37–45 (2019)
12. Silberstein, A., Braynard, R., Ellis, C., Munagala, K., Yang, J.: A sampling-based approach to optimizing top-k queries in sensor networks. In: 22nd International Conference on Data Engineering (ICDE 2006), p. 68. IEEE Computer Society, Washington DC (2006)
13. Guo, L., Beyah, R., Li, Y.: SMITE: a stochastic compressive data collection protocol for mobile wireless sensor networks. In: 2011 Proceedings IEEE INFOCOM, pp. 1611–1619. IEEE Press, Piscataway (2011)
14. Wang, K., Chen, F., Chen, Y.: Directly compute curvatures on point-based surface. Mini-Micro Syst. **26**(5), 813–817 (2005). (in Chinese)
15. Meyer, M., Desbrun, M., Schröder, P., Barr, A.H.: Discrete differential-geometry operators for triangulated 2-manifolds. In: Hege, H.C., Polthier, K. (eds.) Visualization and Mathematics III, pp. 35–60. Springer, Heidelberg (2003). https://doi.org/10.1007/978-3-662-05105-4_2
16. Roughan, M., Zhang, Y., Willinger, W., Qiu, L.: Spatio-temporal compressive sensing and Internet traffic matrices (extended version). IEEE/ACM Trans. Netw. **20**(3), 662–676 (2012)
17. Kong, L., Xia, M., Liu, X.Y., Wu, M.Y., Liu, X.: Data loss and reconstruction in sensor networks. In: 2013 Proceedings IEEE INFOCOM, pp. 1654–1662. IEEE Press, Piscataway (2013)
18. Rallapalli, S., Qiu, L., Zhang, Y., Chen, Y.C.: Exploiting temporal stability and low-rank structure for localization in mobile networks. In: Proceedings of MobiCom 2010, pp. 161–172. ACM, New York (2010)

Outlier Detection of Internet of Vehicles

Yingming Zeng[1], Huanlei Zhao[2], Haibin Zhang[2(✉)], and Qian Zhang[2]

[1] Beijing Institute of Computer Technology and Applications, Beijing 100854, China
yingmingblue@163.com
[2] School of Cyber Engineering, Xidian University, Xi'an 710071, Shaanxi, China
hlzhao_1@stu.xidian.edu.cn, hbzhang@mail.xidian.edu.cn, zqrose41@163.com

Abstract. With the development of the Internet of Things (IoT) and automobile industry in recent years, the Internet of Vehicle (IoV) has become a future direction of automobile development. Due to the large amount of vehicles, the opening of wireless media, the high-speed movement of vehicles and the impact of the environment, it is inevitable to produce abnormal data in IoVs including data tampering, loss, disorder and so on. However, there are few systematic research results for outlier detection of IoVs. The usability of the existing outlier detection schemes and their performances are not yet evaluated. To this issue, we select six applicable schemes and propose the outlier detection process for IoVs. Then we evaluate the comparison performances of the proposed schemes on real vehicle data collected by a Focus car.

Keywords: Internet of Things · Internet of vehicles · Abnormal data · Outlier detection · Comparison performance

1 Introduction

With the rapid development of modern automobile manufacturing technology, sensor technology and wireless communication technology, new concept of driving has been constantly put forward and put into use gradually in recent years. As an important area of the Internet of Things, the Internet of Vehicles plays an increasingly important role in the intelligent transportation.

IoVs is an integrated intelligent decision system which utilizes on-board sensor devices, wireless communication, vehicle navigation, intelligent terminals and information processing system to achieve the bidirectional data interchange and sharing between Vehicle to Internet (V2I), Vehicle to Vehicle (V2V), Vehicle to Person (V2P) and Vehicle to Road Infrastructure (V2R) [1]. Vehicles can collect various information of their environment, operation status and the relevant data of neighboring vehicles by GPS, RFID, sensor, camera image processing and other devices. These large amounts of vehicle information can be analyzed and processed to calculate the best route for different vehicles, timely report the traffic conditions and reasonably arrange the signal cycle [2]. Therefore, the Internet of Vehicles can effectively alleviate traffic pressure and improve people's life travel.

© Springer Nature Switzerland AG 2019
G. Wang et al. (Eds.): SpaCCS 2019 Workshops, LNCS 11637, pp. 185–196, 2019.
https://doi.org/10.1007/978-3-030-24900-7_15

However, due to the wireless transmission media, the large amount of nodes, the high-speed moving of the vehicles, the characteristics of roads and even the interference of artificial information, the data collected by vehicle sensors are easy to suffer the risk of modifying, falsifying and replacing, which may cause serious harm to traffic security. If the distance information of the ahead vehicle can not be collected correctly, traffic collision may be caused which can seriously threaten the safety of the drivers and passengers. Therefore, outlier detection is extremely important to ensure the reliability and accuracy of vehicle data.

As we know, there are few achievements for outlier detection of IoVs. The current researches mainly diagnose abnormal vehicles considering the vehicle communication aspect like packet loss. In view of the special routing protocols of the Internet of Vehicles, Praba *et al.* in [3] provided a scheme using enhanced Robust Ad-hoc On Demand Distance Vector (RAODV) protocol to detect abnormal vehicles with the speed mutation, the registration time expiring, no message exchanging with trusted vehicles, Road Side Unit (RSU) and Central Authority (CA). The simulation results showed that the scheme had a high detection rate, but there might be some problems such as lower message delivery rate, increased routing overhead with the increasing of abnormal vehicles. Alheeti *et al.* in [4] proposed an Artificial Neural Network (ANN) for outlier detection of DoS attacks in the IoVs. Yang *et al.* in [5] put forward a trust management mechanism based on Affinity Propagation (AP) clustering algorithm. Considering the constant changing of the topology structure in IoVs, abnormal vehicles could be detected gradually in the process of continuous iteration of messages by the dynamic AP clustering algorithm and mutual monitoring model.

There are lots of outlier detection achievements for traditional wireless sensor networks. However, these schemes can not be used directly for outlier detection of the IoVs due to its unique characteristics. In this paper, we first reform six existing outlier detection schemes for traditional wireless sensor networks to enable them applicable for outlier detection of IoVs, and then evaluate the comparison performances of these schemes to give an assistant reference of scheme selection for outlier detection of IoVs. The main contributions of this paper are given as follows.

- We select six outlier detection schemes and propose the process of how to use them to detect outliers of IoVs. We first propose the parament learning for constructing outlier detection models of these schemes using training data, and then give the outlier detection process using the trained models.
- To evaluate the performance of proposed outlier detection schemes, we conduct a real dataset obtained by a Fucos car travelling on an expressway. We first inject outliers to the dataset, then detect the artificial outliers using those schemes and show their comparison performances for outlier detection scheme selection reference of IoVs.

The rest of this paper is organized as follows. Section 2 proposes six outlier detection schemes for IoVs. Section 3 evaluates the comparison performances of the proposed outlier detection schemes. In Sect. 4 we conclude this paper.

2   Outlier Detection Processes

In this section, we select six outlier detection schemes which are suitable for the application scene of the IoVs, and then propose the detail processes of how to detect outliers in IoVs.

2.1   Exponential Smoothing Scheme

The exponential smoothing scheme is a special weighted moving average method, which gives a larger weight to the historical dataset that is nearer to the distance, and gives a relatively small weight that is far away from the distance. The exponential smoothing scheme can be divided into the one-time exponential smoothing scheme, the quadratic exponential smoothing scheme and the triple exponential smoothing scheme by the number of smoothing times [6].

One-Time Exponential Smoothing Scheme. Let $X = \{x_1, \cdots, x_n\}$ be set of time series, the basic formula of one-time exponential smoothing scheme is

$$y_{t+1} = \alpha x_t + y_t \tag{1}$$

where y_{t+1} is the estimated value at time $t+1$, and α is a smoothing coefficient with $0 < \alpha < 1$.

Quadratic Exponential Smoothing Scheme. One-time exponential smoothing is only suitable for the prediction of horizontal historical data, which will produce a lot of errors when it is used for the prediction of historical data with slope linear trend. For this issue, we can use the quadratic exponential smoothing scheme which is expressed as

$$S_t^{(2)} = \alpha S_t^{(1)} + (1 - \alpha)S_{t-1}^{(2)} \tag{2}$$

where $S_t^{(2)}$ is the second exponential smoothing value of the first t period, $S_t^{(1)}$ is the first exponential smoothing value of the t period, and $S_{t-1}^{(2)}$ is the second exponential smoothing value of the first $t - 1$ period. Then we can establish a corresponding predictive mathematical model as

$$\hat{Y}_{t+T} = m_t + n_t \cdot T \tag{3}$$

in which

$$\begin{cases} m_t = 2S_t^{(1)} - S_t^2 \\ n_t = \frac{\alpha}{1-\alpha}\left(S_t^{(1)} - S_t^{(2)}\right) \end{cases} \tag{4}$$

Triple Exponential Smoothing Scheme. The one-time and quadratic exponential smoothing schemes are only suitable for linear time prediction. The triple exponential smoothing scheme is required for the trend of the nonlinear change. Similarly, the essence of the scheme is smoothed on the basis of the quadratic exponential smoothing

$$S_t^{(3)} = \alpha S_t^{(2)} + (1 - \alpha)S_{t-1}^{(3)} \tag{5}$$

The corresponding mathematical prediction model is

$$\hat{Y}_{t+T} = m_t + n_t \cdot T + k_t \cdot T^2 \tag{6}$$

in which

$$\begin{cases} m_t = 3S_t^{(1)} - 3S_t^{(2)} + S_t^3 \\ n_t = \frac{\alpha}{2(1-\alpha)^2}\left[(6 - 5\alpha)S_t^{(1)} - 2(5 - 4\alpha)S_t^{(2)} + (4 - 3\alpha)S_t^3\right] \\ k_t = \frac{\alpha^2}{2(1-\alpha)^2}\left[S_t^{(1)} - 2S_t^{(2)} + S_t^{(3)}\right] \end{cases} \tag{7}$$

For outlier detection of IoVs with exponential smoothing scheme, we first learn the smoothing coefficient of the model with history training data, and then use the trained model calculate the predicted value Y. If the deviation between the predicted value Y and the actual reading H is greater than a preset threshold, the sensor reading H is determined as a fault value.

2.2   Linear Least-Squares Estimation Scheme

Linear Least-Squares Estimation (LLSE) is an important mathematical tool which seeks the best function matching of data by minimizing the square of the error [7]. Suppose that the values reported by sensors Z_1 and Z_2 in IoVs are correlated, $\hat{s}_1 (s_2)$ is the estimate value of the sensor Z_1 based on the sensory reading s_2 reported by Z_2, and s_1 is the sensory reading reported by Z_1. The specific formula is as

$$\hat{s}_1(s_2) = m_1 + \frac{\lambda_{12}}{\lambda_2}(s_2 - m_2) \tag{8}$$

$$m_1 = \frac{1}{n}(s_{11} + s_{12} + \cdots + s_{1n}) \tag{9}$$

$$\lambda_{12} = cov(s_1, s_2) = \frac{1}{n-1}\sum_{i=1}^{n}(s_{1i} - m_1)(s_{2i} - m_2) \tag{10}$$

$$\lambda_2 = var(s_2) = \frac{1}{n-1}\sum_{i=1}^{n}(s_{2i} - m_2)^2 \tag{11}$$

where $s_1 = \{s_{11}, \cdots, s_{1n}\}$, $s_2 = \{s_{21}, \cdots, s_{2n}\}$ are reading sequences of two sensor data with spatial correlation, m_1 and m_2 are the average values of Z_1 and Z_2 respectively, λ_{12} is the covariance between the readings of Z_1 and Z_2, and λ_2 is the variance of the readings of Z_2.

For outlier detection of IoVs with LLSE scheme, we first train the curve fitting function using history data, and then calculate the prediction value $\hat{s}_1$ using Eq. (8). If $|s_1 - \hat{s}_1| > \delta$ for the preselected threshold δ, we classify the sensory reading s_1 as a fault.

2.3 Neural Network Classification Scheme

Artificial neural network is an algorithm developed according to the process of human cognition. In this scheme, we only need to know the input data and the corresponding output data, and we do not need to know the mechanism of getting the output data from the input data. Artificial neural networks are trained on their own according to input and output data. The training process is that the neural network adjusts the weights of the adjacent connected nodes in the network according to the errors of the obtained output data and the real output data, and continuously runs iteratively until the errors reach the experimental allowable range [8]. In this way, when the training is over, we give an input, and the network will calculate the output according to its own adjusted weights, which is the simple principle of the neural network model.

In our experiment, the first step is to train the neural network. We collect the speed, rotation rate and distance at time t through the sensors, and then we input the three kinds of data information into the training file for data training to obtain the speed information at time $t + 1$. The training file will adjust the connection weights inside the neural network according to the errors of the result, and then the training file will use the data for training again. The program runs iteratively until the resulting errors are minimized. After the training is completed, we can input the data collected at time t containing errors into the neural network for error detection. The speed, rotation rate and distance at time t are used as input layer, and the speed at time $t + 1$ is used as output layer. When the deviation between the predicted speed value at time $t + 1$ and the collected speed value is greater than a certain threshold, the collected data is considered to be wrong.

2.4 K-Nearest Neighbor Classification Scheme

KNN algorithm is an anomaly detection algorithm based on distance. Its main principle is to judge the type of data according to the data type of the $K - Neighborhood$ of the point to be measured [9]. Firstly, we construct the data we collected at the same time into a data point X, and all the data points are constructed into a data point library X_n. Then we can check all points in the database for errors. If we want to check the correctness of point p, we first need to find the distance between point p and other points, which is recorded as $d(o, p)$, where o is any point in the vector database. Then we need to determine the K distance of point p, which is recorded as $d_k(p) = d(p, o)$, where the distance from p to o ensures that only K points in the database are in this range. At the same time, we call the point within the $K - th$ distance of the point p the $K - th$ neighborhood of p, which is denoted as $N_k(p)$. Then we need to find the

$K - reachable$ distance between all points in the $K - Neighborhood$ of point p and point p, which is denoted as $reach - dist_k(p, o) = max\{d_k(o), D(p, o)\}$. Then we can find the local reachable density of point p, which is recorded as:

$$lrd_k(p) = 1 / \left(\frac{\sum_{o \in N_k(p)} reach - dist_k(p, o)}{|N_k(p)|} \right) \tag{12}$$

Then the local anomaly factor can be calculated according to the local reachable density, which is recorded as:

$$LOF_k(p) = \frac{\sum_{o \in N_k(p)} \frac{lrd_k(o)}{lrd_k(p)}}{|N_k(p)|} \tag{13}$$

This factor represents the average of the ratio of the local reachable density of the neighboring point $N_k(p)$ of point p to the local reachable density of point p. If the ratio is less than 1, it means that the local reachable density of p is higher than that of its neighborhood, and that p is a dense point. If the ratio is greater than 1, it means that the local reachable density of p is less than that of its neighborhood, so p is more likely to be an anomaly point. After that, we correct the errors by using the method of selecting the weight of the nearest neighbor value of the distance ratio and using the repair algorithm to repair the data to get the repair result $\hat{v}$. The repair algorithm uses K groups of nearest neighbor data sets to repair the abnormal data value, that is:

$$\hat{v} = \sum_{i=1}^{k} \alpha_i v_i \tag{14}$$

where v_i is the sub-data in the ith state point in the database corresponding to the abnormal data; α_i is the weight of the sub-data in the ith state point in the database corresponding to the abnormal data; $\hat{v}$ is the repaired abnormal data.

2.5   Dynamic Bayesian Network Model

The Dynamic Bayesian Network (DBN) is actually a kind of Bayesian network with time factor whose core idea is to connect the data of two adjacent time slices. We can use DBN model to describe the vehicle data change process in any time slice, which contains two kinds of nodes in each time slice: one is the actual values and the other is the readings of vehicle sensors.

The process of building DBN model is actually the process of structure learning and parameter learning. We use PSO algorithm in [10] to learn the structure and EM algorithm in [11] to learn the parameters. For some vehicle sensor reading Y_{ti} at time t, we first calculate the probability $P(X_{ti}|Y)$ for each possible value of X_{ti} using the trained DBN model, and then select a value X_{ti} which can maximize the probability $P(X_{ti}|Y)$ as the estimated value H_{ti} for X_{ti}, where X_{ti} represents the actual value of the diagnosed sensor at time t and Y denotes all sensor readings during the t time interval. If the deviation of H_{ti} and Y_{ti} is greater than a predefined threshold, the sensor reading Y_{ti} is diagnosed as a fault.

2.6   ESTI-CS Scheme

Environmental Space Time Improved Compressive Sensing (ESTI-CS) algorithm is an algorithm based on Compressed Sensing algorithm, which combines minimum rank estimation and spatiotemporal feature interpolation algorithm to repair data. In our experiment, we first need to construct the benchmark data set, because there are data errors in the original data, so we preprocess the data and extract the data of as long as possible time series collected by sensors of 50% nodes from the original data, which can be used as the benchmark data set.

After that, we use Principal Component Analysis (PCA) to analyze the structure and temporal-spatial relationship of the data, because the data we collected includes three kinds of physical quantities, we need to use PCA to reduce the dimension for analysis. We get that the structure feature of the benchmark data set is that the benchmark data set conforms to the low rank feature, and the spatiotemporal relationship feature is that the data measured by the node sensors with similar physical location at the adjacent time are not very different. Next, we use the Compressed Sensing algorithm to process the benchmark data set and get the preliminary prediction of the complete data set. After the complete data set is obtained, the spatiotemporal feature interpolation algorithm is used to improve the data set, and the final complete data set is obtained. Assuming that the original data set is G, and we get the prediction data set $\hat{G}$, then we calculate $\left\| G - \hat{G} \right\|_F$, where $\|\cdot\|_F$ is the Frobenius norm, which is used to represent the recovery error of $\hat{G}$. The calculation rule is $\|X\|_F = \sqrt{\sum_{i,j}(x(i,j))^2}$. When the value of $\left\| G - \hat{G} \right\|_F$ is greater than the selected threshold, we think the data collected is wrong.

3   Experimental Results

In this section, we evaluate the comparison performances of the proposed outlier detection schemes on a real vehicle dataset.

3.1   Experiment Settings

To collect the sensor data used in the experiment, we prepare a Ford car to start from the Xi'an University of Electronic Science and Technology and arrive at Huayin Toll Station via the Lianhuo Expressway with the trajectory shown in Fig. 1. The vehicle data of this car is transmitted to the computer through the OBD interface. In addition, we use a synchronized smartphone to get GPS latitude and longitude information. The vehicle operating data contain information such as speed, rotation rate, temperature and so on. We mainly focus on three attributes: speed, rotation rate and GPS.

To conduct the experiment, we first translate the GPS data to distance by calculating the Euclidean distance of the GPS data between two time slots. We use one car to carry out the experiment and diagnose the abnormal value of

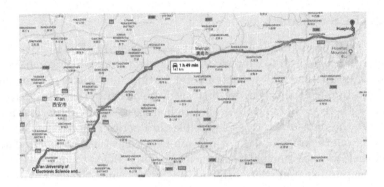

Fig. 1. The trajectory of experimental vehicle.

the experimental data of the car. However, we have collected a lot of data, and the results of experiments are also representative. We select 1200 of them as the experimental data (1000 experimental data as training data and the other 200 experimental data as diagnosed data) and artificially modify some data to produce injected outliers. The locations and the values of injected outliers are produced by random numbers. There is a certain relationship among the three physical quantities we measured, and they are not included in each other and are relatively equal. So we can inject error data into any one physical quantity, and then use the experimental data of the other two physical quantities to detect outliers. In our experiment, we select the speed for outlier detection and respectively inject 5%, 10%, 15%, 20%, 25%, 30%, 35% and 40% outliers into the speed data to evaluate the performances of the proposed schemes. To better compare the performances of the proposed methods, we use the same data in each method. In addition, we also need to set the values of two parameters, which are the smoothing factor and the optimal threshold.

Smoothing Coefficient. From the formula of the exponential smoothing, we can see that the choice of the smoothing coefficient plays an important role in the prediction effect of the exponential smoothing scheme. The general selection principle is: α should take a smaller value (generally 0.1–0.3) when the change trend of the time-series dataset is stable; α should take the median (generally 0.3–0.5) for a long-term trend; α should take a larger value (generally 0.6–0.8) when the data have a significant upward or downward trend. In the actual prediction experiment, we take several smoothing coefficient values for comparison and select the α value that makes the error smallest.

Optimal Threshold. The threshold is a decisive criterion for outlier detection. In our experiment, we use the following two heuristics for threshold selection.

– Maximum Error: If the training data has no faulty samples, we can set δ to be the maximum estimation error for the training dataset, i.e. $\delta = max\left\{|s_1 - \hat{s}_1| : s_1 \epsilon S\right\}$ where S is set of all samples in the training dataset.

– Confidence Limit: In practice, the training dataset will have faults. If we can reasonably estimate, e.g., according to historical information, we can set the proportion of error data in training samples as $p\%$, we can set δ to be the upper confidence limit of the $(1-p)\%$ confidence interval for the LLSE estimation errors on the training dataset.

3.2   Evaluation Metrics

To evaluate the performance of the proposed fault detection scheme, we define three metrics, which are outlier detection rate, false alarm rate and posterior outlier rate.

fault detection rate α it is the correctly diagnosed outlier rate, which is

$$\alpha = \frac{TP}{TP + FN} \tag{15}$$

false alarm rate β it is correct data rate that are incorrectly diagnosed as outliers, which is

$$\beta = \frac{FP}{FP + TN} \tag{16}$$

posterior fault rate σ it is the fault rate after the fault detection process, which is

$$\sigma = \frac{FP + FN}{TP + TN + FP + FN} \tag{17}$$

where TP denotes the number of detected outliers, FP denotes the number of incorrectly diagnosed outliers, TN denotes the number of correct data that are not incorrectly diagnosed as outliers, and FN denotes the number of outliers that are not detected.

3.3   Comparison Performances of the Proposed Schemes

To evaluate the comparison performances of the proposed schemes, we fix the outlier rates of rotational speed and distance at 5% and then inject outlier to the training and diagnosed data. The performance results of the proposed outlier detection schemes are the average performances of 100 times random experiments.

Figure 2(a) shows the comparison performances of outlier detection rate for the proposed schemes. We can see that the DBN has the highest outlier detection rate in most cases. And the comparison performance is quite obvious when the outlier rate relatively small. The performance of outlier detection for the exponential smoothing scheme is not ideal which has the worst outlier detection rate among the proposed schemes. The outlier detection rate of the KNN scheme exceeds that of the DBN scheme when the outlier rate reaches 40%, which shows that the KNN scheme has a better outlier detection performance when the outlier rate is high.

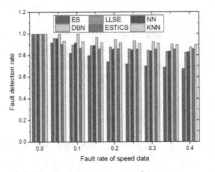

(a) Fault detection rate histogram.

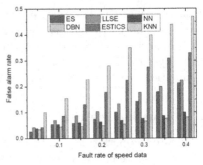

(b) False alarm rate histogram.

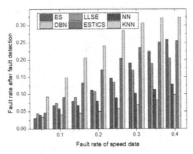

(c) Overall error rate histogram.

Fig. 2. Fault detection rate, false alarm rate and overall error rate histogram.

Figure 2(b) gives the comparison performance of the false alarm rates of the proposed schemes, which shows that the KNN scheme has the highest false alarm rate, which is even close to 50% when the outlier rate reaches 40%. The false alarm rate of the ESTI-CS scheme is the second highest which increases n quickly during the increasing of outlier data. The artificial neural network scheme is relatively stable in terms of false alarm rate, which keeps at a low level. The DBN scheme has the best performance of false alarm rate compared to other schemes, whose the comparison performance is even better when the outlier rate is higher. In addition, the neural network scheme has the second best performance of false alarm rate which is close to that of DBN.

Figure 2(c) presents the comparison performances of the overall outlier rates after outlier detection process of the proposed schemes, which tells us that KNN scheme has the posterior outlier rate. The main reason is that its false alarm rate is too high although it has the best performance of outlier detection rate. The performance of the DBN scheme is very stable which is not sensitive with the outlier rate, and its the overall outlier rate after outlier detection process maintains at a very low level. This is mainly because its false alarm rate is the lowest while it has almost the best performance of outlier detection rate. The neural network scheme has a better performance close to that of DBN, as its also has a low false alarm rate while its outlier detection performance is still good.

Discussion: Simulation results tell us that the neural network and the DBN schemes are suitable for outlier detection of IoVs with better comparison performances. But their shortcomings are that the model training needs very large computing resources. The KNN scheme is not suggested for outlier detection of IoVs although it is very simple for model training and outlier diagnosis. The LLSE scheme has the advantage of simple model training and convenient application, but it has a higher false alarm rate and posterior outlier rate. However, it is very suitable for outlier detection when the outlier rate is low (no more than 10%).

4   Conclusions

We selected six specific algorithms for simulation. In addition, we compared the error detection and correction effects of the six algorithms under different data error rates. Most of the methods used in our paper are based on thresholds, but we have not given a theoretical solution to the optimal threshold, which will be our future work.

Acknowledgments. Part of this work has been supported by National Natural Science Foundation of China (No. 61771373, 61771374, 61601357), China 111 Project (No. B16037), in part by the Fundamental Research Fund for the Central Universities (No. JB181508, JB171501, JB181506, JB181507), and "13th Five-Year" Plan Equipment Pre-Research Foundation of China (No. 6140134040216HT76001).

References

1. Zhou, Z., Gao, C., Xu, C., et al.: Social big-data-based content dissemination in internet of vehicles. IEEE Trans. Ind. Inf. **14**(2), 768–777 (2018)
2. Lu, N., Cheng, N., Zhang, N., et al.: Connected vehicles: solutions and challenges. IEEE Internet Things J. **1**(4), 289–299 (2014)
3. Praba, V.L., Ranichitra, A.: Isolating malicious vehicles and avoiding collision between vehicles in VANET. In: IEEE International Conference on Communication & Signal Processing, pp. 811–815 (2013)
4. Alheeti, K.A., Gruebler, A., Mcdonaldmaier, K.D.: An intrusion detection system against malicious attacks on the communication network of driverless cars. In: IEEE Consumer Communications and Networking Conference, pp. 916–921 (2015)
5. Zhang, M., Chen, C., Wo, T., et al.: SafeDrive: online driving anomaly detection from large-scale vehicle data. IEEE Trans. Ind. Inf. **13**(4), 2087–2096 (2017)
6. Ebrahim, B., Ozgul, S., Muammer, E.: Exponential smoothing of multiple reference frame components with GPUs for real-time detection of time-varying harmonics and interharmonics of EAF currents. IEEE Trans. Ind. Appl. **54**, 6566–6575 (2018)
7. Ballal, T., Suliman, M.A., Al-Naffouri, T.Y.: Bounded perturbation regularization for linear least squares estimation. IEEE Access **5**, 27551–27562 (2017)

8. Hayashi, H., Shibanoki, T., Shima, K., et al.: A recurrent probabilistic neural network with dimensionality reduction based on time-series discriminant component analysis. IEEE Trans. Neural Netw. Learn. Syst. **26**(12), 3021–3033 (2015)
9. Zhang, S., Li, X., et al.: Efficient kNN classification with different numbers of nearest neighbors. IEEE Trans. Neural Netw. Learn. Syst. **9**, 1774–1785 (2018)
10. Kosasih, K., Abeyratne, U.R., Swarnkar, V., et al.: Wavelet augmented cough analysis for rapid childhood pneumonia diagnosis. IEEE Trans. Biomed. Eng. **62**(4), 1185–1194 (2015)
11. Xing, Y.Y., Wu, X.Y., Jiang, P., et al.: Dynamic Bayesian evaluation method for system reliability growth based on in-time correction. IEEE Trans. Reliab. **59**(2), 309–312 (2010)

Review of Power Spatio-Temporal Big Data Technologies, Applications, and Challenges

Ying Ma[1], Chao Huang[2]($\boxtimes$), Yu Sun[3], Guang Zhao[2], and Yunjie Lei[1]

[1] Xiamen University of Technology, Xiamen 361024, China
{maying,yjl}@xmut.edu.cn
[2] Xiamen Great Power GeoInformation Technology Co., Ltd., Xiamen 361008, China
{yunjielei,gzhao}@yeah.net
[3] National Tsing Hua University, Hsinchu 30013, Taiwan
sunyu6336@163.com

Abstract. The spatio-temporal big data of the power grid has experienced explosive growth, especially the development of various power sensors, smart devices, communication devices, and real-time processing hardware, which has led to unprecedented opportunities and challenges in this field. This paper firstly introduces Power Spatio-Temporal Big Data (PSTBD) technologies based on the characteristics of grid spatio-temporal big data, followed by a comprehensive survey of relevant articles analysis in this field. Then we compare the difference between traditional power grid and PSTBD platform, and focus on the key technologies of current PSTBD and corresponding typical applications. Finally, the development direction and challenges of PSTBD are given. Through data analysis and technical discussion, we provided technical supports and decision supports for relevant practitioners in PSTBD field.

Keywords: Spatio-temporal · Security control · Power grid ·
Big data · Sensors

1 Introduction

Spatio-temporal large data of power grid refers to the collection of massive spatio-temporal data involving the safe and stable operation of power grid, energy-saving economic dispatch, power supply reliability, economic and social development analysis and so on, through various data acquisition channels such as sensors, intelligent equipment, video surveillance equipment, audio communication equipment and mobile interruption. The characteristics of Power Spatio-Temporal Big Data (PSTBD) meet the "5V3E" characteristics, as shown in Fig. 1. In addition to "3E" which is energy, exchange, and empathy, the "5V" is as follows.

Volume: Conventional power dispatching system includes hundreds of thousands of data collection points; the number of power distribution data centers often reaches tens of millions; data volume is often above TB and PB.

G. Wang et al. (Eds.): SpaCCS 2019 Workshops, LNCS 11637, pp. 197–206, 2019.
https://doi.org/10.1007/978-3-030-24900-7_16

Velocity: Decision support requires analysis of large amounts of data in a fraction of a second; real-time processing requires continuous real-time data generation.

Variety: Data types are structured, semi-structured, and unstructured data, including real-time data, historical data, text data, multimedia data, time series data and so on;

Value: Electric power enterprises realize business trend analysis, prediction and decision support, through a series of means such as data mining.

Veracity: Due to the generation technologies, acquisition means and various forms, there are a large number of inferior data in power data.

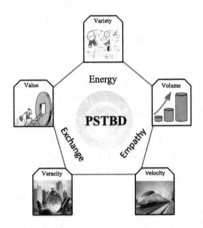

Fig. 1. Power spatio-temporal big data features

The engineering application of PSTBD technologies involves user behavior analysis, demand response analysis, equipment risk analysis, system risk assessment, energy efficiency analysis, decision support and other fields.

Most counties have formed a comprehensive and controllable big data and large grid intelligent monitoring system comprehensive solution, technical system and (international) standard specifications, environmental awareness, special communication, intelligent cloud, intelligent analysis, intelligent service, etc.

2   Relevant Articles Analysis

In order to investigate the existing research in power spatio-temporal big data, a article analysis was conducted on 14 April 2019 using the well-established and acknowledged databases, Web of Science (WoS). The query for WoS is as follows:

R1: TS = (power temporal AND big data)
R2: TS = (electric temporal AND big data)
R3: TS = (energy temporal AND big data)

R4: TS = (smart grid temporal AND big data)
R5: TS = (smart grid spatial AND big data)
R6: TS = (energy spatial AND big data)
R7 TS = (electric spatial AND big data)
R8: TS = (power spatial AND big data)
R9: TS = (electric AND big data AND spatio-temporal)
R10: TS = (power AND big data AND spatio-temporal)
R11: TS = (energy AND big data AND spatio-temporal)
R12: TS = (smart grid AND big data AND spatio-temporal)

The final query is R = (R12 OR R11 OR R10 OR R9 OR R8 OR R7 OR R6 OR R5 OR R4 OR R3 OR R2 OR R1).

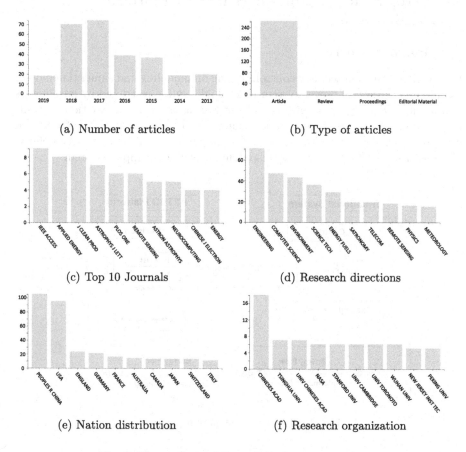

(a) Number of articles

(b) Type of articles

(c) Top 10 Journals

(d) Research directions

(e) Nation distribution

(f) Research organization

Fig. 2. The analysis of the articles in query results

The number of the articles reached 277 from 2013 to 2019 in the query results. Figure 2(a) depicts the number of the articles published every year. Almost all of these articles are research paper, as shown in Fig. 2(b). From Fig. 2(c), among the top 10 most popular journals in this field, IEEE access is ranked no. 1. Although not a traditional journal, it is a interdisciplinary field, which makes this journal a natural outlet for power spatio-temporal big data analysis.

We can see that the engineering and computer science are the largest two group among all research directions, from the Fig. 2(d). It can be seen from Fig. 2(e) that the number of articles in China has exceeded that of the United States, reaching more than 100 articles. Globally, the number of papers in China and the United States accounts for about 70% of the entire paper. Research institutions in this field have published the most papers for the Chinese Academy of Sciences, far exceeding other institutions, as shown in Fig. 2(f).

3   Power Spatio-Temporal Big Data Platform Architecture

3.1   Platform Goal

Under the traditional security control, relying on modeling and simulation model, the intelligent level of power system is not high, and is restricted by parameters and models. The depth of mining wide-area measurement information is insufficient, and timeliness is difficult to guarantee. The above aspects of research will provide basic theoretical support for the online intelligent security defense of large grid based on smart grid dispatching technical support system.

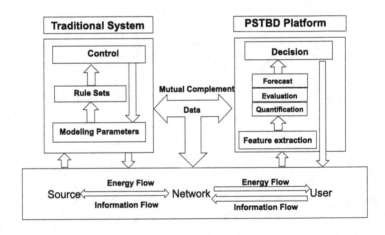

Fig. 3. Platform construction purpose.

The main goal of establishing an information-driven model based on big data technology is to meet the efficient analysis and processing of large-scale spatio-temporal sequence data of large power grids, and to dynamically track the evolution of space-time sequences of power grids. At the same time, it combines the theory of machine learning and complex network to quantitatively evaluate the multi-dimensional spatio-temporal dynamic behavior of large power grids and adaptive wide-area coordinated control.

As shown in Fig. 3, the traditional system and PSTBD platform are combined with each other to complement each other, which can further explore spatio-temporal sequence information and the evolution characteristics of the grid.

3.2 Platform Architecture

Based on the wide-area space-time sequence data of the power grid, a data analysis platform centered on Spark is constructed, as shown in Fig. 4, which mainly includes the following levels.

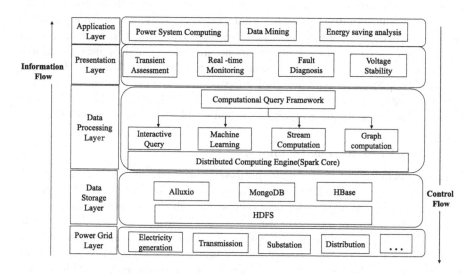

Fig. 4. Power spatio-temporal big data platform.

The platform aims to build an information-driven grid information-physical coupling system, extract key features of the dominant grid operating state from complex information networks, and utilize information-physical interactions by computation, communication, and control technologies. Further, it can improve the intelligent real-time perception of the power grid and wide-area coordinated control capabilities to ensure the safe and stable operation of the power grid.

Application layer: is an abstraction layer of communication methods designed for the processes of the entire internet computer network.

Presentation layer: graphically displays the calculation results, allowing dispatchers to visually identify the real-time operating status of the grid.

Data processing layer: is the core part of the platform. The computing framework adopts a unified programming mode, and the input and output data between components can be seamlessly shared without the need for format conversion.

Data storage layer: uses such as Hadoop distributed file system (HDFS) as the underlying distributed storage. The system, combined with a variety of NoSQL databases, provides a powerful underlying support for large-scale mass data storage.

Power grid layer: can use the business insights obtained from the data processing layer for grid abnormal event monitoring and real-time decision making to control the physical layer of the grid in real time.

4 Algorithms for PSTBD

4.1 Anomaly Data Detection Technology

Wide area measurement system coverage has also theoretically realized considerable real-time monitoring of the whole network, making real-time stability analysis and control of power grid possible [1]. At present, the data processing of wide-area measurement systems at home and abroad mainly uses the global positioning system (GPS) synchronous clock technology to transmit the voltage and phase angle measurement information of each measurement node to the dispatch center. After processing the phase angle information in the dispatch center, phase angle monitoring and transient stability control are performed.

4.2 Data Presentation Technology

Dynamic visualization can display spatio-temporal data by various means such as dynamic map and 3D GIS. The spatio-temporal data is presented in a dynamically changing map or three-dimensional scene, which can visually and vividly represent the changing process of various spatial information [2–4]. Visualization technology is widely used in smart grids to monitor and control the operation of the grid in real time, which can effectively improve the automation level of the power system [5]. Spatial information flow display technology is usually embodied in the fusion of grid parameters and existing GIS, such as three-dimensional display technology and virtual reality technology. Historical flow display technology is often applied to grid historical data management and display. It can realize real-time monitoring data of power production site or forecasting function of data trend such as power grid planning and load forecasting data. It can be seen that this technology has great application value.

4.3 Transmission and Storage Technology

Sadiq, Cai, and Zhong et al. mainly solved several key problems of big data storage, representation, processing, reliability and effective transmission, by developing reliable distributed file system, energy-optimized storage, big data duplication and efficient low-cost big data storage technology [6, 7]. And the researchers make a breakthrough on distributed non-relational big data management and processing technology; data fusion and data organization technology; research big data modeling technology; big data index technology; big data backup, copy and other technologies [8–10].

4.4   Parallel Analysis of Time and Space Big Data

Parallel analysis can minimize data migration, thereby reducing the occurrence of network contention, which will ultimately improve the efficiency of the cloud system. The two main mechanisms that must be explicitly considered are:

(1) A data location aware scheduling algorithm;
(2) Application-specific resource allocation mechanism.

In order to make the MapReduce parallel programming model easier to use, there are a variety of big data processing advanced query languages, such as Facebook's Hive [11], Yahoo's Pig [12], Sawzall [13] and so on. These high-level query languages parse the query into a series of MapReduce jobs through a parser and execute them in parallel on a distributed file system. Compared with the basic MapReduce system, the high-level query language is more suitable for users to perform parallel processing of large-scale data.

4.5   Heterogeneous Multi-data Source Processing Technology

For efficient integration, it is necessary to propose a scalable data fusion technology for multi-source and multi-layer heterogeneous data to provide resource intensive configuration for smart grid [14, 15]. According to the heterogeneous and massive characteristics of electric big data, and the data access mode of typical business applications, we can study the scalable, highly reliable and efficient power big data management technology. For the different data of different sources of supply and external non-power data in terms of data size, structural characteristics and value density, research is suitable for the optimization of the use of electrically structured, semi-structured, unstructured data.

4.6   Data Processing Technology

With the development of the Internet of Things, various large-scale real-time data processing based on real-time sensor data is becoming the key to the current EPC (epcglobal network) application construction [6]. Academia, industry and even government agencies have begun to pay close attention to big data issues and have generated a strong interest. Kiran et al. [17] implemented the operation of processing Amazon datasets using batch computing techniques. Researchers have conceptualized and abstracted this setup in the flow model [18]. In this model, data runs at high speed, one instance at a time, and the algorithm must process it under very strict spatial and temporal constraints. Streaming algorithms can use probabilistic data structures to provide quick approximation answers.

5   State of Applications

Typical applications based on PSTBD technology cover all aspects of power industry such as energy management, transmission operation, wide area control, state estimation, system monitoring, security defense, load forecasting, demand response, real-time energy management, analyzing user behavior, real-time pricing and so on, as shown in Fig. 5. Strategies, end-user real-time power demand, real-time price forecasting and other areas have achieved good application results. With the further advancement of smart grid construction, PSTBD technology will play an increasingly important role in the smart grid [19–21].

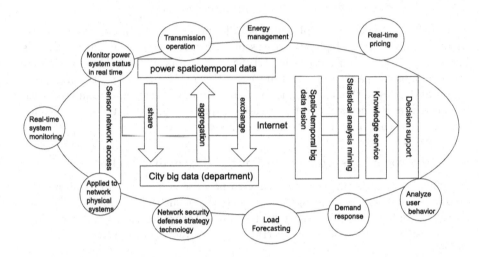

Fig. 5. Applications of PSTBD technologies.

6   Challenges and Research Directions

The concept of big data is not new, it can be used to create transparency, reveal requirements, and replace manual decisions. However, big data technology applied to power systems is still in its infancy and there is still a long way to go. We point out some of the challenges of PSTBD technology [22].

Multi-source data integration and storage. Traditional data analysis typically processes data from a single domain, so a fusion method for multiple source data sets must be found, which has different modalities, formats, and representations. In terms of big data storage, although systems such as the Hadoop distributed system seem to be viable, they still need to be customized and modified to fit the big data on the grid.

Real-time data processing technology. For some emergency applications, such as fault detection and transient oscillation detection, the response time scale is milliseconds. While cloud systems can provide fast computing services, network congestion, complex algorithms, and large amounts of data can still cause delays. A memory-based database seems to be a viable solution to this problem, and the memory-based database is used to process large amounts of kilowatt table data to better distribute power flow.

Data compression. Data compression technology is essential in wide area surveillance systems. It needs to develop its own characteristics to meet high demands of PSTBD. In addition, in order to detect transient disturbances while achieving a high compression ratio, some special compression methods are needed.

Big data visualization technology. Visualized graphs and charts provide operators with refinement and explicit changes in voltage and frequency. However, how to effectively discover and represent the correlation or trend between multi-source data is a huge challenge. Other challenges are visualization algorithms, involving information extraction, rendering, and image synthesis.

Data privacy and security. Legacy systems and inter-operability through APIs expose the grid to dangerous scenarios such as metadata spoofing, packaging, and phishing attacks. On the customer side, since data is shared between different entities, private data leaks can be a disaster and lead to cascading problems.

Acknowledgments. This work was supported in part by the National Natural Science Foundation of China (Grant No. 61502404), Natural Science Foundation of Fujian Province of China (Grant No. 2019J01851), Distinguished Young Scholars Foundation of Fujian Educational Committee (Grant No. DYS201707), Xiamen Science and Technology Program (Grant No. 3502Z20183059), and Open Fund of Key Laboratory of Data mining and Intelligent Recommendation, Fujian Province University. We thank the anonymous reviewers for their great helpful comments.

References

1. Liu, D., Xu, P., Ren, L.: TPFlow: progressive partition and multidimensional pattern extraction for large-scale spatio-temporal data analysis. IEEE Trans. Vis. Comput. Graph. **25**(1), 1–11 (2019)
2. Lu, M., Pebesma, E., Sanchez, A., Verbesselt, J.: Spatio-temporal change detection from multidimensional arrays: detecting deforestation from MODIS time series. ISPRS J. Photogram. Remote Sens. **117**, 227–236 (2016)
3. Idehen, I., Wang, B., Shetye, K., Overbye, T., Weber, J.: Visualization of large-scale electric grid oscillation modes. In: 2018 IEEE North American Power Symposium (NAPS), pp. 1–6 (2018)
4. Li, Y., Wang, Z., Hao, Y.: A hierarchical visualization analysis model of power big data. In: IOP Conference Series: Earth and Environmental Science, vol. 108, no. 5, pp. 52–64 (2018)
5. Yu, N., Shah, S., Johnson, R., Sherick, R., Hong, M., Loparo, K.: Big data analytics in power distribution systems. In: 2015 IEEE Power and Energy Society Innovative Smart Grid Technologies Conference (ISGT), pp. 1–5 (2015)
6. Sadiq, B., et al.: A spatio-temporal multimedia big data framework for a large crowd. In: 2015 IEEE International Conference on Big Data (Big Data), pp. 2742–2751 (2015)
7. Cai, H., Xu, B., Jiang, L., Vasilakos, A.V.: IoT-based big data storage systems in cloud computing: perspectives and challenges. IEEE Internet Things J. **4**(1), 75–87 (2017)

8. Zhong, R.Y., Newman, S.T., Huang, G.Q., Lan, S.: Big data for supply chain management in the service and manufacturing sectors: challenges, opportunities, and future perspectives. Comput. Ind. Eng. **101**, 572–591 (2016)

9. Tao, F., Cheng, J., Qi, Q., et al.: Digital twin-driven product design, manufacturing and service with big data. Int. J. Adv. Manuf. Technol. **94**(9–12), 3563–3576 (2018)

10. He, X., Ai, Q., Qiu, R.C., Huang, W., Piao, L., Liu, H.: A big data architecture design for smart grids based on random matrix theory. IEEE Trans. Smart Grid **8**(2), 674–686 (2017)

11. Thusoo, A., Sarma, J., Jain, N., et al.: Hive warehousing solution over map-reduce framework. In: Proceedings of the 35th International Conference on Very Large Data Bases (VLDB), Lyon, France, pp. 1626–1629. VLDB (2009)

12. Christopher, O., Benjamin, R., Utkarsh, S.: Pig Latina not-so-foreign language for data processing. In: Proceedings of the 2008 ACM SIGMOD International Conference on Management of Data, Vancouver, Canada, pp. 1099–1110. ACM (2008)

13. Rob, P., Sean, D., Robert, G., et al.: Interpreting the dataparallel analysis with Sawzall. Sci. Program. **13**(4), 277–298 (2005)

14. Prahlad, A., Gokhale, P., Kottomtharayil, R., et al.: Data mining systems and methods for heterogeneous data sources. U.S. Patent 9,405,632 (2016)

15. Kong, C., Gao, M., Xu, C., Qian, W., Zhou, A.: Entity matching across multiple heterogeneous data sources. In: Navathe, S.B., Wu, W., Shekhar, S., Du, X., Wang, X.S., Xiong, H. (eds.) DASFAA 2016. LNCS, vol. 9642, pp. 133–146. Springer, Cham (2016). https://doi.org/10.1007/978-3-319-32025-0_9

16. Wang, Y., Chen, Q., Kang, C., et al.: Clustering of electricity consumption behavior dynamics toward big data applications. IEEE Trans. Smart Grid **7**(5), 2437–2447 (2017)

17. Marinakis, V., Doukas, H., Tsapelas, J., et al.: From big data to smart energy services: an application for intelligent energy management. Future Gener. Comput. Syst. (2018). S0167739X17318769

18. Shi, H., Xu, M., Ran, L.: Deep learning for household load forecasting novel pooling deep RNN. IEEE Trans. Smart Grid **99**(1), 1 (2017)

19. Guo, B., Liu, Y., Ouyang, Y., et al.: Harnessing the power of the general public for crowdsourced business intelligence: a survey. IEEE Access **7**, 26606–26630 (2019)

20. Zhang, Y., Wang, J.: A distributed approach for wind power probabilistic forecasting considering spatio-temporal correlation without direct access to off-site information. IEEE Trans. Power Syst. **33**(5), 5714–5726 (2018)

21. Wang, J., Wang, Y., Zhang, D., et al.: Energy saving techniques in mobile crowd sensing: current state and future opportunities. IEEE Commun. Mag. **56**(5), 164–169 (2018)

22. Hossain, E., Khan, I., Un-Noor, F., et al.: Application of big data and machine learning in smart grid, and associated security concerns: a review. IEEE Access **7**, 13960–13988 (2019)

CP-MCNN: Multi-label Chest X-ray Diagnostic Based on Confidence Predictor and CNN

Huazhen Wang, Junlong Liu, Sisi Lai, Nengguang Wu, and Jixiang Du$^{(\boxtimes)}$

Huaqiao University, Xiamen 361021, China
jxdu@hqu.edu.cn

Abstract. Chest X-ray as a sensing mode is worthwhile to be paid attention in terms of its conversation and prevalence, and it as a typical multi-label problem where each example is represented by a single instance while associated with a set of labels simultaneously. Early researches on chest X-ray mainly using Convolutional Neural Network (CNN), although it has outperformance in experiment, diagnosis of chest x-ray as a typical high-risk problem, CNN lacks confidence evaluation its output to make a judgment. To solve this problem, we propose a new framework of Confidence Prediction-Multi-label Convolutional Neural Network (CP-MCNN) that plugs MCNN into Confidence Predictor. It can provide calibrated confidential evaluation for MCNN. On chestx-ray14 dataset, the experimental results show that CP-MCNN performs better than MCNN in terms of Sub-accuracy, Hamming-loss, Ranking-loss and Average Precision. Moreover, CP-MCNN can provide well-calibrated confidence prediction on chest X-ray sensor picture in order to enhance its reliability and interpretability.

Keywords: Sensor · Chest X-ray · Conformal predictor · CNN · Multi-label

1 Introduction

X-ray CT sensor is a medical sensor. The working process is as follows: firstly, X-ray CT is irradiated. Then if the X-rays are absorbed by certain parts of the human tissue, it can be detected by abnormalities in the human body (bleeding, tumors, etc.). Finally, the output size of the sensor is displayed in the form of a image. X-ray CT sensors are commonly used in Chest X-ray. Chest X-ray has the best clinical basis for lung lesions. And clinical examination of chest X-ray is a typical multi-label classification problem. Multi-label classification means that a sample can belong to multiple categories (or labels), and different categories are correlated.

Deep learning has achieved prevalent success in chest X-ray fields [9]. Among them, in 2018, Abiyev and Ma'aitah noticed that the Convolutional Neural Network (CNN) was capable of gaining a better generalization power than that

© Springer Nature Switzerland AG 2019
G. Wang et al. (Eds.): SpaCCS 2019 Workshops, LNCS 11637, pp. 207–217, 2019.
https://doi.org/10.1007/978-3-030-24900-7_17

achieved by any other deep learning [7]. CNN as for the excellent framework in deep learning, showing the characteristics of high efficiency and low error rate in the ImageNet images classification and recognition competition [16]. Thus, a new framework of Multi-label CNN (MCNN) which incorporates CNN with Multi-label learning [2,4,6,17] has been proposed. MCNN has good performance in Multi-label learning.

However, beside the significantly achievement, there is room for improvement. Diagnosis of the chest X-ray is a typical high-risk problem, which would lead to serious consequences in case of failure diagnosis. Therefore, in 2017, Iwata and Ghahramani put forward that it urgently needs confidence assessment to ensure AI security [11]. Although MCNN can automatically extract feature on data and complete very accurate pattern discrimination without manual operation, People can not control the classification process from another perspective. Consequently, MCNN lacks interpretability with respect to the effective characteristics which makes MCNN output a judgment [2]. Additionally, MCNN generally uses a fixed threshold i.e., 0.5 to obtain a multi-label prediction set without consideration the calibration of its prediction [3]. In the nutshell, the absence of calibrated confidence evaluation for MCNN hinders its effective practice.

Shafer and Vovk [10] put forward that Conformal prediction (CP) is a confidence machine that can incorporates traditional algorithms and make its output with confidence evaluation. The lack of a calibrated confidence evaluation of CNN will hinder its effective practice for high-risk medical image analysis problems e.g. chest X-ray diagnosis. CP can be applied to improve the security of single-label CNN, and it should be a promising hint of confidence prediction for MCNN [2].

Therefore, we propose a new framework CP-MCNN that plugs MCNN into the framework of CP, which not only provides multi-label prediction but appends a valid confidence to the prediction. Specially, the whole given dataset is divided into two parts, with the former is applied to construct the MCNN modeling and the latter is used to confidence prediction.

To summarize, we make the following contribution:

(1) An incidental confidence evaluation scheme for chest radiography is proposed to solve high-risk medical problems such as diagnosis of chest X-ray.
(2) We propose a new framework CP-MCNN that plugs MCNN into CP, it can further solve the problem of the absence of calibrated confidence evaluation for Multi-label CNN.
(3) We regulate the output of MCNN for nonconformity measure, which make the nonconformity score of each example agrees very well with the i.i.d characteristic.

2 Related Work

2.1 X-ray CT Sensor Principle

X-ray CT sensor is a kind of medical sensor, which transforms the physiological information of human body into electrical information with definite function relation. It extracts the body's physiological information and outputs electrical signals. The main principle is that, first of all, after the X-ray passes through the human body, a sensor is used to check the intensity of the X-ray as the output signal. Then, after X-ray CT irradiation, X-rays are absorbed in certain parts of human tissue. Finally, according to the output of the sensor, with the help of the computer, a partial image of the human body is generated. An abnormality of the body (bleeding, tumor, etc.) can be detected by an image. And in 2018, X-ray CT sensors were used as the primary test for screening patients for lung nodules [5].

2.2   Conformal Predictor

Vock et al. [13] have proposed Conformity Predictor to predict the traditional single-label instance with a well-calibrated prediction. CP infers confidece prediction p-value of each label by algorithmic randomness test, then selects those labels whose p-value greater than pre-defined significance level as region prediction [10,13]. The novelty of CP can be characterized by the calibration property of the region prediction, i.e. the accuracies of CP region prediction can be limited by the confidence level. According to CP, given the training data sequence $Z^{(t-1)} = (z_1, z_2, ..., z_{t-1})$ and the testing instance x_t, CP assumes all the possible labels $\{y : y = 1, 2, ..., Q\}$ (Q is the number of classes) being the candidate label for x_t. Thus, Q test data sequences are constructed as follows,

$$Z^{(t)y} = \{(z_1, z_2, ..., z_{n-1}, z_t^y), y = 1, 2, ..., Q\} \tag{1}$$

The p-value p_t^y is then applied to measure the degree that $Z^{(n)y}$ conforms to the independent and identical distribution (i.i.d.). Intuitively, a small p-value means that $Z^{(n)y}$ may not be an i.i.d. data sequence. It further implies that the corresponding candidate label may not be the true label.

In order to obtain the p-value p_n^y, CP designs a nonconformity measurement function $\Lambda : Z^{(n)y} \rightarrow \alpha^{(n)y}$, which maps each example z_i to a single-value nonconformity score α_i, which forms the following sequence:

$$\alpha^{(n)y} = \{(\alpha_1, \alpha_2, ..., \alpha_{n-1}, \alpha_n^y), y = 1, 2, ..., C\} \tag{2}$$

where α_i measures the degree of the nonconformity between z_i and $Z^{(n)y}$. Based on $\alpha^{(n)y}$, p-value is defined as follows:

$$p_n^y = \frac{|\{i = 1, 2, ..., n-1 : \alpha_i \geq \alpha_n^y\}| + 1}{n} \tag{3}$$

Given a significance level , which reveals the smallest threshold of the acceptation of a particular testing data sequence $Z^{(n)y}$ being the i.i.d., CP outputs region-prediction instead of point- predictions for x_n as follows,

$$\tau_n^\varepsilon = \{y : p_n^y > \varepsilon, y = 1, 2, ..., C\} \tag{4}$$

An error occurs when the prediction set τ_n^ε does not contain the true label y_n of the testing instance x_n. It has been proven that in online learning setting the error rate of CP is not greater than significance level ε, that is,

$$P\{p_n^y(z_1, z_2, ..., z_{n-1}, z_n^y) \le \varepsilon\} \le \varepsilon \tag{5}$$

3   The Framework of CP-MCNN

3.1   The Theory of CP-MCNN

In this paper, a new framework CP-MCNN that plugs MCNN into the CP framework is proposed (see Fig. 1).

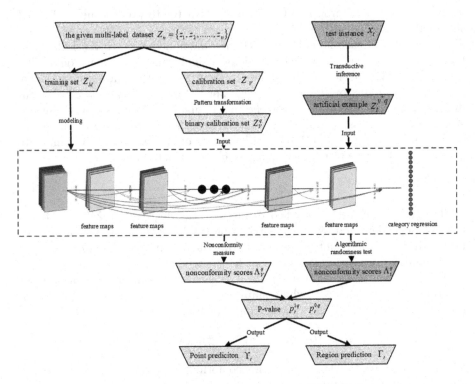

Fig. 1. The theoretical framework of CP-MCNN

Learning Setting. Given a serial of data: $Z_n = \{z_1, z_2, ..., z_n\}$ and a testing instance x_t, where the data $z = (x, Y)$ is represented by a high-dimensional instance and a label vector $Y = \{y^q : q = 1, 2, ..., Q\}$, with Q being the size of multi-label set and $y^q \in \{0, 1\}$ being the indicator of the existence of the qth label. Then Z_n is further divided into two parts, the training dataset $Z_M = \{z_1, z_2, ..., z_m\}$ where $m < n$ and the validation dataset

$Z_V = \{z_{m+1}, z_{m+2}, ..., z_n\}$. Based on Z_M , the MCNN model is constructed using Eq. (1). Then the algorithmic randomness test is executed based on Z_V and x_t, where the nonconformity scores are supported by the hidden information (i.e.,MCNN model) from Z_M. It is clear that CP-MCNN utilizes the information of all the serial of data Z_n for confidence prediction.

Pattern Transformantion. At this stage, the multi-label learning problem is decomposed into Q independent classification problems. All the data of qth class in Z_V is recorded as Z_V^q, where $Z_V = \{Z_V^q, q = 1, 2, ..., Q\}$. For the qth classification, the serial of set nonconformity scores is denoted as $\Lambda_V^q = \{\alpha_l^q, l = m + 1, m + 2, ..., n : q = 1, 2, ..., Q\}$. For the x_t, $z_t^{y^*q} = \{y = 0, 1 : 1 = 1, 2, ..., Q\}$,where y^* represents label $y^q = 0$ or $y^q = 1$ respectively. Thus the corresponding nonconformity scores are termed as $\Lambda_t^q = \{\alpha_t^y q, y = 0, 1; q = 1, 2, ...Q\}$.

Compututation P-Value. A label-wise p-value is computed by selecting different set of nonconformity scores according to label. The p-value for each possible classification is formalized as follows:

$$p_t^{1q} = \frac{\left|\left\{i = 1, 2, ..., h^1 : a_i^{1q} \geq a_t^{1q}\right\}\right| + 1}{h^1 + 1} \tag{6}$$

$$p_t^{0q} = \frac{\left|\left\{i = 1, 2, ..., h^0 : a_i^{0q} \geq a_t^{0q}\right\}\right| + 1}{h^0 + 1} \tag{7}$$

where h^1 is the size of the subset whose label is $y^q = 1$ in Z_V and h^0 is that of example with label being $y^q = 0$, therefore,$h^1 + h^0 = n - m$. Douding the smallest threshold of the acceptation of artificial label y^* being true label for test instance x_t. Thus, both the binary relevance p-value p_t^{1q} and $p_t^0 q$ are compared by ε. The region prediction will be formed $\Gamma_t = \{\{y : p_q^y > \varepsilon, y = 0, 1\}, q = 1, 2, ...Q\}$. The region prediction for the qth binary classification is characterized as confidence prediction of CP-MCNN.

3.2 Nonconformity Measure of CP-MCNN

The key technique of CP-MCNN is the nonconformity measure which maps an example to a score $\Lambda : Z_M \times z \to \mathbb{R}$. The significance behind the nonconformity score $\Lambda(Z_M, z)$ is that it should measure how strange z to the training dataset Z_M. A standard choice of $\Lambda(Z_M, z)$ is $\Lambda(\{Z_M, z) := \Delta(y, o^y)$ where o^y is the label-conditional output based on the category regression of MCNN model, i.e., o^y is the 1 minus regression probability of MCNN if the true label y is o. The specification of CP-MCNN lies on the trick which takes the label y and the output value o^y into account. The detailed assignments are shown as follows:

$$\Lambda(Z_M, z) := \Delta(y, o^y) := \begin{cases} \alpha = \frac{1}{o^y + r} & o^y \geq 0.5, y \in \{0, 1\} \\ \alpha = \frac{1}{1 - o^y + r} & o^y < 0.5, y \in \{0, 1\} \end{cases} \tag{8}$$

where $r \in [0, 1]$ is a smooth parameter.

3.3   The Algorithmic Schema of CP-MCNN

The algorithmic schema of CP-MCNN is formalized as Algorithm 1:

Algorithm 1: CP-MCNN

Input: the given dataset $Z_n = \{z_1, z_2, ..., z_n\}$ and a testing instance x_t,
   where $z = (x, Y)$, $Y = \{y^q : q = 1, 2, ..., Q\}$, $y^q \in \{0, 1\}$
Output: point-prediction Υ_t or region-prediction Γ_t

1. **Dataset division:**
   Dividing $Z_n = \{z_1, z_2, ..., z_n\}$ into $Z_M = \{z_1, z_2, ..., z_m\}$ where $m < n$ and
   the validation dataset $Z_V = \{z_{m+1}, z_{m+2}, ..., z_n\}$.
2. **MCNN modeling:**
   Based on Z_M, the MCNN model is constructed by ChexNet introduced in
   Section 2.1.
3. **Pattern transformation:**
   Decomposing Z_V into Q independent binary classification problems.
4. **Nonconformity measuremet:**
   for $q = 1$ **to** Q **do**
   Computing the serial of single-value nonconformity scores $\Lambda_V^q = \{\alpha_l^q, l = m+1, ..., n\}$, Using Equation (9)
   end
   for $q = 1$ **to** Q **do**
   Assigning both artificial label $y^q = 0$ and $y^q = 1$ to test instance x_t respectively, then computing two nonconformity scores $\Lambda_t^q = \{\alpha_t^{yq}, y = 0, 1\}$, using
   Equation (9)
   end
5. **P-value computation:**
   for $q = 1$ **to** Q **do**
   Computing the label-wise p-values p_t^{1q} and p_t^{0q} for the test instance x_t using
   Equation (7-8)
   end
6. **Point-prediction output:**

$$\Upsilon_t = \{y : \max p_t^{yq}, y = 0, 1; q = 1, 2, ...Q\} \tag{9}$$

7. **(optional)Region-prediction output:**
   For given significance level ε, the output is:

$$\Gamma_t = \{\{y : p_q^y > \varepsilon, y = 0, 1\}, q = 1, 2, ...Q\}d \tag{10}$$

Point-Prediction. In the case of point-prediction of CP-MCNN, the prediction(output) $\Upsilon_t = \{y : \max p_t^{yq}, y = 0, 1; q = 1, 2, ...Q\}$ forms a Q-dimension vector according $q^t h$ being 1 or 0, i.e. the presence or absence of the $q^t h$ classification. Then CP-MCNN is applied to test T instances with 5 Multi-Label learning evaluation metrics [12,15], i.e. Subset Accuracy, Hamming-loss, Coverage, Ranking-loss and Average precision, are used to measure the performance of CP-MCNN.

Region-Prediction. In the case of region-prediction of CP-MCNN, the output prediction $\Gamma_t = \{\{y : p_q^y > \varepsilon, y = 0,1\}, q = 1,2,...Q\}$ forms Q region-predictions according Q separate category. For the qth category, the region-prediction $\Gamma_t^q = \{y : p_q^y > \varepsilon, y = 0,1\}$ belongs to binary classification with candidate label 0 or 1. Then CP-MCNN is applied to test T instances according four efficiency metrics, i.e., certain prediction, favorite prediction, empty prediction, and the performance of CP-MCNN for each category can be demonstrated by Accuracy [1].

4 Experiments and Discussion

4.1 Experimental Setup

Experimental Setup. Experiment CP-MCNN based on ChestX-ray [14]. Each image scaled to 224 * 224 and normalized on the mean and standard deviation of ImageNet training set. At the same time, we also augment the number of training data by random horizontal fillping. Entire dataset is divided into 70% for training, 20% for validation and 10% for testing.

Constructed MCNN model make reference to CheXNet [8] with similar structure configuration, except the network weights are randomly initialized, and the Adam is used to optimize network with parameter $\beta_1 = 0.9$ and $\beta_2 = 0.999$, and the batch size is 32, and the initial learning rate is 0.001.

There are two parameters of CP-MCNN is important: the size of Z_v and smooth parameter γ for nonconformity measurement in CP-MCNN algorithm. Optimal setting is picked by grid searching, i.e. 20%, 15%, and 12% is used for selecting Z_v and the smooth parameter is 0, 0.1, and 0.5.

4.2 Experimental Performance of CP-MCNN

Given testing chest x-ray image as the input of CP-MCNN. CP-MCNN will output two types output, point-prediction and region prediction. We show the experimental results of two samples in Fig. 2, the result of point-prediction is a 14 dimensional vector. the result of region-prediction is a 14-dimensional vector with each element as a set.

The Performance of Point-Prediction. The experimental results are based on the test dataset, i.e. 1504 instances. The performance of MCNN serves as the baseline for CP-MCNN. The traditional MLL evaluation metrics are computed and demonstrated in Table 1.

It concludes that the p-value of CP-MCNN instead of the softmax probability of MCNN serves as the category regression is also effective in term of point-prediction.

Image	Point Prediction	Region Prediction($\varepsilon = 0.05$)
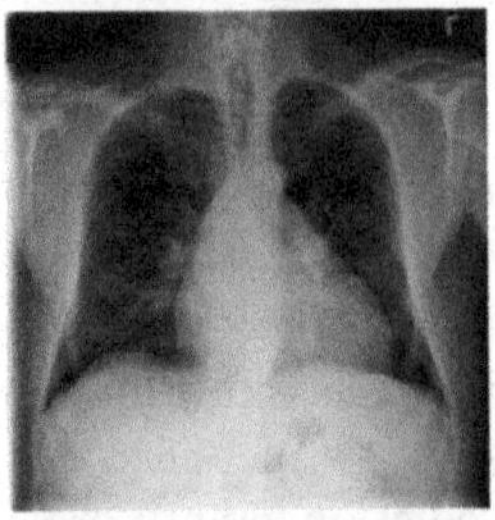	{1, 0, 0, 1, 1, 1, 1, 0, 0, 0, 0, 1, 0, 0}	{ {0}, {0}, {0}, {0,1}, {0}, {0}, {0}, {0}, {0}, {0}, {0}, {0,1}, {0}, {0}, {0} }
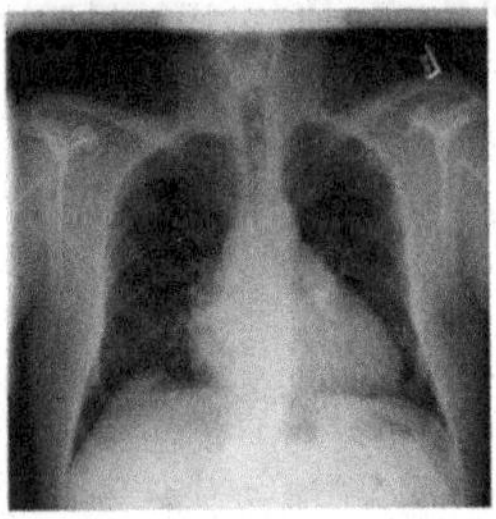	{1, 1, 1, 0, 1, 1, 0, 1, 1, 0, 1, 1, 1, 0}	{ {1,0}, {1,0}, {0}, {0,1}, {0}, {0}, {0}, {0}, {0}, {0}, {0}, {0,1}, {0}, {0}, {1,0} }

Fig. 2. Comparison of point prediction and region prediction

Table 1. The comparison of CP-MCNN and MCNN

Algorithims	Evaluation metrics				
	Subset-Accuracy	Hamming-loss	Coverage	Ranking-loss	Average precision
CP-MCNN	**0.3238**	**0.1186**	**5.5365**	0.3428	**0.6252**
MCNN	0.1655	0.2725	4.7034	**0.2921**	0.6167

The Preformance of Region Prediction. In this section, the empirical result of the calibration of CP-MCNN is demonstrated for Chestx-ray14 binary classification. For the sake of comparison, we proposed the calibrate of MCNN, using its softmax regression as teh counterpart of p-value of CP-MCNN.

Recalling the significance level and confidence are complementary, with the sum of them being 1. The distributions of accuracy against confidence can be depicted in line with the x-axis referring confidence and the y-axis referring the accuracy. Limited by space, we take the results of pleural Thickening as an example.

Figure 3 demonstrates the calibration lines of CP-MCNN and MCNN against the baseline of diagonal line. The calibration distribution of CP-MCNN is overwhelmingly high over the baseline, which reveals conservative valid property. On the contrary, the calibration line runs across the baseline calibration, which reveals non-validity property. Although the validity property of MCNN can be found in some binary classifications, but the validity of CP-MCNN has been demonstrated on allover binary classifications which validates the theoretically proven valid calibration.

Except for the test calibration property, the prediction efficiency is another main consideration of CP-MCNN algorithm. We focus on three confidence-dependent efficiency criteria in terms of certain prediction, favorite prediction and empty prediction. The comparative results of CP-MCNN against the baseline MCNN are depicted in Figs. 4, 5 and 6 respectively. It can be seen from Figs. 3, 4 and 5, CP-MCNN prevalently outperforms MCNN with respect to efficiency metric. In terms of certain prediction, the higher value is preferred. The distribution of certain prediction of CP-MCNN hangs over that of MCNN, which reveals only one candidate label in the binary region-prediction and reduces the users confusion for select the true label. Similarly, the distribution of favorite prediction of CP-MCNN dramatically hangs over that of MCNN, which reveals that most of the only candidate label in the binary region-prediction is exactly true and guarantees the practicable effectiveness. On the other way, the lower position of empty prediction line is preferred. The performance of CP-MCNN also demonstrates the rare cases of both p-values being small, i.e. taking advantage

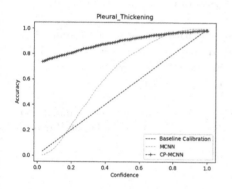

Fig. 3. Calibration

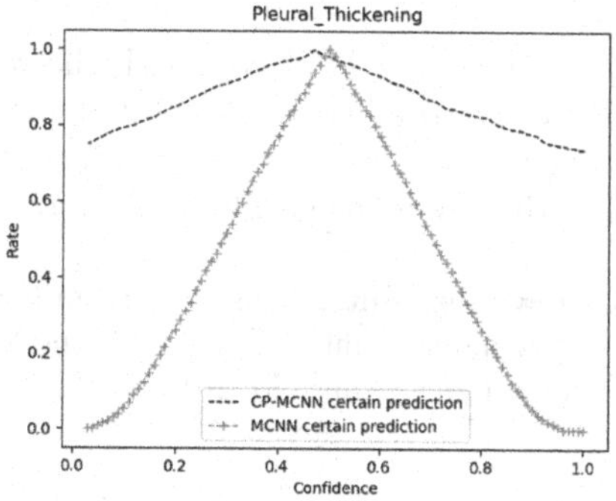

Fig. 4. Certain prediction

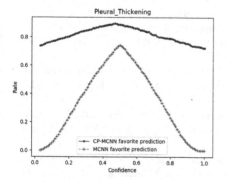

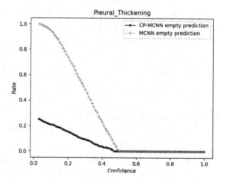

Fig. 5. Favorite prediction

Fig. 6. Empty prediction

of the label-wise p-value computation, CP-MCNN can always specify different label with distinct p-value and also support the practicable effectiveness.

5 Conclusion

In order to solve the problem that the absence of confidence of MCNN, a new framework of CP-MCNN is proposed for abnormal detection of Lung disease in Chest X-ray image, which not only provides multi-label prediction but appends a valid confidence to the prediction. Accordingly, a label-wise p-value computation method is developed to promote the prediction efficiency. The results of Chest X-ray data set shows that CP-MCNN is superior to MCNN in terms of Subset-Accuracy, Hamming-loss, Coverage and Average Precision. With the results of their evaluation indicators are respectively 0.3239, 0.1186, 5.5365, 0.6252, while in MCNN they are 0.1655, 0.2725, 4.7034, 0.6167. As for region prediction, CP-MCNN prevalently outperforms MCNN with respect to efficiency metric. Similarly, the distribution of favorite prediction of CP-MCNN dramatically hangs over that of MCNN, which reveals that most of the only candidate label in the binary region-prediction is exactly true and guarantees the practicable effectiveness.

With the CP-MCNN model, the relevant algorithms will be more reliability and interpretability and this model can be applied to medical sensing field. In the future, we will design more accurate nonconformity measure functions to make the confidence evaluation more reliable in chest X-ray.

Acknowledgments. This work is supported by National Natural Science Foundation of China under Grant No. 61673186, the Natural Science Foundation of Fujian Province in China under Grant No. 2012J01274.

References

1. Balasubramanian, V., Ho, S.S., Vovk, V.: Conformal prediction for reliable machine learning: theory, adaptations and applications (2014)
2. Gao, L., Wang, J., Fan, Y., Chen, N.: Robust visual tracking based on convolutional neural networks and conformal predictor. Acta Optica Sinica **37**(8), 0815003 (2017)
3. Madjarov, G., Kocev, D., Gjorgjevikj, D., Džeroski, S.: An extensive experimental comparison of methods for multi-label learning. Pattern Recogn. **45**(9), 3084–3104 (2012)
4. Li, Z., Zheng, Y., Zhang, C., Shi, Z.: Combining deep feature and multi-label classification for semantic image annotation. J. Comput.-Aided Des. Comput. Graph. **30**(2), 318 (2018)
5. Dewey, M., Kachelrieß, M.: Fundamentals of X-ray computed tomography: acquisition and reconstruction. In: Sack, I., Schaeffter, T. (eds.) Quantification of Biophysical Parameters in Medical Imaging, pp. 325–339. Springer, Cham (2018). https://doi.org/10.1007/978-3-319-65924-4_14

6. Mojoo, J., Kurosawa, K., Kurita, T.: Deep CNN with graph laplacian regularization for multi-label image annotation. In: Karray, F., Campilho, A., Cheriet, F. (eds.) ICIAR 2017. LNCS, vol. 10317, pp. 19–26. Springer, Cham (2017). https://doi.org/10.1007/978-3-319-59876-5_3
7. Abiyev, R.H., Ma'aitah, M.K.S.: Deep convolutional neural networks for chest diseases detection (2018)
8. Rajpurkar, P., et al.: CheXNet: radiologist-level pneumonia detection on chest x-rays with deep learning 1711, 1 November 2017. http://adsabs.harvard.edu/abs/2017arXiv171105225R
9. Schmidhuber, J.: Deep learning in neural networks: an overview (2014)
10. Shafer, G., Vovk, V.: A tutorial on conformal prediction. J. Mach. Learn. Res. **9**, 371–421 (2008). <Go to ISI>://000256642000002
11. Iwata, T., Ghahramani, Z.: Improving output uncertainty estimation and generalization in deep learning via neural network Gaussian processes (2017)
12. Tsoumakas, G., Katakis, I.: Multi-label classification: an overview. Int. J. Data Warehouse. Mining (IJDWM) **3**(3), 1–13 (2007)
13. Vovk, V., Gammerman, A., Shafer, G.: Algorithmic Learning in a Random World. Springer, New York (2005). https://doi.org/10.1007/b106715
14. Wang, X., Peng, Y., Lu, L., Lu, Z., Bagheri, M., Summers, R.M.: Chestx-ray8: hospital-scale chest x-ray database and benchmarks on weakly-supervised classification and localization of common thorax diseases. In: IEEE Conference on Computer Vision and Pattern Recognition (CVPR), pp. 3462–3471 (2017)
15. Zhang, M., Zhou, Z.: A review on multi-label learning algorithms (2013)
16. Zhao, H.J.W.C.C.: Pulmonary tuberculosis detection model of chest x-ray images using convolutional neural network, 8 July 2018
17. Zhu, J., Liao, S., Yi, D., Lei, Z., Li, S.Z.: Multi-label CNN based pedestrian attribute learning for soft biometrics. In: International Conference on Biometrics, pp. 535–540 (2015)

Naïve Approach for Bounding Box Annotation and Object Detection Towards Smart Retail Systems

Pubudu Ekanayake[1]([✉]), Zhaoli Deng[1], Chenhui Yang[1]([✉]), Xin Hong[2]([✉]), and Jang Yang[3]

[1] Computer Science Department, School of Information Science and Engineering, Xiamen University, Xiamen 361005, China
`pubudu1ekanayake@gmail.com`, `304628356@qq.com`, `chyang@xmu.edu.cn`
[2] College of Computer Science and Technology, Huaqiao University, Xiamen 361021, China
`xinhong@hqu.edu.cn`, `10409035@qq.com`
[3] Cognitive Science Department, Sixth College, University of California, San Diego, CA 92092, USA

Abstract. It is becoming a trend that companies use smart retail stores to reduce the selling cost, by using the sensor technologies. Deep convolutional neural network models which are pre-rained for the Object detection task achieve state-of-the-art result in many benchmark. However, when applying these algorithms to the intelligent retail system to help automated checkout, we need to reduce the manual labelling cost of making retail data sets, and to achieve real-time demand while ensuring accuracy. In our paper, we propose a naive approach to get first portion of the bounding box annotations for a given custom image dataset in order to reduce manual cost. Experimental results show that our approach helps to label the first set of images in short time of period. Further, the custom module we designed helped to reduce the number of parameters by 41.77% for the YOLO model maintaining the original model's accuracy (85.8 mAP).

Keywords: Smart retail system · Object detection · Bounding box annotation · Convolutional neural network · YOLO

1 Introduction

Some tech companies such as Amazon and Orange do researches and developments of smart retail stores with combining with the cutting edge technologies to reduce the selling cost. These newest technologies include the sensor technology, computer vision technology, AI technology and much more as either stand alone or a combination. Unlike in traditional retail stores, in smart retail stores the store automatically identifies and calculate the price for the products in a buying process. By implementing the smart retail stores, they help to reduce

G. Wang et al. (Eds.): SpaCCS 2019 Workshops, LNCS 11637, pp. 218–227, 2019.
https://doi.org/10.1007/978-3-030-24900-7_18

the requirement of human employees in the selling activities for a store. Further, the requirement of monitoring the products will also be reduced due to the monitoring capabilities of a smart retail store.

When considering the smart retail stores, much literature can be found which uses RFID technology [1]. When use RFID sensors we need to tag each object with the RFID sensors. However, with the development of the AI field and computer vision techniques, now most of the companies try to attach the innovations from the AI to smart retail stores. Paper [2] discusses about the technologies used in the Amazon go smart store. The research paper [3] has developed a smart checkout system using the object detection and classification algorithms. They have used YOLO [4,5] object detection algorithm and another trained classifier to identify the object category type. Further, much work can be found under the product detection and classification in the recent past years. Paper [6] tried to categorize thousands of fine-grained products with few training samples. Nonparametric probabilistic models were used for initial detections and then used CNNs where applicable. Paper [7] used active learning process to improve the recognitions in their models continuously. Papers [8–10] focus about recognizing and finding the misplaced products in the shelves using different techniques such as BoW techniques, classical feature extraction procedures (SIFT,HoG), DNN, etc. Image annotations, many approaches were taken to reduce the bounding box annotation cost in recent past years. Few are box verification series [11], point annotations [12,13] and eye tracking [14]. Among above the paper [11] has produces much quality detectors at low cost. Apart from above mentioned approaches human supervision methods also used for bounding box annotation [15–17].

Our designed solution includes a camera to capture the moving object/product in the smart store environment. It removes some of the issues of shelf monitoring methods had. In the coming phases, we will improve our project by applying motion sensors and heat sensors to improve the current results. Further, we will experiment with Reinforcement Learning methods by using RFID sensors to train models. Experimental results show that our designed custom module helped to reduce the number of parameters in the YOLO object detection model by 41.77% while maintaining the original accuracy.

2   System Design of Smart Retail Store

Our system (prototype) consists of a shelf equipped with image sensor, object detection model, product dataset and cloud server.

Our dataset is made up of product images. As shown in the red box in the Fig. 1, we make a training dataset based on our method. The original image dataset is not labelled, and our method used to annotate the bounding boxes for original images and generate the annotation files (.xml). The advantage of our method is that it can reduce the cost of manual labelling.

At the moment, Our prototype is only equipped with image sensors. As shown in the green box in the Fig. 1, Our sensor will capture images when customers shop. These images will be passed as input to our object detector. Then the detector outputs the category type of the product and its coordinates on of the detected frame, and the output is further analyzed to obtain the user's purchase list. Our main contribution is to design a new module to reduce the computational complexity of the model. Most importantly we placed our sensors to avoid some complexities such as monitoring the shelf, counting the number of products inside the shelf, etc. However, in an indirect manner our solution helps to monitor the shelves.

As we know the packaging of the product is frequently updated. So our model also needs to be updated. However to avoid the problems occurred for updating the system regular basis will be handled by uploading the trained model to a cloud server. Hence, we can train the models for new data in the back-end and update the cloud server model without stopping the smart retail system in the front-end, which leads to encourage the small retail companies to grab the new technology.

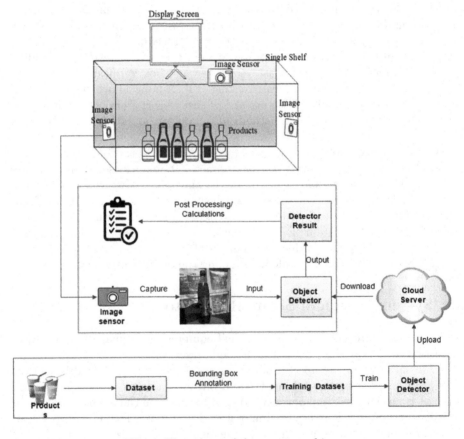

Fig. 1. Flow chart of the smart cambin.

3   Proposed Method

In this section, we will introduce our method and algorithm details.In addition,we will introduce the module we designed to reduce the computational complexity.

3.1   Naïve Bounding Box Annotation

Our approach requires a pre-training model, a feature extractor and trained a simple classifier. Its procedure is shown in Fig. 2. Image dataset which is required to be annotated will be fed into the pre-trained object detection model. From the pre-trained object detector we get the top-left and bottom-right corner coordinates of the detections. Then we crop image based on these coordinates. Next we extract feature vectors from cropped images by using the feature extractor (VGG16 [18]). Then we use simple classifiers to classify (we already trained a logistic regression classifier from very small number of cropped images) these features to get their classification categories. Finally it generates the annotation file (in .xml format) containing the coordinate information and the object category.

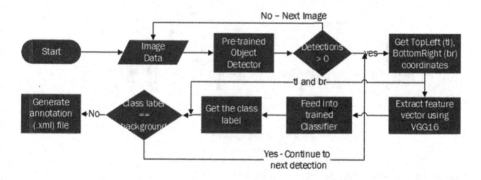

Fig. 2. Naïve bounding box annotation approach–flow chart.

The public pre-trained object detection model mentioned before is trained on large datasets such as COCO [19], iNaturalist Species Detection Dataset [20], etc. When training the simple classifiers, approximately 50 good-cropped images were selected for each category type and 446 cropped images as background including the hard negatives. 1266 total cropped images were used in training the simple feature classifier.

We extract feature maps for cropped images. Features are extracted for the images to train a simple classifiers (SVM/Logistic Regression). We use VGG16 [18] model (without the final fully connected layers) which is trained on "ImageNet" [21] dataset as the feature extractor. Pre-training model is used to extract feature maps with rich features, which our small dataset does not represent. We used data augmentation method while extracting the feature vectors. Hence, we were able to increase the number of extracted feature samples for training the classifier that led to increase the accuracy of the classifier almost by 4.0% compared to the feature set, which used without data augmentation.

Manual annotation is reduced by this method. After the annotation, we have done a human supervision and incorrectly, annotated images and annotations (xml files) were removed. Using the annotated images, we can start training our object detector to annotate the rest of the images (similar to active learning approaches) and the procedure mentioned in [22].

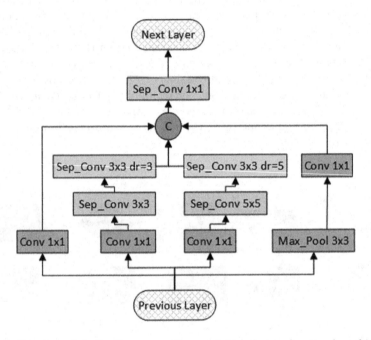

Fig. 3. Designed module for the proposed convolutional neural network architecture. dr = dilation rate.

3.2 Custom Module

Basically to design our proposed architecture we have used the YOLOV2 [4] (tiny-yolo version) algorithm. We have tried out few different architectures for the feature extraction part of the network while using the yolo algorithm itself (loss function). For the proposed module and the architecture from us, used the concept about depthwise convolutions followed by pointwise convolutions mentioned in the MobileNetV1 [23] and paper [24] to reduce the computational complexity of the model by decreasing the number of matrix multiplicative operations. Further, we modified the architecture to focus on nearby features aswell using the dilated convolutions with normal convolutions inspired by the paper RFBNet [25]. However, to reduce the computational complexity we have followed the concept of Depthwise Convolutions from [25] for the dilated convolutions as well for designed module. Output number of activations were decided by considering the paper [26] and multiplying the values mentioned in the original paper by factor 1/2. We could not do any more experiments on fine-tuning those values. Hence modules designed (Fig. 3) by us is basically the combination of Depthwise Convolutions [23] and Dilated Convolutions [25] which used in a manner in the paper GoogleNet [26] with 2 branches.

Model Serving. Should be done in a cloud platform and while maintaining a model in the local machines when considering the smart retail system. Once the smart retail system is up and running we should perform model training and model updating in the backend without stopping the smart retail system. We happened to found that the best way to perform this task is using a cloud platform. Train the models, update the weight files in the backend, and update it in the cloud system. Therefore, without any interruptions and with very small delay we can update the local machines in the smart retail system.

4   Result

In this section, we show some results on the experiments conducted during working on the project.

Table 1. Accuracies for cropped image classifier – Naïve bounding box annotation

	Accuracy	
Classifier model	W/O augmentation	Augmentation
SVM	88.30%	92.00%
Logistic regression	88.41%	92.00%
CNN	-	92.91%

4.1   Simple Classifiers

We have trained Simple classifiers to classify the cropped images. As shown in the Table 1 there is a significant improvement of the accuracy when using the features extracted with the data augmentation. However, we have not noticed any significant different of training SVM model, Logistic Regression model and CNN model. For our project we choose the Logistic Regression model as the classifier. In generally we suggest it would be much easier to go with logistic regression model than other two models as the SVM took considerably large amount of time to train.

Fig. 4. Some image results obtained from Naïve bounding box annotation.

Naive Bounding Box Annotation. Figure 4 shows some of the results taken from the naive bounding box annotation experiments. As we can see that for the custom image datasets, the proposed naïve bounding box annotation method could be used and obtained some good results. Object localization was done using the pre-trained object detector, and classification was done using the trained logistic regression model. Sample results show, two bounding boxes in each image. One is the ground-truth bounding box, which was drawn by the humans manually. The other bounding box and the label was predicted by our naive bounding box annotation approach.

Table 2. Results for naive bounding box annotation

Model	Image dataset	Detections	(%)	Time(h)
mask_rcnn_inception_resnet	RPC [27]	14,921	27.76	8.6
mask_rcnn_inception_resnet	Custom dataset	734	56.38	0.3
faster_rcnn_resnet50_coco	Raccoon dataset	112	56.00	0.02

Table 2 depicts the results, if IoU (intersection over union) of the detections/predicted boxes and the ground truth boxes are equal or greater than 0.75. Last column represents the time taken to perform the bounding box annotations for the image datasets in hours. The results suggests that specially for a large image dataset we can use our naive image bounding box annotation approach to get the first set of bounding box annotations for a custom image dataset. We used only singe objects training images from RPC [27] image dataset. Since the RPC [27] image dataset has 53,739 training images in total.

4.2 Results for Some Experiments Conducted on Object Detection

Object detection was done using a video stream taken from single camera. As shown in the Table 3 the best mAP results are achieved by the Tiny YoloV2 [6] model. It has the second highest number of parameters and second slowest FPS speed among the experimented object detection models. For the real time applications mobilentV2 [23] is quite good with considerably low number of parameters and a better speed compared to the other models. The model we proposed has very low number of parameters and competitive mAP percentage

Table 3. Comparisons done within smaller one-stage object detectors, which our custom data set trained.

Model	Input layer size	mAP (%)	FPS	# of parameters (millions)
Tiny yolo v2	416 × 416	85.80	2.02	15.8
SSDMobilenetV2	300 × 300	68.04	7.06	(approximately) 3.4
SSD (VGG16 backbone)	300 × 300	68.31	0.80	25.7
MobilenetV2 (as backend)	301 × 301	67.02	3.56	3.4
Ours	416 × 416	77.47	2.16	1.2
Ours	301 × 301	69.84	3.93	1.2

Table 4. Effectiveness of the custom module.

Model	Input layer size	mAP (%)	FPS	# of parameters (millions)
Tiny yolo v2	416 × 416	85.80	2.02	15.8
Tiny yolo v2 – replaced module	416 × 416	86.32	2.41	9.2

to SSDMobilenetV2 model architecture and having much faster frame rate compared to Tiny Yolo V2 [6]. Comparing our model which has 416 × 416 input layer size and the Tiny YoloV2 model, our model got low accuracy while passing the FPS speed and maintaining very low number of learning parameters (almost 90% reduction) which indicates it required very small storage capacity. Hence, we hope this model architecture can be used in mobile applications. We hope the FPS speed can be increased by replacing the 5 × 5 Seperable Convolutions in the early phase of our designed network with the 3 × 3 seperable convolutions.

Original tiny yolo uses size 416 for the input image size while SSD MobileNet models used 300 and our model used 301 as input image size. We believe that input image size and the higher number of parameters lead to achieve higher number of mAP for the Tiny Yolo V2 model. MobileNetV2 architecture design used only 3 × 3 kernel sizes and 1 × 1 kernel sizes.

Effectiveness of the Custom Module. We performed a simple experiment to check the effectiveness of the designed custom module. We replaced last second and third to the last layers of the original Tiny-YOLO model with the designed custom module. Comparison results with the original Tiny-YOLO model was given in the Table 4. We have used the custom image dataset for this experiment. According to the results, we were able to reduce the number of parameters of the model by 41.77% while maintaining the original result with a slight increase of the FPS speed.

5   Conclusion

We have proposed a system architecture for a smart retail system in this paper and further made 3 major contributions in this paper: (1) propose a naïve approach to get first portion of the bounding box annotations for a given custom image dataset. (2) A shallower and lightweight network architecture. (3) Novel module design considering the receptive fields of convolutions more at the end of the architecture. While discussing above major facts we describe the application of Convolutional Neural Networks and Object tracking to build a Smart Retail store. Using our proposed naïve bounding box annotation method, it reduces largely manual work, which has to be done.

We have used a simple camera to capture the environment and performed object detection. Further, we have used another camera to detect the face of a customer which we have not discussed in detail in this paper. In future work, the trained model will be further tested by hosting in a cloud server and add the data mining section to suggest products using the age and gender predictions while continue to improve the accuracy on both models for object detection and face, gender classification. Further, we will use motion sensors, more cameras to localize the moving object which will help to improve the accuracy of the smart retail store.

References

1. Domdouzis, K., Kumar, B., Anumba, C.: Radio-frequency identification (RFID) applications: a brief introduction. Adv. Eng. Inf. **21**(4), 350–355 (2007)
2. Wankhede, K., Wukkadada, B., Nadar, V.: Just walk-out technology and its challenges: a case of Amazon go. In: 2018 International Conference on Inventive Research in Computing Applications (ICIRCA). IEEE (2018)
3. Wu, B.-F., et al.: An intelligent self-checkout system for smart retail. In: 2016 International Conference on System Science and Engineering (ICSSE). IEEE (2016)
4. Redmon, J., Farhadi, A.: YOLO9000: Better, faster, stronger. arxiv (2016). arxiv preprint arXiv:1612.08242
5. Redmon, J., et al.: You only look once: unified, real-time object detection. In: Proceedings of the IEEE Conference on Computer Vision and Pattern Recognition (2016)
6. Karlinsky, L., et al.: Fine-grained recognition of thousands of object categories with single-example training. In: Proceedings of the IEEE Conference on Computer Vision and Pattern Recognition (2017)
7. George, M., et al.: Fine-grained product class recognition for assisted shopping. In: Proceedings of the IEEE International Conference on Computer Vision Workshops (2015)
8. Tonioni, A., Di Stefano, L.: Product recognition in store shelves as a sub-graph isomorphism problem. In: Battiato, S., Gallo, G., Schettini, R., Stanco, F. (eds.) ICIAP 2017. LNCS, vol. 10484, pp. 682–693. Springer, Cham (2017). https://doi.org/10.1007/978-3-319-68560-1_61
9. Franco, A., Maltoni, D., Papi, S.: Grocery product detection and recognition. Expert Syst. Appl. **81**, 163–176 (2017)

10. Solti, A., et al.: Misplaced product detection using sensor data without planograms. Decision Support Syst. **112**, 76–87 (2018). S0167923618301039
11. Papadopoulos, D.P., et al.: We don't need no bounding-boxes: training object class detectors using only human verification. In: Proceedings of the IEEE Conference on Computer Vision and Pattern Recognition (2016)
12. Mettes, P., van Gemert, J.C., Snoek, C.G.M.: Spot on: action localization from pointly-supervised proposals. In: Leibe, B., Matas, J., Sebe, N., Welling, M. (eds.) ECCV 2016. LNCS, vol. 9909, pp. 437–453. Springer, Cham (2016). https://doi.org/10.1007/978-3-319-46454-1_27
13. Papadopoulos, D.P., et al.: Training object class detectors with click supervision. In: Proceedings of the IEEE Conference on Computer Vision and Pattern Recognition (2017)
14. Papadopoulos, D.P., Clarke, A.D.F., Keller, F., Ferrari, V.: Training object class detectors from eye tracking data. In: Fleet, D., Pajdla, T., Schiele, B., Tuytelaars, T. (eds.) ECCV 2014. LNCS, vol. 8693, pp. 361–376. Springer, Cham (2014). https://doi.org/10.1007/978-3-319-10602-1_24
15. Vedaldi, A., Bilen, H.: Weakly supervised deep detection networks. In: Institute of Electrical and Electronics Engineers (2016)
16. Kantorov, V., Oquab, M., Cho, M., Laptev, I.: ContextLocNet: context-aware deep network models for weakly supervised localization. In: Leibe, B., Matas, J., Sebe, N., Welling, M. (eds.) ECCV 2016. LNCS, vol. 9909, pp. 350–365. Springer, Cham (2016). https://doi.org/10.1007/978-3-319-46454-1_22
17. Zhu, Y., et al.: Soft proposal networks for weakly supervised object localization. In: Proceedings of the IEEE International Conference on Computer Vision (2017)
18. Simonyan, K., Zisserman, A.: Very deep convolutional networks for large-scale image recognition. arXiv preprint arXiv:1409.1556 (2014)
19. Lin, T.-Y., et al.: Microsoft COCO: common objects in context. In: Fleet, D., Pajdla, T., Schiele, B., Tuytelaars, T. (eds.) ECCV 2014. LNCS, vol. 8693, pp. 740–755. Springer, Cham (2014). https://doi.org/10.1007/978-3-319-10602-1_48
20. Van Horn, G., et al.: The inaturalist species classification and detection dataset. In: Proceedings of the IEEE Conference on Computer Vision and Pattern Recognition (2018)
21. Russakovsky, O., et al.: Imagenet large scale visual recognition challenge. Int. J. Comput. Vis. **115**(3), 211–252 (2015)
22. King, D.E.: Dlib-ml: a machine learning toolkit. J. Mach. Learn. Res. **10**(7), 1755–1758 (2009)
23. Howard, A.G., et al.: MobileNets: efficient convolutional neural networks for mobile vision applications. arXiv preprint arXiv:1704.04861 (2017)
24. Chollet, F.: Xception: deep learning with depthwise separable convolutions. In: Proceedings of the IEEE Conference on Computer Vision and Pattern Recognition (2017)
25. Liu, S., Huang, D., Wang, Y.: Receptive field block net for accurate and fast object detection. In: Ferrari, V., Hebert, M., Sminchisescu, C., Weiss, Y. (eds.) ECCV 2018. LNCS, vol. 11215, pp. 404–419. Springer, Cham (2018). https://doi.org/10.1007/978-3-030-01252-6_24
26. Szegedy, C., et al.: Going deeper with convolutions. In: Proceedings of the IEEE Conference on Computer Vision and Pattern Recognition (2015)
27. Wei, X.-S., et al.: RPC: A Large-Scale Retail Product Checkout Dataset. arXiv preprint arXiv:1901.07249 (2019)

Evaluation of Face Recognition Techniques Based on Symlet 2 Wavelet and Support Vector Machine

Zhipeng Li, Xuesong Jiang[✉], and Yewen Pang

School of Computer Science and Technology, Qilu University of Technology
(Shandong Academy of Sciences), Jinan 250353, China
lizhipengqilu@gmail.com, jxs@qlu.edu.cn

Abstract. In this study, we analyze and study the feature extraction method based on wavelet transform and Principal Component Analysis (PCA), and propose a method combining symlet 2 wavelet (sym2) and Support Vector Machine (SVM) for face recognition. Firstly, the sym2 is used to wavelet decomposition of the original image, and the decomposed low-frequency information is selected for image reconstruction. Then, the reconstructed data is multi-classified using support vector machine. Experiments were carried out using the internationally published ORL face recognition database, and compared with some classical methods used in ORL face recognition. The experimental results show that the recognition success rate increases with the increase in the training set. When 7 poses are selected for each face (A total of 280 photos are used as training sets) in the data set, the recognition success rate reaches 100%. Therefore, the method proposed in this paper is better than the previous method.

Keywords: Symlet 2 wavelet · Support Vector Machine ·
ORL face recognition, feature extraction · Principal component analysis

1 Introduction

With the rise of artificial intelligence and big data technology, the research and application of face recognition technology has been promoted. In recent years, domestic and foreign scholars have proposed some feasible algorithms for face recognition technology. Such as eigenface method, neural network, wavelet transform, support vector machine, hidden Markov and other methods [1]. Most algorithms currently require hardware and long training time. Generally, the face recognition method commonly uses wavelet transform for feature extraction and dimensionality reduction or PCA for feature dimensionality reduction and for performing classification operations using a neural network. In this paper, we use wavelet transform and PCA for image feature extraction and dimensionality reduction. Wavelet transform is a major breakthrough after Fourier analysis in recent years. The multi-resolution analysis of wavelet has good localization characteristics of space and frequency, and the detailed analysis of the object can be realized by adopting gradually detailed step size for the high-frequency part of the signal. Therefore, wavelet transform is especially suitable

© Springer Nature Switzerland AG 2019
G. Wang et al. (Eds.): SpaCCS 2019 Workshops, LNCS 11637, pp. 228–239, 2019.
https://doi.org/10.1007/978-3-030-24900-7_19

for the processing of non-stationary signals such as images [2]. PCA is a commonly used method for feature dimension reduction. The basic idea is to extract the main information of the data, and then discard the redundant information to achieve the purpose of compression. SVM is a common classification algorithm in machine learning. For multi-classification problems, SVM maps data from low-dimensional to high-dimensional space by introducing kernel functions, so as to achieve linear divisibility and achieve multi-classification goals. In this paper, we use the international standard universal face recognition library which is ORL face recognition data set. The ORL face database consists of a series of face images, with 40 objects of different ages, genders and races. Each person's 10 images consists of a total of 400 grayscale images, the image size is 92 × 112, and the image background is black, as shown in Fig. 1. In this paper, we introduce the feature extraction methods using PCA and wavelet transform, respectively, and use SVM for classification and recognition. The structure of this paper is as follows. Section 2 introduces the feature extraction method wavelet transform and PCA. In Sect. 3, we introduced the classification algorithm SVM. In Sect. 4, we detail the experimental process and experimental results. Finally, In Sect. 5, we draw conclusions.

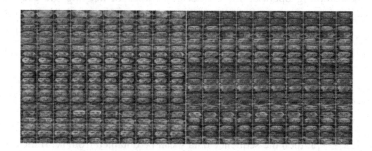

Fig. 1. ORL face recognition data set

2 Feature Extraction Method

2.1 Wavelet Transform

Wavelet transform is applied to face recognition, mainly because the resolution of the subgraph is reduced in different directions after the wavelet image is decomposed by wavelet, and the computational complexity is reduced accordingly [3]. At the same time it provides good local information in both the airspace and the frequency domain. The low frequency portion of the face image information describes the overall shape of the image. The high frequency part describes the details of the image. The face low frequency information obtained by wavelet transform can better describe the face features useful for classification [4].

In our study, we used a multi-layer (4-layer) SWT (stationary wavelet transform) wavelet decomposition on the image set. SWT consists of two opposite processes of decomposition and reconstruction, where the decomposition is the time series data y (recorded as a^0) through J iterations. Transform into a set of wavelet coefficients distributed in J + 1 wavelet metrics

$$c_y = \left[a^J, b^J, b^{J-1}, \cdots, b^1\right] \tag{1}$$

$$\begin{cases} a^j = H^{[j-1]}a^{[j-1]}, b^j = G^{[j-1]}a^{[j-1]} \\ H^{[j]} = U_o H^{[j-1]}, G^{[j]} = U_o G^{[j-1]} \end{cases} \tag{2}$$

In the above formula, decomposition series $j = 1, 2, \cdots, J$; $H^{[0]}$ and $G^{[0]}$ are wavelet low pass, high pass decomposition filters. U_o indicates that zeros are inserted after each coefficient of the filter to double the filter length. a^j and b^j are called the j level low frequency scale and the high frequency scale, respectively. Through wavelet decomposition, different frequency band components in y are separated into different scales in c_y. The above formula is therefore called multi-scale analysis.

Unlike DWT, each wavelet scale of SWT is the same length as y, so SWT is a redundant transform [5]. $H^{[j-1]}$, $G^{[j-1]}$ decomposing a^{j-1} into (a^j, b^j) is non-orthogonal. Its inverse transformation is not unique. But if defined D_0 and D_1 perform a downsampling operator for the second choice of keeping the even and odd terms. Then transforms $(D_o H^{[j-1]}, D_o G^{[j-1]})$ and $(D_1 H^{[j-1]}, D_1 G^{[j-1]})$ are orthogonal transforms, and gives the even and odd terms of a^j and b^j respectively. Therefore, if we remember that the inverse transformation of the two is $R_0^{[j-1]}$ and $R_1^{[j-1]}$. Then refactored SWT is

$$a^{j-1} = \frac{1}{2}\left(R_0^{[j-1]} + R_1^{[j-1]}\right)\left(a^j, b^j\right) \tag{3}$$

If $j = 1, 2, \cdots, J$, then the sequence data y can be obtained from c_y. If the coefficient of the partial scale in c_y is kept unchanged, and the coefficient of the remaining scale. The discarding scale is set to zero, it is a partial scale reconstruction.

Because it is a redundant transform, SWT retains more information than DWT and has translation invariance, which is more conducive to time series analysis [6]. However, if the length of y is 2^J, the complexity of SWT decomposition J is $O(J2^J)$, which is larger than $O(2^J)$ of DWT.

For simple calculation, use W to represent J-level SWT decomposition, which is $c_y = Wy$. Use W^- to indicate the corresponding refactoring, which is $y = W^- c_y$. The use of S_0 for partial scale reconstruction adds zero to the coefficient of the discarding scale.

Replace DWT with SWT and use wavelet sym2 to study wavelet extraction [7]. Sym2 is an approximate symmetric wavelet function with better symmetry, which can reduce the phase distortion when analyzing and reconstructing signals to a certain extent.

2.2 Principal Component Analysis

Principal Component Analysis (PCA) is the most commonly used linear mapping method in pattern recognition analysis [8]. It is based on the position distribution of sample points in multi-mode space, and the maximum direction of sample points in space. The direction with the largest variance is used as the discriminant vector to achieve feature extraction [9].

Face frequency map as raw data of PCA [10]. Let a known low-frequency sub-graph form a column vector whose size $D = M \times N$ is a dimension. Let n be the number of training samples, and X_i denote the face vector formed by the i-th face low-frequency sub-graph, then the covariance matrix of the required samples is

$$S_r = \sum_{i=1}^{n} (X_i - \mu)(X_i - \mu)^T \tag{4}$$

Where u is the average image vector of the training sample

$$\mu = \frac{1}{n} \sum_{i=1}^{n} x_i \tag{5}$$

Let $A = [x_1 - \mu, X_2 - \mu, \cdots X_n - \mu]$, there is $S_r = AA^T$, and its dimension is $D \times D$. According to the K-L transform principle [11], the new coordinate system to be required is composed of the feature vectors corresponding to the non-zero eigenvalues of the matrix AA^T.

The calculation of direct calculation is relatively large, so the eigenvalues and eigenvectors of AA^T are obtained by solving the eigenvalues and eigenvectors of $A^T A$ using the SVD (singular value decomposition) theorem.

According to the SVD theorem, let $\lambda_i = (i = 1, 2, \cdots, r)$ be the r non-zero eigenvalues of matrix $A^T A$. v_i is the eigenvector of $A^T A$ corresponding to λ_i, then the orthogonal normalized eigenvector μ_i of AA^T is

$$\mu_i = \frac{1}{\sqrt{\lambda_i}} \tag{6}$$

Then the feature face subspace is $\omega = (\mu_1, \mu_2, \cdots, \mu_r)$. The training sample is projected into the feature face subspace, and a set of projection vectors $W = w^T \mu$ is obtained to form a database for face recognition [12]. When identifying, each image of the face to be recognized is first projected into the feature face subspace, and is identified as input data of the SVM classifier.

3 Classification and Recognition Based on SVM

Support Vector Machine is a learning method based on statistical learning theory developed [13] in the 1990s. The generalization ability of machine learning is improved by seeking the minimum of structured sorting, and the empirical risk and confidence range are minimized. In the case of a small amount of statistical samples, good statistical laws can also be obtained.

In the training data, each data has n attributes and a second class of category markers, we can think of these data in an n-dimensional space. Our goal is to find an n-1 dimensional hyperplane. This hyperplane divides the data into two parts, each of which belongs to the same category. In fact, there are many such hyperplanes, we have to find the best one [14]. Therefore, a constraint has been added, the distance from this hyperplane to the nearest data point of each class is the largest.

A linearly separable data set $\{(\vec{x_1},y_1),(\vec{x_2},y_2),\cdots,(\vec{x_N},y_N)\}$, ample feature vector $\vec{x} \in D^T$, that is, $\vec{x}$ is a vector in the D-dimensional real space. Class label $y \in \{-1,+1\}$, that is, there are only two types of samples. Usually, a sample with a class label of $+1$ is a positive example, and a sample with a class label of -1 is a counterexample. Now classify these two types of samples [15]. The goal is to find the optimal segmentation hyperplane, i.e. the segmentation hyperplane of the largest classification interval determined from the training samples. We sct the equation for the optimal hyperplane as $\vec{w}^T \vec{x} + b = 0$. According to the point-to-plane distance formula, the distance between sample $\vec{x}$ and the best hyperplane $(\vec{w},b)$ is $\frac{\vec{w}^T \vec{x} + b}{\|\vec{w}\|}$. By scaling the vector $\vec{w}$ and the deviation term b proportionally, there are many solutions to the optimal hyperplane. The hyperplane is normalized to select the sample $\vec{x}_k$ that is closest to the hyperplane to satisfy $\vec{w}$ and b of $\left| \vec{w}^T \vec{x}_k + b = 0 \right| = 1$. We can get normalized sample hyperplane. The distance from the nearest sample to the edge is

$$\frac{\vec{w}^T \vec{x} + b}{\|\vec{w}\|} = \frac{1}{\|\vec{w}\|} \tag{7}$$

And the classification interval becomes

$$m = \frac{2}{\|\vec{w}\|} \tag{8}$$

In fact, it can be seen from the above formula that the most critical point for finding the support vector is to find the upper method to maximize the normal vector $\vec{w}$. Put $\vec{w}$ with a relationship $\vec{w}^T \vec{x} + b = 1$ to get b. The key to the entire support vector is to find the following objective function:

$$\arg\max_{\vec{w},b} \left\{ \frac{1}{\|\vec{w}\|} \min_i \left[y_i \left(\vec{w}^T \vec{x}_i + b \right) \right] \right\} \tag{9}$$

Find the maximum spacing of the nearest support vector points for the two types of data, and satisfy the conditions $\underset{w}{\rightarrow}$ and b. At the same time, there is a constraint on this formula:

$$y_i\left(\underset{w}{\rightarrow}^T \underset{x_i}{\rightarrow} + b\right) \geq 1 \tag{10}$$

At this point, the problem of finding support vector points is transformed into an extremum problem of a function with constraints. For the problem of this kind, we can solve it by Lagrangian multiplier method to get the following formula:

$$L\left(\underset{w}{\rightarrow}, b, \alpha\right) = \frac{1}{2}\left\|\underset{w}{\rightarrow}\right\|^2 - \sum_{i=1}^{N} \alpha_i\left[y_i\left(\underset{w}{\rightarrow}^T \underset{x_i}{\rightarrow} + b\right) - 1\right], \alpha_i > 0 \tag{11}$$

Find the partial conductance of L on $\underset{w}{\rightarrow}$ and b make it equal to zero.

$$\frac{\partial\left(L, \underset{w}{\rightarrow}, b, \alpha\right)}{\partial \underset{w}{\rightarrow}} = 0 \Rightarrow \underset{w}{\rightarrow} = \sum_{i=1}^{N} \alpha_i y_i \underset{x_i}{\rightarrow} \tag{12}$$

$$\frac{\partial\left(L, \underset{w}{\rightarrow}, b, \alpha\right)}{\partial b} = 0 \Rightarrow \sum_{i=1}^{N} \alpha_i y_i = 0 \tag{13}$$

Bring the above two styles into the following formula.

$$L\left(\underset{w}{\rightarrow}, b, \alpha\right) = \frac{1}{2}\underset{w}{\overset{T}{\rightarrow}}\underset{x}{\rightarrow} - \sum_{i=1}^{N} \alpha_i y_i \underset{w}{\overset{T}{\rightarrow}} x_i - b\sum_{i=1}^{N} \alpha_i y_i + \sum_{i=1}^{N} \alpha_i \tag{14}$$

Find the support vectors of the two types of data sets by finding $\underset{w}{\rightarrow}$ and b that satisfy the maximum value of the above formula.

The commonly used kernel functions are linear kernel function, polynomial kernel function, Gaussian kernel function (RBF kernel function) and sigmoid kernel function [16]. The choice of kernel function has a great influence on the classifier. We compare and analyze the following kernel functions [17].

The mapping function corresponding to the RBF kernel function projects the sample into an infinite dimensional space, and performs a polynomial expansion on the RBF kernel function to obtain the result. Second, after mapping to the new space, all sample points are distributed over a 1/4 sphere with a radius of 1 at the origin as:

$$K\left(x_i, x_j\right) = \exp\left(-\frac{\left\|x_i - x_j\right\|^2}{2\sigma^2}\right) \tag{15}$$

Linear kernel are mainly used for linear separability. We can see that the dimension of the feature space to the input space is the same. Its parameters are less fast, and for linearly separable data, the classification effect is very good, so we try to use linear kernel function to do classification as:

$$K(x, x_i) = x \cdot x_i \tag{16}$$

Polynomial kernel functions can map low-dimensional input spaces to high-dimensional feature spaces, but the polynomial kernel function has many parameters. When the order of the polynomial is relatively high, the element values of the kernel matrix will tend to infinity or infinitesimal. The computational complexity is too large to calculate as:

$$K(x, x_i) = ((x \cdot x_i) + 1)^d \tag{17}$$

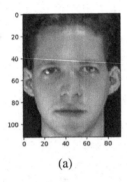

(a)

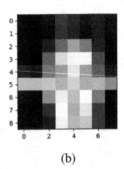

(b)

Fig. 2. (a) The original image; (b) Decompose the original image to the image of the fourth layer based on sym2 wavelet;

4   Experimental Results and Analysis

We first used wavelet transform to extract features. Wavelet transform can reduce dimension while extracting features, and the extracted feature data was classified by SVM. In this experiment, we use python language for code writing, wavelet transform USES the third-party package pywt in python, and SVM USES the popular third-party machine learning extension library scikit-learn in python. The experimental hardware environment we used was inter(R) Core(TM) i7-8700k CPU @3.70 ghz processor, 32G RAM and 1080TI GPU.

In this study, we used the standard face recognition data set ORL. In this data set, each person has 10 different pose faces and 40 people have 400 photos. During the experiment, we selected one, two, three, four, five, six and seven face poses of each person as the training set, and the rest as the test set.

In the experimental process, we use the sym2 wavelet base in the pywt library. The Symlets wavelet system is a finitely tightly supported orthogonal wavelet, which has strong localization ability in the time domain and frequency domain, especially in the wavelet decomposition process of the signal. Actually more specific digital filters, so the sym2 wavelet base in the Symets wavelet system was chosen to perform wavelet transform on image features. In the experiment, we use wavelet to decompose the original image into the fourth layer which as shown in Fig. 2. The feature data after wavelet decomposition is used. The image before and after decomposition is shown in Fig. 3. For the feature data after wavelet transform, we use SVM for multi-classification. The prediction and real results of SVM classification test set are shown in Fig. 4. In SVM, we set the value of parameter c to 1000. C is the error item. Penalty factor. The larger C, the greater the degree of punishment for the fault-divided sample, so the higher the accuracy in the training sample, but the lower the generalization ability, that is, the classification accuracy of the test data is reduced. Conversely, if C is reduced, there are some misclassification errors in the training samples, and the generalization ability is strong. For the case where the training sample is noisy, the latter is generally used, and the sample that is misclassified in the training sample set is used as noise. The kernel functions we can use are 'linear', 'poly', 'rbf', etc. We set the kernel function coefficient gamma to 0.001.

All figures and tables should be cited in the main text as Fig. 1, Table 1, etc.

In the experiment, we also tried to use PCA as image feature extraction. We use the PCA in scikit-learn for dimension reduction. The feature data before and after dimension reduction is shown in Fig. 5. We set the value of n_components in sklearn.decomposition.PCA to be equal to 0.9, which is to retain 90% of the principal components. Then we use SVM to complete the classification identification. We also use wavelet transform for feature extraction, using the PCA for dimension reduction (the dimensionality reduction method is the same as above), and then using SVM to complete the classification and recognition. After three different methods of testing, we obtained the experimental results shown in Table 1.

From Table 1, we can see that the four-layer wavelet decomposition and SVM face recognition using Sym2 are better than the other two methods. With the increase of training samples, when the sample pose is increased to 7, the recognition rate classified by the method proposed in this paper can reach 100%.

Consider previous studies [18]. Comparing the proposed method with the previous method, we plot the recognition rate of two different methods using different kernel functions, as shown in Fig. 6 (RBF kernel), Fig. 7 (LINEAR kernel) and Fig. 8 (POLY kernel). When the face number of each training set is less than 2 (80 in total), the support vector machine with three different kernel functions is higher than the previous method. When the training set selects less than 4 faces per face (160 total), the previous method is superior to this method. When the training set is greater than 160, the recognition rate of this method is significantly higher than the previous method.

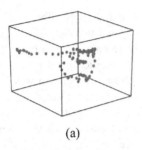
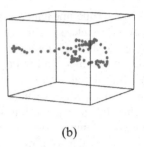

(a)   (b)

Fig. 3. (a) The distribution of the features of the first primitive face (the first one on the left in Fig. 2) in space; (b) The distribution of the features of the first original face after four layers of wavelet transform (the graph on the right in Fig. 2)

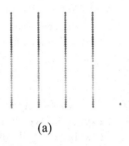
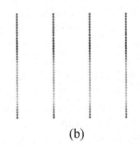

(a)   (b)

Fig. 4. (a) Training sample 240, test sample 160, when inputting test sample predicted classification result; (b) Training sample 240, test sample 160, when entering the correct classification result of the test sample

Table 1. Recognition rates of applied techniques according to increasing pose count

Technique	Pose count per individual in training (number of test images)						
	1/360	2/320	3/280	4/240	5/200	6/160	7/160
	%	%	%	%	%	%	%
Sym2_SVM(rbf)	77.22	85.62	91.43	96.67	98.50	99.38	100.0
Sym2_SVM(linear)	77.22	85.62	91.43	95.83	99.00	99.38	100.0
Sym2_SVM(poly)	76.94	86.56	90.00	95.42	99.00	99.38	100.0
PCA_SVM(rbf)	69.17	86.56	89.64	95.00	95.50	96.88	98.33
PCA_SVM(linear)	69.17	86.56	89.64	94.58	96.00	96.88	98.33
PCA_SVM(poly)	34.44	52.19	58.21	76.25	83.00	86.88	89.17
Sym2_PCA_SVM(rbf)	72.22	82.81	88.93	96.67	97.50	98.75	99.17
Sym2_PCA_SVM(linear)	72.22	82.81	88.57	96.25	97.50	98.12	98.33
Sym2_PCA_SVM(poly)	60.00	71.25	81.43	92.08	94.00	94.38	96.67

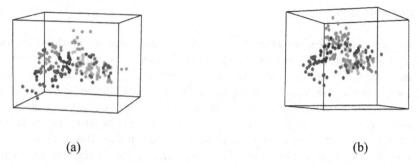

(a)   (b)

Fig. 5. (a) The spatial distribution of the training set before dimension reduction; (b) After the dimension reduction, the training set is spatially distributed.

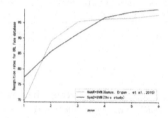

Fig. 6. Comparison of two methods based on RBF kernel function recognition rate

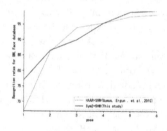

Fig. 7. Comparison of two methods based on LINEAR kernel function recognition rate

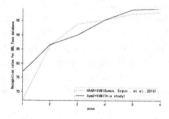

Fig. 8. Comparison of two methods based on POLY kernel function recognition rate

5 Conclusions

In this paper, we propose a method based on Sym2 based wavelet transform and face recognition. This method is validated on the ORL data set. We select the feature data of the face through the wavelet transform of the 4-layer sym2 wavelet, and then use svm to complete the classification and recognition. We use three different kernel functions and compare them with the other two methods (One is using pca and svm, another is using wavelet transform, pca and svm). The experimental results show that the method is better than due to two other methods. This paper also compares this method with the previous method. With the increase of training samples, the recognition rate of this method is higher than the previous method. When the training sample reaches 280, the recognition rate of this method reaches 100%.

Acknowledgments. This work was supported by Key Research and Development Plan Project of Shandong Province, China (No. 2017CXGC0614).

References

1. Chen, X., Wu, W., Fan, J.: Overview of face recognition technology. In: China Academic Association of Instrumentation Youth Conference (2010)
2. Mi, C., Wei, F.: Application of Haar wavelet transform in image processing. Ningxia Eng. Technol. **2**, 70–72 (2003)
3. Eslami, R., Radha, H.: Wavelet-based contourlet transform and its application to image coding. In: International Conference on Image Processing, Singapore, p. 3189. IEEE (2004)
4. Wang, Y., Chen, J., Wu, Q., Castleman, K.R.: Fast frequency estimation by zero crossings of differential spline wavelet transform. EURASIP J. Appl. Signal Process. **2005**, 1251 (2005)
5. Alickovic, E., Kevric, J., Subasi, A.: Performance evaluation of empirical mode decomposition, discrete wavelet transform, and wavelet packed decomposition for automated epileptic seizure detection and prediction. Biomed. Signal Process. Control **39**, 94 (2018)
6. Ma, L., Stückler, J., Wu, T., Cremers, D.: Detailed Dense Inference with Convolutional Neural Networks via Discrete Wavelet Transform (2018)
7. Bhattacharyya, A., Sharma, M., Pachori, R.B., Sircar, P., Acharya, U.R.: A novel approach for automated detection of focal EEG signals using empirical wavelet transform. Neural Comput. Appl. **29**, 47 (2018)
8. Mavroeidis, D., Vazirgiannis, M.: Stability based sparse LSI/PCA: incorporating feature selection in LSI and PCA. In: Kok, J.N., Koronacki, J., Mantaras, R., Matwin, S., Mladenič, D., Skowron, A. (eds.) ECML 2007. LNCS (LNAI), vol. 4701, pp. 226–237. Springer, Heidelberg (2007). https://doi.org/10.1007/978-3-540-74958-5_23
9. Lee, M.-S., Chen, M.-Y., Lin, F.-S.: Face recognition under variant illumination using PCA and wavelets. In: Salberg, A.-B., Hardeberg, J.Y., Jenssen, R. (eds.) SCIA 2009. LNCS, vol. 5575, pp. 341–350. Springer, Heidelberg (2009). https://doi.org/10.1007/978-3-642-02230-2_35
10. Poon, B., Amin, M.A., Yan, H.: Performance evaluation and comparison of PCA Based human face recognition methods for distorted images. Int. J. Mach. Learn. Cybern. **2**, 245 (2011)

11. Caballero-Morales, S.-O.: Noise-removal markers to improve PCA-based face recognition. In: Martínez-Trinidad, J.F., Carrasco-Ochoa, J.A., Olvera-Lopez, J.A., Salas-Rodríguez, J., Suen, C.Y. (eds.) MCPR 2014. LNCS, vol. 8495, pp. 192–200. Springer, Cham (2014). https://doi.org/10.1007/978-3-319-07491-7_20

12. Biswas, S., Sil, J., Maity, S.P.: PCA based face recognition on curvelet compressive measurements. In: Mandal, J.K., Dutta, P., Mukhopadhyay, S. (eds.) CICBA 2017. CCIS, vol. 775, pp. 217–229. Springer, Singapore (2017). https://doi.org/10.1007/978-981-10-6427-2_18

13. Schuldt, C., Laptev, I., Caputo, B.: Recognizing human actions: a local SVM approach. In: Proceedings - International Conference on Pattern Recognition, vol. 3, p. 32. Institute of Electrical and Electronics Engineers Inc., Cambridge (2004)

14. Sadeghi, M.T., Khoshrou, S., Kittler, J.: SVM-based selection of colour space experts for face authentication. In: Lee, S.-W., Li, S.Z. (eds.) ICB 2007. LNCS, vol. 4642, pp. 907–916. Springer, Heidelberg (2007). https://doi.org/10.1007/978-3-540-74549-5_95

15. Kar, N.B., Babu, K.S., Sangaiah, A.K., Bakshi, S.: Face expression recognition system based on ripplet transform type II and least square SVM. Multimedia Tools Appl. **78**, 4789 (2019)

16. Manolova, A., Neshov, N., Panev, S., Tonchev, K.: Facial expression classification using supervised descent method combined with PCA and SVM. In: Cantoni, V., Dimov, D., Tistarelli, M. (eds.) Biometric Authentication. LNCS, vol. 8897, pp. 165–175. Springer, Cham (2014). https://doi.org/10.1007/978-3-319-13386-7_13

17. Li, M., Yu, X., Ryu, K.H., Lee, S., Theera-Umpon, N.: Face recognition technology development with Gabor, PCA and SVM methodology under illumination normalization condition. Cluster Comput. **21**(1), 1117–1126 (2017)

18. Gumus, E., Kilic, N., Sertbas, A., Ucan, O.N.: Evaluation of face recognition techniques using PCA, wavelets and SVM. Expert Syst. Appl. **37**, 6404 (2010)

The 11th International Symposium on UbiSafe Computing (UbiSafe 2019)

UbiSafe 2019 Organizing and Program Committee

General Chairs

Shuhong Chen	Guangzhou University, University of Florida, China, USA
Bowen Du	Beihang University, China
Xiaoyong Li	Beijing University of Posts and Telecommunications, China

Program Chairs

Fuhua Lin	Athabasca University, Canada
Zhangbing Zhou	China University of Geosciences, TELECOM SudParis, China, France

Program Committee

Ali, Asim	Bahria University, Pakistan
Deize Ceng	China University of Geosciences, China
Xianhao Chen	University of Florida, USA
Yihai Chen	Shanghai University, China
Wei Cheng	Virginia Commonwealth University, USA
Hongning Dai	Macau University of Science and Technology, SAR China
Judith Molka-Danielsen	Molde University College, Norway
Shuiguang Deng	Zhejiang University, China
Ali Dewan	Athabasca University, Canada
Hong Feng	Ocean University of China, China
M Tahir Fattani	SSUET, Pakistan
Kehua Guo	Central South University, China
Noman Hasany	Sir Syed University of Engineering and Technology, Pakistan
Patrick C. K. Hung	University of Ontario Institute of Technology, Canada
Shiraz Latif	Sheridan College, Canada
Ren Lei	Beihang University, China
Shu Lei	Nanjing Agricultural University, China
Bing Li	Wuhan University, China
Zhou Li	National University of Defense Technology, China
Heng Rong Lin	Beijing University of Posts and Telecommunications, China
Meng Lin	Ritsumeikan University, Japan
Zhibo Pang	ABB Corporate Research, Sweden
ChingYeh Shih	Fudan University, China
Neeraj Singh	University of Toulouse, France
Changai Sun	University of Science and Technology Beijing, China

Qing Tan	Athabasca University, Canada
Zhiyuan Tan	Edinburgh Napier University, UK
Kevin I-Kai Wang	The University of Auckland, New Zealand
Shanguang Wang	Beijing University of Posts and Telecommunications, China
Shengke Wang	Ocean University of China, China
Jun Wei	Institute of Software Chinese Academy of Sciences, China
Di Wu	Norwegian University of Science and Technology, Norway
Xue Xiao	Tianjin University, China
Zheng Yan	Xidian University, China
Geng Yang	Zhejiang University, China
Guoxian Yu	Southwest University, China
Zhang Yu	Hainan University, China
Ming Zhan	Southwest University, China
Wenbo Zhang	Institute of Software Chinese Academy of Sciences, China
Xuyun Zhang	The University of Auckland, New Zealand
Ao Zhou	Beijing University of Posts and Telecommunications, China
Xiaokang Zhou	Shiga University, Japan
Ying Zou	Queen's University, Canada

Publicity Chairs

Hao Wang	Norwegian University of Science and Technology, Norway
Sheng Wen	Swinburne University of Technology, Australia

Web Chairs

Yao Li	Guangzhou University, China
Junqiu Lai	Guangzhou University, China

An Approach of ACARS Trajectory Reconstruction Based on Adaptive Cubic Spline Interpolation

Lan Ma[2], Shan Tian[1], Yang Song[1], Zhijun Wu[1(✉)], and Meng Yue[1]

[1] School of Electronic Information and Automation,
Civil Aviation University of China, Tianjin 300300, China
zjwu@cauc.edu.cn
[2] School of Air Traffic Management, Civil Aviation University of China,
Tianjin 300300, China

Abstract. Trajectory reconstruction is one of the key technologies to achieve flight trajectory and ensure the safety of flight. Aircraft Communication Addressing and Reporting System (ACARS) is a digital data link system that transmits short messages by radio or satellite between aircraft and ground station. In this paper, an approach based on adaptive cubic spline interpolation is proposed for ACARS trajectory reconstruction. The ACARS data points of different flight phases are reconstructed, and the appropriate trajectory curve is obtained. This approach is verified in simulation platform by using true flight historical data. Experimental results show that this approach obtained better smoothness and lower error precision than that of traditional trajectory reconstruction algorithm, especially in take-off and landing phases. Improving the degree of cure smoothing and decreasing its error are helpful to the accurate trajectory and position of the flight, which provides a guarantee for the safe operation of the air traffic.

Keywords: Flight safety · ACARS · Trajectory reconstruction · Adaptive · Cubic spline

1 Introduction

Aircraft Communication Addressing and Reporting System (ACARS) is a data link system which is widely used in international civil aviation. It is used to monitor the aircraft in real time. Since Malaysia Airlines MH370 incident occurred in March 8, 2014, in order to ensure the safe operation of air transport, the International Civil Aviation Organization (ICAO) and the aviation industry attached great importance to trajectory the global flight by using the ACARS data [1].

In the era of rapid development of communication network, the core of the next generation aviation transportation system-Next Generation Air Transportation System (NextGen) is Trajectory-based Operational [2, 3]. Trajectory reconstruction is one of the core technologies of the Trajectory-based Operational. In the operation and management of the trajectory, the trajectory reconstruction can accurately predict the current position and future position of the civil aviation aircraft in high density airspace, and solve the Airspace utilization and improve the flight safety and operational

© Springer Nature Switzerland AG 2019
G. Wang et al. (Eds.): SpaCCS 2019 Workshops, LNCS 11637, pp. 245–252, 2019.
https://doi.org/10.1007/978-3-030-24900-7_20

efficiency of the civil aviation aircraft [4, 5]. It is a technical problem that needs to be solved urgently at present.

Besada, et al. presented a method of air traffic control trajectory reconstruction for sensor and trajectory performance evaluation [6]. Sotiriou et al. studied an adaptive time-series probabilistic framework for 4-D trajectory conformance monitoring [7]. The trajectory reconstruction of aircraft was studied in Nanjing University of Aeronautics & Astronautics, but they had some defects. Wang used the traditional cubic spline interpolation and linear interpolation to reconstruct the trajectory [8]. The smoothness and accuracy of the trajectory obtained was not good through two algorithms. Lu did not launch a specific study of different flight stages (take-off, cruise and landing) [9].

This paper proposes adaptive cubic spline algorithm which uses ACARS data link technology to carry on the trajectory reconstruction, improve the accuracy of trajectory, reduce the estimation error, and achieve the purpose of flight trajectory.

2 Adaptive Cubic Spline Interpolation Algorithm

In order to ensure the real-time performance of the aircraft, it is needed to fit the accurate trajectory of the aircraft. Therefore, we propose an adaptive cubic spline interpolation based ACARS trajectory reconstruction algorithm, which can be used to reconstruct the real time flight path of the aircraft. The basic idea of this method is that the number and the initial value of spline are given by the algorithm. The initial node vector is used to construct B spline basis functions and the coefficients of the basis functions are obtained. Then the spline function values are obtained by the least square method to solve the B spline curve equation. Then we calculate the error of the spline function and the original data. If it is less than the specified error, the trajectory can be constructed to meet the requirements, if the error is greater than the specified error, the initial value of the node is changed or the number of the nodes is changed, and the operation is carried out until it meets the requirements [10, 11].

In the adaptive trajectory reconstruction, the initial value N is given, and the data points $\{t_i\}_{i=0}^{N}$ are constructed according to the message. These data points are within the range of [A, B], among them, $t_0 = A, t_N = B$. We select N − 1 random number $\{r_i\}_{i=1}^{N-1}, 0 < r_i < 1$. We can use the formula $t_i = r_i t_{i-1} + (1 - r_i)t_{i+1} \quad i = 1, \ldots, N - 1$ to get the monotonically increasing random sequence $\{t_i\}_{i=0}^{N}$. We take this sequence as the sequence of the spline. Solving tri-diagonal equations as follows.

$$\begin{pmatrix} -1 & 1-r_1 & & & & \\ r_2 & -1 & 1-r_2 & & & \\ & \ddots & \ddots & \ddots & & \\ & & r_{N-2} & -1 & 1-r_{N-2} \\ & & & r_{N-1} & -1 \end{pmatrix} \begin{pmatrix} t_1 \\ t_2 \\ \vdots \\ t_{N-2} \\ t_{N-1} \end{pmatrix} = \begin{pmatrix} -r_1 A \\ 0 \\ \vdots \\ 0 \\ -(1-r_{N-1})B \end{pmatrix} \tag{1}$$

We construct the cubic B-spline by using the node vector, and determine whether the accuracy is up to the requirement. If the accuracy does not meet the requirements, we select another set of random number and reconstruct the curve. In order to get the node vector with the specified accuracy, this process is repeated several times. If we do not meet the requirements at the number of nodes, the number of nodes will change (the number of nodes increased by 1 in turn). Then repeat the above process until the requirements are met [2, 12].

The main steps of the algorithm are as follows:

Step 0 (initialization): (a) Original points $\{x_i, y_i, z_i\}_{i=1}^{w}$. (b) Number of nodes N. (c) Under the fixed length, nodes were selected randomly Num times (Num represents the maximum value possible). (d) Specified accuracy e.

Step 1. Selecting random number $\{r_i\}_{i=1}^{N-1}$. If min $r \to 0$ or max $r \to 1$, we select the random number.

Step 2. Using formula 1 to get the internal node $\{t_i\}_{i=1}^{N-1}$.

Step 3. If $|t_{i+1} - t_i| < \theta, \theta = 1.0 \times 10^{-4}$, We remove a node.

Step 4. Node normalization.

Step 5. Construct cubic B-spline basis function.

Step 6. The ACARS data parameter values are brought into the basis function, and the coefficient matrix is obtained.

$$
\begin{cases}
N_{i,0}(t) = \begin{cases} 1 & if \ t_i \leq t < t_{i+1} \\ 0 & other \end{cases} \\
N_{i,k}(t) = \frac{(t-t_i)N_{i,k-1}(t)}{t_{i+k}-t_i} + \frac{(t_{i+k+1}-t)N_{i+1,k-1}(t)}{t_{i+k+1}-t_{i+1}} & k > 0 \\
0/0 = 0
\end{cases}
\tag{2}
$$

Step 7. Solving equations

$$
\begin{pmatrix} y_1 \\ \vdots \\ y_w \end{pmatrix} = \begin{pmatrix} N_{0,k}(x_1) & \cdots & N_{n,k}(x_1) \\ \vdots & \vdots & \vdots \\ N_{0,k}(x_w) & \cdots & N_{n,k}(x_1) \end{pmatrix} \begin{pmatrix} \beta_0 \\ \vdots \\ \beta_n \end{pmatrix} + \delta
\tag{3}
$$

Step 8. Determine whether the error is less than precision. Yes, step 10; No, step 9.

Step 9. $num = num + 1$. If $num < Num$, to perform step 1; if $num \geq Num$, so $N = N + 1, num = 1$.

Step 10. End of program.

3   Experiment and Result Analysis

In this paper, the experimental system is using a PC machine and MATLAB simulation software for data processing. In order to ensure the reliability of the experiment, the original data of this paper originates from the domestic real flight data of an airline [13, 14].

The experimental scheme of trajectory reconstruction is shown in Fig. 1.

In order to carry on the comparative analysis, the experiment uses three kinds of flight path methods, as follows.

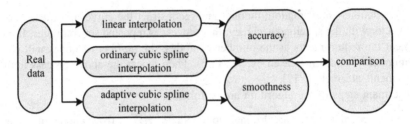

Fig. 1. Experimental scheme of trajectory reconstruction

- Adaptive cubic spline interpolation
- Linear interpolation
- Ordinary cubic spline interpolation

The trajectory of the three methods are compared and analyzed.

Using the historical flight data, three methods are used to reconstruct the trajectory, and the results are shown in Fig. 2.

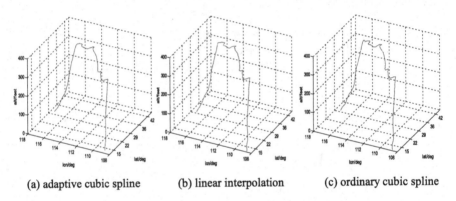

(a) adaptive cubic spline   (b) linear interpolation   (c) ordinary cubic spline

Fig. 2. Reconstructed trajectory

As shown in Fig. 2(a), (b) and (c), in the reconstruction of ACARS trajectory, adaptive cubic spline has a higher accuracy than ordinary cubic spline interpolation and linear interpolation. In the smoothness of the trajectory, the trajectory has an advantage by adopting the adaptive cubic spline function, and it is more flexible in the curve reconstruction.

In order to explain the effect of interpolation function and the accuracy of each flight phase, we have to make the interpolation operation for each stage of the flight (take off, cruise and landing) [15, 16].

1. Take-off phase

In the take-off phase, the flight path of the three methods is shown in Fig. 3.

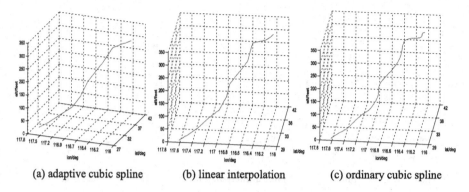

(a) adaptive cubic spline   (b) linear interpolation   (c) ordinary cubic spline

Fig. 3. Trajectory in the take-off stage

As shown in Fig. 3(a), (b) and (c), the smoothness of ordinary cubic spline is significantly better than the linear interpolation in the take-off stage, but obviously worse than the adaptive cubic spline.

2. Cruise phase

In the cruise phase, the flight path of the three methods is shown in Fig. 4.

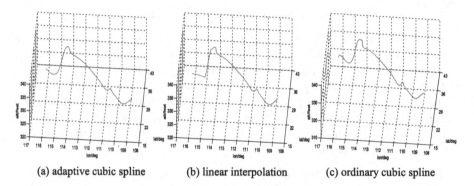

(a) adaptive cubic spline   (b) linear interpolation   (c) ordinary cubic spline

Fig. 4. Trajectory in the cruise stage

As shown in Fig. 4(a), (b) and (c), due to the original trajectory data is relatively flat, the effect of three methods is similar in the cruise phase. However, in the relatively large fluctuations of the trajectory stage, the smoothness of the adaptive cubic spline curve is better than the ordinary cubic spline curve, and the ordinary cubic spline curve is better than the linear interpolation curve.

3. Landing phase

In the landing phase, the flight path of the three methods is shown in Fig. 5.

As shown in Fig. 5(a), (b) and (c), we can see that the smoothness of the cubic spline curve is still better than the linear interpolation curve in the landing phase of the

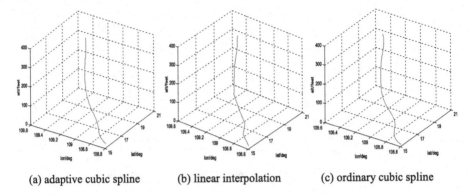

(a) adaptive cubic spline   (b) linear interpolation   (c) ordinary cubic spline

Fig. 5. Trajectory in the landing stage

trajectory, and the adaptive cubic spline curve is better than the ordinary cubic spline curve.

The smoothness of the trajectory fitting curve and the precision of the reconstructed trajectory are two important parameters in the trajectory of real-time monitoring applications. Through the analysis of the experimental results, this paper analyzes the smoothness of the trajectory fitting curve and the accuracy of the reconstructed trajectory.

Contrast the smoothness of the trajectory in the three stages:

- Due to the location of the data has a good stability in the cruise phase, results of the three methods are smooth. In the large deflection of the trajectory segment, the adaptive cubic spline interpolation is still relatively smooth.
- During take-off and landing stage, some of the changes in the technical indicators of the aircraft is relatively large (such as flight altitude, flight speed), resulting in a complex distribution of trajectory points. Compared with the other two interpolation methods, the reconstructed trajectory obtained by the adaptive cubic spline method has obvious advantages.

In order to get the precision of the reconstructed trajectory, the root mean square error (RMSE) is used as the criterion to evaluate the accuracy of the trajectory. The trajectory data is used as the reference value, and the accuracy of the trajectory is calculated by the three algorithms (see Table 1).

Table 1. Trajectory interpolation contrast experiment (%)

Error	Take-off stage			Cruise stage			Landing stage		
	a	o	l	a	o	l	a	o	l
Lat	1.04	10.9	17.5	0.05	0.43	0.61	0.49	4.78	19.5
Lon	0.16	0.81	1.57	0.28	0.80	1.08	0.12	0.43	1.09
Alt	0.27	0.88	1.53	0.42	1.37	2.06	0.13	0.40	0.88

Lat, Lon, Alt denote Latitude, Longitude, Altitude respectively.
l, o, a denote linear, ordinary and adaptive respectively.

From Table 1 we can reach the following conclusions.

- In the cruise phase, due to the flight data is relatively stable, the reconstruction of the trajectory does not show a greater difference in accuracy, the three methods have shown a better performance.
- Due to the irregular flight data, the accuracy of the cubic spline curve is still better than the ordinary cubic spline curve in the take-off and landing phases and the ordinary cubic spline curve is better than the linear interpolation curve.

The algorithm of this paper is different from others. According to the different trajectory curves, the distribution of nodes is not the same. In the large deflection, the distribution of nodes is relatively large, so that the error of the trajectory is small. In the small deflection, the distribution of nodes is relatively small. Under the premise of ensuring the accuracy, in order to improve the efficiency of the algorithm and ensure accurate trajectory of flights, the number of nodes is less as far as possible. Therefore, the experimental results show that the adaptive cubic spline algorithm has a good performance of the flight trajectory in the range of error allowed.

4 Conclusion

We get the better smoothness and higher accuracy of the trajectory by using the method, this method meets the International Civil Aviation Organization (ICAO) latest implementation of the global flight trajectory standards. By using the flight data transmitted by ACARS system to reconstruct the flight path, it can provide accurate flight information to the global flight trajectory, realize the accurate positioning of the flight, and provide guarantee for the safe operation of the air traffic.

In the actual flight, the flight time is relatively short, and the interval between the messages sent by ACARS is relatively long, so there are not many available trajectory points, so the accuracy of the reconstructed trajectory needs to be further improved. Due to the randomness of node selection in this method, the precision and time of the reconstructed trajectory can be better. Therefore, the selection and optimization of the node is the focus of the research in future.

References

1. Andrienko, G., Andrienko, N., Fuchs, G., Garcia, J.M.C.: Clustering trajectories by relevant parts for air traffic analysis. IEEE Trans. Vis. Comput. Graph. **24**(1), 34–44 (2018)
2. Hong, Y., Choi, B., Lee, K., Kim, Y.: Conflict management considering a smooth transition of aircraft into adjacent airspace. IEEE Trans. Intell. Transp. Syst. **17**(9), 2490–2501 (2016)
3. Jackson, M.R.C.: Role of avionics in trajectory-based operations. IEEE Aerosp. Electron. Syst. Mag. **25**(7), 12–19 (2010)
4. Ellerbroek, J., Visser, M., van Dam, S.B.J., Mulder, M., van Paassen, M.M.: Design of an airborne three-dimensional separation assistance display. IEEE Trans. Syst. Man Cybern. Part A Syst. Hum. **41**(5), 863–875 (2011)

5. Radišić, T., Novak, D., Juričić, B.: Reduction of air traffic complexity using trajectory-based operations and validation of novel complexity indicators. IEEE Trans. Intell. Transp. Syst. **18**(11), 3038–3048 (2017)
6. Besada, J., Soto, A., de Miguel, G., García, J., Voet, E.: ATC trajectory reconstruction for automated evaluation of sensor and trajectoryer performance. IEEE Aerospace Electron. Syst. Mag. **28**(2), 4–17 (2013)
7. Sotiriou, D., Kopsaftopoulos, F., Fassois, S.: An adaptive time-series probabilistic framework for 4-D trajectory conformance monitoring. IEEE Trans. Intell. Transp. Syst. **17**(6), 1606–1616 (2016)
8. Wang, X.: Research on key techniques of real-time monitoring for aircraft flight safety. Nanjing University of Aeronautics and Astronautics (2008)
9. Lu, H., Deng, X.: Real-time flight trajectory security monitoring technology based-on ACARS. Aircraft Des. **6**, 52–56 (2009)
10. Dai, S.: Study of adaptive cubic spline interpolation approximation algorithm. Dalian University of Technology (2008)
11. Li, X.: An adaptive algorithm for knots of cubic B-spline in data fitting. Dalian University of Technology (2008)
12. Chaimatanan, S., Delahaye, D., Mongeau, M.: A hybrid metaheuristic optimization algorithm for strategic planning of 4D aircraft trajectories at the continental scale. IEEE Comput. Intell. Mag. **9**(4), 46–61 (2014)
13. Wang, X., Shirinzadeh, B.: Nonlinear multiple integrator and application to aircraft navigation. IEEE Trans. Aerospace Electron. Syst. **50**(1), 607–622 (2014)
14. Margellos, K., Lygeros, J.: Toward 4-D trajectory management in air traffic control: a study based on monte carlo simulation and reachability analysis. IEEE Trans. Control Syst. Technol. **21**(5), 1820–1833 (2013)
15. Tang, J.: Review: analysis and improvement of traffic alert and collision avoidance system. IEEE Access **5**, 21419–21429 (2017)
16. Pritchett, A.R., Genton, A.: Negotiated decentralized aircraft conflict resolution. IEEE Trans. Intell. Transp. Syst. **19**(1), 81–91 (2018)

Lightweight Distributed Attribute Based Keyword Search System for Internet of Things

Jiahuan Long[1], Ke Zhang[2,3], Xiaofen Wang[2(✉)], and Hong-Ning Dai[4]

[1] School of Information and Communication Engineering,
University of Electronic Science and Technology of China,
Chengdu 611731, China
jhlong@std.uestc.edu.cn
[2] School of Computer Science and Engineering,
University of Electronic Science and Technology of China,
Chengdu 611731, China
{kezhang,xfwang}@uestc.edu.cn
[3] Science and Technology on Electronic Information Control Laboratory,
Chengdu 610000, China
[4] Department of Information Technology,
Macau University of Science and Technology, Macau, China
hndai@must.edu.mo

Abstract. Internet of Things (IoT) is a promising networking paradigm that connects various kinds of sensors and exchanges data from smart devices. Since IoT always related to user's daily life, the problems of security and privacy are of great importance. Presently, the attribute based encryption (ABE) is a popular solution to guarantee the fine-grained sharing of encrypted data in IoT. In this paper, an attribute based keyword search with lightweight decryption in multi-authority (ABKS-LD-MA) is proposed. Our system supports multi-keyword search in cloud by using searchable attribute based encryption. We also integrate the lightweight decryption to searchable ABE scheme that largely reduces the computing overhead for users. Furthermore, our ABKS-LD-MA scheme supports multi-authority scenario, which is more adaptive to the real IoT environment. The experiment analysis shows that our scheme has relatively lowered the communication cost on IoT devices.

Keywords: ABE · Multi-keyword search · Multi-authority ·
Lightweight decryption · IoT

1 Introduction

1.1 Background

Internet of things (IoT) is a network combining devices, e.g. smart phones, industrial electronic devices and home appliances, and allows these things to connect,

© Springer Nature Switzerland AG 2019
G. Wang et al. (Eds.): SpaCCS 2019 Workshops, LNCS 11637, pp. 253–264, 2019.
https://doi.org/10.1007/978-3-030-24900-7_21

interact and exchange data. However, User information stored on IoT devices or in the ecosystem may be acquired by unauthorized users. Thus, more and more users and companies encrypt their data that they collect from the sensor network before uploading it to the clouds.

Unfortunately, traditional public key encryption schemes are not suitable for distributed IoT environments. To solve the problem of data security and IoT data access control in distributed IoT system, attribute based encryption (ABE) have been proposed due to its advantage in realizing the fine-grained data access control in the cloud storage. The concept of ABE was proposed by Sahai et al. [1]. ABE schemes are classified into two classes: ciphertext-policy ABE (CP-ABE) [2] and key-policy ABE (KP-ABE) [8]. CP-ABE is more practical for designing an access control system in a cloud environment, as it gives the data owner more direct control on access policies. Bethencourt et al. [2] designed the first CP-ABE encryption scheme, where ciphertext can be decrypted only if the attributes embed in the private key satisfy the access structure for computing the ciphertext. These ABE schemes have been focusing on the single-authority scenario, where all attributes' authorization is managed by a single authority.

However, in our real world, each user's attributes are from different authorities, and the data owner can share data with the users from different authorities. In order to solve this problem, Chase et al. [5] constructed the first multi-authority CP-ABE scheme, where multi-independent authorities manage the attributes and distribute keys to the users. To prevent the collusion attack from corrupted authorities, Lewko and Waters [12] proposed a secure multi-authority ABE construction, where the dual system encryption methodology is used to realize safety proof.

Although the encryption-before-outsourcing scheme can guarantee the IoT data privacy, it makes the data search over encrypted IoT data extremely difficult. Therefore, searchable encryption (SE) is proposed to maintain keyword search over encrypted data. The first public key encryption scheme with keyword search (PEKS) was constructed by Boneh et al. [3], which enables user to securely retrieve files of interest over encrypted data according to user-defined keyword. In practice, to further achieve fine-grained access control in the SE schemes, the attribute based keyword search (ABKS) schemes were proposed [6,11,14]. However, these methods only support single keyword search. To enable multi-keyword search with fine-grained access control, Li et al. [13] proposed an improved ABKS scheme.

One of the main drawbacks of CP-ABE is that the decryption overhead on authorized users is tremendous. To improve the efficiency of decryption on authorized users, Green et al. [9] proposed CP-ABE scheme, where the main part of the decryption is done by the cloud and the remainder part is done at the user end. Therefore, the computation cost of decryption at the user end is greatly lowered while the confidentiality of the message is still protected against the cloud.

1.2   Contribution

In this paper, we propose a novel scheme: attribute based keyword search and lightweight decryption in multi-authority system ABKS-LD-MA, which has the following contributions:

Multiple Keyword Search. Our scheme supports multi-keyword search in cloud by using searchable attribute based encryption. It enables end users to search ciphertext of interest according to a series of keywords.

Lightweight Computation on End Users. Our scheme reliefs the large computational burden from resource-constrained devices. Specically, we outsource the main computation of the decryption to the cloud without loss any data condentially. the user need only compute one exponentiation and no pairings to recover the message.

Decentralizing Attribute Based Encryption. Our scheme design an efficient multi-authority access control scheme for cloud storage. There is no requirment for any central authority, which can avoid placing absolute trust in a single authority which must remain active and uncorrupted throughout the lifetime of the system.

Functionality and Practicability. The performance analysis demonstrates that our system is efficient and feasible in IoT environment.

2   Definition of ABKS-LD-MA

2.1   System Model of ABKS-LD-MA

The system model of ABKS-LD-MA for distributed IoT is presented in Figure 1. The system comprises of six entities, whose responsibilities and interactions are described below.

IoT Node (Data Owner). There are various types of IoT network systems, e.g. smart home, smart industry and remote health care system. Intelligent devices in these systems connect and communicate with each other, collecting and transmitting data. For example, the monitors in smart home are used to monitor home state and the body sensors in remote health care system are used to detect heart rate, body temperature and blood pressure. These private information are formed into files. Then the keywords are extracted from each file, and then the file and the keywords are both encrypted by the IoT node and later sent to the cloud server.

Certificate Authority (CA). CA is not involved in any key distribution and it is only responsible to generate the initial set of common reference parameters and the global user identity (UID) for the authorized user.

Attribute Authority (AA). There exists multiple attribute authorities (AA) in the distributed IoT system. Every AA generates the attribute public key (APK) and the attribute secret key (ASK) for each attribute it manages, and it give respectively APK and ASK to the data owner.

Cloud Server (CS). The cloud sever has huge storage space and the massive computing power, which helps user store ciphertexts. Moreover, the cloud server needs to provide the keyword search query for the data users. The cloud server is regarded as honest-but-curious, who honestly executes the assigned calculation, but is curious to the user's private information.

Auxiliary Cloud Server (ACS). The Auxiliary Cloud Server (ACS) will help the users to complete a part of the decryption calculation with the user's transformation key as input.

Data User (User). Each data user has the UID assigned by the CA and get the attribute secret key from some authorities according to the attributes it has. To search the ciphertext, user chooses a keyword set that he wants to search. Then, a trapdoor is computed from the keywords and uploaded to the cloud server. If the trapdoor satisfies the encrypted index, the data user blinds his secret key and transfers it to a random transformation key. The auxiliary cloud server can use the transformation key to partially decrypt ciphertext if the attributes embed in the private key satisfies the access structure embed in the ciphertext. Upon receiving the partially decrypted ciphertext, the data user runs decrypt algorithm to recover the file.

2.2   Framework of ABKS-LD-MA

Global Setup $(\kappa) \rightarrow (PP, MSK)$. Global setup algorithm takes as input the security parameter κ, and it outputs public parameters PP for the system, the master secret key MSK for each authority and global identity GID for the legal user.

Authority Setup $(PP) \rightarrow (APK_{i,j}, ASK_{i,j})$. Each authority A_j runs the authority setup algorithm, which takes public parameters PP as input and generates a attribute public key $APK_{i,j}$ and a attribute secret key $ASK_{i,j}$ for each attribute i it manages.

SecretKeyGen$(MSK, i, PP, GID, ASK_{i,j}) \rightarrow SK_{i,GID}$. The SecretkeyGen algorithm takes as input an identity GID, the global parameter PP, an attribute

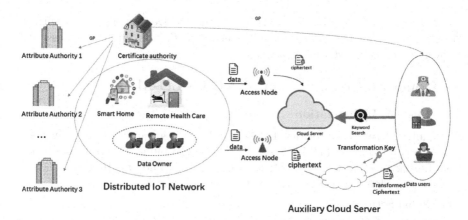

Fig. 1. System model of ABKS-LD-MA

i belonging to some authority, and the attribute secret key $ASK_{i,j}$ for this authority. It produces a secret key $SK_{i,GID}$ for this attribute and send it to the data user.

Encrypt $(M, (A, \rho), KW, PP, \{APK_{i,j}\}) \rightarrow CT$. Data owner runs the Encrypt algorithm, which take as input the file M, the access policy (A, ρ), a keyword set KW, the global parameters PP and the set of attribute public keys $APK_{i,j}$ for relevant authorities. It output the ciphertext CT, which contains encrypted file C_M and encrypted secure index I.

Trapdoor $(\{SK_{i,GID}\}, KW', PP) \rightarrow T_{KW'}$. Data user runs the rapdoor algorithm, which take as input the secret key set, query keyword set KW' and the global parameters PP, and outputs the keyword trapdoor $T_{KW'}$.

TransKeyGen $(\{SK_{i,GID}\}, z) \rightarrow TK_{GID}$. Data user runs the TransKeyGen algorithm, which take as input the secret key set and a blind value z, and outputs the transformation key TK_{GID}. Then, the data user submits $T_{KW'}$ to the cloud server.

Search $(CT, T_{KW'}) \rightarrow 1/0$. The cloud server executes the search algorithm with the trapdoor $T_{KW'}$ and the ciphertext CT as input. If output is "1", the query is successful and the cloud server runs transform algorithm. If output is "0", the transform algorithm will not be run.

Transform $(CT, TK_{GID}) \rightarrow CT_{out}/ \perp$. The cloud runs the partial decrypt algorithm, which takes the transformation key TK_{GID} and the ciphertext CT as input. If the search algorithm output is "1" and attributes embedded in the transformation key satisfies the access structure of the ciphertext CT, the cloud will returns the transformed ciphertext CT_{out} to the user. Otherwise, it outputs $\perp$.

Decrypt $(z, CT_{out}) \to M$. The data user runs the Decrypt algorithm with its blind value z and the transformed ciphertext CT_{out} as input. The user can recover the message M with lightweight decryption.

3   Concrete Construction of ABKS-LD-MA

3.1   System Initialization

S_A denote the set of authorities. Let $\mathbb{G}$ be a bilinear group of prime order p and g be a generator of $\mathbb{G}$. Let $e : \mathbb{G} \times \mathbb{G} \to \mathbb{G}_T$ be the bilinear map. Choose three hash functions $H' : \{0,1\}^* \to \mathbb{Z}_p^*$, $h : \{0,1\}^* \to k$, and $H : \{0,1\}^* \to \mathbb{G}$ that maps global identities $GID \in \{0,1\}^*$ to an element of $\mathbb{G}$.

(1) Global Setup

The certification authority CA inputs a security parameter κ and runs the algorithm Global Setup. Then it chooses a random element $\lambda \in \mathbb{Z}_p^*, f \in \mathbb{G}$, and set the public parameter and master secret key of the system as

$$PP = (f, g, g^\lambda), MSK = \lambda \tag{1}$$

(2) Authority Setup

Each authority takes the global public parameters as the input and runs the Authority Setup. Let S_A denote the the set of attribute authorities. Each authority $A_j(A_j \in S_A)$ has a set of attributes L_j. For different attribute authorities, they manage different attributes. Therefore, for any $A_i, A_j \in S_A$ ($i \neq j$), $L_i \cap L_j = \varnothing$.

For each $i \in L_j$, the authority A_j also chooses two random exponents $a_i, y_i \in \mathbb{Z}_N$ as its attribute secret key, i.e.

$$ASK_{i,j} = \{a_i, y_i, \beta_i\}_{i \in L_j, j \in S_A} \tag{2}$$

and sets the attribute public key as

$$APK_{i,j} = \{e(g,g)^{a_i}, g^{y_i}, g^{\beta_i}\}_{i \in L_j, j \in S_A} \tag{3}$$

3.2   Key Generation

(1) SecretKeyGen

User U_{GID} receives a set of attribute $I[j, GID]$ from authority A_j, and the corresponding secret key is $SK_{i,GID}$. For each $i \in I[j, GID]$, authority A_j computes $K_{1,i} = g^{\frac{a_i}{\lambda + \delta}}$, $K_{3,i} = H(GID)^{y_i}$, $K_{4,i} = g^{a_i} H(GID)^{\beta_i}$.

$$SK_{i,GID} = \{K_{1,i}, K_{3,i}, K_{4,i}\}_{i \in I[j,GID], j \in S_A} \tag{4}$$

(2) TransKeyGen

The data user U_{GID} chooses a random value $z \in \mathbb{Z}_p^*$, and computes $K_2' = H(GID)^z$, $K_{3,i}' = H(GID)^{zy_i}$, $K_{4,i}' = g^{za_i} H(GID)^{z\beta_i}$. It computes the transformation key:

$$TK_{GID} = (K_2', \{K_{3,i}', K_{4,i}'\}_{i \in I[j,GID], j \in A_{GID}}) \tag{5}$$

where A_{GID} denotes the set of authorities that issued the secret keys to the user U_{GID}.

3.3 Trapdoor Generation

If the user wants to find all data owner's file that contain a certain keyword set $KW' = \{kw_1, kw_2...kw_{l_2}\}$, he randomly chooses $u, \varrho_2 \in \mathbb{Z}_p^*$ and generates a keyword trapdoor T'_{KW} using his secret key as follows: $T_{1,i} = K^u_{1,i}$, $T_2 = H(GID)$, $T_3 = u\varrho_2 l_2^{-1}$, $T_{4,x} = \varrho_2^{-1}\Sigma_{x=1}^{l_2}H'(kw_i)^x$, $T_5 = e(g, f)^u$. The keyword trapdoor $T_{KW'}$ is

$$T_{KW'} = (\{T_{1,i}\}_{i \in I[j, GID], j \in A_{GID}}, T_2, T_3, T_5, \{T_{4,x}\}_{x \in \{0,1,...,l_1\}}) \qquad (6)$$

3.4 Encryption

(1) File Encryption

Data owner encrypts the file M with secret key $k_{SE} = h(\Upsilon)$ and Υ is randomly selected element from $\mathbb{G}_T^*$. The encrypted file is denoted as

$$C_M = SEnc'_{k_{SE}}(M) \qquad (7)$$

(2) Index Encryption

The data owner extracts a keyword set $KW = \{kw_1, kw_2...kw_{l_1}\}$ from the file M. Let A be an $n \times l$ matrix and ρ be the function that associated rows of A to attributes. The access policy is represented as (A, ρ). The concrete encryption algorithm is described below.

1. It chooses a random $s \in \mathbb{Z}_p$ and a random vector $v \in \mathbb{Z}_p^n$. Note that s is the first entry of v. For each $i \in [l]$, $\lambda_i = A_i \cdot v$, where A_i is the ith row of A.
2. Construct an l_1 degree polynomial $r(x) = \eta_{l_1}x^{l_1} + \eta_{l_1-1}x^{l_1-1} + ... + \eta_0$, such that $H'(kw_1), ..., H'(kw_{l_1})$ are the l_1 roots of the equation $r(x) = 1$.
3. Randomly picks $\varrho_1, b \in \mathbb{Z}_p^*$ and generate the secure index by computing $I_i = \Upsilon \cdot e(g, g)^{s\alpha_{\rho(i)}}$, $I_0 = g^b$, $I_1 = g^{\lambda b}$, $I_2 = g^s$, $I_3 = g^{\varrho_1}$, $I_{4,i} = g^{\beta_{\rho(i)}\lambda_i}g^{-\varrho_1 y_{\rho(i)}}$ $I_{5,x} = \varrho_1^{-1} \cdot \eta_x$, $E_1 = e(g, f)^{\varrho_1}$, $E_{2,i} = e(g, g)^{\alpha_{\rho(i)} b \varrho_1}$.
4. Outsource the ciphertext CT to the cloud, where

$$CT = (I_0, I_1, I_2, I_3, E_1, \{I_i, I_{4,i}, E_{2,i}\}_{i \in [l]}, \{I_{5,x}\}_{x \in \{0,1,...,l_1\}}, C_M) \qquad (8)$$

3.5 Retrieve Matching Files and Outsourced Computing

When the cloud server receives the keyword trapdoor and transformation key from the data user, it retrieves the data owner's encrypted files to find the matching documents by running the following two phase: Search phase and Transform phase.

In the search phase, if the searched keyword set in keyword trapdoor is a subset of that in the secure index, it means the encrypted file matches the trapdoor.

In the transform phase, the cloud can transform the ciphertext CT to the partial decrypted ciphertext and sent it to the user.

(1) Search
   1. Suppose the attributes embedded in TK_{GID} satisfy the access structure associated with CT. Let $N \subset [l]$ be defined as $N = \{i : \rho(i) \in S\}$. There exists a set of constants $\{w_i \in Z_p\}_{i \in N}$ so that $\Sigma_{i \in N} w_i A_i = (1, 0, ..., 0)$.
   2. The cloud verifies whether the following equation holds

$$T_5 \cdot e(\Pi_{i \in N} T_{1, \rho(i)}, I_0^{T_2} I_1) = (E_1 \cdot \Pi_{i \in N} E_{2,i})^{T_3 \cdot (\Sigma_{x=1}^{l_1} I_{5,x} T_{4,x})}. \qquad (9)$$

If the equation holds, it outputs 1 indicating that $KW' \subset KW$. Otherwise, it outputs 0.

(2) Transform
   1. If the output of *Search* algorithm is 0 or the attributes associated with TK_{GID} does not satisfy the access structure associated with CT, *Transform* algorithm outputs $\bot$.
   2. If the output of *Search* algorithm is 1 and the attributes associated with TK_{GID} satisfy the access structure associated with CT, the cloud computes

$$I' = \frac{e(\Pi_{i \in N} K'_{4, \rho(i)}, I_2)}{e(I_3, \Pi_{i \in N} K'^{w_i}_{3, \rho(i)}) \cdot e(\Pi_{i \in N} I^{w_i}_{4,i}, K'_2)}$$

$$= \frac{e(g, g)^{sz \Sigma_{i \in N} \alpha_{\rho(i)}} e(g, H(GID))^{sz \Sigma_{i \in N} \beta_{\rho(i)}}}{(\Pi_{i \in N} e(g, H(GID))^{\beta_{\rho(i)} z \lambda_i w_i})}$$

$$= e(g, g)^{sz \Sigma_{i \in N} \alpha_{\rho(i)}} \qquad (10)$$

$$I'' = \Pi_{i \in N} I_i = \Pi_{i \in N} (\Upsilon \cdot e(g, g)^{s \alpha_{\rho(i)}}) = \Upsilon^{|N|} e(g, g)^{s \Sigma_{i \in N} \alpha_{\rho(i)}} \qquad (11)$$

The *transform* algorithm outputs $CT_{out} = (C_M, I', I'')$. CT_{out} is the transformed ciphertext which is sent to data user.

3.6   Decryption

In this algorithm, the data user takes as input the blind value z and the transformed ciphertext CT_{out}, and recovers the plaintext as

$$(I''/(I')^{1/z})^{1/|N|} = (\Upsilon^{|N|})^{1/|N|} = \Upsilon \qquad (12)$$

$$k_{SE} = h(\Upsilon) \qquad (13)$$

$$M = SDec'_{k_{SE}}(C_M) \qquad (14)$$

As the ciphertext is already partially decrypted by the cloud server, in this phase the data user only needs to compute a simple exponentiation and division operation to recover the plaintext file, which is very efficient.

4   Performance Analysis

In this section, we analyze the performance of ABKS-LD-MA from the following parts. On the one hand, we analyze the functions of ABKS-LD-MA with existing schemes as shown in Table 1. On the other hand, we also evaluate the computing overheads of ABKS-LD-MA and other schemes on an experimental workbench (Table 2).

Table 1. Function comparison

	[4]	[10]	[18]	[9]	[17]	[20]	[15]	[22]	[21]	[16]	Our
Fine-grained access control	×	√	√	√	√	√	√	√	√	√	√
Multi-keyword search	√	×	√	×	√	×	×	√	×	×	√
Lightweight decryption	×	×	×	√	×	×	√	×	×	×	√
Decentralized system	×	×	×	×	×	√	×	×	√	√	√

Table 2. Computing overhead comparison

Scheme	KeyGen	Encryption	Trapdoor	Search	Decryption
[19]	$(|S|+4)E$	$P + E_T$ $+(5l+2)E$	$\perp$	$\perp$	$(3|S|+1)P$ $+(|S|+1)E$
[11]	$4|S|E$	$2P+(l+6)E$ $+E_T$	$8|S|E$	$2P+2lE$	$4P+E_T$ $+(3|S|+5)E$
[10]	$(4|S|+3)E$	$(5l+1)E+E_T$	$\perp$	$\perp$	$(4|S|+1)P$
Our	$4|S|E$	$3E_T+(2l+1)P$ $+(2l+4)E$	$(|S|+1)E+P$	$3P+3E_T$ $+(2l+1)E$	$2E_T$

4.1   Experimental Analysis

To evaluate the performance, we leverage Java Pairing Based Cryptography (JPBC) Library [7] on PC to implement ABKS-LD-MA and other available schemes used for comparison. The PC used for conducting experiment is running Windows 10 64-bit operation system with the following configurations: Intel core i7 CPU @ 2.60 GHZ, 16 GB RAM.

Figure 2 shows the computation overheads of decryption algorithms. In decryption phase, our ABKS-LD-MA scheme outsources a large number of computations to cloud, so the use can only consume 44 ms to decrypt the ciphertext. However, the schemes in [10,11,19] has more greater computations than our scheme.

The above analysis shows that ABKS-LD-MA has efficiency significantly better than the other schemes.

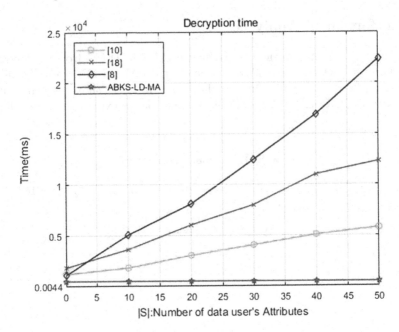

Fig. 2. Computing overhead

5   Conclusion

In this paper, we propose ABKS-LD-MA, lightweight attribute based search encryption in multi-authority. ABKS-LD-MA seamlessly integrates a number of key security functionalities, such as multi-keyword search, fine-grained access control, lightweight decryption. Futhermore, the scheme also supports multi-authority scenario, which is more suitable for the Internet of Things environment. The function analysis showed that ABKS-LD-MA is superior to most of the existing systems. Peformance analysis demonstrated that our schemes is very practical.

Acknowledgments. The paper is partially supported by the Sichuan Science and Technology Program (No. 2019YFG0405), the 6th Innovation and Entrepreneurship Leading Talents Project of Dongguan, the Project of Science and Technology on Electronic Information Control Laboratory, the National Natural Science Foundation of China under Grants U1833122, and the Macao Science and Technology Development Fund under Grants 0026/2018/A1.

References

1. Sahai, A., Waters, B.: Fuzzy identity-based encryption. In: Cramer, R. (ed.) EURO-CRYPT 2005. LNCS, vol. 3494, pp. 457–473. Springer, Heidelberg (2005). https://doi.org/10.1007/11426639_27
2. Bethencourt, J., Sahai, A., Waters, B.: Ciphertext-policy attribute-based encryption. In: 2007 IEEE Symposium on Security and Privacy (SP 2007), pp. 321–334. IEEE, Berkeley, May 2007. https://doi.org/10.1109/SP.2007.11, http://ieeexplore.ieee.org/document/4223236
3. Boneh, D., Di Crescenzo, G., Ostrovsky, R., Persiano, G.: Public key encryption with keyword search. In: Cachin, C., Camenisch, J.L. (eds.) EUROCRYPT 2004. LNCS, vol. 3027, pp. 506–522. Springer, Heidelberg (2004). https://doi.org/10.1007/978-3-540-24676-3_30
4. Boneh, D., Waters, B.: Conjunctive, subset, and range queries on encrypted data. In: Vadhan, S.P. (ed.) TCC 2007. LNCS, vol. 4392, pp. 535–554. Springer, Heidelberg (2007). https://doi.org/10.1007/978-3-540-70936-7_29
5. Chase, M.: Multi-authority attribute based encryption. In: Vadhan, S.P. (ed.) TCC 2007. LNCS, vol. 4392, pp. 515–534. Springer, Heidelberg (2007). https://doi.org/10.1007/978-3-540-70936-7_28
6. Cui, J., Zhou, H., Zhong, H., Xu, Y.: AKSER: attribute-based keyword search with efficient revocation in cloud computing. Inf. Sci. **423**, 343–352 (2018). https://doi.org/10.1016/j.ins.2017.09.029. http://linkinghub.elsevier.com/retrieve/pii/S0020025516311215
7. De Caro, A., Iovino, V.: JPBC: Java pairing based cryptography. In: Proceedings of the 16th IEEE Symposium on Computers and Communications, ISCC 2011, Kerkyra, Corfu, Greece, 28 June–1 July, pp. 850–855 (2011)
8. Goyal, V., Pandey, O., Sahai, A., Waters, B.: Attribute-based encryption for fine-grained access control of encrypted data. In: Proceedings of the 13th ACM conference on Computer and communications security - CCS 2006, Alexandria, Virginia, USA, p. 89. ACM Press (2006). https://doi.org/10.1145/1180405.1180418, http://portal.acm.org/citation.cfm?doid=1180405.1180418
9. Green, M., Hohenberger, S., Waters, B., et al.: Outsourcing the decryption of ABE ciphertexts. In: USENIX Security Symposium, vol. 2011 (2011)
10. Hohenberger, S., Waters, B.: Online/offline attribute-based encryption. In: Krawczyk, H. (ed.) PKC 2014. LNCS, vol. 8383, pp. 293–310. Springer, Heidelberg (2014). https://doi.org/10.1007/978-3-642-54631-0_17
11. Liang, K., Susilo, W.: Searchable attribute-based mechanism with efficient data sharing for secure cloud storage. IEEE Trans. Inf. Forensics Secur. **10**(9), 1981–1992 (2015). https://doi.org/10.1109/TIFS.2015.2442215. http://ieeexplore.ieee.org/document/7118738/
12. Lewko, A., Waters, B.: Decentralizing attribute-based encryption. In: Paterson, K.G. (ed.) EUROCRYPT 2011. LNCS, vol. 6632, pp. 568–588. Springer, Heidelberg (2011). https://doi.org/10.1007/978-3-642-20465-4_31
13. Li, H., Liu, D., Jia, K., Lin, X.: Achieving authorized and ranked multi-keyword search over encrypted cloud data. In: 2015 IEEE International Conference on Communications (ICC), London, pp. 7450–7455. IEEE, June 2015. https://doi.org/10.1109/ICC.2015.7249517, http://ieeexplore.ieee.org/document/7249517/
14. Li, J., Zhang, L.: Attribute-based keyword search and data access control in cloud. In: 2014 Tenth International Conference on Computational Intelligence and Security, Kunming, Yunnan, China, pp. 382–386. IEEE, November 2014. https://doi.org/10.1109/CIS.2014.113, http://ieeexplore.ieee.org/document/7016922/

15. Li, J., Yao, W., Zhang, Y., Qian, H., Han, J.: Flexible and fine-grained attribute-based data storage in cloud computing. IEEE Trans. Serv. Comput. **10**(5), 785–796, September 2017. https://doi.org/10.1109/TSC.2016.2520932, http://ieeexplore. ieee.org/document/7390098/

16. Li, M., Yu, S., Zheng, Y., Ren, K., Lou, W.: Scalable and secure sharing of personal health records in cloud computing using attribute-based encryption. IEEE Trans. Parallel Distrib. Syst. **24**(1), 131–143 (2013). https://doi.org/10.1109/TPDS.2012. 97. http://ieeexplore.ieee.org/document/6171175/

17. Miao, Y., Ma, J., Liu, X., Li, X., Jiang, Q., Zhang, J.: Attribute-based keyword search over hierarchical data in cloud computing. IEEE Trans. Serv. Comput. 1–14 (2017). https://doi.org/10.1109/TSC.2017.2757467, https://ink.library.smu. edu.sg/sis_research/3856

18. Miao, Y., Ma, J., Liu, X., Li, X., Liu, Z., Li, H.: Practical attribute-based multi-keyword search scheme in mobile crowdsourcing. IEEE Internet Things J. 1 (2017). https://doi.org/10.1109/JIOT.2017.2779124

19. Ning, J., Dong, X., Cao, Z., Wei, L., Lin, X.: White-box traceable ciphertext-policy attribute-based encryption supporting flexible attributes. IEEE Trans. Inf. Forensics Secur. **10**(6), 1274–1288 (2015). https://doi.org/10.1109/TIFS.2015.2405905

20. Ruj, S., Nayak, A., Stojmenovic, I.: DACC: distributed access control in clouds. In: 2011 IEEE 10th International Conference on Trust, Security and Privacy in Computing and Communications, Changsha, China, pp. 91–98. IEEE, November 2011. https://doi.org/10.1109/TrustCom.2011.15, http://ieeexplore.ieee.org/document/ 6120807/

21. Wei, J., Liu, W., Hu, X.: Secure and efficient attribute-based access control for multiauthority cloud storage. IEEE Syst. J. **12**(2), 1731–1742 (2018). https://doi. org/10.1109/JSYST.2016.2633559. http://ieeexplore.ieee.org/document/7792622/

22. Zhang, W., Lin, Y., Xiao, S., Wu, J., Zhou, S.: Privacy preserving ranked multi-keyword search for multiple data owners in cloud computing. IEEE Trans. Comput. **65**(5), 1566–1577 (2016). https://doi.org/10.1109/TC.2015.2448099. http://ieeexplore.ieee.org/document/7130597/

Continuous Objects Detection
Based on Optimized Greedy Algorithm
in IoT Sensing Networks

Jin Diao[1], Deng Zhao[1], Jine Tang[2], Zehui Cheng[3], and Zhangbing Zhou[1,4(✉)]

[1] School of Information Engineering, China University of Geosciences,
Beijing 100083, China
{diaojin,zbzhou}@cugb.edu.cn, dengzhao.cugb@gmail.com
[2] School of Artificial Intelligence, Hebei University of Technology,
Tianjin 300401, China
tangjine2008@163.com
[3] Computer Science Department, University of California,
Santa Cruz, CA 95064, USA
evelynchengze@gmail.com
[4] Computer Science Department, TELECOM SudParis, Évry, France

Abstract. Sensing network of the Internet of Things (IoT) has become the infrastructure for facilitating the monitoring of potential events, where the accuracy and energy-efficiency are essential factors to be considered when determining the boundary of continuous objects. This article proposes an energy-efficient boundary detection mechanism in IoT sensing network. Specifically, a sleeping mechanism is adopted to detect the relatively coarse boundary through applying the convex hull algorithm. Leveraging the analysis of the relation for corresponding boundary nodes, the area around a boundary node is categorized as three types of sub-areas with descending possibility of event occurrence. An optimized greedy algorithm is adopted to selectively activate certain numbers of 1-hop neighboring IoT nodes in respective sub-areas, to avoid the activation of all 1-hop neighboring nodes in a flooding manner. Consequently, the boundary is refined and optimized according to sensory data of these activated IoT nodes. Experimental results demonstrate that our method can achieve better detection accuracy, while reducing energy consumption to a large extent, compared to the state of arts.

Keywords: Boundary detection · Continuous objects ·
IoT sensing networks · Energy efficiency · Greedy algorithm

1 Introduction

The rapid proliferation of smart devices envisions IoT sensing network as a novel infrastructure to facilitate applications in various domains. Generally speaking, IoT sensing network enables the collaboration, cooperation, and communication

G. Wang et al. (Eds.): SpaCCS 2019 Workshops, LNCS 11637, pp. 265–278, 2019.
https://doi.org/10.1007/978-3-030-24900-7_22

among a large number of smart things, and forms self-organizing and adaptive sub-networks based on edge network intelligence [1]. Due to its advantage of providing affordable, lightweight and flexible solutions for early warning, data analysis, knowledge aggregation, and remote monitoring, IoT sensing network has been paid more attention in many fields, especially in physical sensing and monitoring [2]. One example is the gas leakage boundary detection specifically for toxic gases. It is essential to identify the boundary of the object to make the retreat and rescue more effective and prompter [3]. Sensing devices, such as wireless sensors, play a vital role in collecting physical information in a real-time situation, but they are usually powered by battery resources and hardly to be recharged in most cases especially when urgent [4]. Although there are some techniques proposed for energy saving and harvesting, maximizing and extending the network lifecycle remains challenging, and energy efficiency is also one of the most significant research questions in IoT sensing network [5]. Consequently, techniques that can facilitate the boundary detection efficiently and accurately, and prolong the network lifetime as much as possible, are fundamental.

The frequent occurrence of gas leakage especially toxic gases causes severe loss of life and property. Therefore, researchers from both the industrial and academic are devoted to a practical solution for gas leakage boundary detection and monitoring. Several methods were proposed in recent decades. Some researchers suggested to leverage the planarization algorithm, allowing for an accurate boundary based on the boundary faces defined by boundary nodes [6]. However, the real networks are usually more complicated, so the assumptions of these planarization algorithms are not met. Besides, it is always difficult to solve the determination of the network partitioning granularities based on the boundary faces. The authors [7] attempting to adopt the greedy algorithm found an accurate boundary based on the sensory data of all 1-hop neighbors of abnormal nodes. All abnormal nodes can be detected using the greedy method, so the accuracy of the detection result is very high. However, greedy algorithm usually causes excessive detection during the iteration process and unnecessary network energy consumption. Other researchers aimed to integrate traditional stable nodes with mobile nodes to achieve better detection of the boundary where mobile nodes are moving around to sense and collect more critical information effectively [8]. The technique is promising but may incur higher cost since mobile nodes are usually more expensive, which may result in a limited number of mobile nodes, which are supposed to drain more energy when moving, sensing and collecting data continuously. Moreover, the technique seems to be unadaptable when mobile nodes are used in mountains and other areas with poor transportation. These techniques achieve acceptable performance based on certain assumptions but may not function well in complex or real-world cases. Besides, energy efficiency was not emphasized in some techniques.

To mitigate this problem, we aim to explore an accurate and energy-efficient method to detect the continuous object boundary leveraging the Optimized Greedy Algorithm (OGA), where only partial 1-hop neighbors of abnormal nodes are involved in the detection to achieve higher accuracy and energy-efficiency.

The network is deployed with three kinds of nodes: (i) *Base Station* (*BS*), (ii) *Relay Nodes* (*RNs*) and (iii) *Terminal Nodes* (*TNs*), where rely nodes collect sensory data from corresponding local terminal nodes, communicate with each other, and forward the information to base station, to provide a more flexible means of abnormal nodes detection and boundary supervision. The contributions of this technique are presented as follows:

- A sleeping mechanism is adopted, such that *RNs* in the network activate periodically for the detection of abnormal situations, to reduce unnecessary energy consumption. The detected leakage is forwarded to *BS* from corresponding *RNs*. The initial gas leakage boundary, which is defined by a set of boundary nodes, is determined in *BS* through adopting the widely-adopted convex hull algorithm.
- Based on the positional relations between the boundary node and its left/right closest neighbors, areas around each boundary node are categorized as three sub-areas with descending possibilities of gas leakage: (i) most possible leakage area, (ii) possible leakage area and (iii) non-possible leakage area. Different numbers of 1-hop neighbors in these sub-areas are activated accordingly concerning optimized greedy algorithm, to avoid activating all 1-hop neighbors in a flooding manner. This strategy can reduce unnecessary energy consumption and ensure high accuracy.
- The initial boundary is updated according to sensory data of selective 1-hop neighbors from a slightly rough boundary to an accurate one, where the farthest and nearest neighbors of boundary nodes are generally taken into account to improve the boundary accuracy.

2 Preliminaries

2.1 IoT Sensing Networks and Network Nodes

IoT sensing network is composed of a large number of smart devices, varying in computational and storage capacities, and remaining energy [1,9]. A network is defined as a graph as follows:

Definition 1. *IoT Sensing Network. An IoT sensing network SN_{IoT} is a tuple (ND, LnK), where (i) ND is a set of IoT smart things including base station, relay nodes, or terminal nodes, and (ii) LnK is a set of links between smart things in ND, and a link connects two smart things when their geographical distance is within the pre-specified communication radius.*

Generally, there is only one base station (BS) with no capacity limitation. Relay nodes have a particular capability for local sensory data preprocessing. Terminal nodes are usually deployed in a relatively dense fashion, aiming to sense and detect the occurrence of potential events. An IoT smart thing corresponds to a network node defined as follows:

Definition 2. *Network Node. A network node nd is a tuple (id, loc, cr, engy, typ, stat, hid, val), where:*

- id is the unique identifier.
- loc is the geographical location obtained by GPS technology, composed of its latitude and longitude.
- cr is the communication radius which is unique to different types of nodes.
- engy is the current remaining energy of nd. Same type of node has the same initial energy. Initial energy of relay node is higher than that of terminal node. Zero energy of nd suggests the dead status of that nd.
- typ is the type of nd, which can be BS, RN, or TN, where RN stands for relay node, and TN means terminal node.
- stat has two values, active and inactive.
- hid is the id of the relay node to which nd belongs. It should be noted that the hid of RN is the id of BS, and the hid of BS is empty. Each terminal node is supposed to send data to its upper-level relay node.
- val indicates sensory data.

We used an experiment-set threshold trd to determine whether a node is abnormal. When the detected value of a node in the network is higher than the trd, we concluded that the node detects the object and it is an abnormal node.

2.2 Energy Model

We applied a widely-adopted radio energy dissipation model proposed in [10]. Further changes were made to the model considering different experimental backgrounds. A description of model parameters is shown in Table 1. The energy consumption formula of a relay node is constructed as:

$$E_R = nE_{elec}N_{nonR} + nE_{DA}(N_{nonR} + 1) + nE_{elec} + n\epsilon_{mp}d_{toBS}^4 \tag{1}$$

Terminal nodes transmit data to the relay node which it belongs to, so its energy consumption formula is:

$$E_{nonR} = nE_{elec} + n\epsilon_{fs}d_{toR}^2 \tag{2}$$

If N nodes are uniformly distributed in the $M \times M$ square area, d_{toBS} and d_{toR} can be shown as [11]:

$$d_{toBS} = \int_{M^2} \sqrt{x^2 + y^2}\frac{1}{M^2}dM^2 = 0.3825M \tag{3}$$

$$d_{toR} = \sqrt{\int\int (x^2 + y^2)\rho(x,y)dxdy} = \frac{M}{\sqrt{2\pi k}} \tag{4}$$

3   Initial Boundary Detection

3.1 Abnormal and Boundary Nodes

We divide nodes into three types: *Abnormal Nodes (ANs)*, *Boundary Nodes (BNs)* and *Normal Nodes (NNs)*. Nodes located inside a continuous object are stored in ANs to reflect the inner situation of the object. The boundary nodes obtained in the current detection phase are stored in BNs. The set is constantly updated through continuous iterative detecting process. Normal nodes those close to the object boundary, and at least one of its neighbors is an abnormal node inside the object or a boundary node are stored in NNs. Details of the probing process, based on the three sets described above, are described in the following sections.

Table 1. Parameters in the energy model.

Name	Description
n	The number of bits in each data message
E_{elec}	The energy consumed to transmit or receive data for per bit
N_{nonR}	The number of terminal nodes which belong to a relay node
E_{DA}	The data aggregation cost which this relay node manages
ϵ_{mp}	The transmitting and amplifying parameter
d_{toBS}	The average distance between relay nodes and BS
ϵ_{fs}	The transmitting and amplifying parameter
d_{toR}	The average distance between terminal nodes and the relay node which they belong to
x	The latitude of the node
y	The longitude of the node
k	The number of relay nodes
E_R	The energy consumption of each relay node
E_{nonR}	The energy consumption of each terminal node

3.2 Initial Boundary Generation

For all abnormal nodes that currently detect the object, BS uses the convex hull algorithm to select the boundary nodes to generate an initial boundary. Details of the initial detection algorithm are given as Algorithm 1:

When some nodes detect the object, they send packets which include subsets of BNs to BS (lines 1–3), as shown in Fig. 1-START. BS obtains basic information of the boundary node such as id and loc through received data packet. First, BS stores all boundary nodes into the $SBNs$ (line 4) and selects the node rn_i with the smallest y-coordinate. This node is considered as the origin p_0 of Cartesian coordinate system (lines 5–10). Then calculate the angle between the remaining nodes and the origin and sort nodes counterclockwise (lines 11–14). If the angles are the same, then nodes closer to the origin are placed in front, as shown in Fig. 1-(1). The top three nodes of $SBNs$ are stored in CHNs (line 15). For remaining nodes in $SBNs$, it is sequentially determined whether the vector formed by the current rn_i and the latest node in CHs are deflected to the right relative to the vector formed by the latest node and the second new

Algorithm 1. Initial Object Detection

Require:
- RNs: a set of relay nodes which detect the object.

Ensure:
- BNs: initial boundary nodes.
- ANs: abnormal nodes inside the object.

1: **for all** abnormal $rn_i \in RNs$ **do**
2:     $SBNs_i \leftarrow SBNs_i \cup \{rn_i\}$
3: **end for**
4: $SBNs \leftarrow SBNs_1 \cup SBNs_2 \cup ... \cup SBNs_n$
5: $p_0 \leftarrow rn_0$
6: **for all** $rn_i \in SBNs$ **do**
7:     **if** $rn_{i+1}.getY < rn_i.getY$ **then**
8:         $p_0 \leftarrow rn_{i+1}$
9:     **end if**
10: **end for**
11: **for all** $rn_i \in SBNs$ **do**
12:     calculate the polar angle between rn_i and p_0
13: **end for**
14: sort counterclockwise $SBNs$ according to the polar angle
15: CHNs $\leftarrow \{rn_0\} \cup \{rn_1\} \cup \{rn_2\}$
16: **for all** rn_i of others **do**
17:     $p_x \leftarrow$ CHNs[|CHNs|-2]; $p_y \leftarrow$ CHNs[|CHNs|-1]
18:     **while** ($\overrightarrow{p_y rn_i}$ is right-turned relative to $\overrightarrow{p_x p_y}$) **do**
19:         CHNs $\leftarrow$ CHNs-{CHNs[|CHNs|-1]}
20:         $p_x \leftarrow$ CHNs[|CHNs|-2]; $p_y \leftarrow$ CHNs[|CHNs|-1]
21:     **end while**
22:     CHNs $\leftarrow$ CHNs$\cup\{rn_i\}$
23: **end for**
24: $ANs \leftarrow ANs\cup(SBNs$-CHNs)); $BNs \leftarrow BNs\cup$CHNs

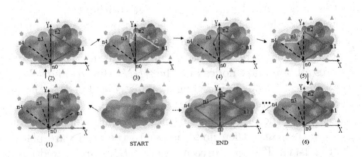

Fig. 1. A sample of initial object boundary generation procedure.

node in CHs. If so, the latest node of CHs is deleted(lines 16–21). Otherwise, the current rn_i is inserted into CHs (line 22). All nodes included in $SBNs$ but not included in CHNs are inserted into ANs (line 24). All nodes included in CHNs are inserted into BNs (line 24). This process is shown as Fig. 1-(2)-END.

4   Boundary Detection Optimization

4.1   Priori Condition for Activating Nodes

To detect the detail of object, areas around each boundary node are categorized as three kinds: (i) most possible leakage area (denoted as vnt), (ii) possible leakage area (denoted as vnt_p) and (iii) non-possible leakage area (denoted as vnt_{pn}) with different importance defined based on the object boundary. The discipline of continuous object diffusion makes vnt_{pn} the most likely diffusion area of the object. vnt_p is less important, but it still has higher detection value than vnt. Selecting a different number of neighbor nodes to activate in each part can reduce energy waste caused by invalid activation behavior. It's shown as Fig. 2.

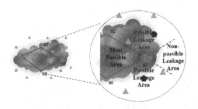

Fig. 2. A sample for dividing the surrounding area of a boundary node.

4.2   Object Boundary Optimization

Leveraging the initial boundary of the object afore-generated, this section aims to improve object boundary accuracy considering the priori condition.

As presented in Algorithm 2, for each node in the initial boundary of the object, its neighboring area is divided into three types four parts according to the initial object boundary. We find the left neighbor, the right neighbor, the diagonal point of left neighbor, and the diagonal point of the right neighbor of the current boundary node (lines 1–3). Store all neighbors of the current boundary node into NEI (line 4). We determine which part of each neighbor node is located around the current node and store it in the corresponding set (lines 5–15). Since vnt_{pn} is the area that needs to be emphasized during the detection process, vnt_{pn} of the current node is divided into k equal sub-areas based on the origin to make sure the omnidirectional detection (lines 16–18). And the nk_i is the k equal point.

Algorithm 2. Boundary Optimization Based on Priori Conditions

---

Require:
- BNs: current boundary nodes.

Ensure:
- BNs: new boundary nodes.
- ANs: abnormal nodes inside the object.
- NNs: normal nodes near the boundary.

1: **for all** node $n_i \in BNs$ **and** n_i.flag is $true$ **do**
2:     $s_0, s_1 \leftarrow$ left and right neighbors of n_i
3:     $s_2, s_3 \leftarrow$ diagonal point of s_0, s_1
4:     $NEI \leftarrow n_i$.getnei()
5:     **for all** node $ne_i \in NEI$ **do**
6:         **if** ($\overrightarrow{s_0 ne_i}$ rotates counterclockwise with respect to (denoted as :$\circlearrowleft$) $\overrightarrow{n_i s_0}$) and ($\overrightarrow{s_1 ne_i}$ rotates clockwise with respect to (denoted as :$\circlearrowright$) $\overrightarrow{n_i s_1}$) **then**
7:             $ENs \leftarrow ENs \cup \{ne_i\}$
8:         **else if** ($\overrightarrow{s_1 ne_i}$:$\circlearrowright$ $\overrightarrow{n_i s_1}$) and ($\overrightarrow{s_2 ne_i}$:$\circlearrowright$ $\overrightarrow{n_i s_2}$) **then**
9:             $BNs1 \leftarrow BNs1 \cup \{ne_i\}$
10:         **else if** ($\overrightarrow{s_2 ne_i}$:$\circlearrowright$ $\overrightarrow{n_i s_2}$) and ($\overrightarrow{s_3 ne_i}$:$\circlearrowright$ $\overrightarrow{n_i s_3}$) **then**
11:             $NN \leftarrow NN \cup \{ne_i\}$
12:         **else**
13:             $BNs2 \leftarrow BNs2 \cup \{ne_i\}$
14:         **end if**
15:     **end for**
16:     nk_1.setX, nk_2.setX, ..., nk_{k-1}.setX $\leftarrow$ (s2.getX+s3.getX)/k, 2(s2.getX+s3.getX)/k, ..., (k-1)(s2.getX+s3.getX)/k
17:     nk_1.setY, nk_2.setY, ..., nk_{k-1}.setY $\leftarrow$ (s2.getY+s3.getY)/k, 2(s2.getY+s3.getY)/k, ..., (k-1)(s2.getY+s3.getY)/k
18:     split NN into k subsets by comparing loc of nk_i and loc of node$\in NN$ as lines 10-11.
19:     find the farthest 1-hop neighbor of n_i in each set.
20:     **if** fn.value $\geq trd$ and the part is vnt **then**
21:         $SANs_i \leftarrow SANs_i \cup \{fn\}$
22:     **else if** fn.value $\geq trd$ and the part is not vnt **then**
23:         $SBNs_i \leftarrow SBNs_i \cup \{fn\}$
24:     **else**
25:         $SNNs_i \leftarrow SNNs_i \cup \{fn\}$
26:     **end if**
27:     **if** ($\forall$ value of activated nodes in $vnt_{pn} < trd$) or ($\nexists$ nodes can be activated) **then**
28:         n_i.flag $\leftarrow false$
29:     **end if**
30: **end for**
31: $ANs \leftarrow SANs_1 \cup SANs_2 \cup ... \cup SANs_{|SANs|}$
32: $NNs \leftarrow SNNs_1 \cup SNNs_2 \cup ... \cup SNNs_{|SNNs|}$
33: $SBNs \leftarrow SBNs_1 \cup SBNs_2 \cup ... \cup SBNs_{|SBNs|}$
34: $BNs \leftarrow BNs \cup SBNs$.CH(); $ANs \leftarrow ANs \cup (SBNs-SBNs$.CH())

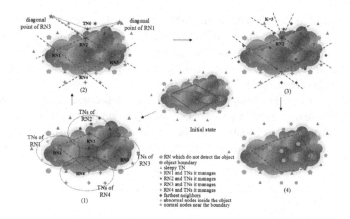

Fig. 3. A sample for the optimization based on farthest neighbors of object boundary.

Firstly, we activate the farthest 1-hop neighbor node fn with a true detection flag from each part (line 19). If fn is abnormal and located in vnt, the relay node which governs fn inserts it to the subset of ANs. If it is abnormal but not located in vnt, it is inserted into the subset of BNs. If it is normal, it is inserted into the subset of NNs (lines 20–26). If all activated nodes in vnt_{pn} are normal nodes, or none of nodes can be activated in all sub-areas, the detection flag of this node is set to false (lines 27–29). After one round of detection, each relay node uploads its subsets and sends them to BS. BS integrates all subsets and updates ANs, BNs and NNs (lines 31–35). For each node in the former BNs, if it is not the node of the current boundary, it is inserted into ANs (Fig. 3).

Now we are further optimizing the boundaries. Repeat lines 1–15 in Algorithm 2 to divide the area around the boundary node. But we divide vnt_{pn} into l equal parts which is not less than k to conduct more detailed detection of the most important area. Moreover, we no longer detect the farthest 1-hop neighbor but detect the nearest 1-hop neighbor. If the node is abnormal and located in vnt, the relay node which governs this node inserts it into the subset of ANs. If it is abnormal but not located in vnt, it is inserted into the subset of BNs. If it is normal, it is inserted into the subset of NNs. When all activated nodes in vnt_{pn} are normal nodes, or none of the nodes can be activated in all sub-areas, for each boundary node, current detection process ends and the detection flag of this node is set to false. After each detection process, ANs, BNs and NNs are updated by BS, and BS generates new boundaries.

5   Implementation and Evaluation

5.1   Experiment Settings

Experiments were conducted on a desktop with an Intel i7-6700 processor at 3.40 GHz and 3.41 GHz, 8.00 GB memory, and a 64-bit Windows 10 operating system. We used Java to program simulation experiments.

In the initial network, there are 2000 nodes, of which 100 uniformly distributed relay nodes are active, and the remaining 1900 terminal nodes are in a dormant state. Table 2 shows the parameter settings of our experiments. In all experiments, we took the circular area, as a continuous object, whose center is the center of the network and radius is 145.

We evaluate the performance of our boundary detection algorithm by experiments. The whole experiment process consisted of two parts. In the first part, we explore the impact of important variables in the algorithm. In the second part, the efficiency of the algorithm is evaluated by comparison with the baseline.

Table 2. Parameter settings

Parameter name	Value
Region size	700 m × 700 m
Threshold of detection event (trd)	$210 \, \text{mg/m}^2$
Communication radius of relay sensor (r)	100 m
Communication radius of terminal sensor (r)	50 m
E_{elec}	50 nJ/bit
ϵ_{mp}	$0.1 \, \text{nJ}/(\text{bit} \times \text{m}^2)$

5.2 Variables Affecting Detection Efficiency Evaluation Results

We develop this section separately in three parts: terminal node number, the value of k and the value of l.

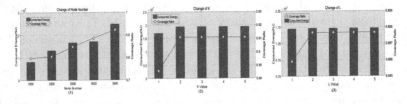

Fig. 4. The effect of variable changes on coverage ratio of the detected object and the real object and energy consumption.

First, we set TNs number to 1400, 1900, 2400, 2900, and 3400, respectively, to make total nodes number to 1500, 2000, 2500, 3000, 3500. And we set both k and l to 1. In Fig. 4-(1), as the number increases, energy costs also increase. The reason is that the more nodes there are, the more neighbors need to be detected and the more energy the network consumes. There are many popular interpolation algorithms IDW, Spline and Kriging. Since IDW [12] is more advantageous for evenly arranged scenes, we use this method to plot concentration equivalents as shown in Fig. 5. According to the figure, the corresponding event processing measures can be well formulated.

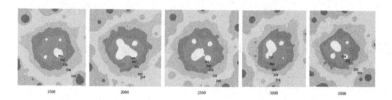

Fig. 5. Concentration contour map drawn by IDW, when the node number is set to 1500, 2000, 2500, 3000 and 3500, respectively.

Second, we discussed the impact of different k-value as 1, 2, 3, 4 and 5 respectively. We set the total number of nodes to 3000, and l to 1. In Fig. 4-(2), as the value of k continues to increase from 1 to 5, the energy overhead of the network increases first and then stabilizes. The reason is that, as the number of sub-parts increases, more nodes need to be activated which leads to more energy overhead. Then, due to the limited number of neighbor nodes, no more nodes need to be detected. Similar to the energy consumption, the coverage ratio does not increase continuously, too. The result shows that the effect of vnt_{pn} segmentation is limited, and excessive division does not necessarily lead to better detection results. We also used IDW interpolation to plot the concentration contours. In the Fig. 6, as k changes, the detection result changes first, but when k reaches a specific value, the detection result remains.

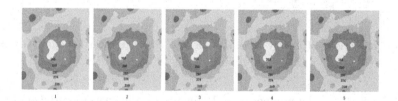

Fig. 6. Concentration contour map drawn by IDW, when the parameter k is set to 1, 2, 3, 4 and 5, respectively.

Third, we discussed the different l-values as 1, 2, 3, 4 and 5 respectively. We also set total nodes number to 3000, and k to 1. In Fig. 4-(3), as l continues to increase, the energy consumed and the coverage ratio increase first and then remain unchanged. The reason for this phenomenon is similar to the second experiment. The division of sub-parts should be adjusted according to the total number of nodes in the network and cannot be divided excessively. We used IDW interpolation to plot the concentration contours, as shown in Fig. 7.

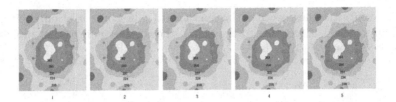

Fig. 7. Concentration contour map drawn by IDW, when the parameter l is set to 1, 2, 3, 4 and 5, respectively.

5.3 Comparison with Other Methods

The following two methods are chosen as the baseline:

- *Lei's method*: We chose the greedy method proposed by Lei [7] as a baseline. This method obtains the final object boundary by detecting the situation of all boundary nodes' neighbours. Although it causes a lot of energy overhead, the detection effect is very accurate.
- *RNG planarization method*: The planarization algorithm is another commonly used detection method. We choose the most universal RNG algorithm [13] to planarize the network to detect object boundaries. Use this method as another baseline.

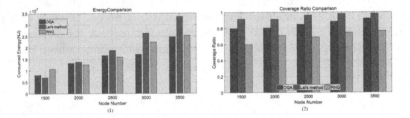

Fig. 8. Comparison of energy consumption and coverage ratio for our OGA, Lei's method and RNG.

In Fig. 8-(1), as the number of nodes increases, the energy overhead of these three algorithms increases. But the more nodes, the energy cost of the other two will be much lower than Lei's method. It is because selective detection nodes avoid unnecessary overhead. In Fig. 8-(2), the more nodes, the higher the coverage ratio. Lei's method has always been the most accurate, but our method is getting closer to him. Combining the two results, our algorithm saves overhead while ensuring the detection effect as much as possible.

6 Related Works

As the scale of WSNs continues to expand, the disadvantages high energy consumption and high latency of it are becoming more and more obvious. The edge intelligence of the network was promoted to address the above issues [1]. The edge intelligent nodes in IoT sensing network shortens the data transmission distance considerably. However, the energy of most nodes in the network is still limited, and it is still necessary to consider the energy efficiency to extend the network lifecycle.

Detecting and tracking continuous harmful object in IoT sensing networks is vital to guide the transfer of personnel and property. The planarization algorithm is commonly used for boundary detection of continuous objects. In [14], based on the activation state network nodes, authors use the planarization algorithm to construct the boundary surfaces of continuous objects, estimate their sensory data by spatial interpolation, and select more suitable boundary candidate nodes. However, whether the planarization of the network is reasonable affects the efficiency of the object detection.

In [8], the authors proposed a new mechanism for detecting the boundary of continuous objects when there is a perceived hole in the deployed fog computing network. Using the sensing data collected by the mobile node, an interpolation algorithm is applied to estimate the sensory data of specific geographic locations to estimate a more accurate boundary. However, not all scenarios are suitable for arranging dynamic nodes, for example, mountains.

Due to limited energy, most of the above methods use a sleep mechanism to extend the network lifecycle. In [15], authors used a suitable diffusion model to predict the diffusion of continuous objects. During the detection process, the nodes are usually in a sleep state and are activated for detection at specific intervals. This mechanism reduces the nodes' energy costs. However, the method of transferring all data to the sink for unified processing still causes a large amount of transmission overhead and delay.

7   Conclusion

With the wide-deployment of IoT smart things, adopting IoT sensing networks to monitor and detect the occurrence of potential events becomes a reality. Continuous objects, which reflect the potential events, should be detected in an accurate and energy-efficient manner. The article explores the energy- and performance-efficient continuous object detection in the IoT sensing network. Compared with the method that transfers sensory data to the sink, the reasonable use of edge intelligent nodes that relay nodes can save a lot of network transmission overhead. Meanwhile, we proposed a method for activating the node by using the current boundary to divide the area around the boundary node and assign each sub-part a different importance value. Based on the importance value, we selectively deactivate nodes to reduce the energy cost of detecting some unnecessary nodes. We also draw the network concentration equivalent map, which visually displays the concentration distribution in the network. Experimental results demonstrate that our method achieves better detection accuracy, while reducing energy consumption to a large extent, in comparison with the state of arts.

Acknowledgments. This work was supported by the National Natural Science Foundation of China (Grant no. 61772479 and 61662021).

References

1. Xiong, S., Ni, Q., Wang, X., Su, Y.: A connectivity enhancement scheme based on link transformation in iot sensing networks. IEEE Internet Things J. **4**(6), 2297–2308 (2017)
2. Kavitha, B.C., Vallikannu, R.: IoT based intelligent industry monitoring system. In: 2019 6th International Conference on Signal Processing and Integrated Networks (SPIN), pp. 63–65 (2019)
3. Dong, L., et al.: The gas leak detection based on a wireless monitoring system. IEEE Trans. Ind. Inf. (2019)
4. Chao, C., Jiao, S., Zhang, S., Liu, W., Feng, L., Wang, Y.: TripImputor: real-time imputing taxi trip purpose leveraging multi-sourced urban data. IEEE Trans. Intell. Transp. Syst. **99**, 1–13 (2018)
5. Olatinwo, S.O., Joubert, T.H.: Energy efficient solutions in wireless sensor system for monitoring the quality of water: a review. IEEE Sens. J. (2018)
6. Shu, L., Chen, Y., Sun, Z., Tong, F., Mukherjee, M.: Detecting the dangerous area of toxic gases with wireless sensor networks. IEEE Trans. Emerg. Top. Comput. (2017)
7. Lei, F., Yao, L., Zhao, D., Duan, Y.: Energy-efficient abnormal nodes detection and handlings in wireless sensor networks. IEEE Access **5**, 3393–3409 (2017)
8. Zhang, Y., Wang, Z., Meng, L., Zhou, Z.: Boundary region detection for continuous objects in wireless sensor networks. Wirel. Commun. Mob. Comput. (2018)
9. Hong, Z., Wang, R., Li, X.: A clustering-tree topology control based on the energy forecast for heterogeneous wireless sensor networks. IEEE/CAA J. Autom. Sinica **3**(1), 68–77 (2016)
10. Heinzelman, W.B., Chandrakasan, A.P., Balakrishnan, H.: An application specific protocol architecture for wireless microsensor networks. IEEE Trans. Wirel. Commun. **1**(4), 660–670 (2002)
11. Bandyopadhyay, S., Coyle, E.J.: Minimizing communication costs in hierarchically-clustered networks of wireless sensors. Comput. Netw. **44**(1), 1–16 (2004)
12. Bartier, P.M., Keller, C.P.: Multivariate interpolation to incorporate thematic surface data using inverse distance weighting (IDW). Comput. Geosci. **22**(7), 795–799 (1996)
13. Li, X.Y., Calinescu, G., Wan, P.J., Wang, Y.: Localized delaunay triangulation with application in ad hoc wireless networks. IEEE Trans. Parallel Distrib. Syst. **14**(10), 1035–1047 (2003)
14. Ping, H., Zhou, Z., Shi, Z., Rahman, T.: Accurate and energy-efficient boundary detection of continuous objects in duty-cycled wireless sensor networks. Pers. Ubiquit. Comput. **22**(3), 597–613 (2018)
15. Liu, L., Han, G., Shen, J., Zhang, W., Liu, Y.: Diffusion distance-based predictive tracking for continuous objects in industrial wireless sensor networks. Mob. Netw. Appl. 1–12 (2018)

The 11th International Workshop on Security in e-Science and e-Research (ISSR 2019)

ISSR 2019 Organizing and Program Committees

Steering Committee

Guojun Wang (Chair)	Guangzhou University, China
Wei Jie (Chair)	University of West London, UK
Aniello Castiglione	University of Naples Parthenope, Italy
Liang Chen	University of West London, UK
Kim-Kwang Raymond Choo	University of Texas at San Antonio, USA
Scott Fowler	Linkoping University, Sweden
Jiankun Hu	UNSW Canberra, Australian Defence Force Academy, Australia
Georgios Kambourakis	University of the Aegean, Greece
Peter Komisarczuk	Royal Holloway, University of London, UK
Gregorio Martinez	University of Murcia, Spain
Kouichi Sakurai	Kyushu University, Japan
Sabu M. Thampi	Indian Institute of Information Technology and Management, India
Lizhe Wang	China University of Geosciences, China
Carlos Becker Westphall	Federal University of Santa Catarina, Brazil
Jeff Yan	Lancaster University, UK
Deqing Zou	Huazhong University of Science and Technology, China

General Chairs

Shaobo Zhang	Hunan University of Science and Technology, China
Alinani Karim	Hunan University of Science and Technology, China

Program Chairs

Wanlei Zhou	Deakin University, Australia
Indrakshi Ray	Colorado State University, USA

Program Committee

Marios Anagnostopoulos	Singapore University of Technology and Design, Singapore
Elena Apostol	Politehnica University of Bucharest, Romania
Junaid Arshad	University of West London, UK
Bruce Beckles	University of Cambridge Information Services, UK

Nik Bessis	Edge Hill University, UK
Andrea Bruno	University of Salerno, Italy
Pinial Khan Butt	Sindh Agriculture University, Pakistan
Arcangelo Castiglione	University of Salerno, Italy
Dan Chen	China Wuhan University, China
Xu Chen	Sun Yat-Sen University, China
Zesheng Chen	Indiana University, Purdue University Fort Wayne, USA
Zuguo Chen	Hunan University of Science and Technology, China
Chang Choi	Chosun University, South Korea
Chao Gong	University of Mary Hardin-Baylor, USA
Ying Guo	Central South University, China
Guangjie Han	Hohai University, China
Su Xin	Hohai University, China
Wolfgang Hommel	University der Bundeswehr, Germany
Frank Jiang	University of Technology Sydney, Australia
Wenjun Jiang	Hunan University, China
Pankoo Kim	Chosun University, South Korea
Hoon Ko	Sungkyunkwan University, South Korea
Saru Kumari	Chaudhary Charan Singh University, India
Juan Li	North Dakota State University, USA
Xiong Li	Hunan University of Science and Technology, China
Jing Liao	Hunan University of Science and Technology, China
Chi Lin	Dalian University of Technology, China
Qin Liu	Hunan University, China
Sofia Anna Menesidou	Democritus University of Thrace, Greece
Francesco Palmieri	University of Salerno, Italy
Dimitrios Papamartzivanos	University of the Aegean, Greece
Raffaele Pizzolante	University of Salerno, Italy
Yizhi Ren	Hangzhou Dianzi University, China
Sai Wang	Macau University of Science and Technology, SAR China
Yupeng Wang	Shenyang Aerospace University, China
Sheng Wen	Swinburne University of Technology, Australia
Chao Wu	Tsinghua University, China
Dengfeng Xiao	Hunan University of Science and Technology, China
Peiyin Xiong	Hunan University of Science and Technology, China
Ming Xu	Hangzhou Dianzi University, China
Xiaodan Yan	Beijing University of Posts and Telecommunications, China
Wencheng Yang	Edith Cowan University, Australia
Congxu Zhu	Central South University, China

Publicity Chairs

Thomas Tan	Edinburgh Napier University, UK
Yang Xu	Central South University, China

Webmaster

Jiating Huang	Hunan University of Science and Technology, China

Software Quality Assurance: Tools and Techniques

Allah Bachayo Brohi[1], Pinial Khan Butt[1(✉)], and Shaobo Zhang[2]

[1] Information Technology Centre, Sindh Agriculture University Tandojam,
Hyderabad 70060, Sindh, Pakistan
allahbachayo101@gmail.com, pinial@yahoo.com
[2] School of Computer Science and Engineering, Hunan University of Science
and Technology, Xiangtan 411201, China
shobozhang@hnust.edu.cn

Abstract. Software products are tested using various techniques. These techniques are mostly based on technical and technological diligence and verification which are conducted by an experienced examiner and the absence of which may cause quality assurance issues. Such hindrances may be tackled by using software testing processes. Currently, two most important basic processes exist in software testing industry: manual and automated testing process. The manual process is not recommended when iterative tasks are performed. Additionally, automated testing has many advantages it is time and cost effective with lesser human interference. Selection of an appropriate testing tool is still in infancy way which may lead to problems with any software company. In this research, we propose a quality framework of selection of an appropriate self-driven software quality optimization tools for regression testing by focusing on quality of the final product.

Keywords: Software tools · Software quality · Software engineering ·
Automation testing · Software behavior

1 Introduction

Software Testing is a process or method to identify software bugs in a program or application. We know that the process of testing never ends, it is important to identify the starting and ending phase before going into the testing phase [1]. One of the most important aspects to be considered as a major objective when developing any software is to meet emerging market requirements. Moreover, the quality of software product basically determines the success or failure of a product. It is rare that developed product is a bug free. Therefore, software industry focuses on testing of the product parallel with the various software development phases. One of the most important testing, quality framework used in parallel to the software development life cycle is V-model [2]. It's purely testing model, in which each phase of software life cycle has a V model testing phase, once the tester is satisfied with the outcome of the software development phase than the next phase may be stated. The model may also be read as verification and validation model. Each stage in verification has a corresponding stage in the

G. Wang et al. (Eds.): SpaCCS 2019 Workshops, LNCS 11637, pp. 283–291, 2019.
https://doi.org/10.1007/978-3-030-24900-7_23

validation in the model. The V-model is very helpful for practical software testing industry and it's an applied model. The manual testing is a more traditional way of testing. Tester mostly do all tests manually, i.e.; it checks the requirement documents, reports and evaluate test results. Tester specifies the System under Test (SUT) and test cases are defined in a best way to identify bugs. In addition, the bugs can be fixed before releasing the software product. The quality framework used software development life cycle is V-model as shown in Fig. 1. It's purely testing model, in which each phase in software life cycle has a V-model testing phase, once the tester is satisfied with the outcome of the software development phase than next phase may be stated. The model may also read as verification and validation model. Each stage in verification has correspondence stage in the Validation in the model. The V-model is very helpful in practical software testing industry and it's an applied model.

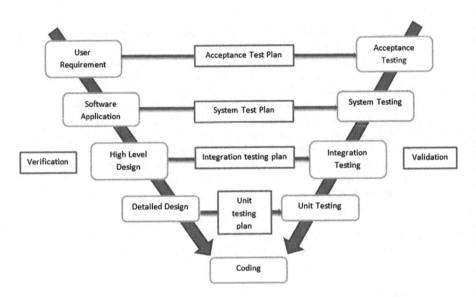

Fig. 1. V model

Software testing is mainly divided into two categories: manual and automated Testing. Manual testing is more traditional way of testing in which all tests are conducted manually i.e. tester check the requirement documents, reports and evaluate test results. Tester specifies the System Under Test (SUT) and test cases are defined in a best way to identify bugs. So, the bugs can be fixed before releasing the software product. Automation is one of the most popular among the companies that reduces the testing effort, which ultimately saves time and cost of the companies. Mainly automated testing is used to execute manual tests quickly in a cost-effective manner without human interventions. One of the important factors, where the automated tests are much suitable where the same tests are executed repeatedly this method or re-run tests that have been previously executed is known as regression testing to validate the functional correctness of the desired application. For example, we want to validate the username and password of 10,000 users, manually it will be an exhaustive approach to do this, here automated testing will save time, effort and cost to automate this type of test cases.

There are various open source testing tools as well as commercial testing tools available these days, for example: Selenium, HP UFT, QTP, WATIR and WinRunner.

2 Review of Literature

The presented a new concept using an artificial neural network as an automated oracle for a tested software system and since the objective of testing is ensured the conformity of an application [3, 4]. They used an automated test oracle to reduce human intervention and reduces the actual cost of the testing and maintenance. The [5] proposed methodology to automate their test cases using Selenium and WinRunner, and they compared both tools, the results are better in Selenium in most situations, however, their methodology does not focus any quality framework for comparison of both tools, they executed only test scripts in selenium as well as in WinRunner.

To compared manual with automation testing and found that automation is useful that saves time and effort of the developers, they used selenium and the old QTP (Quick Test Professional) tool for automation purpose and did not focus on quality aspects of testing [6–8]. A study to identifying defects or error an early stage will definitely save maintenance cost; however, they do not focus on quality framework [9, 10].

The proposed various characteristics to evaluate the automation tool such as Test Complete based on their recording efficiency, capabilities, reusability and cost, while these quality characteristics may not enough to provide a complete quality framework for evaluation of any automated testing tool [11–13].

A case study focused on certain characteristics on bio, e-commerce, and travel website for automated testing [14]. The Selenium automated tool to automate the whole process using the applied case studies and similar study conducted to measures the performance and accuracy characteristics, which is having some impact on quality of tests [15].

Multiple instances of browser on single time test for selenium. The instances are kept in Selenium's BD management System such as Oracle and SQL server, the accuracy and efficiency were observed, and some Client libraries are used to test the accuracy [16].

Load runner, QTP and recording aspects of automated tools used against the defined test cases; [17] and these test cases are executed in both Load runner and QTP. However, they proposed that Load runner is a bit difficult in learning and QTP is a bit easier to learn, the documentation is widely available for the QTP compared to the load runner. Some other factors are also focused by these authors such as cost and speed. It proposed that the criteria to identify the reliability of the testing tools, interesting to note that based on their criteria open source testing tools have very good ratings for the reliability attribute. QTP, Selenium and WATIR are compared with Islam, [18] based on the integral phases of the software development life cycle. They also used some quality attributes for comparing these testing tools such as learnability and usability.

3   Quality Model for Regression Testing

In this section, we proposed a quality framework to evaluate/select the proper auto-mated testing tool for regression testing. Sometime, software testing professionals have a difficulty in selecting the appropriate tool for regression testing, whether they use open source or commercial based automated testing tool. We proposed a framework that will help the software testers to select the appropriate testing tool from huge list available online.

Our proposed quality framework for testing tool is adapted from ISO/IEC 9126, the main quality characteristics adopted from ISO 9126 model are Functionality, Testa-bility, Learnability and Maintainability on the first layer of the quality framework, on second layer each quality character is further divided into sub-characteristics/attribute, these attributes will help us to measure or assess the testing tool based on the metrics. Our proposed quality model is shown in Fig. 2. Additionally, the results of these metrics will help us to compare and recommend the best automated testing tool for regression testing.

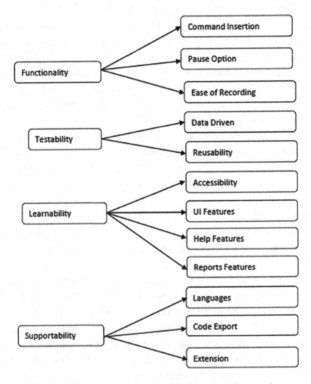

Fig. 2. Proposed quality model for regression testing

The Fig. 2 main quality attributes of the proposed model are functionality, testability, learnability and supportability. These quality attributes are further divided into sub-attribute or metrics to evaluate the main quality characteristics.

Functionality of the automated tool is calculated based on the combination of metrics such as command insertions, pause options and ease of recording and threshold for the functionality are scaled from 1 to 10, where 1 is at the bottom and 10 is on the excellent quality scale. In continuation to functionality Testability is another main character that is further divided to measure the quality of automated tool based on data driven and reusability metrics. Learnability is measured with Accessibility, UI, Help and report features of the available in the automation tools, these are also measured on the same scale as described for the functionality. The last main quality attributes are suitability which is further measured based on languages, code export and extension supported by the automated tools. In addition, the metrics thresh hold is scaled from 1 to 10 as described in the functionality.

3.1 Functionality

Functionality is defined as set of attributes of the testing tool, which allow existence of set functions and their properties. Functions are those which basically satisfy the tester needs. Functionality is measured based on the set of functions that hold by the testing tool. The metric can be calculated as follows:

$$Functionality = \frac{Command\ Insertion\ (CI) + Pause\ Options(PO) + Ease\ of\ Recording(ER)}{3}$$

CI = *Total Number of commands inserted during activity.*
PO = *Total Number of pause option performed during activity.*
ER = *Total Number of Times recording activity is performed.*

3.2 Testability

Testability is defined as how much the testing tool allows the access of data from external resources and how much it allows changing the data. The metric can be calculated as follows:

$$Testability = \frac{Data\ Driven\ (DD) + Reusability}{2}$$

DD = *Total number of times the data exported from external resource for the activity.*
$Reusability$ = *Total number of times the test case is reused during the activity.*

3.3   Learnability

Learnability is defined as set of attribute or properties that automated testing tool provide easy access to the learning. It means tool vendors should provide user manual, online help, easy to learn the reports and easy to understand the formation of test cases. This attribute further divided based on the automation testing tool features and properties that can be used to access the automation testing tool. The metric can be calculated as follows:

$$Learnability = \frac{Accessibility + User\ Interface\ Features + Help\ Features + Report\ Features}{4}$$

Accessibility = *Total number of features easy to obtain, learn and understand for the activity.*
UI features = *Total number of user interface features.*
Help features = *Total number of helps features.*
Reports Feature = *Total number of features of automated testing tool.*

3.4   Supportability

Supportability is defined as degree to which the automation testing tool supports other languages, export method and other extension. These features help the automation testing tool more advanced and can be used in connection or can be integrated to different languages and also can be extended or add to be as part of the web browsers or applications. The metric can be calculated as follows:

$$Supportability = \frac{Supported\ languages + Code\ Export + Extensions}{3}$$

Supported Languages = *Total number of languages supported by the automation testing tool for regression testing.*
Code Export = *Total number of steps code can be exported from the automated testing tool.*
Extension = *total number of extensions supported by the automated testing tool.*

4   Results and Discussions

The results are shown in Table 1. The table shows the metric name and the corresponding results of metrics applied to the automated testing tools: Selenium and HP UFT tool.

Table 1. Summary of results

Metric name	Selenium	HP UFT
Functionality	4.6	3.5
Testability	6	4.5
Learnability	4	6
Supportability	9	1

The results shown in the Table 1 are further described here, the functionality metric for Selenium are better than HP UFT. This metric described various parameters, they are tested on the web-based application, where three test cases are executed automatically with Selenium as well as on HP UFT, the metric shows slightly better functionality of the Selenium.

Testability metric results are much better than Selenium as an automated tool. The three test cases show encouraging results for the Selenium, while HP UFT has weak support for testability, however, it is good at Microsoft platform if testability metrics are applied with visual studio.

Learnability metric has better support for HP UFT because it is a commercial product, it provides standard tutorials and with good community support. The product updates are fully supported in previous versions, while in case of open source product such as Selenium, it does not provide stable support for previous versions. Supportability metric for Selenium shows much better results than an HP UFT tool, because UFT only supports VB scripts, while open source Selenium supports 9 different languages that makes a more suitable automated platform for supportability. These results are visually described in bar graph as shown in the Fig. 3 below. It shows clear Fig. 3 that Selenium is a much better tool for the automated testing while HP UFT is a commercial tool, it provides better support and learnability environment to limited community, which is the main disadvantage of this tool.

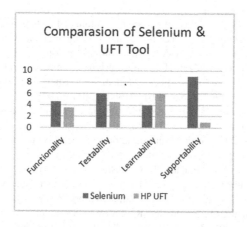

Fig. 3. Comparison of selenium & UFT tool

5 Summary and Outlook

The research conducted in the software testing domain, where we have chosen automated testing tools for regression testing, for this we studied and compared open source and commercial automated testing tool. We selected Selenium as an open source tool and HP UFT as a commercial tool. First, we conducted studies and then we proposed quality framework for our hypothesis testing. Our quality model is based on four specialized metrics chosen for ISO/IEC 9126 generic quality model these are: functionality, Testability, Learnability and Supportability metrics and applied with one of the famous case studies (Mercury Tours provided by the HP UFT tool). We found that Selenium has better functionality, testability and supportability features while on other hand HP UFT is a commercial tool and based on Microsoft languages and tools, so it has limited functionality, testability and supportability features, while as it has excellent learnability features. The quality model proposed in this research requires further investigation on various other open source and commercial automated testing tools available in the market. The quality model may also further extend for continuous quality improvement techniques as well as for the fourth and fifth generation languages.

Acknowledgements. This work is supported in part by the Hunan Provincial Education Department of China under Grant Numbers 18B200.

References

1. Paternoster, N., Giardino, C., Unterkalmsteiner, M., Gorschek, T., Abrahamsson, P.: Software development in startup companies: a systematic mapping study. Inf. Softw. Technol. **56**(10), 1200–1218 (2014). https://doi.org/10.1016/j.infsof.2014.04.014
2. Morandini, M., Nguyen, D.C., Perini, A., Siena, A., Susi, A.: Tool-supported development with tropos: the conference management system case study. In: Luck, M., Padgham, L. (eds.) AOSE 2007. LNCS, vol. 4951, pp. 182–196. Springer, Heidelberg (2008). https://doi.org/10.1007/978-3-540-79488-2_14
3. Tian, Y., Pei, K., Jana, S., Ray, B.: Deeptest: automated testing of deep-neural-network-driven autonomous cars. In: Proceedings of the 40th International Conference on Software Engineering, pp. 303–314. ACM, May 2018. https://doi.org/10.1145/3180155.3180220
4. Kıraç, M.F., Aktemur, B., Sözer, H.: VISOR: a fast image processing pipeline with scaling and translation invariance for test oracle automation of visual output systems. J. Syst. Softw. **136**, 266–277 (2018). https://doi.org/10.1016/j.jss.2017.06.023
5. Garousi, V., Elberzhager, F.: Test automation: not just for test execution. IEEE Softw. **34**(2), 90–96 (2017). https://doi.org/10.1109/MS.2017.34
6. Bhargava, S., Jain, P.B.: Testing connect automated technologies. i-Manag. J. Softw. Eng. **13**(2), 18 (2018). https://doi.org/10.26634/jse.13.2.15225
7. Manoj, G., Beeranur, R.K., Prakash, K.R.: Designing a software test automation framework for windows application using coded UI in visual studio tool and page object design. i-Manag. J. Softw. Eng. **12**(4), 1 (2018). https://doi.org/10.26634/jse.12.4.14703
8. Kasurinen, J., Taipale, O., Smolander, K.: Software test automation in practice: empirical observations. Adv. Softw. Eng. (2010). http://dx.doi.org/10.1155/2010/620836

9. Ahad, A., Ullah, Z., Tariq, L., Niaz, S.: Software inspections and their role in software quality assurance. Am. J. Softw. Eng. Appl. 6(4), 105–110 (2017). https://doi.org/10.11648/j.ajsea.20170604.11
10. Bahamdain, S.S.: Open source software (OSS) quality assurance: a survey paper. Procedia Comput. Sci. 56, 459–464 (2015). https://doi.org/10.1016/j.procs.2015.07.236
11. Ma, L., et al.: Secure Deep Learning Engineering: A Software Quality Assurance Perspective. arXiv preprint arXiv:1810.04538 (2018)
12. Durak, U., Stürmer, I., Pawletta, T., Mahmoodi, S.: Quality assessment and quality improvement in model engineering. In: Model Engineering for Simulation, pp. 209–231. Academic Press (2019)
13. Chen, Y., Chen, J., Gao, Y., Chen, D., Tang, Y.: Research on software failure analysis and quality management model. In: 2018 IEEE International Conference on Software Quality, Reliability and Security Companion (QRS-C), pp. 94–99. IEEE, July 2018
14. Ten, A.C., Paz, F.: A systematic review of user experience evaluation methods in information driven websites. In: Marcus, A., Wang, W. (eds.) DUXU 2017. LNCS, vol. 10288, pp. 492–506. Springer, Cham (2017). https://doi.org/10.1007/978-3-319-58634-2_36
15. Raulamo-Jurvanen, P., Kakkonen, K., Mäntylä, M.: Using surveys and web-scraping to select tools for software testing consultancy. In: Abrahamsson, P., Jedlitschka, A., Nguyen Duc, A., Felderer, M., Amasaki, S., Mikkonen, T. (eds.) PROFES 2016. LNCS, vol. 10027, pp. 285–300. Springer, Cham (2016). https://doi.org/10.1007/978-3-319-49094-6_18
16. Virk, R., Malhotra, N.: Extension of Selenium Db for Better Compatibility with the Database for Web Based Application Testing (2014)
17. Uppal, N., Chopra, V.: Design and implementation in selenium ide with web driver. Int. J. Comput. Appl. 46, 8–11 (2012)
18. Just, R., Jalali, D., Inozemtseva, L., Ernst, M.D., Holmes, R., Fraser, G.: Are mutants a valid substitute for real faults in software testing? In: Proceedings of the 22nd ACM SIGSOFT International Symposium on Foundations of Software Engineering, pp. 654–665. ACM, November 2014. https://doi.org/10.1145/2635868.2635929

A Campus Carpooling System Based on GPS Trajectories

Xuesong Wang[1,2], Yizhi Liu[1,2(✉)], Zhengtao Jiang[1], You Peng[1],
Tianhao Yin[1], Zhuhua Liao[1,2], and Jingqiang Zhao[3]

[1] School of Computer Science and Engineering, Hunan University of Science
and Technology, Xiangtan 411201, China
yizhi_liu@sina.cn
[2] Key Laboratory of Knowledge Processing and Networked Manufacturing
in Hunan Province, Xiangtan 411201, China
[3] Network Information Center, Hunan University of Science and Technology,
Xiangtan 411201, China

Abstract. College students are special because they relatively have tighter in economy but have greater consistency in leisure time. They prefer to go out together with schoolfellows due to higher trusts and closeness. Moreover, the electronic map is difficult to be updated. Campus-roads recently are updated rapidly. And many alleys in campuses are not shown in the electronic map. Therefore, we devise and implement a campus carpooling system based on GPS trajectories. It includes three parts. Firstly, the campus road network is extracted based on GPS trajectories. Next, the shortest sharing path in the campus is computed in terms of the campus road network. Then, passengers are matched automatically by the carpooling matching algorithm (CMA) in our system. Experiments show that our system is able to provide a safer and more comfortable carpooling experience for college students.

Keywords: Trajectory mining · Campus carpooling ·
Road network extraction · Carpooling matching algorithm (CMA) ·
The shortest sharing path

1 Introduction

Ridesharing is popular among travelers because it can reduce their travel costs, and it also holds the potential to reduce travel time, congestion, air pollution, and overall fuel consumption [1, 2]. Contemporary college students have more travel activities, greater consistency in leisure time, and limited economic conditions. Many college students (especially girls) are more concerned about the object of carpooling, whether it will affect the carpooling experience. With the widespread use of carpooling service, many taxi accidents have occurred on the carpooling process when passengers are traveling alone (especially women). Therefore, students are paying more and more attention to the safety of taxi travel. College students prefer to travel with schoolfellows because they have higher trust and closeness. Therefore, compared with other social groups, the need for college students to carpool is more urgent. As we all know, there are many

G. Wang et al. (Eds.): SpaCCS 2019 Workshops, LNCS 11637, pp. 292–301, 2019.
https://doi.org/10.1007/978-3-030-24900-7_24

alleys on campus, which are accessible to vehicles. Since the electronic map update is not timely, the campus road is relatively updated relatively quickly, which causes many campus alley information not to be on the electronic map.

Aim to the above problems, we design and implement a system for the campus carpooling of college students. We extract the campus road network information by processing the GPS trajectory dataset and make campus path planning according to the road network information to reduce the carpool time. We propose a carpooling matching algorithm (CMA) to match users.

Ridesharing applications have enhanced the travel experience for many people [3]. He et al. [4] developed three frequency-correlated algorithms for route mining, rider selection, and route merging in an urban carpool service. Jiau et al. [5] proposed appropriate matches by using the proposed Low-Complexity and Low-Memory Car-pool Matching method combined with the compact genetic algorithm. Huang et al. [6] combined carpooling services with rich geographic, traffic and social information, and propose a genetic-based carpooling route and matching algorithm. Huang et al. [7] proposed a fuzzy-controlled genetic-based carpool algorithm by using the combined approach of the genetic algorithm and the fuzzy control system. Ma et al. [8] designed a taxi-sharing system based on mobile cloud architecture. The cloud-first uses the taxi search algorithm supported by the space-time index to quickly find a taxi ride request for the candidate taxi. Luo [9] proposes a regional transfer service based on taxi carpooling to solve the problem of taxiing. Nie et al. [10] proposed a taxi sharing mode and discussed related scheduling processes, pricing standards, and revenue analysis. Huang et al. [11] considered the two factors of passengers' travel waiting time and service time, matched the carpool passengers through the dynamic tree algorithm. Zhang et al. [12] developed the NP-hard path calculation problem under different practical constraints to plan the path. In the literature [13, 14], the pick-up point was obtained by performing spatiotemporal analysis on the trajectory data. Zhang et al. [15] fused the driver's location, distance, and other geographic information into the hidden semantic model to provide the driver with a pick-up area.

The main contributions of this paper are:

- This is a campus carpooling system specially designed for college students, which can provide a safer and more economical carpooling experience for college students.
- Extract campus road network information through datasets, including small roads. The extraction of small roads provides a faster path for carpooling.
- This paper combines R-tree and Dijkstra algorithm to plan the route of taxis on campus, reducing passenger waiting time and increasing taxi pick-up speed.

2   Campus Carpooling System

The system performs offline processing on the GPS dataset, clusters and generates high-frequency stay area of the passengers in the campus, and counts the information of the road network within the campus. A carpool request is sent by the campus pas-sengers to the database, and the matching algorithm is used to match the users on the campus. After the match is succeeded, the system sends the order to the driver and recommends a suitable sharing point for the carpool user. After the driver receives the order, the system plans an optimal campus route for the driver. Finally, after the order is completed, the passengers pay for this carpooling with the corresponding fee. Figure 1 shows the system framework.

Definition 1. Stay area. In the process of security personnel patrolling, there are a lot of waiting, rest areas, the GPS recorder generates a large number of trajectory points in the range. We refer to these areas as the stay area. We use the TJ-cluster density clustering algorithm to obtain the stay area in the security patrol.

Definition 2. Sharing point. The same pick-up point of the carpool users is called the sharing point. The candidate sharing point is usually the center point of the stay area during the security patrol and is close to the main road section or the inflection point.

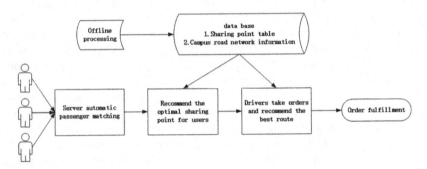

Fig. 1. System framework

3   Our Methods

3.1   Carpooling Matching Algorithm

Ridesharing systems match travelers with similar trajectories [16]. Fixed on a campus range, limited area this characteristic, we put forward a new carpooling matching algorithm (CMA) to find the same carpool group of passengers. The server traverse nearby sharing points, calculates the distance between each sharing point and the starting point of each carpool passenger, take the point with the smallest distance sum as the sharing point. The carpool passenger arrives at the sharing point before the agreed time. The passenger matching algorithm is as follows:

Step 1: passenger makes a carpool request in a certain location within the campus, and the server receives the request and sends the current location and destination location information as well as the departure time domain acceptable to users (the earliest departure time to the latest departure time) to the server.

Step 2: The server takes out the passenger to be processed according to the processing order of the first in first out, searches for the endpoint of other passengers in the radius threshold r. If the match is succeeded, the system follows the principle of proximity to select the appropriate number of matching passengers, otherwise, other passenger information is put at the end of the team to the next match via repeating step two.

Step 3: The passenger group information is sent to the passenger. According to the passenger sharing point and the driver's entrance location to the school, the server recommends the planned path to the driver.

Step 4: If the order is succeed, the selected passengers are formed to be a carpooling group. Then it jumps to step two.

3.2   Campus Road-Network Extraction

Accurate extraction and timely updating of road network information is essential for road planning and vehicle navigation [17]. We use the road network extraction method based on the pedestrian GPS trajectory to extract the campus road network which includes some small roads. The small roads provide a more convenient route for our path planning in the campus, saving the carpooling process time. The basic idea is to automatically generate the road center line based on the GPS trajectory. The left and right sides of Fig. 2 show the results diagram after the trajectory point clustering and the centerline fitting respectively. The details are described below.

Fig. 2. The resulting diagram after trajectory point clustering and centerline fitting

The trajectory data are basically distributed along the road. Therefore, this paper uses a rolling clustering algorithm, which is to obtain cluster points along the extending direction of the trajectory data. Set the number of trajectory points m and the cluster radius d as the constraints of the cluster. If the number of points in the d neighborhood of each trajectory point is greater than m, the trajectory points included in the d neighborhood are converted into cluster points by a clustering algorithm. The coordinate values of the cluster points are determined by all the trajectory points in the neighborhood.

The clustering point segmentation can make each segmented clustering point can be fitted with a curve function to obtain a curve to represent the corresponding road centerline. In this paper, the basis of segmentation is determined by the size of the corners of the cluster points and the distance between adjacent cluster points. The corner of the trajectory refers to the steering angle of the adjacent trajectory segment. We set the distance threshold D_{min} and the angle threshold θ. When the distance between the trajectory points p_n and p_{n+1} is greater than D_{min} and the angle is greater than θ, we consider this to be an inflection point (that is, what we call "intersection"), extracted from the Hunan University of Science and Technology road network inflection point data. We define the threshold radius R, then calculate the number n of trajectory points in the radius R onto the trajectory data of the security patrol for each road segment, average the n to gets N, calculate the road segment. The length L, the weight of each road segment is calculated as shown in the formula (1).

$$weight = L * (1 + (1/N))$$ (1)

Because of the complexity of the shape of the road, this paper uses a quasi-uniform B-spline curve fitting method to generate a curve that can represent the centerline of the road. Compared with the B-spline curve, the quasi-uniform B-spline curve overcomes the disadvantage that the head and tail ended points are not on the curve, that is, N degree of repetition is done at the head and tail end points. At the same time, it also has the characteristics of local modification and closer to the feature polygon. The obtained target curve is a smooth piecewise polynomial function. Its mathematical expression is as follows:

$$P(t) = \sum_{i=0}^{n} P_i N_{i,k}(t)$$ (2)

$$N_{i,k}(t) = \frac{1}{k!} \sum_{j=0}^{k-i} (-1)^j C_{K+1}^j (t + k - i - j)^n$$ (3)

After the Central Line fitting process, vectorization tool provided by ArcGIS is directly used to convert them into linear vector files, and then vector road network information under the same coordinate system can be obtained through coordinate transformation and registration.

3.3 Path Planning

Through the road network extraction part, we can get the topology between the roads. Here, we use the R-D shortest network distance algorithm planning path. We combine the R-tree with the Dijkstra algorithm and use the acquired campus road network data to achieve the shortest network distance recommendation. We use the spatial segmentation of the R tree to limit the segment search for a certain range, reducing the search volume and improving the search efficiency. The specific practices are as follows:

The road network is divided, and the road network is divided into multiple rectangular regions $R_i(i = 1, 2, 3, \ldots)$. The principle of division is that multiple rectangular areas divided must contain all the inflection points in the road network, and there must be no omissions. Connectivity should be maintained between the individual rectangular areas, so there is an overlap between the rectangular areas.

Search the user's carpool sharing point and the starting position of the taxi in the campus through the R tree, a new rectangular region R' is created with these two positions coordinates, and the shortest path is found using the Dijkstra algorithm in the rectangular region R' and the rectangular region intersecting it.

Let us give an example to illustrate the R-D algorithm. Detailed as shown in Fig. 3. Suppose there is a graph, in which there are a large number of inflection points and edges. At this time, we need to find the shortest path from $V1$ to $V2$ in the graph. This is only to illustrate the idea of an algorithm, so the specific distribution of inflection points and edges in the graph and the weight of edges are not given. In this graph, we divide a total of 9 regions, namely 9 data rectangles: $R0$, $R1$, $R2$...., $R7$, $R8$, and construct R trees based on these data rectangles. Suppose the starting point and ending point is $V1$ and $V2$ respectively, draw a rectangle R' with the line of $V1$ and $V2$ as the diagonal line, the solid line in the figure represents the data rectangle, and the dotted line represents the rectangle R'; It can be seen from the figure that in addition to the rectangles $R7$ and R8 where the starting inflection point is located, the data rectangle intersecting R' also includes $R2$, $R3$, $R4$, and $R5$. Finally, the Dijkstra algorithm is used to find the shortest network distance from the data onto these data rectangles.

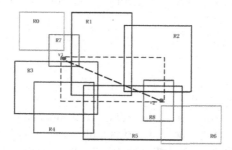

Fig. 3. The example of algorithm

4 Experiment

4.1 Dataset, Reducing Redundant Data, Filter Processing

With the popularity of GPS devices with positioning functions, lots of trajectories have been generated [18]. This project selects the security patrol trajectory data of Hunan University of Science and Technology in March 2011. As shown in Fig. 4, the data contains more than 2.5 million trajectory points, covering the entire campus, data size is 195 M, this sampling frequency is once per second, each piece of data contains information such as time, longitude, latitude, altitude, and speed.

When the signal of the GPS receiver is suddenly interrupted, it will repeatedly record the last received positioning data in a short time. At low speeds, the GPS receiver still receives positioning data based on the set acquisition frequency. These unnecessary, large amounts of redundant positioning data seriously interfere with the efficiency of the algorithm. The reduction of redundant data can improve the accuracy of the algorithm. We set the adjacent trajectory points p_i and p_{i+1}, and if the distance D_i is smaller than the threshold D_{min}, it indicates these records are invalid.

INDEX	TRACK NUMBER	UTC DATE	UTC TIME	LOCAL DATE	LOCAL TIME	LATITUDE	N/S	LONGITUDE	E/W	ALTITUDE	SPEED
1	1	2011/2/26	18:01:56	2011/2/27	2:01:56	27.909637	N	112.904427	E	86.203735	0
2	1	2011/2/26	18:01:57	2011/2/27	2:01:57	27.909637	N	112.904427	E	86.205688	0
3	1	2011/2/26	18:01:58	2011/2/27	2:01:58	27.909637	N	112.904427	E	86.205688	0
4	1	2011/2/26	18:01:59	2011/2/27	2:01:59	27.909637	N	112.904427	E	86.205688	0.036
5	1	2011/2/26	18:02:00	2011/2/27	2:02:00	27.909637	N	112.904427	E	86.207642	0.036
6	1	2011/2/26	18:02:01	2011/2/27	2:02:01	27.909637	N	112.904427	E	86.209595	0
7	1	2011/2/26	18:02:02	2011/2/27	2:02:02	27.909637	N	112.904427	E	86.211548	0.18
8	1	2011/2/26	18:02:03	2011/2/27	2:02:03	27.909637	N	112.904427	E	86.211548	0.072
9	1	2011/2/26	18:02:04	2011/2/27	2:02:04	27.909637	N	112.904427	E	86.213501	0.036
10	1	2011/2/26	18:02:05	2011/2/27	2:02:05	27.909637	N	112.904427	E	86.213501	0.072

Fig. 4. Data set

Through the filtering process, the random error of the GPS trajectory portion can be eliminated, the effect of smoothing the original GPS trajectory is achieved, and the relative smoothness of the overall trajectory is ensured. The Gaussian filtering method is used to smooth the data, and the filtering parameters are designed to be 5 times the sampling frequency of the GPS device, thereby avoiding unnecessary influence on the normal trajectory point. The Gaussian filtering calculation formula is shown as follows:

$$(x', y') = \frac{\sum_i k(t_i)(x_{t_i}, y_{t_i})}{\sum_i k(t_i)} \tag{4}$$

$$k(t_i) = e^{-\frac{(t_i - t)^2}{2\sigma^2}} \tag{5}$$

Here, x' and y' are coordinate values subjected to smoothing operation, $k(t_i)$ is the Gaussian kernel function at time t_i, and σ is a filter parameter.

Figure 5 shows comparison between the original trajectories and that after pre-processing. It can be clearly observed in the figure that most of the erroneous trajectory data has been deleted after pre-processing, and the trajectory data of the upper right corner of the two figures is obviously contrasted. The trajectory data is smoother and more accurate.

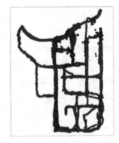

Fig. 5. Comparison between the original trajectories and that after preprocessing

4.2   Experience

In this section, we will verify the effectiveness of the campus carpooling algorithm by verifying the performance of the road network extraction and path planning algorithms.

We carry out a quantitative evaluation on the road network extraction. The basic idea is to obtain the set of road networks that match the experimental results with the road network on Baidu Map and then to evaluate the extraction performance of the road network in this paper by referring to coverage α and false detection rate β [10]. Its definition is shown in Eqs. (6) and (7).

$$\alpha = \frac{\sum_{P \in \sigma} len(P)}{\sum_{P \in \phi} len(P)} \tag{6}$$

$$\beta = 1 - \frac{\sum_{P \in \sigma} len(P)}{\sum_{P \in \psi} len(P)} \tag{7}$$

Based on the buffer method proposed by l. Zhang et al. [19], this paper took the road network of Baidu Map as the object of buffer analysis and obtained the road network set within each buffer radius that the road network extracted in this paper and the road network of Baidu Map match each other. As shown in Table 1, when the buffer radius is 10 meters, the road network coverage rate and false detection rate of this method are 98.73% and 18.84%, respectively. While the road network coverage rate and false detection rate extracted in literature [20] are respectively 93% and 5%. One of the main reasons for the high false detection rate in this paper is that the roads that are not updated in the Baidu Map road network are identified in our method.

Table 1. Road network extraction quantitative evaluation results

Buffer radius/m	Experimental results in this paper (including new main roads and path)		Experimental results in this paper (removal of new trunk roads and path)		The method of Zhang et al. [19]
	Coverage	False detection rate	Coverage	False detection rate	Coverage
2	45.04%	62.99%	44.67%	55.08%	27.40%
5	86.07%	29.25%	84.89%	14.64%	61.70%
7	92.20%	24.21%	**90.47%**	**9.02%**	73.90%
10	**98.73%**	**18.84%**	**96.21%**	**3.26%**	

We select 30 sharing points in the campus. These points are crowd gathering points, such as the gates of student dormitories or teaching buildings. These 30 points are randomly combined with the campus's four exits, combining 120 point-pairs (start-end point). For the 120 point-pair data, the shortest path is calculated by the R-D algorithm and the Dijkstra algorithm respectively, the shortest path calculation time of the algorithm is recorded. As shown in Fig. 6, as the shortest network distance between pairs increases, the time difference between the R-D algorithm and the Dijkstra algorithm increases gradually. It can conclude that the R-D algorithm is feasible and has high efficiency.

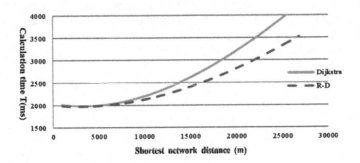

Fig. 6. Calculation time comparison chart

5 Summary

This paper provides a campus carpooling platform system that increases the occupancy rate of taxis and enables multiple passengers to "share" a taxi. There are already many carpooling systems on the market, but there is currently no carpooling system for college students. This article is specifically aimed at college students who are most concerned about carpooling: safety, comfort, economy, convenience and design and implementation of a carpooling system, it is expected to have a large user base in the market. At the same time, it also provides a platform for drivers to achieve a win-win situation for users and drivers, with good market prospects and economic benefits. In the next step, we will consider a kind of taxi searching algorithm by using the spatiotemporal indexing technology in order to quickly find the candidate taxis for users.

Acknowledgments. This work is supported by National Nature Science Foundation of China (Grant No. 41871320); the Provincial and Municipal Joint Fund of Hunan Provincial Natural Science Foundation of China (Grant No. 2018JJ4052); Hunan Provincial Natural Science Foundation of China (Grant No. 2017JJ2099 and 2017JJ2081); Hunan Provincial Education Department of China (Grant No. 18B200, 17C0646, and 10C0688); Undergraduate Scientific Research Innovation Plan of Hunan University of Science and Technology (Grant No. SYZ2018042).

References

1. Chen, L., et al.: Price-and-time-aware dynamic ridesharing. In: IEEE 34th International Conference on Data Engineering (ICDE), Paris, France, pp. 1061–1072 (2018)
2. Bozdog, N., Makkes, M., Halteren, A., Bal, H.: RideMatcher: peer-to-peer matching of passengers for efficient ridesharing. In: 18th IEEE/ACM International Symposium on Cluster, Cloud and Grid Computing (CCGRID), Washington, DC, USA, pp. 263–272 (2018)

3. Madria, S., Yeung, S., Ward, K.: Ridesharing-inspired trip recommendations. In: 19th IEEE International Conference on Mobile Data Management (MDM), Aalborg, Denmark, pp. 34–39 (2018)
4. He, W., Hwang, K., Li, D.: Intelligent carpool routing for urban ridesharing by mining GPS trajectories. IEEE Trans. Intell. Transp. Syst. **15**(5), 2286–2296 (2014)
5. Jiau, M.K., Huang, S.C.: Services-oriented computing using the compact genetic algorithm for solving the carpool services problem. IEEE Trans. Intell. Transp. Syst. **16**(5), 2711–2722 (2015)
6. Huang, S.C., Jiau, M.K., Lin, C.H.: A genetic-algorithm-based approach to solve carpool service problems in cloud computing. IEEE Trans. Intell. Transp. Syst. **16**(1), 352–364 (2015)
7. Huang, S.C., Jiau, M.K., Lin, C.H.: Optimization of the carpool service problem via a fuzzy controlled genetic algorithm. IEEE Trans. Fuzzy Syst. **23**(5), 1698–1712 (2014)
8. Ma, S., Zheng, Y., Wolfson, O.: Real-time city-scale taxi ridesharing. IEEE Trans. Knowl. Data Eng. **27**(7), 1782–1795 (2014)
9. Luo, X.: Regional transfer service based on taxi carpooling. Sun Yat-Sen University (2015). (in Chinese)
10. Nie, C., Tang, D., Xu, T.: Research on taxi mixing scheduling mode based on calling platform. J. Wuhan Univ. Technol. (Transp. Sci. Eng.) **39**(04), 807–809 (2015). (in Chinese)
11. Huang, Y., Favyen, B., Jin, R., Wang, X.S.: Large scale realtime ridesharing with service guarantee on road networks. In: Proceedings of the 40th International Conference on Very Large Data Bases, Hangzhou, China, vol. 7, no. 14 (2014)
12. Zhang, D., He, T., Zhang, F., et al.: Carpooling service for large-scale taxicab networks. ACM Trans. Sensor Netw. **12**(3), Article 18 (2016)
13. Liu, Y., Liu, J., Liao, Z., Tang, M., Chen, J.: Recommending a personalized sequence of pick-up points. J. Comput. Sci. **28**, 382–388 (2018)
14. Zhang, M., Liu, J., Liu, Y., Hu, Z., Yi, L.: Recommending pick-up points for taxi-drivers based on spatio-temporal clustering. In: Proceedings of the 2nd International Conference on Cloud and Green Computing (CGC 2012), pp. 67–72 (2012)
15. Zhang, J., Liao, Z., Liu, Y.: Fusing geographic information into latent factor model for pick-up region recommendation. In: Proceedings of 6th IEEE International Workshop on Mobile Multimedia Computing in conjunction with ICME 2019, Shanghai, China (2019)
16. Blerim, C., Athina, M., Nikolaos, L.: SORS: a scalable online ridesharing system. In: IWCTS 2016, Burlingame, CA, USA (2016)
17. Hong, O.Y., Liu, J.X., Liu, Y.Z.: Road network extraction method based on walking GPS trajectory. J. Comput. Mod. **222**(2), 124–128 (2014). (in Chinese)
18. Li, H., Liu, J., Liu, Y., Jin, L.: Evaluating roving patrol effectiveness by GPS trajectory. In: DASC 2011, pp. 832–837 (2011)
19. Zhang, L., Thiemann, F., Sester, M.: Integration of GPS traces with road map. In: Proceedings of the Second International Workshop on Computational Transportation Science, pp. 17–22. ACM (2010)
20. Liu, X., Zhu, Y., Wang, Y.: Road recognition using coarse-grained vehicular traces. Technical report HPL-2012-26, HP Labs (2012)

The 2019 International Workshop on Cybersecurity Metrics and Risk Modeling (CMRM 2019)

CMRM 2019 Organizing and Program Committees

General Chairs

David Maimon	Georgia State University, USA
Robert Harrison	Georgia State University, USA

Program Chairs

David Maimon	Georgia State University, USA
Robert Harrison	Georgia State University, USA
William L. Harrison	Oak Ridge National Laboratory, USA
Yubao Wu	Georgia State University, USA

Program Committee

Flavio Villanustre	LexisNexis Risk Solutions, USA
Bill Sabol	Georgia State University, USA
Richard Baskerville	Georgia State University, USA
Max Garcia	Primerevenue Inc, USA
David F. Katz	Adams and Reese LLP, USA
Kausar Kenning	SunTrust, USA
Benoit DuPont	Université de Montréal, Canada
David Maimon	Georgia State University, USA
Robert W. Harrison	Georgia State University, USA
Yubao Wu	Georgia State University, USA
Marie Ouellet	Georgia State University, USA
Donald Edward Hunt	Georgia State University, USA
William L. Harrison	Oak Ridge National Laboratory, USA

Web Chairs

David Maimon	Georgia State University, USA
Yubao Wu	Georgia State University, USA

Steering Committee

David Maimon (Chair)	Georgia State University, USA
Robert Harrison (Chair)	Georgia State University, USA
David Maimon	Georgia State University, USA
Robert Harrison	Georgia State University, USA
William L. Harrison	Oak Ridge National Laboratory, USA
Yubao Wu	Georgia State University, USA

Web-Based Intelligence for IDS

Christopher B. Freas and Robert W. Harrison[✉]

Department of Computer Science, Georgia State University, Atlanta, USA
{cfreas,rharrison}@cs.gsu.edu

Abstract. We and others have shown that machine learning can detect and mitigate web-based attacks and the propagation of malware. High performance machine learning frameworks exist for the major computer languages used to program both web servers and web pages. This paper examines the factors required to use the frameworks as an effective distributed deterrent.

Keywords: Networks · Attack detection · Machine learning · Application level intelligence · Security

1 Introduction

Current tools for mitigating web-based attacks usually live on the network border. These tools are often single function hardware appliances. Examples include Intrusion Detection Systems (IDS), Intrusion Prevention Systems (IPS), and firewalls. Other commercial offerings include "traffic scrubbers". These devices ingest live network traffic and remove known attack traffic from the traffic flow. The cleaned traffic is then injected back into the network. Unified Threat Management (UTM) systems combine the above functions into a single appliance.

While effective, these systems do have caveats. Updated attack signatures and policy changes must be constantly deployed. Appliances often do not scale to high speeds, and if they do, it is at significant cost. To effectively guard against attacks, these systems must be deployed to all ingress points at the network border. Doing so imposes significant costs in licensing, operations, and physical footprint.

Machine learning is being applied to problems in many domains. As a result, several popular frameworks have gained popularity. Many of these frameworks provide APIs for programming languages such as Python. This can enable the creation of powerful threat detection agents.

This paper explores the factors required to create intelligent distributed threat detection agents. These agents are capable of performing the roles of the hardware appliances at the application level. They are tightly integrated into the various components of the web application stack. They distribute valuable information on attacks as they are mitigated. The agents integrate modern machine learning into web servers and web applications.

© Springer Nature Switzerland AG 2019
G. Wang et al. (Eds.): SpaCCS 2019 Workshops, LNCS 11637, pp. 307–316, 2019.
https://doi.org/10.1007/978-3-030-24900-7_25

We describe several web-based attacks to provide context to our proposed solution. We discuss two popular Python-based machine learning frameworks. These frameworks can be used to build intelligent threat detection agents. We propose a distributed threat detection model for the contemporary web application stack. Finally, we discuss the potential challenges of such a model.

2 Related Work

Research in using machine learning for threat detection abounds. In [7], Miller et al. propose a cloud-based model for detecting the use of proxy services. Attackers often obscure their true location by hiding behind one or more proxy services. Detecting the use of a proxy server is an important first step in mitigating potentially malicious network traffic.

Event correlation is crucial to any threat detection system. A security analyst saves considerable time remediating intrusion events for real threats. In [16], Zomlot et al. show that machine learning can be applied to event correlation graphs to filter out events that do not need to be acted upon.

We show in our own work that it is possible to discriminate between benign and malicious network traffic [4]. We applied conventional machine learning to two important data sets. The first is the well-known KDD '99 network intrusion data set [1]. The second is the Intrusion Detection Evaluation Data set (CIC-IDS) published by Sharafaldin et al. in [11]. This data set consists of 15 different attacks over a week of collection. After obtaining high accuracy on both data sets, we broke the CIC-IDS data into non-overlapping sets per day of collection. Machine learning accuracy deteriorates when attacks are present only in the test data. This lead us to conclude that the data are non-stationary. This means that conventional machine learning algorithms cannot reliably detect malicious network flows.

Threat detection tools must adapt to changes in attacks while maintaining accuracy. Signature-based tools, currently in use by most commercial vendors, are not able to adapt to changes in a timely manner. Machine learning can be a valuable aid to threat detection, but it must be applied carefully.

3 Threat Analysis

It is important to understand common threats to understand the potential use of distributed intelligence. The number of web-based attacks is numerous and growing, so we describe a few common attacks here.

One of the most common web attacks leverages improper or altogether missing form validation in a web application. A number of potent attacks are possible when form inputs are not properly validated [13]:

- Injection of SQL code, which enables an attacker to run arbitrary SQL commands on the backend database of the website

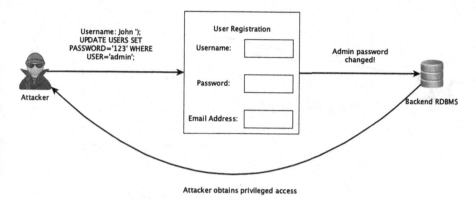

Fig. 1. A SQL injection attack. The attacker sends a crafted payload and obtains privileged access to the back end database.

- Cross-site scripting, which enables an attacker to post arbitrary data to a website
- Header injection, which allows an attacker to exploit forms in order to send spam

An illustration of a SQL injection attack is shown in Fig. 1. To carry out the attack, the attacker includes valid SQL code in the form submission. The result of the attack depends on the payload. The attacker could corrupt the database. Sensitive data could be stolen. The attacker could gain privileged access to carry out further attacks. Form validation restricts the type of data that can be entered into a form. Input checks ensure the input data is valid for what is being requested in a given form field. Research into the prevention of such attacks is active [10,14].

Another common attack is a Cross-Site Request Forgery (CSRF) attack. CSRF attacks are a type of confused deputy attack. The forged requests leverage the authentication and authorization of the victim [8]. A CSRF attack adds extra commands to a user's request. The extra commands perform any actions for which the user is authorized. Attacks can change the user's credentials. If the current user has sufficient privileges, other users can be impersonated. These actions are performed without the user's knowledge or consent.

Figure 2 shows a generalized CSRF attack. The attacker first embeds a malicious payload into the website's Hypertext Markup Language (HTML) code. The code could be as trivial as adding a password change request query as the source to an HTML image tag. Once logged in, the victim's web browser fetches the contents of the image tag. The victim's password is changed to the password specified by the attacker in the query. The victim has no knowledge that this has occurred. The victim is a valid user so the password change request appears legitimate from the perspective of the website.

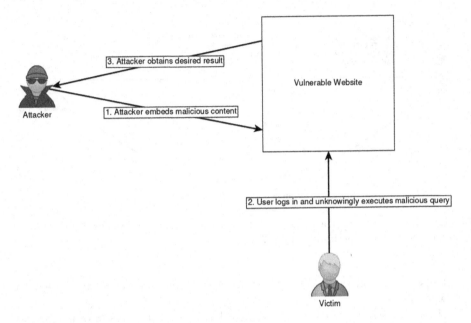

Fig. 2. A CSRF attack. The attacker embeds a malicious payload into the website. When the user logs in, their web browser automatically executes the malicious query. The attacker obtains the result.

There are many defenses against CSRF attacks [2]. The most common is to embed a secret validation token in any requests. If a request is missing the token or the token does not match the expected value, the server rejects the request.

These two brief examples share a caveat with the hardware appliances mentioned before. Because the mitigations work only with known attacks, any unknown attack is likely to succeed. The use of machine learning can help to mitigate known and unknown attacks.

4   Using Machine Learning Frameworks

Machine learning at the application layer can reduce many of the drawbacks of hardware and software solutions. Security can be moved from the network perimeter to host systems. The software solutions described in Sect. 3 gain greater protection. Training application-layer security against application layer threats improves the quality of the decisions.

Host-based application-layer security can substantially reduce license and operational costs for hardware appliances. The physical footprint of the network can thus be scaled down. Throughput scaling becomes less of a concern since host systems perform traffic inspection. Constant signature updates on security devices is reduced or eliminated altogether. However, our proposed model requires updates to traffic that is considered benign. Generative machine learn-

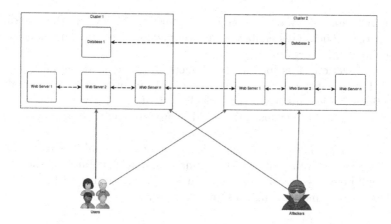

Fig. 3. An intelligent threat mitigation model for a web application. The dashed lines indicate the distribution of threat intelligence. User traffic is permitted while attacker traffic is not.

ing models such as the restricted Boltzmann machine (RBM) are a solution to this. Application throughput is thus limited to the host system's bandwidth.

Many popular Open Source frameworks exist and are compatible with the application layer. We briefly describe two popular frameworks.

Scikit-learn supports many supervised and unsupervised machine learning models. Other supporting functionality includes data preparation and model validation. Scikit-learn provides a Python API and is easy to learn. The use of Graphics Processing Units (GPU) is not supported. CPU-optimized versions of the Numpy library can provide some performance gains. Limited support for basic neural networks is available. Neural networks are not the main focus of the library.

TensorFlow was released by the Google Brain team in 2015. In contrast to Scikit-learn, TensorFlow operates with or without a GPU. Using the GPU results in significant speedups in learning. It is intended to be a general-purpose numerical computation library. Like Scikit-learn, TensorFlow can execute "shallow learning" tasks. Support for all major neural network models is included.

5   A Mitigation Model

Intelligent agents can be incorporated into any component of the web application infrastructure. Figure 3 illustrates intelligent agents in multiple layers of the web application infrastructure. The intelligent agents run on each of the components. The dashed lines indicate the distribution of threat intelligence among the components. Note that there is no inter-component communication. Different components face different threats. Threat detection models thus protect specific components. A compromise of any single component's agents does not affect the agents for other components.

The inclusion of multiple component clusters highlights the distributed nature of the model. This enables a geographically dispersed infrastructure for sharing threat information.

The next sections describe intelligent agents for specific web application components. The use of the Python-based frameworks mentioned in Sect. 4 make the serialization of object instances (i.e. "pickling an object") trivial. Mitigation systems using either of the frameworks could be updated asynchronously while still running.

Training and validation of machine learning models could be carried out in a non-production environment, and the updated models supplied to the applications. It will be necessary to sign the updates to ensure security. Python libraries exist that support modern digital signature algorithms.

5.1 Flask

Flask is a Python-based web framework used to build APIs, websites, and more. In the model shown in Fig. 3, an instance of Flask would run on every web server. Building an intelligent agent using either of the two frameworks in Sect. 4 is trivial. An intelligent agent need only check incoming requests to see if they're potentially malicious. Requests with suspicious content are dropped and an error is returned to the user. This results in just two classes of requests and a linear model on which to learn.

Stochastic gradient descent (SGD) is a simple binary classification model that uses convex optimization as a loss function. SGD outperforms models such as Support Vector Machines (SVM), especially on large data sets. The intelligent agent is first trained using SGD. Once trained, it transforms an incoming request into a feature vector, classifies it, and returns the result. If the feature vector belongs to the malicious class, the request is dropped and an error is returned to the user.

5.2 Databases

The database intelligent agent checks incoming SQL queries before running them. Unusual or never-before-seen queries are potentially malicious. For example, if no user management exists in the web application, the agent should never receive queries against such tables. Queries of this type are malicious and are dropped.

Building an intelligent agent for the database component using either of the two frameworks in Sect. 4 would require more effort. The agent would receive incoming SQL queries, classify them, then pass along queries classified as benign to the SQL database. The intelligent agent thus acts as a reverse proxy between the client applications (e.g. the web servers in Fig. 3) and the database.

The number of possible requests is small relative to those seen by the Flask component. As a result, most database queries are benign. In this case, the use of an SVM is appropriate. As before, the intelligent agent is first trained. Once trained, it transforms an incoming SQL query into a feature vector, classifies it, and returns the result. If the feature vector belongs to the malicious class, the SQL query is not passed along to the database and an error is returned to the user.

5.3   Web Servers

Web servers are the most outward facing component of the web application. Protecting them against attacks is vitally important. Attacks against web servers tend to focus on the web server itself instead of the content it serves. Fuzzing is a common technique where invalid or unexpected data is provided to an application and the result is observed [9]. Attackers combine fuzzing and known vulnerabilities into attack tool kits. Automated scanners and bots use these tool kits to exploit known and unknown vulnerabilities.

Web servers are typically written in languages such as C to maximize performance. Python-based frameworks such as Flask typically use library functions, written in C and integrated into Python, to optimize performance by speeding up critical bottlenecks to performance. Therefore integrating a Python-based machine learning package, one that also uses low-level C libraries, into a Python-based web-server is fully viable.

An intelligent agent could either be integrated into the web server software itself or act as a reverse proxy like the database model. An agent acting as a reverse proxy only checks incoming Hypertext Transfer Protocol (HTTP) requests. An integrated agent would need to check incoming network packets as well since attacks might target lower level functionality of the web server.

The attack surface of the web server could be quite large depending on how the agent is integrated. In both cases, SGD would be a good fit for a machine learning model.

5.4   Web Browsers

The focus of this paper is on the web application infrastructure. We mention web browsers only briefly here to provide a more thorough discussion of the web application ecosystem. A web browser presents a large attack surface on the user's device. This is due to the complexity of modern web browsers. They parse HTML and Javascript code, render audio and visual content, cope with third party extensions, and talk securely to web sites. Most contemporary web browsers include protections for users. While this paper focuses on Python frameworks, machine learning frameworks exist for Javascipt, including TensorFlow [5] and mljs [15].

- Tracking protection prevents a user from being profiled
- Protection against dodgy downloads prevents the user from installing malware
  Blocking pop-up windows protects the user against potentially malicious advertisements
- Disabling third party cookies prevents some user tracking and CSRF attacks

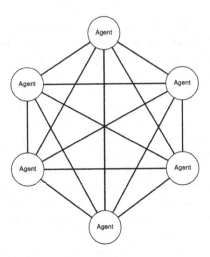

Fig. 4. A DHT for distributing threat intelligence.

– Private browsing sandboxes the user's session and prevents user cookies from being stolen

Even with the above protections, web browsers still have drawbacks. The above features mostly guard against known attacks. New attacks can wreak havoc until the browser vendor updates the software. Web browsers offer no protection against potentially malicious content in web pages. A good example of this is the CSRF attack detailed in Sect. 3. A web browser agent would see the unusual content in the image tag and refuse to execute it. Modern firewalls block all communication by default. Trusted communication, defined by policy, may pass through. Web browsers allow all communication by default until the user configures content blocking.

6   Distributing the Intelligence

Trained models can be easily distributed using peer-to-peer (P2P) network technology. Modern P2P networks implement a distributed hash table (DHT). This provides robust, fault-tolerant, distributed delivery of resources [6,12]. However, some environments need strict security controls. In such environments, a private bootstrap host can be used to connect the private peers to each other.

A DHT for distributing threat intelligence is shown in Fig. 4. The intelligent agents discussed in Sect. 5 are depicted in the figure. The DHT can serve several functions. It can distribute signed trained model data. It can distribute the public keys used to validate the signed training data. Potential threats that agents have seen but could not correctly classify can be distributed and analyzed.

The types of threats that could be handled using the DHT depend on the placement of the intelligent agents. In the model shown in Fig. 3, each layer of components runs a separate DHT. In general, any anomalous behavior can be identified and remediated. The default response of the components should be to drop the anomalous traffic. Requests that could not be clearly identified could be quarantined similar to the model seen in email spam filtering. The anomalous request is moved to a secure sandbox until an administrator can identify it. Once identified, the request becomes part of the training data and shared with the agents via the DHT.

7   Challenges

From a software engineering and implementation viewpoint, the use of integrated machine learning at the application level is attractive. Several challenges remain.

Obtaining training data, and especially labeled training data, is problematic. A combination of honeypots, monitoring software, and unsupervised classification could be used to find classes of data. The data would then require evaluation to see if it is malicious or benign. Partially trained models could be used to "bootstrap" a system by flagging suspicious, but uncertain, data for further evaluation.

User adoption is another major challenge. It will be necessary to make the addition of the models to existing systems as seamless as is possible and to convincingly demonstrate that the systems provide real benefits to the users. Since, even with advanced machine learning, the problem of deciding what code actually does without executing it, being isomorphic to the stopping problem is formally undecidable, it is critical to tune the machine learning to give a small number of false positives without giving too many false negatives. A system that "cries wolf" too often will inhibit security as users will learn to ignore it.

Another challenge is the validation and update of training models. Distributed and custom training on individual machines may seem an ideal model, but it introduces the possibility of a "false oracle" attack where the adversary spoofs the machine learning until it ignores real threats while focusing on noise. Therefore, training probably should be separate from the online application so that the training can be supervised and performed in a secure and reliable manner. The models themselves would need to be updated, asynchronously and securely, to the users. ClamAV [3] is an example of an open-source anti-virus program which demonstrates that this is an achievable goal.

8   Conclusions

This position paper has examined the factors needed to integrate machine-learning into application level security. While technical challenges remain, there is no fundamental architectural reason why this could not be done. What remains to be demonstrated is that this can be achieved with a useful level of accuracy while not degrading computational performance.

References

1. ACM SIGKDD: KDD Cup 1999: Computer network intrusion detection. http:// www.kdd.org/kdd-cup/view/kdd-cup-1999/Data
2. Barth, A., Jackson, C., Mitchell, J.C.: Robust defenses for cross-site request forgery. In: Proceedings of the 15th ACM Conference on Computer and Communications Security, pp. 75–88. ACM (2008)
3. ClamavNet: ClamAV is an open source antivirus engine for detecting trojans, viruses, malware & other malicious threats. https://www.clamav.net/. Accessed 26 May 2019
4. Freas, C.B., Harrison, R.W., Long, Y.: High performance attack estimation in large-scale network flows. In: 2018 IEEE International Conference on Big Data (Big Data), pp. 5014–5020. IEEE (2018)
5. Google: Tensorflow for Javascript. https://www.tensorflow.org/js. Accessed 26 May 2019
6. Maymounkov, P., Mazières, D.: Kademlia: a peer-to-peer information system based on the XOR metric. In: Druschel, P., Kaashoek, F., Rowstron, A. (eds.) IPTPS 2002. LNCS, vol. 2429, pp. 53–65. Springer, Heidelberg (2002). https://doi.org/10.1007/3-540-45748-8_5
7. Miller, S., Curran, K., Lunney, T.: Cloud-based machine learning for the detection of anonymous web proxies. In: 2016 27th Irish Signals and Systems Conference (ISSC), pp. 1–6. IEEE (2016)
8. Muscat, I.: What is cross-site request forgery? June 2017. https://www.acunetix.com/blog/articles/cross-site-request-forgery/
9. Oehlert, P.: Violating assumptions with fuzzing. IEEE Secur. Priv. 3(2), 58–62 (2005)
10. Scholte, T., Robertson, W., Balzarotti, D., Kirda, E.: Preventing input validation vulnerabilities in web applications through automated type analysis. In: 2012 IEEE 36th Annual Computer Software and Applications Conference, pp. 233–243. IEEE (2012)
11. Sharafaldin, I., Lashkari, A.H., Ghorbani, A.A.: Toward generating a new intrusion detection dataset and intrusion traffic characterization. In: Proceedings of Fourth International Conference on Information Systems Security and Privacy, ICISSP (2018)
12. Stoica, I., Morris, R., Karger, D., Kaashoek, M.F., Balakrishnan, H.: Chord: a scalable peer-to-peer lookup service for internet applications. ACM SIGCOMM Comput. Commun. Rev. 31(4), 149–160 (2001)
13. Syronex: Why is Form Validation Needed? https://formsmarts.com/form-validation
14. Xu, W., Bhatkar, S., Sekar, R.: Practical dynamic taint analysis for countering input validation attacks on web applications. Technical report SECLAB-05-04, Department of Computer Science (2005)
15. Zasso, M.: Machine learning and numerical analysis tools in Javascript for node.js and the browser. https://github.com/mljs. Accessed 26 May 2019
16. Zomlot, L., Chandran, S., Caragea, D., Ou, X.: Aiding intrusion analysis using machine learning. In: 2013 12th International Conference on Machine Learning and Applications, vol. 2, pp. 40–47, December 2013. https://doi.org/10.1109/ICMLA.2013.103

Predictably Deterrable? The Case of System Trespassers

David Maimon[1(✉)], Alexander Testa[2], Bertrand Sobesto[3],
Michel Cukier[4], and Wuling Ren[5]

[1] Department of Criminology and Criminal Justice, Georgia State University,
Atlanta, USA
dmaimon@gsu.edu
[2] Department of Criminal Justice, University of Texas at San Antonio,
San Antonio, USA
[3] Division of Information Technology, University of Maryland,
College Park, USA
[4] A. James Clark School of Engineering, University of Maryland,
College Park, USA
[5] College of Computer and Information Engineering,
Zhejiang Gongshang University, Hangzhou, China

Abstract. Can computing environments deter system trespassers and increase intruders' likelihood to cover their tracks during the progression of a system trespassing event? To generate sufficient empirical evidence to answer this question, we designed a series of randomized field trials using a large set of target computers built for the sole purpose of being infiltrated. We configured these computers to present varying levels of ambiguity regarding the presence of surveillance in the system, and investigated how this ambiguity influenced system trespassers' likelihood to issue clean tracks commands. Findings indicate that the presence of unambiguous signs of surveillance increases the probability of clean tracks commands being entered on the system. Nevertheless, even when given clear signs of detection, we find that intruders are less likely to use clean tracks commands in the absence of subsequent presentations of sanction threats. These results indicate that the implementation of deterring policies and tools in cyber space could nudge system trespassers to exhibit more cautiousness during their engagement in system trespassing events. Our findings also emphasize the relevance of social-science models in guiding cyber security experts' continuing efforts to predict and respond to system trespassers' illegitimate online activities.

Keywords: System trespassing · Deterrence · Randomized trial · Ambiguity

1 Introduction

System trespassing (i.e. the unauthorized use of a computer system) [1] has become a common global problem; in 2013, over 740 million records were exposed in the U.S. alone as a result of numerous system trespassing incidents targeting governmental and private organizations [2]. Moreover, users of private computers, smartphones, and even medical devices increasingly report infiltration of their devices by illegitimate users [3].

© Springer Nature Switzerland AG 2019
G. Wang et al. (Eds.): SpaCCS 2019 Workshops, LNCS 11637, pp. 317–330, 2019.
https://doi.org/10.1007/978-3-030-24900-7_26

Thus, it comes as no surprise that Americans are today more worried about having their computers or smartphones hacked than about falling victim to any other types of crime [4]. These concerns seem to be well funded given recent knowledge regarding numerous system trespassing events into governmental computers, that are likely more secured than systems of regular users. Acknowledging the potential risks posed to U.S. national security and Internet users' privacy by the growing number of system trespassing events and other cyber threats, President Obama recently determined that the activities elaborated in the Comprehensive National Cyber security Initiative (CNCI) should evolve to become the key elements of the U.S.'s national cyber security strategy [5]. One key activity in the CNCI highlights the development of deterrence strategies designed to prevent and mitigate the consequences of cyber attacks against U.S. organizations and individuals. The rationale behind the implementation of this activity is embedded in the expected utility model's (also known as the rational choice model) prediction that when the costs of behaviors outweigh the benefits, individuals will refrain from acting all together [6, 7]. Nevertheless, despite the emphasis placed on cyber deterrence, the effectiveness of deterrence-based strategies for preventing and mitigating the occurrence of malicious cyber activities is theoretically challenging [8–11].

On one hand, several scholars believe that the implementation of deterrence-based strategies and tools like surveillance and sanctions in cyber space is prone to failure, since the inherently anonymous nature of cyber space increases system trespassers' ability to avoid detection and escape penalties for their illegitimate online behaviors [8–10]. This theoretical claim receives some support from empirical research that indicates mixed evidence regarding the effectiveness of surveillance measures (for instance, CCTV cameras) and sanction threats (for instance, warnings) in preventing the occurrence of non-cyber criminal behaviors [12, 13]. These inconsistent findings are generally attributed to the limited capability of the criminal justice system to detect and punish all criminal events that occur in our world [14, 15]. Accordingly, potential offenders learn through trial and error that the certainty of being detected and punished for a criminal act is relatively low, and therefore, initiate illegitimate behaviors. Since the certainty of detection and punishment of a system trespassing event is even lower than the certainty of detection of a non-cyber criminal event (it is very difficult for the average computer user to detect malicious activity on a computer system promptly), the implementation of surveillance measures and sanction threats in a computing environment is predicted to play an insignificant role in preventing the occurrence of cyber attacks.

In contrast, other scholars contend that it is unnecessary to identify specific individuals in order for deterrence to take effect in cyber space [11]. Accordingly, the introduction of situational deterrence cues in an attacked computer environment could be sufficient to entice a predictable avoidance response from system trespassers, and consequently attenuate the consequences of a computer attack. For instance, since detection of a system trespassing event results in increased efforts by legitimate users to deny trespassers access to the attacked computer [16], implementing surveillance measures in a computing environment may lead system trespassers to overestimate the risk of detection on the system, devote increased efforts toward avoiding detection and hiding their presence, and even reduce harmful activity on the system. Therefore, even though implementation of surveillance measures will not necessarily prevent the occurrence of a system trespassing event and result in official sanction, it will increase system trespassers' efforts to avoid detection of their presence and to restrict the scope of their illegitimate activity on the attacked system during the progression of a system trespassing event.

Two important lines of research support this claim. First, accumulating empirical evidence suggests that system trespassers are rational decision makers that direct their efforts towards targets that provide the maximum return and involve a minimum level of risk [17, 18]. Second, although past research reveals mixed evidence regarding the effects of detection and punishment on the *occurrence* of a criminal event, several studies reveal consistent evidence regarding the effectiveness of deterring cues (for instance, CCTV cameras or police patrols) in shaping criminals' behaviors *during the progression* of a criminal event. Specifically, this line of research shows that the presentation of situational deterring cues in the environment increases offenders' efforts to avoid detection, attenuate the volume of their repeat offending, and reduce the severity of the crimes they commit [19–21]. Therefore, it is possible that manipulation of the computing environment to influence system trespassers into believing that attacking the system is too risky and subject to quick detection and potential sanctions will increase their efforts to avoid detection on the system [22, 23]. Our work seeks to delve into this theoretical debate, in an effort to determine whether the design of deterring computer environments could trigger system trespassers' cautious online behaviors during the progression of a system trespassing event.

One avenue through which perceived risk of detection and punishment could be elevated and incorporated in the environment involves the introduction of information regarding the risk of surveillance and sanctions [15]. Nevertheless, whether such information should be presented in a vague or clear manner is debatable. On one hand, since most decision makers are ambiguity averse in their decision-making processes (i.e. they opt for prospects with known risks as opposed to unknown risks [24–26]), the introduction of ambiguous information (i.e. incomplete information that hinders decision makers' ability to estimate the distribution around the probability of an event [24, 27]) regarding the implementation of surveillance and sanctions in an attacked computer system may disrupt system trespassers' estimates of the low risks of getting caught, increase their uncertainty regarding the perceived risk of detection and punishment, and make them more cautious during system trespassing events [15, 28]. In contrast, several scholars contend that while decision makers are ambiguity averse for gains, they tend to be ambiguity seeking for losses [24, 25, 29]. In that case, ambiguity regarding the presence of surveillance, and regarding the prospects of detection and sanction of system trespassing events, should attenuate the deterrent potential of surveillance and punishment and entice risky behaviors from system trespassers during system trespassing events.

In this study we identify the monitoring of an attacked computer environment as a key potentially deterrent process in cyber space, and examine whether ambiguous information regarding the presence of surveillance in the attacked computer system increases system trespassers' efforts to avoid detection during system trespassing events.

2   Experimental Design

We designed and implemented three randomized controlled field trials that allowed the collection of data on system trespassing events while preserving the unique computing environment in which they occurred. The experiments were conducted on the Internet infrastructure of one American and one Chinese academic institution, where we set up networks of several hundred target-computers (i.e. honeypots [28]), and waited for system trespassers to find and infiltrate our systems. The three experiments followed the same general experimental design. Our target computers were set up as computer systems with the Linux Ubuntu 10.04 operating system. In order to gain access to these computers system trespassers first had to find them (by scanning the Internet and finding open computer ports that are configured to accept information from the Internet [30]), and then had to employ special software-cracking tools in order to guess the "correct" password to the computers and infiltrate them. Once they gained access to the target computers, system trespassers were randomly assigned to either control or treatment computers, which were manipulated to include indicators of surveillance and sanction threats. Following assignment to the experimental conditions, trespassers were allowed access to the target computers and could initiate repeated system trespassing incidents for a period of 30 days. During this time system trespassers were free to use the honeypot computer as they liked, but a firewall was employed to ensure that they did not engage in activities dangerous to other systems. We recorded all the computer commands entered by the system trespassers on the target computers during each system trespassing event. As a dependent variable, we observed the relative number of target computers on which system trespassers entered "clean tracks" commands during the 30-day period. These commands are entered on Linux computers in order to remove users' traces from the system and complicate system administrators' efforts to identify illegitimate activity on the system. The specific clean tracks commands we looked for were "remove files" (*rm-rf*), "clear bash history" (*history-c*) and "delete history variables" (*unset*)).

3   Results

3.1   Study 1

Our first study was designed to investigate whether a generic warning banner employed by network administrators, one which incorporates ambiguous information regarding surveillance processes on the system and a clear sanction threat, increases system trespassers' efforts to avoid detection on the system. US federal security guidelines recommend that such a banner be installed on all government-owned computers [31]. The setting for this experiment was the Internet infrastructure of a large US university. We deployed our target computers and waited for system trespassers to find and infiltrate our systems. In order to ensure that technical components of the computing environment did not condition the effect of the intervention, we employed a 2 (warning banner, no banner) × 2 (low [512 Mbytes] RAM, high [2.25 Gbytes] RAM) × 2 (Low [128 Kbits/s] bandwidth, high [512 Kbits/s] bandwidth) × 2 (low [5 Gbytes] disk space, high [30 Gbytes] disk space) factorial design in this experiment.

The warning message that appeared on the system trespassers' screens under the warning condition reads as follows: "*The actual or attempted unauthorized access, use, or modification of this system is strictly prohibited. Unauthorized users are subject to institutional disciplinary proceedings and/or criminal and civil penalties under state, federal, or other applicable domestic and foreign laws. The use of this system is monitored and recorded for administrative and security reasons. Anyone accessing this system expressly consents to such monitoring and is advised that if monitoring reveals possible evidence of criminal activity, the Institution may provide the evidence of such activity to law enforcement officials*". Importantly, investigation of the whole poll of computer commands entered into the systems by system trespassers revealed that none of the computer commands entered by system trespassers on the system could reveal the three technical configurations (i.e. RAM size, disk space, and bandwidth capacity) of the computing environment. Therefore, we only test for differences in the influence of the warning message on the presence of clean tracks commands.

Overall, 221 target computers were infiltrated by system trespassers and were used for entering commands; 111 of the computers presented the warning banner, while the other 110 did not. These target computers experienced a total of 2,141 trespassing incidents during the experimental period.

First, investigating the prevalence of target computers with clean tracks commands reveals that 58.4% of the target computers recorded at least one command designed to remove system trespassers' tracks from the attacked system. The most common clean tracks command was "remove a file" (entered on 52.5% of the target computers), followed by "delete history variables" (entered on 27% of the target computers), and then the "clear bash history" command (entered on 14% of the target computers). Next, we test whether the presence of a generic warning banner containing ambiguous information regarding surveillance in the system yet a clear sanction threat influences the presence of clean tracks commands. Findings from this analysis are presented in Fig. 1. As indicated in the figure, there are no statistically significant differences between the proportion of warning and no-warning target computers that were attacked by system trespassers and that had clean tracks commands entered. This pattern is consistent across the three unique clean tracks commands we explored, as well as an overall "clean track" measure we composed to indicate the presence of at least one clean track command on the attacked computers. These findings suggest that the presentation of ambiguous information regarding surveillance processes on the system with a clear sanction threat does not increase system trespassers' efforts to avoid detection on the system.

Based on these findings, we designed our next studies to include varying levels of ambiguity regarding the risk of detection in the system. Specifically, drawing on the assumption that decision makers employ all available information in order to estimate the length of the distribution around the probability of an event to occur [27], we wanted to determine whether altering the level of ambiguity regarding the presence of surveillance in the attacked system increases the likelihood that system trespassers will clean their tracks. Moreover, we sought to understand whether removing ambiguity regarding the risk of detection by alerting system trespassers of their detection on the system increases their probability to enter clean tracks commands.

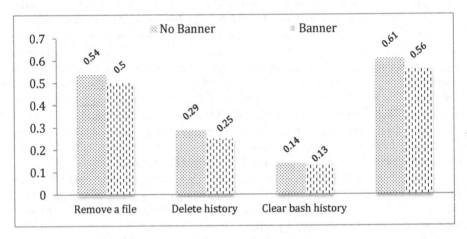

Fig. 1. Differences between the proportions of warning and no-warning target computers with clean track commands. Shown are the proportions of control and experimental target computers that were attacked by system trespassers and that recorded at least one unique clean track command, sorted by warning banner/no warning banner. N = 221 target computers.

3.2   Study 2

In our second study we explored whether the availability of ambiguous information regarding the presence of surveillance influences system trespassers' likelihood to enter clean tracks commands on the attacked computer system. To test this correlation, we targeted system trespassers' ability to assess the distribution around the risk of detection in the attacked system by presenting varying levels of information regarding the presence of surveillance in the system. We redeployed our target computers on the Internet infrastructure of a large American university, and employed a 2 (surveillance banner, no banner) × 2 (surveillance software, no software) factorial design. Consistently with our first study, we deployed our target computers and waited for system trespassers to find and infiltrate our systems. Upon successfully infiltrating our computers, system trespassers were randomly assigned to one of four experimental conditions. In the first treatment group (high ambiguity) we installed an open-source surveillance software (Zabbix) that emulated the process of monitoring on the target computers. Exposure to the surveillance software was possible only upon calling forth a display depicting all the processes running on the target computer. The Linux command to call forth this information is "ps". In the second treatment group (medium ambiguity) the target computers were configured to present the following surveillance banner upon each entry to the system: *"This system is under continuous surveillance. All user activity is being monitored and recorded"*. Similarly to the banner presented in Study 1, this treatment indicated the presence of surveillance in the system, yet did not disclose how active this process was. In the third treatment group (low ambiguity) the target computers were configured to both present the surveillance banner and run the surveillance software.

In addition to the three experimental groups, we incorporated a control condition, in which target computers had neither the surveillance banner nor the surveillance software installed on. Note that since a great deal of information is provided to system trespassers in the third treatment, their ability to estimate a narrower distribution around the probability of detection is greater than in the other treatments and in the control condition [27]. Therefore, there is lower ambiguity regarding the presence of surveillance and the risk of detection in the system. In contrast, in the first treatment, almost no information regarding the presence of surveillance is provided to system trespassers (in fact system trespassers have to actively seek this information). Therefore, system trespassers' ability to estimate a narrower distribution around the probability of detection is smaller here than in the other treatment conditions, causing higher ambiguity regarding the presence of surveillance and the risk of detection in the system.

In total, 458 target computers were infiltrated by system trespassers and were used for entering commands. 124 of the computers ran the surveillance software, 99 of the computers presented the surveillance banner, 116 of the computers presented the banner and ran the software, and 119 computers neither presented the banner nor ran the software. These target computers experienced a total of 2,226 trespassing incidents during the experimental period. Exploring the prevalence of clean tracks commands entered on the target computers reveals similar patterns to those observed in Study 1: almost 54% of the systems recorded clean tracks commands. The most common clean tracks command was "remove a file" (entered on 47% of the target computers), followed by "delete history variables" (entered on 21% of the target computers), and finally the "clear bash history" command (entered on 20% of the target computers).

Importantly, since system trespassers were able to enter commands on the system *after* assignment to one of the experimental conditions, it was impossible to select only system trespassers that typed "ps" for our study and guarantee their exposure to the hidden surveillance software. Therefore, while some of the system trespassers were exposed to the surveillance program (by typing in "ps"), the majority were not; specifically, of the 458 target computers that were infiltrated by system trespassers only 190 command logs (41.5%) contained a "ps" command. Investigating whether the proportion of target computers that recorded the "ps" command was significantly different across the four experimental conditions suggests an insignificant difference between the four groups ($X^2 = 2.82$, $P > 0.1$). However, target computers that recorded the "ps" command were significantly more likely to record the clean track commands as well. Therefore, since some of the system trespassers were fully exposed to the experimental treatment while others were not, we conducted different analyses for computers infiltrated by system trespassers who did not enter the "ps" command, and for computers infiltrated by system trespassers who entered "ps" in the system.

For computers infiltrated by system trespassers who did not enter the "ps" command, we only tested for significant differences between the proportion of target computers with and without the surveillance banner on which clean tracks commands were entered. Specifically, we consolidated the four conditions from the original 2x2 factorial design: the control group and the software only group were consolidated into a single *no banner group*, while the surveillance banner only and the surveillance banner and software groups were consolidated into a *banner group*. Findings from this analysis are presented in Fig. 2. Consistent with our findings in Study 1, there are no statistically significant differences between the proportion of target computers with and without the surveillance banner that had at least one unique clean track command entered.

In contrast, for computers infiltrated by system trespassers who entered the "ps" command (and thus at least theoretically were exposed to the surveillance process), we test whether varying levels of ambiguity regarding surveillance influence the probability of clean tracks commands being entered in the system. Findings from this analysis are presented in Fig. 3, and suggest that attacked computer systems with low levels of ambiguity regarding the presence of monitoring in the system are more likely to record clean tracks commands. This finding is consistent for the unique "remove files" ($X^2 = 9.74$, P < 0.05) and "delete history" ($X^2 = 8.21$, P < 0.05) commands, and for the overall composite "clean tracks" measure we created ($X^2 = 8.59$, P < 0.05). Specifically, while clean tracks commands were entered on 74% and 80%, respectively, of the target computers with moderate and low ambiguity regarding surveillance, only 56% and 60% of the high ambiguity and control computers recorded such commands, respectively.

In order to estimate the effect of different levels of ambiguity regarding surveillance on the probability of at least one clean track commands being entered into the attacked computer system, we estimated a logistic regression and specified the three experimental conditions as predictors for the target computers' probability to record at least one clean tracks command. Results from this model are presented in Table 1, and reveal that the presence of a surveillance banner and software in the system increases the probabillity of target computers to record clean tracks commands by 2.67 fold. These findings suggest that low levels of ambiguity regarding the presence of monitoring in the attacked computer systems increase system trespassers' percepetion of risk, and result in extensive efforts to clean their tracks in order to mask their presence in the attacked computer system.

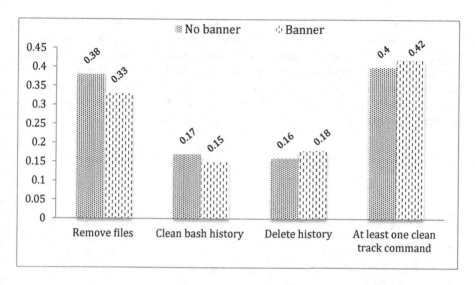

Fig. 2. Differences between the proportions of surveillance banner and no surveillance banner target computers with clean track commands. Shown are the proportions of control and experimental target computers that were attacked by system trespassers who did not check the attacked system processes and who recorded at least one unique clean track command, sorted by surveillance banner/no surveillance banner. N = 268 target computers.

3.3   Study 3

Since findings from Study 2 indicate that less ambiguity regarding the presence of surveillance increases the likelihood of entering clean tracks commands on the attacked computer system, we next investigated whether removing ambiguity regarding surveillance by alerting system trespassers of their detection on the system is sufficient to deter system trespassers. Moreover, we tested whether a sanction threat is necessary in order for deterrence to take effect. For this experiment, we deployed our target computers on the Internet infrastructure of a large Chinese university, and employed a 2 (detection, no detection) × 2 (sanction threat, no sanction threat) factorial design. Since system trespassing is a global phenomenon we have no reason to believe that system trespassers will exhibit different online behaviors on computers hosted by academic institutions located in different geographical regions of the world. Identically to the field experiments we conducted in the U.S., we deployed our target computers and waited for system trespassers to find and infiltrate our systems. Upon successfully infiltrating our systems, system trespassers were randomly assigned to one of four experimental conditions. In the first treatment condition (sanction threat, no detection) the target computers were set to present a 'standard' legal sanction threat identical to that presented in Study 1. In the second treatment condition (detection, no sanction threat) the target computers were configured to present the following message every

326   D. Maimon et al.

time a system trespasser accessed the system: "*Greetings friend, We congratulate you on gaining access to our system, but must request that you not negatively impact our system. Sincerely, Over-worked admin*". In the third treatment condition (detection and sanction threat) the target computers were configured to display the following message: "*We have acquired your IP address. Logout now and there will not be any consequences*". Finally, target computers in the control condition were set to present no messages to trespassers (no detection and no sanction threat).

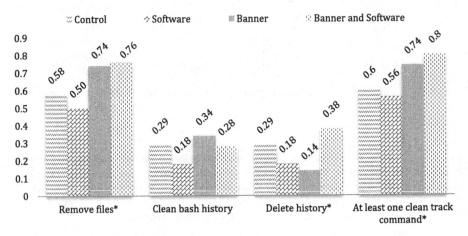

Fig. 3. Differences between the proportions of target computers presenting different levels of ambiguity regarding the presence of surveillance with clean track commands. Shown are the proportions of control and experimental target computers that were attacked by ambiguity-averse system trespassers who checked the attacked system processes and who recorded at least one unique clean track command, sorted by level of ambiguity regarding surveillance in the system. N = 190 target computers, *p < 0.05.

In total, 177 target computers were infiltrated by system trespassers and were used for entering commands. 48 of the computers presented no signs of detection yet threatened system trespassers with potential sanctions, 29 of the computers alerted system trespassers that their presence in the system had been noted yet presented no sanction threat, 49 computers alerted system trespassers that the system trespassing event had been detected and threatened punishment, and 51 computers presented no signs for detection or potential sanctions. Note that although assignment to groups was done completely randomly, it resulted in unequal sample sizes for the different conditions.

To test for potential differences between the group characteristics, we evaluated differences between the origin and timing of system trespassing events initiated against the target computers in each of the experimental conditions. No significant differences were found. These target computers experienced a total of 931 trespassing incidents during the experimental period. Exploring the prevalence of target computers with clean tracks commands entered on reveals that 43% of the systems had clean tracks commands issued. Consistent with the pattern revealed in studies 1 and 2, the most common clean tracks command was "remove a file" (entered on 33% of the target computers), followed by "delete history variables" (entered on 15% of the target computers), and then "clear bash history" (entered on 14% of the target computers).

Table 1. Ambiguity regarding surveillance effect on the presence of clean track commands. Results are from logistic regression of the presence of clean tracks commands on different levels of ambiguity regarding surveillance (treatments) in the attacked system. N = 190 computers, *p < 0.05.

	Odds ratio	Robust SE	95% Confidence	
			Min	Min
Surveillance software	.85	.34	.38	1.84
Surveillance banner	1.92	.92	.75	4.89
Banner and software	2.67*	1.20	1.10	6.43
Constant	1.50	.41	.87	2.57
Log pseudolikelihood	−116.28*			

Examination of the differences between the proportions of target computers that recorded clean tracks commands across the four experimental conditions reveals that simply alerting system trespassers of their detection on the attacked system was insufficient to deter system trespassers. As shown in Fig. 4, clean tracks commands were significantly more likely to be entered on computing environments that notified trespassers of the detection of the system trespassing event and that included a sanction threat. This finding is consistent across the proportions of target computers with the unique "remove files" (X^2 = 9.44, P < 0.05) and "delete history" (X^2 = 6.10, P < 0.1) commands, and for the overall composite "clean tracks" measure (X^2 = 6.35, P < 0.1). Specifically, one may observe that while 57% of the target computers that were infiltrated by system trespassers and were configured to present both detection and sanction threats contained clean track commands, fewer than 40% of the computers configured with the other interventions, including the control group, recorded such commands.

To assess the effect of the three treatments on the probability of target computers to record clean track commands, we estimated a logistic regression predicting the presence of at least one clean track command in the attacked system. Results from this analysis are presented in Table 2. Findings from this analysis suggest that detection and sanction threat increases the probabillity of clean tracks commands being entered in the attacked system by 2.24 fold. In contrast, none of the other experimental conditions yielded significant effect in the model. These findings suggest that signs of detection are not necessarily deterring in and of itself without being accompanied by a sanction threat.

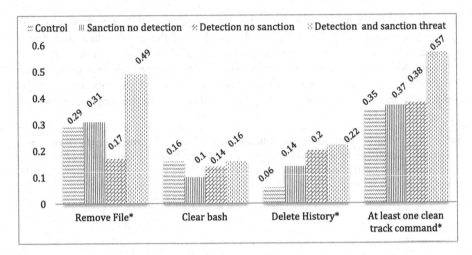

Fig. 4. Differences between the proportions of target computers presenting cues of detection and sanction threats with clean track commands. Shown are the proportions of control and experimental target computers that were attacked by system trespassers and that recorded at least one unique clean track command, sorted by presence of detection alerts and sanction threats in the system. N = 177 target computers, *p < 0.05.

Table 2. Detection and sanction threat effect on the presence of clean track commands. Results are from logistic regression of the presence of clean tracks commands on different detection and sanctions treatments in the attacked systems. N = 153 target computers, *p < 0.05.

	Odds ratio	Robust SE	95% Confidence	
			Min	Min
Sanction threat/No detection	1.03	.49	.40	2.64
Detection/No sanction threat	1.10	.46	.49	2.49
Detection/Sanction threat	2.24*	.92	1.01	5.01
Constant	.59	.17	.33	1.04
Log pseudo likelihood	−118.61			

4 Conclusions

Our conclusion is that low levels of ambiguity regarding the presence of surveillance in an attacked computer system could be useful for deterring system trespassers during the progression of system trespassing events, to the point that tresspassers enter more clean tracks commands in the system. Nevertheless, alerting system trespassers of their detection in the attacked system is insufficient in itself for deterrence to take effect. Such alerts should be accompanied by a sanction threat in order to deter system trespassers. We believe that similar to the way in which system trespassers' deterrability was harnessed to entice efforts to avoid detection in this study, it could be further used to nudge them to engage in other predictable online behaviors during the progression of system trepassing events (for instance typing directly into the system instead of using pre-written scripts, and installing malicious software) that will allow rapid detection of their presence on the system. This quality could support ongoing efforts to develop automated technical tools that will support the detection process and allow more effective mitigation of system trespassing events.

Our findings send a clear message to both policy makers and Information Technology managers in large organizations: the design of more deterrent cyber environments, with clear indications of detection and sanction threats, can push system trespassers to engage in predictable online behaviors. Furthermore, these findings emphasize the importance of integrating soft science models in the development of more sophisticated security solutions and practices to protect against system trespassing events. Finally, our results and research designs emphasize the importance of studying the effect of computing environments on the development and progression of both legitimate and illegitimate online behaviors, while preserving the unique contexts in which those behaviors exist. This issue is of particular relevance to the study of crime in general, and stresses the need to move beyond testing the effect of criminal justice policies on only the occurrence of crime, and to investigate these policies' effects on the progression of criminal events as well.

Acknowledgements. This research was conducted with the support of the National Science Foundation Award 1223634.

References

1. Furnell, S.: Cybercrime: Vandalizing the Information Society. Addison-Wesley, Boston (2002)
2. Online Trust Alliance: Data Protection and Breech: Readiness Guide. Online Trust Alliance (2014)
3. Storm, D.: MEDJACK: hackers hijacking medical devices to create backdoors in hospital networks. Computer World (2015). http://www.computerworld.com/article/2932371/cybercrime-hacking/medjack-hackers-hijacking-medical-devices-to-create-backdoors-in-hospital-networks.html
4. Riffkin, R.: Hacking Tops List of Crimes Americans Worry about Most. Gallup Poll News Service (2014). http://www.gallup.com/poll/178856/hacking-tops-list-crimes-americans-worry.aspx
5. The Comprehensive National Cybersecurity Initiative. The White House. www.whitehouse.gov
6. Becker, G.: Crime and punishment: an economic approach. J. Polit. Econ. **76**, 169–217 (1968)
7. Gibbs, J.: Crime, Punishment, and Deterrence. Elsevier Scientific Publishing Company, New York (1975)
8. Harknett, R.: Information warfare and deterrence. Parameters **26**, 93–107 (1996)
9. Harknett, R., Callaghan, J., Kauffman, R.: Leaving deterrence behind: war-fighting and national cybersecurity. J. Homel. Secur. Emerg. Manag. **7**(1), 1–24 (2010)
10. Denning, D., Baugh, W.: Hiding crimes in cyberspace. In: Thomas, D., Loader, D. (eds.) Cybercrime: Law Enforcement, Security and Surveillance in the Information Age, pp. 105–132. Routledge, London (2000)

11. Goodman, W.: Cyber deterrence: tougher in theory than in practice? Strategic Studies Quarterly Fall, pp. 102–135 (2010)
12. Welsh, B., Farrington, D.: Making Public Places Safer: Surveillance and Crime Prevention. Oxford University Press, New York (2009)
13. Welsh, B., Mudge, M., Farrington, D.: Reconceptualizing public area surveillance and crime prevention: security guards, place managers and defensible space. Secur. J. **23**, 299–319 (2010)
14. Nagin, D.: Deterrence in the twenty-first century. Crime Justice **42**(1), 199–263 (2013)
15. Sherman, L.: Police crackdowns: initial and residual deterrence. In: Tonry, M., Morris, M. (eds.) Crime and Justice: An Annual Review of Research, vol. 12, pp. 1–48. University of Chicago Press, Chicago (1990)
16. Stoneburner, G., Goguen, A., Feringa, A.: Risk Management Guide for Information Technology Systems. NIST Special Publication 800:30 (2002)
17. Png, I., Wang, Q.: Information security: facilitating user precautions vis-à-vis enforcement against attackers. J. Manag. Inf. Syst. **26**, 97–121 (2009)
18. Maimon, D., Alper, M., Sobesto, B., Cukier, M.: Restrictive deterrent effect of a warning banner in an attacked computer system. Criminology **52**, 33–59 (2014)
19. Jacobs, B., Cherbonneau, M.: Auto theft and restrictive deterrence. Justice Q. **31**(2), 1–24 (2014)
20. Jacobs, B.: Crack dealers' apprehension avoidance techniques: a case of restrictive deterrence. Justice Q. **13**, 359–381 (1996)
21. Wright, R., Decker, S.: Burglars on the Job. Northeastern University Press, Boston (1994)
22. Clarke, R.V.: Situational crime prevention. Crime Justice **19**, 91–150 (1995)
23. Cozens, P., Love, T.: A review and current status of crime prevention through environmental design (CPTED). J. Plann. Lit. **30**(4), 393–412 (2015)
24. Ellsberg, D.: Risk, ambiguity, and the Savage axioms. Q. J. Econ. **75**(4), 643–669 (1961)
25. Kahneman, D., Tversky, A.: Prospect theory: an analysis of decision under risk. Econometrica **47**(2), 263–291 (1979)
26. Trautmann, S., Vieider, F., Wakker, P.: Causes of ambiguity aversion: known versus unknown preferences. J. Risk Uncertain. **36**(3), 225–243 (2008)
27. Becker, S., Brownson, F.: What price ambiguity? Or the role of ambiguity in decision-making. J. Polit. Econ. **72**(1), 62–73 (1964)
28. Jacobs, B.: Deterrence and deterrability. Criminology **48**(2), 417–441 (2010)
29. Baillon, A., Bleichrodt, H.: Testing ambiguity models through the measurement of probabilities for gains and losses. Am. Econ. J. **7**(2), 77–100 (2015)
30. Engebretson, P.: The Basics of Hacking and Penetration Testing: Ethical Hacking and Penetration Testing Made Easy. Elsevier, Waltham (2013)
31. National Institute for Standards and Technology: Recommended Security Controls for Federal Information Systems and Organization (U.S. Department of Commerce) (2009)

Author Index

Printed in the United States
By Bookmasters